An INTRODUCTION to MUSIC

An
INTRODUCTION
to MUSIC

MARTIN BERNSTEIN

Professor of Music
New York University

Second Edition

PRENTICE-HALL, INC.

New York

PRENTICE-HALL MUSIC SERIES
Douglas Moore, Editor

First Edition

First Printing...................April 1937
Second Printing.............September 1937
Third Printing ....June 1938
Fourth Printing ....March 1939
Fifth Printing ....June 1939
Sixth Printing ....October 1939
Seventh Printing ....March 1940
Eighth Printing ....February 1941
Ninth Printing ....March 1942
Tenth Printing ....January 1945
Eleventh Printing ....April 1945
Twelfth Printing ....March 1946
Thirteenth Printing ....August 1946
Fourteenth Printing ....July 1947
Fifteenth Printing ....June 1948
Sixteenth Printing ....March 1949
Seventeenth Printing ....December 1949

Second Edition

First Printing ....March 1951
Second Printing ....September 1951
Third Printing ....June 1952
Fourth Printing ....January 1953
Fifth Printing .... November, 1953

PREFACE TO THE SECOND EDITION

THE ORIGINAL purpose of this book has been retained for the second edition: the work remains an introduction to the literature of music. But with the increase of general musical knowledge which the phonograph and radio have brought about, it has seemed necessary to include discussion of additional types of music—hence the expansion of the chapter on contemporary music, the addition of material on Gregorian chant, on polyphonic music of the late Renaissance, and on the Baroque era.

The discussions of some compositions have been expanded from analyses of single movements to detailed treatments of entire works. Bibliographies have been revised and brought up to date. Many corrections and alterations are the result of suggestions kindly made by colleagues at New York University: Professors Philip James and Harold Heeremans and Mr. Jay S. Harrison. Miss Mary S. Schieffelin has again been the indefatigable reader of manuscript and proofs.

Almost every composition mentioned in this book is available in phonograph records. It has not been thought necessary to list these records here, since authoritative evaluations of available materials appear in Irving Kolodin, *The New Guide to Recorded Music* (Garden City, New York, 1950), and David Hall, *Records,* revised edition (New York, 1950).

The book still remains a collection of considered choices of styles, composers, and works—designed to furnish the beginning student with a reasonably adequate orientation. The gratifying extent to which the first edition has been used in American colleges and universities would seem to indicate that these choices have met with general approval and that the grounds for the numerous omissions have been understood.

M. B.

PREFACE TO THE FIRST EDITION

IN THE preparation of this volume the author has had but one objective in mind: the presentation of such information as will make for intelligent listening to the music that is heard today in the concert hall, in the opera house, and through modern instruments of transmission and reproduction. This book is consequently neither a history of music nor a technical manual. In order to concentrate on this objective, the author found certain compromises necessary. There is no discussion of many significant composers and their works, and detailed study begins at so recent a stage in the evolution of the art of music as that represented by the compositions of Johann Sebastian Bach.

It is a familiar axiom that an appreciation of music cannot be acquired by the reading of books. Much space, therefore, has been devoted to discussions of representative works with the hope that they will be read in conjunction with actual hearing of the music. Thematic quotations from an unfamiliar composition have little value; it is only when the reader has had the experience of listening to the work from which they have been extracted that they can be of aid in the recognition of formal outlines.

The writer of a work of this type is often compelled to resort to summary pronouncements and facile generalizations. Lists of suggested readings have therefore been included to enable the reader to find in the books mentioned the necessary expansions and qualifications of the statements made in the text.

For valuable suggestions and friendly interest the author is indebted to his colleagues at New York University, Professor Philip James and Mr. Gustave Reese, and to Doctor Howard Hanson of the Eastman School of Music; and for painstaking assistance in the reading of proofs, to Miss Mary S. Schieffelin. The author wishes especially to express his gratitude to Professor Casper J. Kraemer, Jr. of New York University for the interest he has shown in this volume since its inception, and for his many constructive criticisms of the manuscript.

M. B.

New York University
September, 1936.

ACKNOWLEDGMENTS

Excerpts from Debussy's *L'Après-midi d'un faune* and *Nuages* are reprinted with kind permission of Jean Jobert, of Paris, and Elkan-Vogel Co., Inc., copyright owners in the U. S. A., and excerpts from Debussy's *La Cathédrale engloutie, Jimbo's Lullaby, Voiles, Pelléas et Mélisande,* and Dukas' *L'Apprenti sorcier* with kind permission of Durand & Cie. of Paris, and Elkan-Vogel Co., Inc., copyright owners in the U. S. A.

The excerpt from Vaughan Williams' *Pastoral Symphony* is reprinted by kind permission of J. Curwen & Sons, Ltd., of London.

Excerpts from Sibelius' Symphony No. 2, and Strauss' *Ein Heldenleben* are used by kind permission of the copyright owners, Associated Music Publishers, Inc., New York.

The excerpt from Strauss' *Burleska* is reprinted by special permission of the Society of European Stage Authors and Composers, Inc., of New York, and Steingraeber Verlag, Leipzig.

The excerpts from Křenek's *Twelve Little Piano Pieces,* are used by kind permission of the copyright owners, G. Schirmer, Inc., New York.

TABLE OF CONTENTS

LIST OF ILLUSTRATIONS

FOREWORD—AN APPROACH TO MUSIC

MUSIC, an art that may be considered as a medium of expression utilizing organized sound, has both the strength and the weakness of being inexact in its notation and inexplicit in its communication.

Let us take the famous Fifth Symphony of Beethoven as an example. Just how has the composer set down his expression and what does examination of the printed score reveal?

We can ascertain the following: (1) Beethoven calls his work "Symphony," a usual designation at his time for an orchestral composition in several movements. (2) The ordinal "Fifth" implies that the work was preceded by at least four others of the same type that the composer has seen fit to release. (3) The various orchestral instruments are named; but the exact number of string instruments is not given. (4) Tempo indications, fairly general in character, are supplied for each of the four movements. The first, for example, is directed to be played *Allegro con brio* (fast, with animation). (5) Lastly, there is nothing to indicate what the expressive purpose, that is, the content, of the work is; although the first movement, it is claimed by an untrustworthy associate of Beethoven, contains a theme that the composer described as "fate knocking on the door" (see page 190). Yet no one would deny that this great symphony communicates something to the listener and that hearing it is a profound emotional experience.

Much music, then, has a content that eludes statement in any medium other than the one for which it was created. Whatever Beethoven's expressive purpose was in the creation of this work, it cannot be conveyed by any other communicative method; and granted that the content exists, the perception of it remains the unique prerogative of the listener.

A composition for whose content the composer has given no clue is usually described as *absolute* music, music having no extramusical associations or implications. Typical instances would be the symphony of César Franck or the violin concerto of Brahms.

But there are many compositions whose content may be described with a degree of accuracy, for their composers have given them explicit titles. The Mendelssohn overture to Shakespeare's *A Midsummer Night's Dream* has a demonstrable association with the play; and Strauss' *Don Quixote* clearly states its concern with Cervantes' novel. Similarly, the music of any composition employing the spoken word, a Schubert song or Prokofieff's *Peter and the Wolf,* is fairly explicit in its expression.

Music that has ascertainable extramusical associations is referred to as *program* music. But it cannot be too strongly emphasized that the degree of explicitness of program music varies and that the "program" may consist only of a suggestive title such as heads Schumann's short piano piece, *Träumerei,* or an elaborate literary argument such as accompanies Berlioz' *Fantastic Symphony* (see page 272).

In the light of all the foregoing, the listener might do well to answer these questions before passing judgment on a composition.

(1) What is the title of the work and what are its implications? For example, what does the caption *String Quartet in B Flat Major, Opus 67,* tell us?

(2) Who is the composer of the work? What traits of his personality are reflected in it or shed light on some of its peculiarities? For example, Debussy's virulent anti-Wagnerism explains the quotation of *Tristan und Isolde* in *The Golliwog's Cake-Walk.*

(3) What is the approximate date of the work? What conventions of its period affect its idiom or medium? For example, why a small orchestra for a symphony of Haydn and a large one for a symphony of Tchaikovsky?

(4) What is the function of the composition? Was it designed to be played in a church, a theater, or a concert hall? Was it intended to instill or increase feelings of devotion, entertain, precede a dramatic performance, allow a virtuoso to demonstrate his technical attainments, purvey political or nationalistic sentiments, or serve as a pure medium of expression? And similarly, for what sort of listeners was it intended? (It should be borne in mind that some music—much of the clavier music of Bach, for example—was written purely for the per-

formers thereof; that is, it was music to be played and not to be heard.)
From what social groups were these listeners drawn? What musical
background, if any, did they have? What was their relationship to
the composer and to the performers?

(5) For what medium was the work written, and is it being reproduced today by that medium? For example, what changes foreign to
the composer's intent take place in a Bach organ work when it is arranged for modern symphony orchestra? What deformations of
harpsichord music occur when it is played on a modern piano?

(6) What literary background or other prior information is assumed
of the listener if the full implications of a programmatic composition
are to be realized by him? For example, a richer comprehension of
Beethoven's overture to *Coriolanus* follows from a knowledge of the
tragic story of the Roman general; and similarly, an elementary grasp
of modern European history adds meaning to the quotation of the
Marseillaise in Tchaikovsky's overture *1812.* In other words, if the
work being heard is programmatic, does the listener have a full awareness of the program? An often played work of Richard Strauss, for
example, *Till Eulenspiegel's Merry Pranks,* has a rich literary program
implied by its title. But this remains unknown to most listeners since
the stories of Till and his exploits do not form part of the literary
heritage of America.

And, if a work does have a programmatic title, was that title given
to it by the composer? Beethoven, for example, never called his last
piano concerto *Emperor Concerto,* and the work has no demonstrable
program whatsoever. In fact, the appellation, "Emperor," seems to
be unknown in the German-speaking countries where the work is always represented solely by number and key.

The listener's assimilation of a composer's creation will ultimately
depend on the performer who reproduces it. Obviously then, before
passing judgment on the composer's effort at expression, the listener
must attempt, insofar as possible, to ascertain to what extent the performance (or the recording) is in accord with the composer's intentions, either specifically expressed or implied. Not that all deviations
are of necessity harmful; some may even be desirable. But the listener
should be sure that he is aware of them.

An
INTRODUCTION
to MUSIC

Chapter 1

THE CHARACTERISTICS OF A MUSICAL TONE

THREE men, one in the concert hall listening to a symphony of Beethoven, another in the opera house listening to a presentation of one of Wagner's music-dramas, a third in his own home listening to a sentimental tune sung by a radio performer, are all doing the same thing, or rather, are having the same thing done to them: the atmosphere about them is supplying them with oxygen and transmitting to them waves of compressions and rarefactions set up by certain vibrating bodies. The waves so produced fall on the men's ears, and each of them would describe his own particular sensation as "music." It is obvious that the works that these persons are hearing have certain things in common. No matter what the artistic value of the works performed may be, their renditions consist of successions and combinations of atmospheric disturbances that we designate as *musical tones.* Each and every one of these musical tones has four characteristics: *duration, pitch, intensity,* and *quality.*

The *duration* of a musical tone may be defined purely in terms of the time elapsing between its commencement and its cessation. In actual practice the ear never measures the absolute time interval. It is, however, continually making comparisons between the relative time values of different tones, and between the time values of groups of tones.

The term *pitch* refers to the relative highness or lowness of a tone. The tone of a toy whistle is of high pitch, that of the human voice as used in ordinary speech, of medium pitch, and that of a large church bell, of low pitch. There is, however, an accurate and precise way of describing pitch. The pitch of a musical tone may be shown to depend wholly on the number of vibrations per second set up by the sounding body.   This number of vibrations per second is known as the *frequency* of vibration.   The art of music employs fundamental [1] frequencies ranging from 16 to 4,186 vibrations per second; but the ear can respond to frequencies in the neighborhood of 20,000.   (The modern piano has a range that extends from 27 to 4,186 vibrations per second.)   Precisely as in the case of *duration,* our ears seldom measure the absolute number of vibrations, but rather are continually comparing the relative value of the vibrations of tones sounded either simultaneously or successively. One of the most elementary of these relationships is the *octave*—a ratio of 1:2.

Ex. 1

523.2 vibrations per second

261.6 vibrations per second

Intensity is the measure of the loudness of a tone.   As in the case of the two previously mentioned characteristics, our measurement of intensity is purely relative; acoustical engineers have, however, devised a unit of intensity, the *decibel*.   The loudness of a tone for any given pitch depends on the amplitude of the vibrations: i.e., the extent to which the sounding body moves from its normal position of rest as it vibrates to and fro.   The easiest way to demonstrate this is to strike a key on the piano.   The loudness of the tone will depend entirely on how forcefully the key is depressed, that is, on how far the string is displaced from its position of rest by the blow of the hammer.   The intensity of a tone also depends on its pitch. [2]

The *tone-quality, tone-color,* or *timbre* of a musical tone enables us to distinguish between notes which, although they may possess the same pitch and intensity, are produced by different instruments.   One can very easily distinguish between a bugle-call played on a bugle and the identical notes played on a violin; nor does it take a sensitive ear to recognize a difference in the quality of the tones of two similar instruments, such as two pianos or two violins.   The quality of a musical tone is one of its most interesting and at the same time one of its most

[1] See page 3.

[2] Stated more precisely, the amplitude remaining constant, the intensity of a tone varies as the square of its frequency.   The frequency remaining constant, the intensity varies as the square of the amplitude.

elusive aspects. And there is an infinite variety of tonal qualities. Each and every instrument has its own unique timbre which depends not only on the instrument itself, but also on the skill of the performer. There is no better proof of this than to listen to the same piece of music played in turn on the same instrument by several competent performers.

On what then does the quality of a musical tone depend? Before this question can be answered it will be necessary to investigate in some detail the behavior of a sounding body. Let us take a taut wire as our example. If the wire is plucked, a characteristic sound will be heard. By means of specially devised instruments known as resonators, a physicist could easily demonstrate that this wire was producing not one but many simultaneous sounds; or he could show with equal ease that the wire was vibrating not only as a whole, but also in fractions of itself. The vibrations of the wire as a whole are the strongest vibrations and they produce a tone called the *fundamental*. When we refer to the pitch of a tone we are really referring to the pitch of the fundamental, the loudest of the several tones that we are hearing. The tones produced by the fractional vibrations of the wire are known as *overtones*. These vary in number and intensity, depending on many factors —the composition of the wire, the way in which it is held taut, the manner in which it is sounded, and so forth. The quality of a musical tone depends entirely on the number and the relative intensities of these overtones.

In reality, therefore, when we strike a note on the piano we are hearing not one tone, but several tones. We can readily distinguish the loudest, the fundamental; but many other tones of lesser intensity are also heard, and although we may seem unable to distinguish them from the fundamental, they do nevertheless actuate our ear drums sufficiently for us to be conscious of them. A pure tone, a tone without overtones, can be produced only by a tuning fork or an electronic device. All other sounds that we hear are combinations of a fundamental and numerous overtones. Overtones whose frequencies are exact multiples of the frequency of the fundamental are known as *harmonics*. The harmonics of a violin string may be heard by lightly touching the finger to a point half the string-length from the bridge, a third of the string-length, etc., and by applying the bow. Such tones are frequently used in writing for the violin. An instrument like the flute gives forth a prominent fundamental with but few overtones, most of which are faint. The horn, on the other hand, gives out a prominent fundamental together with more than twenty overtones.

The following illustration will show the series of harmonics that may sound with a given fundamental. These tones are known as the *harmonic series:*

Ex. 2

We have now discussed each individual characteristic of a musical tone. It must be borne in mind, however, that these various aspects cannot be divorced from one another; no one is more important than any other, and with the exception of duration, each is continually influencing the others. A sensitive musical performance consists of a most meticulous regard for these four values. (In the case of instruments like the organ and the piano, however, the performer need not concern himself with the correctness of pitch. This has been attended to in advance by the tuner.) The art of interpretation is largely the performance of each and every individual tone of a composition with what the player or singer deems to be its correct duration, pitch, intensity, and quality.

Suggested Readings

Any standard text book of physics contains a discussion of elementary acoustical phenomena. Dayton C. Miller's treatise, *The Science of Musical Sounds* (New York, 1926), while out-dated in many respects, is a readable and valuable discussion. More recent investigations of a popular nature are John Mill, *A Fugue in Cycles and Bels* (New York, 1935) and Otto Ortmann's article, "What Is Tone-Quality?," in the October 1935 issue of *The Musical Quarterly.* The most useful single volume is Wilmer T. Bartholomew, *Acoustics of Music* (New York, 1942). "American Standard Acoustical Terminology," issued in 1942 by the *American Standards Association* (New York), contains rigorous definitions of acoustic terms.

Chapter II

MUSICAL INSTRUMENTS

MANY of the musical instruments of the Occident are found in a large and diversified aggregation called a "symphony orchestra." [1] The orchestra as we know it today is a comparatively new arrival on the musical scene; for the constitution of the orchestra did not take on any semblance of regularity until the close of the eighteenth century, and many of the instruments in it were not perfected until the nineteenth century.

The instruments of the orchestra may be divided conveniently, although unscientifically, into four large groups—the strings, the woodwinds, the brasses, and the percussion. Of these the string group is the most important. A full-sized symphony orchestra includes about one hundred players, more than half of whom are performers on string instruments.

THE STRING INSTRUMENTS

The string section owes its importance to the fact that it is far superior to any other group in purity of intonation, range of dynamic value, and variety of tone-color. It must not be forgotten that a string instrument is in truth several instruments in one. Each of the strings of the violin, for example, has a different tone-color. The violin may be described, therefore, as four instruments with a common resonator. So versatile is the string group that many works have been written for strings alone. These range, on modern orchestral programs, from the Third and Sixth Brandenburg Concertos of Bach (1721) and the Concerti Grossi of

---

[1] The term *symphony orchestra* is somewhat of a misnomer. It indicates, of course, an orchestra capable of playing music of symphonic dimensions. There is, however, no difference between an opera orchestra and a symphony orchestra.

5

Handel (1739) to the Symphony for Strings of Honegger (1941) and the Concerto for Strings of Stravinsky (1946).

The violin, the best known of the orchestral instruments, achieved its substantially final form under the sensitive hands of a famous Italian, Antonio Stradivarius (1644-1737). The violin bow had to wait almost a hundred years before it was perfected by a Frenchman, François Tourte (1747-1835). While there has been an extensive development of techniques of performance upon the violin, it and its orchestral relatives are unique among orchestral instruments in that they have undergone no significant structural changes in the last two hundred years.

There are usually about thirty-six violins in a symphony orchestra and they are divided into two groups: first and second violins. These designations indicate musical functions of the groups and not the relative competency of the players in them. Second violinists must be every bit as proficient as firsts, and in almost all scores of Wagner and later composers they will be found playing parts of great difficulty. But modern composers have not hesitated to carry the process of division further and have split the violins into many more groups. The most accessible example of violin subdivision may be heard in the long passage for violins in four parts that appears at the beginning of the Prelude to Wagner's *Lohengrin*.

The four strings of the violin are tuned as follows:

The first string, the highest in pitch, is usually of steel wire and gives forth a thin, penetrating, often brilliant tone. The second and third strings, made of sheepgut (not catgut) and often weighted by a wire wrapping, produce a fleshy, warm, and broad tone. The lowest string (the G string) has its weight notably increased by a wire wrapping and can produce a big, tenor-alto sort of tone.

An important determinant of violin tone color is the handling of the bow, essentially a device for scraping the strings with taut horsehairs. The bow may be applied to the strings in a great many ways, each of which will produce a characteristic effect. It may, for example, be drawn across a string rapidly and determinedly, or it may be permitted to bounce lightly and delicately. Or a succession of vigorous chops may be secured through consecutive down bows. Ultra-rapid alternations of short up and down bows produce the exciting *tremolo*.

Pitches produced by the violin as well as the other orchestral string instruments are determined by pressing the string against the finger-board with the finger of the left hand, a procedure known as "stopping." Since the position of the pitch-determining finger is completely under the control of the player, an infinite number of pitches is available within the range of the instrument. This means that minute alterations of pitch can always be effected by the player and, if skillful enough, he can play scrupulously in tune. This freedom from mechanical limitations of pitch adjustment is found in only a few tone-producing media: the human voice, the orchestral stringed instruments, and the trombone. But, as is often the case, freedom begets responsibility and, with irresponsible performers, "out of tune" pitch production by these instruments is all too feasible.

By bowing two strings at once the player can produce "double-stops," and by moving the bow rapidly across the strings "triple-stops" or "quadruple-stops" can be sounded. Hence the orchestral string instruments are not limited to the production of one melodic line, and many-voiced (polyphonic) music may be written for them. This type of writing is well illustrated in the music for unaccompanied violin by Johann Sebastian Bach in which even fugues for solo violin may be found.

If a finger of the left hand is applied very lightly to certain points on the string and the string is bowed, a thin ethereal type of tone will be produced. Such tones are called *harmonics*.[2] A violin harmonic sustained for 53 measures appears at the beginning of Borodin's *From the Steppes of Central Asia*.

Plucking the strings with the fingers is described by the Italian *pizzicato*. Played *pizzicato,* a string instrument becomes an excellent device for producing precisely sounded ultra-short tones. No better example of the *pizzicato* can be cited than the third movement of the Fourth Symphony of Tchaikovsky, the famous *Pizzicato Ostinato* (persistent pizzicato).

By placing a *mute,* a two- or three-pronged clamp, usually of ebony,

[2] See page 3.

on the bridge of a string instrument, its tone is radically thinned though not necessarily softened.

The orchestral range of the instrument is:

The *viola* is held like the violin, and from a distance it looks exactly like one. On comparing the instruments, however, one discovers that the viola is about 1 1/7 times as large. It is pitched four tones lower than its smaller colleague and has a sombre and elegiac tone-quality. It is an instrument of great inherent dignity and nobility, and not at all deserving of the title that has sometimes been bestowed upon it—"a violin in mourning." There are usually ten violas in the orchestra. The orchestral range of the instrument is:

There are prominent passages for the viola in the following works:

Bach—Brandenburg Concerto No. VI
Ippolitoff-Ivanoff—"In the Village" from *Caucasian Sketches*
Strauss—*Don Quixote*

The *cello* (the common abbreviation of *violoncello*) may be readily identified as the only string instrument held between the player's knees, the weight of the instrument being borne by a pin which rests on the floor. It is a vigorous masculine instrument possessing a very expressive, occasionally penetrating tone-quality. The cello is nominally a bass instrument; but so great is its range that it may be consid- a tenor and an alto instrument as well. Modern composers have made excellent use of the versatility of the cellos, and there is hardly a work by composers such as Brahms, Wagner, or Strauss without an outstanding passage for them. There are usually ten cellos in the orchestra. The orchestral range of the instrument is:

Representative passages will be found in the following works:

Rossini—Overture to *William Tell*
Brahms—Symphony No. 3—Third Movement
Wagner—Prelude to *Tristan und Isolde*
Strauss—*Don Quixote*

The *double bass* (known also as bass viol, contrabass, string bass, or bass) is the largest instrument of the string group. It has been so named because for many years it was entrusted with the humble task of doubling in a lower octave the bass of the orchestral harmonies as played by the cellos. The double basses are seldom used independently except for some special effect, but in consort with instruments like the cellos they furnish the orchestra with a rich and firm foundation. Because of its size and the thickness of its strings, the double bass does not lend itself to solo performance. These obstacles, however, have not prevented certain intrepid individuals from becoming virtuoso players on the instrument. There are usually ten double basses in the orchestra. The range of the instrument is:

There are prominent passages for the double bass in the following works:

Beethoven—Symphony No. 5—Third Movement
Beethoven—Symphony No. 9—Fourth Movement
Saint-Saëns—*"L'Eléphant"* from *Le Carnaval des animaux*

THE WOOD-WIND INSTRUMENTS

The name given to this group describes it with some degree of accuracy. All the instruments in it except the flute have air columns which are set in motion by a reed, and each has associated with it one or two related instruments mechanically so similar to it that players can change from one to the other without difficulty. The timbres of the wood-wind instruments are much more striking than those of the strings; but by the same token, the ear tires of them more quickly. They are unique tone-colors which must be handled with circumspection. Like the human voice, the wind instruments have a somewhat different color for each of their several divisions or "registers."

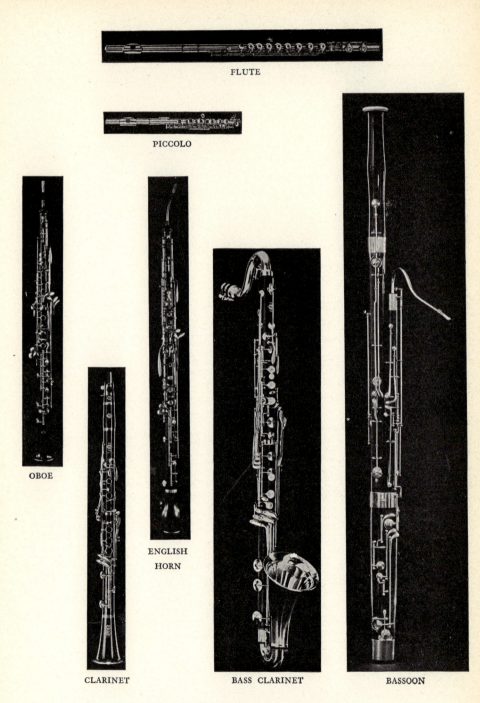

FLUTE

PICCOLO

OBOE

CLARINET

ENGLISH
HORN

BASS CLARINET

BASSOON

Orchestral Wood-Wind Instruments

Scale:—One inch equals 8¾ inches

Courtesy of H. & A. Selmer, Inc.

The *flute* may be very readily identified: it and its related instruments are the only wind instruments that are held parallel to the plane of the floor. It also is the only instrument in this group that is seldom made of wood, silver having been found to be preferable. The flute is made to sound by blowing across a hole, the *embouchure,* at the end of the instrument. The air-column strikes the sharp edge of this hole and sets up vibrations in the flute. The frequency of vibration may be altered by opening or closing the holes drilled in the side of the instrument and by increasing the force of the air-stream blown against the *embouchure* (overblowing).

The flute is an instrument of almost unbelievable agility. No passages are too fast or too complicated for it. Its tone-color is uniformly bright, except in the lowest register where it tends to become somewhat cool and velvety. Because of its lightness and daintiness, the flute is always associated with the elves and fairies of orchestral music, as in the *Scherzo* from Mendelssohn's *Midsummer Night's Dream.* The flute is also used in conjunction with other wood-wind instruments and with the violins to add brilliancy. There are usually three flutists in the orchestra, one of whom will play the related instrument—the *piccolo.* This instrument is half the size of the flute. Its name is an abbreviation of the Italian designation, *flauto piccolo* (little flute). Its tone is extremely penetrating; one piccolo playing loudly can easily make itself heard above the rest of the orchestra. Possessing an ultra-vivid color, the piccolo is usually held in reserve to be unleashed at the crucial moment. The range of the flute is:

and of the piccolo:

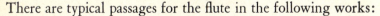

There are typical passages for the flute in the following works:

Mozart—Concerto for Flute in D major (K. V. 314)
Rossini—Overture to *William Tell*
Debussy—*L'Après-midi d'un faune* (see page 417, Example 5)
Ravel—Second Suite from *Daphnis et Chloé*

and for the piccolo in the following works:

Berlioz—"Minuet of the Will-o'-the-Wisps" from *The Damnation of Faust*
Tchaikovsky—"Chinese Dance" from *The Nutcracker Suite*
Sousa—"The Stars and Stripes Forever"
Pierné—"Entry of the Little Fauns" from *Cydalise*

The *oboe* is an instrument of conical bore whose air-column is actuated by a comparatively small double reed held tightly in the mouth of
the player. It is one of the oldest, one of the most difficult, and one
of the most expressive instruments in the orchestra. The difficulty in
playing the instrument arises from the nature and dimensions of the
double reed. This reed, composed of two fine and unusually thin
pieces of cane bound together, is so small that very little breath is
required to make the oboe sound. The oboe player's problem, therefore, is the converse of that of the player of any other wind instrument.
He must have a rest not to fill his lungs, but rather to rid them of the
air that he has been unable to release. The most obvious characteristic
of the instrument is its intensity. No better example could be quoted
than the celebrated passage from the first movement of the Fifth Symphony of Beethoven. The entire orchestra is silent as the oboe sings:

Ex. 1

The tone of the instrument is pungent, nasal, occasionally acrid, and
above all "reedy." This reedy quality will serve to differentiate the
oboe from any other wind instrument. There are usually three oboists
in the orchestra and of these three players, one will play the related
instrument—the *English horn.*

The origin of the name of this instrument is disputed, though one
explanation seems plausible—that the name is a translation of the
French *cor anglais* which in turn is a corruption of *cor anglé* (bent
horn). (The earlier instruments were bent.) No matter what the
explanation for it may be, the name is a complete misnomer. The instrument is neither "English" nor a "horn." It is simply an oboe of
lower pitch, an alto oboe. To be more precise, it bears exactly the same
relationship to the oboe as the viola does to the violin. It is much

longer than the oboe and terminates in a pear-shaped "bell." The double reed is larger than that of the oboe, and the oboe's problems of breath control are not duplicated in the case of its relative. The instrument is one of the most serious and most profound in the entire orchestra. It has about it a reserve, a nostalgia, a gravity, which render it admirably suitable for music of sorrow, of regret, of solitude. There is no better example of the English horn's ability to evoke an atmosphere of forlornness than the melancholy shepherd's tune which is played off-stage after the curtain is raised for Act III of Wagner's *Tristan und Isolde:*

Ex. 2

The range of the oboe is:

and of the English horn:

Characteristic oboe passages are to be found in the following works:

Schubert—Symphony No. 7—Second Movement
Tchaikovsky—Symphony No. 4—Second Movement (see page 372, Example 22)
Brahms—Concerto for Violin—Second Movement (see page 345, Example 23)

Characteristic English horn passages are to be found in the following works:

Wagner—*Tristan und Isolde,* Act III (Shepherd's tune)
Franck—Symphony in D minor—Second Movement (see page 384, Example 16)
Dvořák—Symphony in E minor (*From the New World*)—Second Movement (see page 349, Example 2)
Sibelius—*The Swan of Tuonela*

The *clarinet* is a cylindrical instrument about two feet long, with a large single reed, held with comfort by the player. From a distance it may seem to resemble the oboe; but comparison of the dimensions of the reeds will dispel all doubts. The clarinet is an instrument of considerable agility, of great range, and possessed of a pleasant and, at the same time, variable tone-color. It is so versatile that in arrangements of orchestral music for concert band, it plays all the passages previously executed by violins. The tone of the instrument is smooth and clear, often resembling that of the human voice and possessing a certain feminine quality that has sometimes caused it to be called the prima donna of the orchestra. The player has complete control over the dynamic value of the tone. It can be produced at the level of a whisper, which is more than can be said for any of the other wood-wind instruments. There are usually three clarinetists in the orchestra.

The related instrument, the *bass* clarinet, which might be mistaken for a saxophone if it were not for its wooden pipe, is, as its name indicates, a larger clarinet of lower pitch. Its tone is serious and grave.

Another instrument related to the clarinet appears but rarely. Known as the *E-flat clarinet,* it is a much smaller instrument with a penetrating incisive tone not far removed from a squeal. Richard Strauss uses the instrument in *Till Eulenspiegel's Merry Pranks* to depict the hanging of Till.[3]

The range of the clarinet is:

and of the bass clarinet:

There are prominent passages for the clarinet in the following works:

Mozart—Symphony in E-flat major (K. V. 543)—Trio of the Minuet
Brahms—Symphony No. 1—Third Movement
Brahms—Clarinet Quintet in B minor, Opus 115
Tchaikovsky—Symphony No. 5—First Movement
Sibelius—Symphony No. 1—First Movement

and for the bass clarinet in the following works:

[3] See page 394, Example 8.

Wagner—*Tristan und Isolde*, Act II (King Mark Scene)
Wagner—*Tristan und Isolde*, Act III (Commencement of the *"Liebestod"*)

The *bassoon*, with a double reed, is the bass of the wood-wind family. In appearance it is very much like two long poles bound together; in fact the Italian name for the instrument is *fagotto*, meaning "bundle." The bassoon has a hollow, dry tone, of some seriousness, and possesses quite a degree of flexibility which, coupled with the inherent solemnity of the instrument, enables it to execute complicated passages with cold unconcern. There is no better example of this unique faculty of the bassoon than the commencement of the *Vif* section of Dukas' *L'Apprenti sorcier* (*The Sorcerer's Apprentice*):

Ex. 3

But it must not be thought that the bassoon is limited to macabre music. In its upper register it can well suggest the sound of the human voice, while in its lower register it can be used for clownish effects. It can also intone solemn passages with commensurate gravity. There are usually three bassoonists in the orchestra, one of whom may play the related instrument, the contrabassoon. It is rarely heard independently. The range of the bassoon is:

There are prominent passages for the instrument in the following works:

Rimsky-Korsakoff—*Scheherazade*—Second Movement
Dukas—*L'Apprenti Sorcier*
Tchaikovsky—Symphony No. 6 (*Pathétique*)—First Movement
Stravinsky—*Le Sacre du Printemps*

The essential features of the wood-wind group can be enjoyably learned through listening to Prokofieff's *Peter and the Wolf, A Musical Tale for Children* (1936). Throughout this attractive little work the wood winds remain associated with four characters of the story: the

TRUMPET

HORN

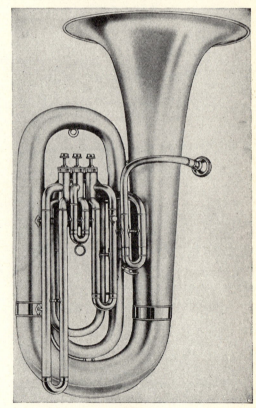

TROMBONE TUBA

Orchestral Brass Instruments
Scale:—One inch equals 8¾ inches

Courtesy of H. & A. Selmer, Inc.

flute personifies the bird; the oboe, the duck; the clarinet, the cat; and the bassoon, the grandfather. (The horns describe the wolf and Peter is portrayed by the strings.)

THE BRASS INSTRUMENTS

The principles underlying the construction and manipulation of brass instruments have been known since ancient times. The walls of Jericho are said to have been blown down by trumpets. Many brass instruments were used by the Romans for military signals. No matter what the shape or dimensions of these instruments have been through the ages, they all depend for their operation on three acoustical facts: (1) that the human lips can be made to act as reeds and that their tension may be varied by means of the facial muscles; (2) that if the taut lips are applied to a tube and air is blown through them, the air-column in the tube commences to vibrate; and (3) that by altering the tension of the lips the frequency of vibration can be changed; but only certain notes can be produced. It will be found that the notes produced from any tube so blown have the same pitch relationship to each other as the notes of the harmonic series given on page 4. Experience has shown that brass is the best material to use; that because of the length of tubing required, the instruments may be rendered more manageable by suitable coiling of their tubes; and that control of the air-column and manipulation of the lips are facilitated by the use of a mouthpiece. The design of the mouthpiece has a great effect on the production of overtones.

This limitation of available notes to the harmonic series is by no means an insuperable one. On examination of the series it becomes apparent that from the first overtone on, it is quite possible to construct simple melodies. For example, on the common bugle, which is nothing more than a coiled brass tube about four feet long, a melody like the following can be played merely by changing the tension of the lips:

Composers found these limitations of the brass instruments irksome, but it was not until the 1830's that the problem was finally solved. The problem was this: to supply the brass instruments with a mechanical device that would (1) enable the player to alter instantaneously the length of the tube, thereby shifting the harmonic series, and (2) allow the player to effect so many of these alterations with their resultant changes of harmonic series that all the notes of the scale could be produced. The solution of this problem was rendered quite difficult because of certain acoustical laws. It was finally effected in this manner—lengths of tubing were added to the instrument and, by means of mechanical devices known as "valves," these additional lengths of tubing could be added to or removed from the main tube at will. It was found that three different lengths of tubing, each with its valve to cut it in or out of the main tube, would, when used in combination, suffice to give every note of the chromatic scale (a scale of half-tones). (See page 38.) The addition of valves to the brass instruments resulted in a conspicuous enrichment of the orchestra's color resources and made possible the opulence and grandeur of sonority that it is now capable of producing.

The *horn* [4] is the most expressive and poetic instrument of this group, and the most difficult to play. The flaring bell and the complicated coils of tubing enable one to identify it easily. Long before the horn was introduced into the orchestra, it was widely used for calls of the hunt. The old French name, *cor-de-chasse* (horn of the chase), and the old German names *Waldhorn* (forest horn) and *Jagdhorn* (hunting horn), tell us much about the use of the instrument, and to this very day the horn retains these associations. Up to the time of Beethoven, composers had to content themselves with horns without valves—the so-called *natural* horns. Here the limitations of the harmonic series were partially overcome by the great range of the horn. Furthermore it was discovered that the length of the tubing might be altered, though somewhat inconveniently, by changing certain sections of pipe—one of the first uses of interchangeable parts. These interchangeable sections of pipe were known as *crooks*. During the performance of a long work such as an opera by Mozart, the horn players would continually be changing crooks between the various numbers.

The following passages will show the style of writing for two natural horns as well as the melodic possibilities of the harmonic series:

[4] Occasionally called the French horn.

Ex. 4. Hunting call.

Ex. 5. Mozart—Symphony in G minor (K. V. 550)—Third Movement.

Ex. 6. Beethoven—Symphony No. 8, in F major—Third Movement.

With the addition of valves, the horn was emancipated and to its capacity for producing a full and warm tone there was added the ability to play a complete scale, and this over a wide range, the widest of any of the brass instruments. So warm and round, that is, so rich in overtones, is the horn tone that the instrument is used very frequently with the string instruments and with the wood winds. Seldom are the horns silent for any length of time. They are in truth instruments of heroic qualities, and many heroes have had their musical portraits drawn by them. There are usually four horns in the orchestra, though as many as eight are called for in some of the operas of Wagner. Haydn, Mozart, and Beethoven usually called for only two. Four horns have become standard equipment, however, since the second decade of the nineteenth century. The range of the instrument is:

There are prominent horn passages in the following works:

Beethoven—Symphony No. 3 (*Eroica*)—Trio of the Third Movement
Wagner—"Siegfried's Rhine Journey" from *Götterdämmerung*
Tchaikovsky—Symphony No. 5—Second Movement
Wagner—*Die Meistersinger*—Prelude to Act III

The instrument that Haydn, Mozart, and Beethoven used, which they called a *trumpet,* would look exactly like a large bugle to us. It was an instrument without valves, a *natural* trumpet. Of much smaller range than the horn, the natural trumpet was used but sparingly by these composers, and found its application principally in military calls like the famous ones in Beethoven's *Leonore No. 3* Overture. It was not until valves were added that the trumpet could be used with any freedom. A brilliant instrument now possessed of great flexibility, it has numerous usages today. It can play broad melodies, complicated and involved passages; it can be serious and dignified one instant, flippant the next. It can intone majestic themes with truly stentorian quality. Then, too, its tone can be completely changed by the insertion of a *mute,* a pear-shaped device made of cardboard. This gives the instrument a pleasantly nasal tone wholly unlike that of the unmuted trumpet. The muted trumpet is familiar through its extensive application in dance music. (Trumpeters in dance orchestras use several different kinds of mutes, each with its characteristic tone.) There are usually three trumpets in the orchestra. The range of the instrument is:

There are prominent passages for the trumpet in the following works:

Beethoven—*Leonore No. 3* Overture
Strauss—*Ein Heldenleben*
Wagner—Prelude to *Parsifal*
Debussy—*Fêtes*

The *trombone* is the simplest of all the brass instruments. In place of a complicated valve mechanism, the trombone has a pair of concentric tubes that slide one over the other. It is a simple matter, therefore, for the player to change the length of tubing. Since the tube is comparatively free from bends and constrictions, the trombone is blown freely and easily, but, unfortunately, with rapid consumption of the player's air-supply. The trombone is inherently stately and dignified. Its tone can be almost overpowering; but never does the instrument belie its native majesty except for purposes of deliberate burlesque.

The best example of the use of the trombone occurs in the well known overture to Wagner's *Tannhäuser*. Here, to the energetic accompaniment of the rest of the orchestra, three trombones peal forth the melody sung in the opera by the chorus of pilgrims. The broad melody comes through above all the excitement of the accompaniment in a manner that seems almost effortless. There are three trombones in the orchestra. The usual range of the instrument is:

There are prominent passages for the trombone in the following works:

Wagner—Overture to *Tannhäuser*
Rimsky-Korsakoff—Overture to *The Russian Easter*
Hindemith—*Mathis der Maler*

The *tuba,* a huge coil of brass ending in an enormous bell, is the double bass of the brass group. Like its string counterpart, it is seldom used independently but serves rather to strengthen the foundations of the orchestral harmonies. As a solo instrument it seems to have definite zoölogical propensities; Wagner uses it to depict the dragon *Fafner* in the *Ring* operas, and Stravinsky uses it to depict the bear in Scene IV of his ballet *Petrouchka*. There is one tuba in the orchestra. The range of the instrument is:

There are prominent passages for the tuba in the following works:

Wagner—Prelude to *Siegfried*
Stravinsky—Suite from *Petrouchka*

The Percussion Instruments

The percussion group, frequently called "the battery," is a section that embraces a host of instruments of diverse shapes and uses, all, however, having one thing in common—they are sounded by being struck.

The *timpani,* or *kettledrums,* are the oldest and most important members of the percussion group. The kettledrums differ from all other drums in that they can be rapidly tuned to definite pitches. Sheep- or calf-skin heads are stretched across large copper "kettles," and are made to sound by striking them with hammers with felt ends. The pitches of the drums may be changed by altering the tension of the heads by means of large screws on the circumferences; though kettledrums that have a foot lever and an internal mechanism to permit faster tuning will frequently be seen.

The performer on the kettledrums must be a very gifted musician. He must, in the first place, possess what is known as absolute pitch, that is, he must know the pitch of any note in the scale. Secondly, he must be able to tune his drums quietly to the required pitch no matter what the rest of the orchestra may be playing. Thirdly, he must count his "rests" while doing all this, so that he may strike his correctly tuned drum at the right moment.

The kettledrums can be used for producing loud thunderous peals, for rhythmic accentuation, and, if enough drums be available, for melodic purposes. Beethoven was one of the first composers to realize the musical potentialities of the kettledrums. They play an important part in the second movement of his Ninth Symphony:

Ex. 7

Richard Strauss, in his *Burleska* for piano and orchestra, allows the principal theme of the work to be announced by four kettledrums:

Ex. 8

There is usually one player assigned to the kettledrums, and he will have from two to four drums under his care. The range of the kettledrums is:

There are prominent passages for the kettledrums in the following works:

Beethoven—Symphony No. 9—Second Movement
Wagner—"Siegfried's Funeral March" from *Götterdämmerung*
Strauss—*Burleska* for piano and orchestra

The rest of the percussion section comprises a great many miscellaneous instruments, too numerous to be described in detail. They are used chiefly to achieve special sound effects. Mere mention and brief description will suffice:

Snare Drum: A small untuned drum played with wooden sticks. It has metallic "snares" that strike against the lower head. A brilliant drum.

Bass Drum: A large untuned drum.

Cymbals: Large, slightly tapered disks of brass that are usually struck together.

Glockenspiel: A series of small tuned metal bars, struck with small hard hammers.

Xylophone: A series of small tuned wooden bars, struck with small hard hammers.

Bells: Large tubes sounding like church bells, struck with a mallet.

Gong: A huge disk of brass giving forth an ominous sound when struck with a large felt-headed stick.

Triangle: A metal bar bent into the shape of a triangle and struck with a small metal rod. It gives forth a pleasant tinkle.

Some other percussion instruments are the *castanets,* the *rattle,* the *wood-block,* the *tambourine,* and the *field-drum.*

Other Instruments of the Orchestra

Instruments Whose Strings Are Plucked

The *harp,* one of the most ancient of instruments, is the only member of this group that has won for itself a permanent place in the orchestra. Like the brass instruments, the harp was not made fully available for orchestral purposes until early in the nineteenth century when the French instrument maker, Sébastien Erard, perfected what is known as the "double-action" mechanism. By means of seven pedals located in the base of the instrument, the pitches of the forty-seven strings of the harp may be raised a half-tone or a whole-tone, thus enabling the instrument to be played in any key. The characteristic musical figure associated with the harp is the wide-spread chord of many notes played not simultaneously, but in quick succession. The name for this figure is *arpeggio* (from the Italian *arpa*). Another idiomatic harp figure is the *glissando*—a quick sweep over the strings. The harp can be used for simple accompaniment, accentuation, and for coloristic purposes. **Wagner** uses six harps in **Das Rheingold** to depict the glittering rainbow on which the gods march into *Walhall*. Some of the most effective harp parts are to be found in the orchestral works of the French composer, Claude Debussy. The range of the harp is:

There are prominent passages for the harp in the following works:

Strauss—*Tod und Verklärung*
Debussy—*L'Après-midi d'un faune*
Ravel—*Introduction and Allegro* for harp, string quartet, and wood winds.

Other instruments in the plucked-string group that are employed in the orchestra only on very rare occasions are the *guitar* and *mandolin*.

Keyboard Instruments

The *celesta* looks like a small portable organ. Its sounding mechanism consists of a series of small metal bars placed over resonators and struck by hammers controlled by a keyboard like that of a piano, but with only about four-sevenths of its range. Its tones, pure and crystalline, resemble those of soft chimes, but lack their dissonant overtones. The most prominent passage for celesta is in the "Dance of the Sugarplum Fairy" from Tchaikovsky's *Nutcracker Suite*.

The *piano* (the common abbreviation for *pianoforte*) is a string instrument whose strings are struck by hammers. These hammers are actuated by the keys on the keyboard, a series of levers faced with ivory or ebony and arranged in two tiers so as to bring a greater number of notes under the hand. The piano has not yet become a regular member of the orchestral forces, though modern composers are employing it with increasing frequency.

The piano is one of the most satisfying musical instruments. It possesses a great range, enables the performer to play many notes simultaneously, and at the same time makes but moderate physical demands. The piano can adequately reproduce many of the sounds of an orchestra and offers more varied possibilities of musical expression than any other single musical instrument.

The *organ* [5] is an instrument composed of literally thousands of pipes

[5] The organ of Bach's day is described on page 92.

of different timbres and pitches, into which air is admitted by valves. These are controlled, usually electrically, by a player performing at the *console,* which is a group of keyboards for both hands and feet. The keyboards actuated by the hands are called *manuals;* the keyboard actuated by the feet is known as the *pedal-board,* or simply, the *pedals.* The organ may be likened to an orchestra composed of many different wind instruments that may be made to sound by mechanical devices and that, by means of various ingenious mechanisms, can be brought under the control of one player. Some large modern organs have as many as one hundred and eighty different kinds of pipes. A set of pipes of one timbre is known as a *stop;* the art of choosing and varying the stops is called *registration.* While the organ offers a greater variety of color and a greater range of gross dynamic value than any other instrument, it suffers from a vital defect: the gap that exists between the player and the sounding medium. Because of the mechanical perfection of the instrument, it is impossible to vary the intensity of individual tones; the dynamic level can be changed only gradually by opening or closing shutters in front of the pipes or by adding or removing stops. When one remembers that the organist's hands and feet are well occupied with the manuals and pedals, and that changes in registration and dynamics have to be sandwiched in while playing, one is inclined to be sympathetic towards the individual who has ventured to play this unwieldy mechanism. Seldom used in orchestral music, its widest application is in church services, where its excellent ability to sustain tones renders it a valuable adjunct to the performance of choral music.

The Orchestra as a Whole

We have now examined the individual components of the orchestral body. The tones of these individual instruments may be likened to primary colors capable of being combined in an infinite number of ways; and these tone-colors must be chosen by the composer with due regard for the limitations of the instruments that produce them. Musical instruments have their unique idioms which, like the idioms of languages, are usually untranslatable. A melody played by a trombone, for example, is not the same music as the identical melody played by a bassoon. There is also the question of blending. The composer must continually ask himself if the colors that he proposes to use will mix. Will the ear hear them as a homogeneous whole or as dissociated sounds? The problem of balance must also be considered, since certain instruments are inclined to be penetrating or overpowering. These are merely a few of the problems involved in *orchestration,* the art of setting music for orchestra, as distinguished from the actual composition of the music.

The appreciation of tone-color is one of the easiest musical habits to acquire. An individual eager to acquire this faculty should, when attending symphony concerts, occupy a seat that will allow him to see the entire orchestra. Before the concert commences he can become acquainted with the appearance of the various instruments. When the music starts, aural identification of the source of the sound may then be confirmed by the eye. A work that may be recommended as an elementary study of orchestration is the *Bolero* of Maurice Ravel. With the exception of a change of key near the end, this composition consists merely of the reiteration, in different orchestral colors, of two themes. Benjamin Britten's *The Young Person's Guide to the Orchestra* (1945) is an engaging set of variations together with a fugue, on a theme of Purcell. It aims, as the composer states, "to introduce to you the instruments of the orchestra."

COÖRDINATION OF THE ORCHESTRAL INSTRUMENTS—
THE CONDUCTOR

To many persons the dominating feature of the orchestra is the conductor. Concert-goers often overestimate the significance of the conductor, and for many individuals he is apparently more important than the composer who has created the music for him to conduct. The prospectus of a symphony orchestra inviting subscriptions for a coming season always gives the names of the conductors; but it seldom, if ever, mentions the compositions that will be performed.

The conductor does three things: he chooses the program, he rehearses the players, and he conducts the concert. The conductor selects the program that he proposes to give, although if a soloist is to be included on the program, the soloist himself usually decides what he will play. Program-making is like arranging a meal; the various courses must be well planned and cannot follow one another haphazardly. More than one new work has been unfavorably received because of its poor position on a program.

After the program has been chosen, the conductor must rehearse the orchestra. Rehearsal is, in fact, instruction; the conductor instructs the orchestra in the performance of the work, explains various passages, clarifies difficulties, makes sure that every individual is playing precisely what the composer has written for his instrument, and adjusts the balance among the various orchestral groups. The greater part of the conductor's task is thus accomplished at the rehearsal.

The concert is largely the product of the rehearsal, for at the concert the conductor cannot speak with his players. Only two media of communication are available: gesture, and facial expression. Gesture is made more visible by use of a baton. The conductor apparently "beats time" with the baton. It would, however, be more accurate to say that with the baton he dictates the speed, that is, the *tempo*[6] of the work being performed. Besides, this tempo is being constantly varied. Given a fine orchestra, the problem of the conductor is largely a choice of the right tempo and of the necessary alterations within that tempo.

Much of the explanation of the art of the conductor, however, rests on a much more intangible basis—personality. The conductor must convey to the players a zeal and enthusiasm for the work in hand; he must make each and every one of the one hundred performers under his control play as if the conductor's eyes were focussed on him and him alone; he must make every instrumentalist outdo himself. The orchestra is really an instrument on which the conductor plays. Concert audiences are prone to judge a conductor by his appearance on the podium, by whether he conducts with or without a score, and so forth, but the only criterion is the quality of the orchestral performance as determined by our ears.

Suggested Readings

The best English account of the development of musical instruments is the authoritative work of Curt Sachs, *The History of Musical Instruments* (New York, 1940). The chapter "Terminology" of this treatise contains a scientific classification of instruments. Orchestration itself is discussed at length in Forsyth, *Orchestration* (London, 1929) and its history in Adam Carse, *The History of Orchestration* (New York, 1925). M. Bernstein, *Score Reading* (New York, 1948) covers orchestral terminology, notation, and transposition.

[6] See page 32.

Chapter III

FUNDAMENTAL MUSICAL
CONCEPTS: RHYTHM AND MELODY

THE CHARACTERISTICS of a single tone and the customary instruments for the creation of tones have been discussed, but as yet we have not dealt with music itself. Tones in themselves are merely raw material; it is not until they are arranged in some systematic manner that they produce what we call music.

Tones may be arranged in meaningful patterns in two ways: they may be heard in succession or they may be heard simultaneously. The first method involves recollection and comparison by the listener of acoustic events presented in sequence. The second demands instantaneous comparison and the resultant perception of pattern.

Two fundamental concepts of music arise from the arrangement of tones in sequence: rhythm and melody. A third concept, harmony, concerns itself with patterns produced by tones sounded simultaneously.

The patterns produced by tones heard successively are often referred to, purely by analogy, as horizontal patterns, while those produced by tones heard simultaneously are often described as vertical ones.

Copious instances of structures possessing both horizontal and vertical patterns can be found in daily life. The façade, stairways, elevator shafts, pipes, and so on, of an apartment house have an essentially vertical organization; the dwelling units, on the other hand, are laid out horizontally.

Similarly, the common sandwich is brought into being by superimposition of a number of horizontal units; but it is consumed as a series of vertical patterns. To use some musical terms that have not yet been defined: The sandwich as made consists of a number of dissimilar layers—horizontal patterns or *melodies;* regular munching of the sandwich results in (a) periodic horizontal flow or *rhythm* as the sandwich moves past the teeth and (b) vertical units or *chords* as the teeth close.

A close study of rhythm, melody, and harmony as found in well known music will serve as a point of orientation in the survey that will be made later in this volume. The primary purpose of this investigation will be clarification; but it should not be forgotten that in the process of analysis each element will be lifted out of its context. Actually, all three are coexistent and are continually interacting on each other.

RHYTHM

If successive sounds appear in some systematic order, the ear will at once be conscious of the existence of a pattern and, in so doing, arrange these sounds in groups. The best proof of this is the manner in which our ears habitually pattern such regularly occurring sounds as those created by the wheels of a rapidly moving railway car as they strike the rail joints. Although the sounds so created may be of equal intensity, the ear in so arranging them either perceives, or imagines that it perceives, an accent on the first sound of the group. Another excellent demonstration is to listen to the absolutely equal beats of a metronome. It will be found impossible not to group the notes and to assign an accent to the first member of each fancied group.

The perception of rhythm in music thus arises in a comparison of the length or duration of tones, or groups of tones; but inasmuch as these groups of tones are marked by stresses or accents, rhythm is concerned at the same time with accentuation.

Careful listening to music will show that of the various successive tones used some are relatively stronger, and that these relatively stronger, that is, accented, tones appear in a fairly regular pattern. The simplest pattern is one in which a strong pulse, or *beat,* alternates with a weak one. The most familiar example of this pattern is the rhythm used for marching, in which the step of the left foot invariably is executed on the strong beat. This rhythm, produced by a group of two pulses, is called duple rhythm. Groups of three pulses produce triple rhythm and those of four pulses, quadruple rhythm.

Our perception of rhythm is heightened when the number of tones appearing between pulses is varied, as is shown by the following example from the *Allegretto* of the Seventh Symphony of Beethoven:

Ex. 1

The following examples illustrate the more fundamental rhythms:

Duple rhythm.
Ex. 2. *Le Pont d'Avignon* (Anonymous).

Triple rhythm.
Ex. 3. *Come, Thou Almighty King* (Giardini).

Quadruple rhythm.
Ex. 4. *Adeste Fideles* (Anonymous).

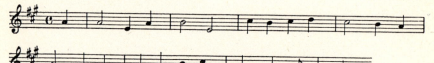

A rhythm based on groups containing five pulses, that is, quintuple rhythm, although common enough in folk music and contemporary music, is seldom found in the works of the earlier masters. The most familiar instance of its use may be found in the second movement of Tchaikovsky's Sixth Symphony (*Pathétique*):

Ex. 5

If groups of pulses are heard rapidly, our ears will tend to simplify matters and arrange these groups into larger, more inclusive patterns. The second movement of Beethoven's Ninth Symphony, for example, is in triple rhythm; but inasmuch as the groups appear in rapid succession, the ear, by a process that might be called "aural accommodation," hears larger groups in a quadruple rhythm:

Ex. 6

In the course of the movement Beethoven changes the rhythmic system so that the groups arrange themselves in triple rhythm:

Ex. 7

Many other examples could be cited of this tendency of the ear to arrange rhythmic groups into larger patterns.

It must not be inferred, however, that the accents of music appear with mechanical regularity, for while the first pulse (beat) of a group (measure) may bear a strong accent, many other secondary accents may be found. And the effect of music played with regular emphasis on the first pulse would be similar to that of reading verse in a sing-song manner that brings out the rhythmic scheme and yet destroys the poetry.

Modern composers are continually striving to expand our concepts of rhythm. An extreme example is the brutal *Danse sacrale* which closes Igor Stravinsky's *Le Sacre du printemps* (*The Rite of Spring*). (See page 421.)

Syncopation, the stressing of one or more normally unaccented beats, is one of the oldest methods of producing rhythmic interest. A few examples, all involving accentuation of the normally unaccented second beat, will demonstrate a simple type of syncopation:

Ex. 8. Beethoven—*Leonore No. 3* Overture:

Ex. 9. Franck—Symphony in D minor—First Movement

Ex. 10. Brahms—Symphony No. 2—Fourth Movement.

Tempo

The rate at which groups of pulses progress is described by the term *tempo*. Tempo and rhythm should not be confused. Rhythm refers to a system of stresses, tempo to the pace at which these stress groups progress. In an artistic rendition of any musical work, one of the chief concerns of the executant is the choice of a proper tempo. Within the confines of this underlying tempo all manner of deviations—slight accelerations at one point, slight retardations at another—are made by an understanding performer.

It is customary on concert programs to describe the several movements of larger works, such as symphonies and concertos, by giving the indications of pace and mood supplied by the composer. The long ascendancy of Italian music and musicians accounts for the predominance of Italian terms. Some of the more frequently employed designations are:

Largo—Slow, slower than *adagio*. Usually broad and stately. (The popular name for the famous aria from a Handel opera is thus only a tempo indication).

Larghetto—Slightly faster than *largo* (literally—diminutive of *largo*).

Lento—Slow

Adagio—Slow (literally *ad agio*—at ease).

Adagietto—Slightly faster than *adagio* (literally—diminutive of *adagio*).

Andante—Rather slow (literally—walking).

Andantino—Slightly faster than *andante* (literally—diminutive of *andante*).

Moderato—Moderate.

Allegretto—Not as fast as *allegro* (literally—diminutive of *allegro*).

Allegro—Fast, lively.

Presto—Quick.

Prestissimo—Very quick.

Con anima—with animation.

Con brio—with spirit.

Con espressione—with expression.

Con moto—with movement.

Cantabile—in a singing style.

Maestoso—majestically.

MELODY

A melody may be defined as a meaningful succession of single tones. The relationships between these tones are those of duration and accent, that is, rhythmic relationship, and those of pitch. (The term *melody* suffers from vagueness of usage and is frequently confused with *tune* or *air,* designations that should be restricted to melodies of a simpler type.) The perception of melody in music demands an ability to sense the relationships between successive tones. Much music that is heard with pleasure today was at first condemned as lacking in melody by auditors unaccustomed to the new relationships involved.

The listener desires melody more than anything else in music. Confusion has arisen, however, from failure to differentiate between the two large types of melodies, *vocal* and *instrumental,* though the characteristics of these types are not so well marked that a hard and fast differentiation may be made. There are, to be sure, hundreds of instrumental melodies that may be sung effectively. Melodies like the following, however, are intrinsically instrumental:

Ex. 11. Bach—Concerto for Two Violins.

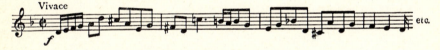

Ex. 12. Beethoven—Symphony No. 9—First Movement.

Ex. 13. Strauss—*Ein Heldenleben.*

Not all melodic relationships make themselves manifest on a first hearing, though some of the world's greatest melodies have been essentially simple. Listeners are prone to call more readily appreciated melodies "tuneful," indicating their quick grasp of the relationships between individual tones; but the effort necessary to perceive more subtle relationships, particularly as found in modern music, should not predispose one to hasty evaluation.

The number of tones available to the composer depends on the vocal or instrumental medium he has chosen. The violin, for example, affords about forty-eight tones, the piano eighty-eight, the average human voice about twenty-four, and the flute thirty-seven.

Scales

Music has much in common with another medium of communication, namely speech. Musical tones may be likened to the letters employed in speech, for just as letters are arranged in an alphabet, the tones used for the construction of melodies are arranged into chains of successive notes that are called *modes* or *scales*.[1] The tone relationships that are felt to exist in most melodies derive in large measure from the scale relationships of the tones employed.

Examination of a few melodies will demonstrate the scales on which they are based. The tones used in *Come, Thou Almighty King* (p. 30) may be systematically arranged as:

Ex. 14

The essential tones employed for this motive from Wagner's *Parsifal*:

Ex. 15
(a)

---

[1] The name is derived from the Latin *scala,* because of an analogy between the steps of a scale and the steps of a ladder. Cf. the German *Tonleiter.*

may be arranged as:

(b)

And the tones employed for Schumann's *The Merry Farmer*:

Ex. 16

(a)

as:

(b)

It will be observed that the tones are arranged within the limits of an octave. Conversely a scale may be defined as the division of the octave for musical purposes; but this definition holds true only for Western music.

It will be noticed in the case of the three examples just given that although their scales commenced on different pitches, they were identical in pattern: each scale consisted of eight tones arranged in wholesteps or half-steps in the following manner:

1–2—whole-step	5–6—whole-step
2–3—whole-step	6–7—whole-step
3–4—*half-step*	7–8—*half-step*
4–5—whole-step	

Any scale may therefore be defined in terms of (a) the tone on which it is based and (b) the arrangement of tones within it. The arrangement that we have just encountered when constructed on any tone produces a *major* scale. The scale on which Schumann's *The Merry Farmer* is based is therefore called the scale of F major.

Another type of scale is called the *minor* scale. A typical form of this scale may be shown by the following model, constructed on the tone A:

Ex. 17

Here there are half-steps between the second and third, fifth and sixth, seventh and eighth tones. For melodic purposes the minor scale is frequently altered and there are as many as three forms.

Western music during the seventeenth, eighteenth, and nineteenth centuries has used the major and minor scales almost exclusively. Prior to this period other scale types were extensively employed. Six of these "modes," often called church modes, although they were used for secular music as well, were:

Ex. 18. The Dorian Mode.

Ex. 19. The Phrygian Mode.

Ex. 20. The Lydian Mode.

Ex. 21. The Mixolydian Mode.

Ex. 22. The Aeolian Mode.

Ex. 23. The Ionian Mode.

The names given to these modes derive from a curious confusion by a medieval theorist of labels used by the ancient Greeks. It is evident that the Ionian mode is identical with our major scale, and that the Aeolian mode is one of the forms of our minor scale. These older scales have come to be called *modal* scales, and music based on them is known as modal music. Many folk songs are modal in character.

Composers of the late nineteenth and early twentieth centuries have manifested considerable interest in the possibilities of modal music, for example:

Ex. 24. Debussy—*Jimbo's Lullaby.*

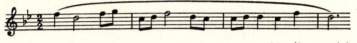

(Aeolian mode)

Ex. 25. R. Vaughan Williams—*Pastoral Symphony*—Third Movement.

(Mixolydian mode)

On playing a scale it will be noticed that certain tones seem to be more important than others and that they possess a marked relationship or affinity to other notes of the scale. The tones of the scale that are most outstanding are the first, the *tonic;* the fifth, the *dominant;* and the seventh, the *leading tone.* The complete list of the names employed for the tones of the scale is: [2]

First tone, *Tonic*	Fifth tone, *Dominant*
Second tone, *Supertonic*	Sixth tone, *Submediant*
Third tone, *Mediant*	Seventh tone, *Leading tone*
Fourth tone, *Subdominant*	Eighth tone, *Octave*

The *interval,* that is, the difference in pitch, between any two tones, is reckoned in terms of the relationship they would possess if arranged in a scale. Intervals are calculated inclusively from the lower note. The actual difference in pitch between C and E, for example, is two whole tones; but, in reckoning the interval, C itself is included so that the interval C-E is called a third. A table of intervals from C is:

[2] It is by no means necessary for the non-professional reader to memorize these names. They are found in program notes, for instance, with a fair degree of regularity and one should at least possess a general, though not necessarily active, knowledge of them.

Ex. 26

The interval between any two tones is, from the standpoint of acoustics, the ratio existing between their rates of vibration, that is to say, between their frequencies. The interval of an octave exists between two tones whose frequencies are to each other as 1:2, the interval of a fifth between two tones whose frequencies are to each other as 2:3, and so on.

The major and minor scales mentioned above are known as *diatonic* scales. But in addition to these scales other divisions of the octave are possible. The *chromatic* scale, for example, is a division of the octave into twelve half-tones:

Ex. 27

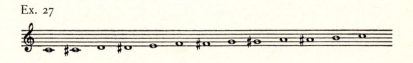

And the *whole-tone* scale is a division of the octave into six whole tones:

Ex. 28

The examples here given, however, by no means exhaust the possibilities of scale formation.

Tonality

The relationships existing between the tones of a melody as summarized in its scale give rise to our feeling for tonality. On playing over the hymn *Come, Thou Almighty King* quoted on page 30, it will be observed that the melody not only employs the scale based on G, but that the tone G serves as a basic note around which the melody gravitates and to which it returns at the conclusion, or more accurately stated, the return to which induces a feeling of rest and termination. The tonality of a composition may therefore be defined in terms of this focal tone, the *tonic,* and the type of scale constructed on it.

Our feeling for tonality is deeply rooted. Although most people cannot describe the tonality of a work in the technical terms employed by musicians, they are keenly aware of its existence and recognize departures from it and the return to it. Our feeling for tonality is an important factor in the formal design of music, as will be shown later. Change of tonality in the course of composition is known as *modulation.* For most purposes, the terms *tonality* and *key* are interchangeable.

SUGGESTED READINGS

Most of the works dealing with the material covered in this chapter presuppose some musical knowledge of their readers. An excellent short treatise is the series of essays edited by Basil Maine, *The Divisions of Music* (London, 1929). A more practical work designed to create an active appreciation of the elements of music is George Wedge, *The Gist of Music* (New York, 1936). This contains many exercises for self-instruction. There are many articles dealing with rhythm, scales, and melody and their various sub-topics in *Grove's Dictionary of Music and Musicians* (New York, 1927), and Willi Apel, *Harvard Dictionary of Music* (Cambridge, 1945).

Chapter IV

THE GOLDEN AGE OF MELODY:
GREGORIAN CHANT

A MAGNIFICENT type of church music that represents the highest point in the development of melody unhampered by considerations of harmony flourished from about the sixth to the twelfth centuries. Associated with the liturgy of the Roman Catholic Church, it is now known as *Gregorian Chant, Plain Chant,* or *Plain Song.* Numbering several thousand melodies, it finds constant use today in the ritual of the Catholic Church in all parts of the world, and alterations and offshoots have found their way into the musical services of other religions as well.

Pope Gregory I, who died in 604 A.D., had concerned himself with the organization of church ritual and the place of music in it. Since he was one of the outstanding personalities of his period, a great mass of legend about him sprang into being after his death. Among other things, he was credited with composition of chants, addition of scales, and so forth. Eventually his name became associated with the entire body of Roman chant. And although it has been shown that Gregory's role was at best that of organizer or editor of the chants, his name still remains coupled with them.

The terms Plain Chant or Plain Song, although of later origin, derive from the fact that the chant was free in its rhythms.

Gregorian Chant differs from most of the music heard today in one vital respect: it is one-line music, a single melody devoid of any accompaniment. Music of this sort may be described as *monody* (from the Greek *monos,* one; *oide,* song) or *monophony* (from the Greek *monos,* one; *phonos,* sound). The latter term is preferable.

Gregorian chants were created to be sung as part of a religious rite. Hence their prime aim was the inculcation of feelings of devotion and piety. They were usually sung by highly skilled male singers, many of whom had as orphans been trained in a special school, the *Schola Cantorum* of Rome, founded in the fourth century. Since the scholars were mostly orphans, the school was sometimes called an *orphanotrophium* (Latin, orphan asylum). The *Schola Cantorum* was thus the antecedent of later famous musical orphanages, the *Conservatorii,* which existed in Naples from the sixteenth to the eighteenth centuries. (Hence the present day term *conservatory* as a designation for a music school.) Upon completion of their training at the *Schola Cantorum* the singers went forth to promulgate the chant all over Europe. Branch schools were also established, notably at St. Gall and Metz. These highly skilled singers were also influential in maintaining a degree of uniformity in the rendition of the chants, for the musical notation of the period was most uncertain and communication by word of mouth was a more reliable means of disseminating music.

The core of the extensive liturgy of the Roman Church is the Mass, an elaborate dramatization involving a symbolic representation of the Last Supper. It is the chief act of Catholic worship.

Finally formulated in the eleventh century, that is, at a late date in the history of Gregorian Chant, the Mass text cannot be said to be the product of any one individual or any one church conference; it is the result of a long process of evolution.

The several sections of the Mass fall into two categories: the Proper (*Proprium Missae*) and the Ordinary (*Ordinarium Missae*). The various parts of the Proper change in accordance with the liturgical implications of the day upon which the Mass is being celebrated. Psalm texts appear frequently in it. With the exception of the first two phrases of the Ordinary, which are in Greek, the entire text of the Mass is in Latin.

The Ordinary, in contrast to the Proper, has an invariable text, non-Biblical in origin. It is divided into five sections known after their initial words as (1) *Kyrie eleison* ("Lord, have mercy"), (2) *Gloria in excelsis deo* ("Glory to God in the highest"), (3) *Credo in unum deum* ("I believe in one God"), (4) *Sanctus* ("Holy, holy, holy"), and (5) *Agnus Dei* ("Lamb of God").

As a purely musical and not a liturgical label, the term Mass indicates a setting of the Ordinary. No other text has been set to music so frequently. Yet the two best known versions, products of a later age, the Mass in B Minor of Bach and the *Missa Solemnis* of Beethoven, have no application in the Catholic Church because of their length as well as their disregard of certain liturgical conventions.

The musical characteristics of Gregorian Chant are easily enumerated. While melodies may vary in complexity from monotones to elaborate patterns of flowing figures, careful attention is usually paid to the expressive intent of the text. Thus the music serves as an auxiliary to the text and aims to enhance its meaning. As already stated, Gregorian Chant is one-line vocal music whose expressiveness is achieved by purely melodic means. But these melodies differ from the majority of conventional ones heard today in two respects: (a) they are modal (see page 36) and (b) their rhythm is "free" and oratorical, unfettered by the demands of a regularly recurring pattern. (It may be observed here that twentieth century composers have also written music devoid of rhythmic regularity. See page 421.) Various contradictory theories concerning the rhythmic interpretations of the chant have been promulgated and the subject still remains one for scholarly dispute.

A typical example of Gregorian Chant is the following excerpt from the Mass, an *Agnus Dei,* given here in the four-line notation of the official Roman version and then in modern notation. The "4." before the music indicates that it is in the fourth (Hypophrygian) church mode.

Ex. 1 (a)

Note: Recorded by the monks of the Abbey of Solesmes in Victor Set M-87.

(b)

(Translation of the text: Lamb of God, Who takest away the sins of the world, have mercy upon us. Lamb of God, Who takest away the sins of the world, grant us peace.)

The Mass for the Dead, the *Requiem Mass* (after its first words *Requiem aeternam dona eis*—Give them eternal rest), has contributed a now famous theme to the music of the nineteenth and twentieth centuries: the melody associated with a section of the Mass, the *Dies Irae* (Day of Wrath), a *sequence* dating from the thirteenth century. For the quotation of this chant in Berlioz' *Fantastic Symphony,* see page 275. Its most recent conspicuous appearance has been in Rachmaninoff's *Rhapsody on a Theme of Paganini,* for piano and orchestra (1934).

Suggested Readings

The best general treatment of Gregorian Chant is the article "Plainsong" in the Introductory Volume of *The Oxford History of Music* (London, 1929). A compendious discussion rich in bibliographical aids can be found in Gustave Reese, *Music in the Middle Ages* (New York, 1940). The significance of music in the liturgy is well discussed in Edward Dickinson, *Music in the History of the Western Church* (New York, 1925). The official Roman interpretation appears in Suñol, *Text Book of Gregorian Chant* (Tournai, 1930). This work embodies the precepts of the Benedictine monks of the Abbey of Solesmes, a group responsible for the revival of Gregorian Chant in the nineteenth century. The best single collection of chants is the *Liber Usualis* of the Catholic Church.

Chapter V

FUNDAMENTAL MUSICAL CONCEPTS: POLYPHONY AND HARMONY

POLYPHONY

THE EARLIEST technical account of music consisting of more than one melodic line dates from about 900 A.D. Many theories have been advanced to explain one of these first forms of melodic combination, a system in which one melody was paralleled by another melody removed from it by intervals, which were most frequently, but not exclusively, fourths and fifths.[1] This procedure was in marked contrast to classical and modern music, which considers thirds and sixths to be consonances.[2] Melodic combination based on fourths and fifths was called *organum* (accented on the first syllable), a simple form of which is shown in the following example:

Ex. 1

Sit glo · ri · a Do · mi · ni in sae · cu · la

It is obvious, however, that the degree of parallelism between the voices of the above-quoted example is too inflexible to permit the added voice to have any individuality.[3] Over two hundred years elapsed before this parallelism yielded to a style that exhibited a marked preference for melodies moving in opposite directions, with the result that these melodies were endowed with a degree of independence and also produced other intervals than the fourth and the fifth. A science of writing combined melodies known as *counterpoint*

---

[1] See page 38.
[2] See page 45.
[3] For the revival of the methods of organum at the end of the nineteenth century see page 414.

(point against point, that is, note against note) developed; and in order to furnish some regulating device with which to synchronize the movement of several melodies, a rhythmic system was evolved. The first great school of polyphonic (many-voiced) writing based on the intervals of fourths and fifths arose in the thirteenth century, with the Cathedral of Notre Dame in Paris as its principal center of activity. A second great school whose standards of consonance were built around the third and the sixth and which reached its height at the close of the sixteenth century will be discussed in the following chapter.

Consonance and Dissonance

For melodies to allow of combination, it is necessary that those pitches that are to sound simultaneously possess certain relationships. These may be classified as consonances or dissonances. No hard and fast definitions of these terms can be given, for standards of consonance have changed considerably throughout the history of music. Hence the essentially subjective descriptions that follow.

Consonances are satisfying, restful combinations that apparently produce an effect of completeness and repose and do not demand that they be followed by some other combination. The following combinations of two notes are consonances:

Ex. 2

Consonantal combinations are not limited to two notes, but can be further enlarged by adding certain other pitches.

Dissonances are not necessarily unpleasant, but they produce a tension that demands progress either immediately, or via other dissonances, to an eventual consonance. This reduction in tension of a dissonance through onward motion is called *resolution*. A few dissonances and the consonances into which they resolve are shown here:

Ex. 3

The problem of the composer of polyphonic music is, therefore, a twofold one. The tones that comprise his work must arrange them-

selves as meaningful successions (melodies) and as logical combinations (consonances and correctly resolved dissonances).[4] The combination of melodies produces *polyphony;* the instantaneous combination
of tones produces *harmony.* Up to about the year 1600 composers
were interested primarily in the flow of melodies, in the motion of
individual parts rather than in the effects of simultaneously sounding
pitches, though, to be sure, these effects had to be taken into consideration.

The Canon

A polyphonic device that has found frequent application is the
canon, a method of polyphonic writing in which there is a literal imitation of one voice by a succeeding voice or voices. An excellent example of the canon is the two-part Invention in F major of Bach:

Ex. 4

The Minuet of the String Quartet in D minor, Opus 76, No. 2, of
Haydn commences with a spirited canon:

Ex. 5

---

[4] See the discussion of the horizontal and the vertical aspects of music on page 28.

A canon, it will be observed, may be regarded as a polyphonic composition in which a melody is combined with succeeding parts of itself. The imitating voices may repeat the melody of the antecedent voice at the unison, the octave, the fifth, or at any other interval; but the first two kinds of imitation are employed most frequently. A *round,* such as the familiar *Three Blind Mice,* is a canon at the unison or octave, in which the performers enter at regular intervals and make the circuit from the beginning to the end and back again without ceasing.

Short passages in a canonic style are frequently found in symphonic music. Beethoven concludes his Fifth Symphony with a triumphant canonic statement of the first theme of the last movement;[5] Franck writes in a similar manner in the first and last movements of his Symphony in D minor.

HARMONY

Polyphony and harmony arose side by side; but since the seventeenth century polyphony has relinquished its former position of priority and harmonic considerations have become important factors in the construction of musical works. The origin of harmony in polyphony may be shown by an examination of the following excerpt from Palestrina's *Stabat Mater* (c. 1590), written in a block-like style in which, since all the voices commence and progress together, their melodic individuality is considerably lessened.

Ex. 6

Despite the fact that these blocks represent cross-sectional cuts made through layers of melody, they possess certain features that have enabled musicians to regard them as separate entities to which the name *chords* has been given.

[5] Quoted on page 194, Example 25.

Homophony

The rapid rise of the opera, dating from about 1600, was responsible for an acceleration in the development of a musical idiom in which emphasis was placed on a single voice accompanied by chords. The polyphonic style, consisting of the interweaving of several independent and equally important melodies, thus gave way to a new method in which one melody predominated while the rest of the musical texture, grouped into chords, fulfilled an auxiliary function. The style is therefore called homophonic because of this emphasis on one voice.

Since the beginning of the seventeenth century, music has been predominantly harmonic in character, but the basic principles of melody formation still govern the progression of chords. The deciding factor between the rival claims on the listener's ear of the harmonic and the polyphonic aspects of any composition is the degree of musical interest, that is, the melodiousness, of its component parts. In the following excerpt from Johann Strauss' *The Beautiful Blue Danube,* for example, the chordal accompaniment which serves as a simple underpinning for the melody possesses largely rhythmic interest:

Ex. 7

But in this excerpt from the chorale that concludes Bach's Cantata No. 72, *Alles nur nach Gottes Willen,* the three accompanying voices not only form chords, but also possess strong melodic individuality: [6]

Ex. 8

Wer Gott ver-traut, fest auf ihn baut, den will er nicht ver - las - - sen.

---

[6] Another Bach chorale will be found on page 98.

Chords

A chord may be defined as a combination of several tones sounded simultaneously. A combination of three tones capable of arrangement as a fundamental note and two superimposed thirds is called a *triad*. A triad composed of a major third and a perfect fifth is called a major triad. The major triad erected on C is:

A minor triad is composed of a minor third and a perfect fifth:

Either of these triads is known as a *common* chord.

The chord of four tones, resulting from the addition of another third to a triad, is called a seventh chord, since it consists of a fundamental, third, fifth, and seventh. The most important of the numerous types of seventh chords is that formed on the dominant (the fifth scale degree) and consequently called the dominant seventh chord. The dominant seventh chord is a dissonant chord of great importance in the definition of tonality. The following illustration shows a seventh chord and a conventional resolution of it:

Additional chords may be created by adding more thirds, raising or lowering the component intervals, or by changing the position of the fundamental tone. The number of possible chords is vast indeed, and new chord-structures and new chord-progressions are continually being evolved.

Chords may be classified as consonant or dissonant, depending on the intervals composing them and the context in which they are found. One dissonant chord is often followed by another, constituting either a new dissonance or a partial resolution, but a state of rest is not reached until a consonant chord is achieved. The art of harmonization consists of the judicious employment of both consonance and dissonance.   Too much consonance is stultifying; too much dissonance is either vitiating or confusing.

It is not necessary that tones be sounded simultaneously to give the effect of a chord.   The ear possesses the faculty of realizing the harmonic implications of successive tones when they are arranged in groups such as:

Ex. 9

This excerpt, the first four measures of the Prelude in C major, Part I, No. 1, of Bach's *The Well-Tempered Clavier,* consists of the elaboration of the following chords by breaking them up into graceful arpeggios:

Melodies themselves often have chordal implications.   The following themes from *Das Rheingold* of Wagner, for example, are based on the notes of the common chord:

Ex. 10

(a)

(b)

A sustained or reiterated bass note over which a series of chords progresses is called a *pedal.* Other names are pedal-point and organ-point. The pedal is an ancient harmonic device tracing its origins to the primitive *drone,* still a distinctive feature of the Scotch bagpipe. The modern name is derived from the custom of sustaining such bass notes by means of the organ pedal.

A pedal sounding throughout the entire fifty-five measures of the middle section of the second movement of the Sixth (*Pathétique*) Symphony of Tchaikovsky begins as follows:

Ex. 11

Almost every major work of Tchaikovsky capitalizes on the tension-creating potentialities of the pedal.

A pedal may also appear in an upper voice, in which case it is called an *inverted pedal.* The following example from the overture to Wagner's opera *Der fliegende Holländer* (The Flying Dutchman) shows an inverted pedal, the effectiveness of which is enhanced by momentary deviation from the pedal tone.

Ex. 12

Suggested Readings

Most of the literature on the subject matter of this chapter presupposes an extensive musical background. For the properly equipped reader, however, there are valuable articles, for example, "Counterpoint," "Harmony," and so forth in *Grove's Dictionary of Music and Musicians* (New York, 1927) and *The Harvard Dictionary of Music* (Cambridge, 1945). Ernest Toch, *The Shaping Forces in Music* (New York, 1948) is a trenchant discussion of fundamental musical concepts. Lawrence Abbot, *The Listener's Book on Harmony* (Philadelphia, 1941) is an enjoyable treatise enlivened by many quotations from popular music.

Chapter VI

THE GOLDEN AGE OF POLYPHONY

THE LONG process of development of the art of writing polyphonic vocal music culminated during the second half of the sixteenth century in what has often been referred to as a "Golden Age."
But great as is the space devoted to the music of this period in various
historical treatises, almost none of it can be said to enjoy any widespread popularity today. And for those who have any interest in this
music, recorded performances constitute practically the sole method of
hearing it. But our modern methods of recording music, despite all
their technical perfection, are for the most part inadequate for reproducing the complexities of vocal polyphony with its emphasis on
equality of musical interest in its constituent parts. Furthermore, it
should be remembered that the choruses that performed this music
differed significantly from those of today: (1) they were all male;
upper parts were sung by the clear, firm voices of boy sopranos; and
(2) choruses were much smaller than those customarily heard today.
(The Papal Choir in Rome numbered 26 performers in 1594.) Hence
all the various simultaneously sounding melodies were much more
apparent to the ear. To sum up, a stylistically correct and mechanically adequate performance of works drawn from this great wealth of
superb music will be a rare experience indeed. The listener should
be wary of formulating adverse critical judgments that are unwittingly
caused more by poor performance than any other single factor.

The approach to the vocal polyphonic music of the sixteenth century should be made with the observation of an astute writer on music,
Sir Donald Francis Tovey, continually in mind: ". . . though the
music of one age or style may at first be unintelligible to a listener who
is accustomed to another style, and though the listener may help him-

self by acquiring information as to the characteristics and meaning of the new style, he will best learn to understand it by merely divesting his mind of prejudices and allowing the music to make itself intelligible by its own self-consistency. The understanding of music thus finally depends neither upon technical knowledge nor upon convention, but upon the listener's immediate and familiar experience of it; an experience which technical knowledge and custom can of course aid him to acquire more rapidly, as they strengthen his memory and enable him to fix impressions by naming them." [1]

The history of European music from 900 to 1600 A.D. concerns itself primarily with the development of the idioms of polyphony. The principal impetus to this development was furnished by composers either born in or resident in the region of northern France and Belgium vaguely referred to as the Low Countries, the Netherlands, Brabant, Flanders, Burgundy, and so on. They are most often described as Flemish composers, though the awkward appellation "Franco-Flemish" would be more accurate. Prominent among these outstanding Flemings were Guillaume Dufay (c. 1400-1474), canon of the cathedral at Cambrai; Jean Ockeghem (c. 1430-1495), *maître de chapelle* to two kings of France, Charles VII and Louis XI; Jacob Obrecht (c. 1430-1505), active at the Cathedral of Antwerp; and Josquin des Prés (c. 1450-1521), for a long time a resident in Italy, like Dufay also in charge of the music at Cambrai, and one of the most famous composers of his epoch.

So great was the artistic proficiency of Flemish musicians that their style set the musical standards for almost all of Europe. As performers and as composers their services were everywhere in demand. Flemish musicians performing music either written by Flemings or composed under their influence could be heard at such important musical centers as the Papal Chapel in Rome, the Cathedral of St. Mark in Venice, the Medici court in Florence, and the Wittelsbach court in Bavaria.

Flemish techniques reached their apex in the works of Philippe de Monte (1521-1603), alternately in the service of the Hapsburg rulers in Vienna and Prague, and Orlandus Lassus (c. 1532-1594), in the service of Duke Albert V at Munich. De Monte's achievements as a creative artist have been rediscovered but recently; the eminence of

[1] See "Music," *Encyclopædia Britannica*, Eleventh Edition. London, 1910.

Lassus, on the other hand, has always been conceded by music historians. The Italian, Giovanni Pierluigi da Palestrina (c. 1525-1594), called after his birthplace, Palestrina, spent over forty years in the service of churches in Rome and eventually became composer to the Papal Choir. Embellished by myth and by romantic adulation, the name of Palestrina is the most frequently mentioned in references to sixteenth-century music. But beautiful and moving though his works may be, they are more the embodiment of the spirit of the Counter-Reformation than of the prevailingly humanistic temper of the Renaissance. If any one composer of the second half of the sixteenth century is to be singled out as most representative of his time, the honor would have to be accorded to Lassus.

A description of the vast corpus of late sixteenth-century music produces at best a series of generalized observations, of limited validity for any individual composition. Nevertheless, it is possible to list some features that will be encountered with a high degree of frequency.

Polyphonic vocal music of this period was closely associated with its text: composers continually strove to find music that would add expressiveness to the words. But, on the other hand, polyphonic textures are often in conflict with the intelligibility of a text. Nor does the prevalence of Latin for sacred music ameliorate the plight of the present-day listener. But it should be borne in mind that the texts used for sacred music at the time were, through frequent repetition, fairly well known to listeners and that problems of intelligibility, vexing as they were in some instances even in the sixteenth century, are greatly increased today. Hence it is of the utmost importance that any present-day listener to polyphonic vocal music be sure that he has prior knowledge of the text he is hearing. For, as will be shown later, the text was usually the all-important factor in determining the structural design of a work.

Sixteenth-century polyphonic works were conceived as patterns of simultaneously sounding melodies. The independence of these melodies was stressed above all. This essential individuality of melodic patterns was achieved most effectively through contrast in their rhythms. The bar line of latter-day music, for example, which more or less dictates uniformity of accentuation in any sort of ensemble music, was not employed in the sixteenth century; and the rhythmic

ORLANDUS LASSUS

stresses of each individual part were determined according to the textual needs of that part rather than by a uniform, all-embracing rhythmic scheme. Thus there is much to be said for the thesis that true polyphony is nothing more or less than polyrhythm.

The melodies in these polyphonic works were almost invariably modal (see p. 36) and involved essentially simple melodic progressions. But the ostensible simplicity of this music as performed today is misleading. There is much evidence to show that singers of the time were expected to take many liberties with the composer's indications and that elaborate alterations and embellishments of melodies were done almost routinely. But in any event the music was eminently singable.

Music written for voices unaccompanied by instruments is described as *a cappella,* an Italian term meaning literally "for the choir." (The primary meaning of the word *cappella* is "chapel," a part of the church where the choir sang. Eventually the word was applied to the choir itself.) Although sixteenth-century polyphonic vocal music was conceived as *a cappella* music by its composers, contemporary paintings show us that some of the voice parts were occasionally doubled by a wide variety of instruments. Duplication of voices by instruments was most common in secular polyphonic music. Today, however, the term *a cappella* is reserved for purely unaccompanied singing.

Continuous overlapping of the melodic entries and closes is common in this music and a melodic idea will often appear in one voice before its termination in a preceding one. This results in a highly pleasing concealment of the ends of structural units and an effective maintenance of listener interest. But to the listener nurtured on music of the late eighteenth and early nineteenth century, Haydn, Mozart, and Beethoven, for example, this absence of well-defined structural landmarks may be disconcerting at first. On the other hand, it should be borne in mind that most works of the sixteenth century are fairly short and that their texts serve to indicate their formal plan.

Above all, it cannot be too strongly emphasized that the simultaneously sounding melodies of these compositions are conceived primarily as melodies and not as aggregations of chords (see page 48). While the simultaneous sounding of them was bound to produce chords, the resultant harmonies were for the most part of secondary interest. Here

again the present-day listener with his extensive experience of music
whose texture and form are determined by chords will have to abandon
his old standards. Later polyphony, that of Bach, for example, is built
on a chordal pattern and its formal plan is always governed by harmonic considerations.

A cardinal principle in sixteenth-century polyphony is that of *imitation*. Imitation consists of the repetition by one voice of a melody that
has already been given out by another. Usually only the initial features of a melody are duplicated. The workings of imitative polyphony are shown in the excerpt from Palestrina printed on page 59.

Here the initial figure:

Ex - al - ta - bo te,

is consistently duplicated, after which literal imitation is abandoned.

Imitation with no alteration other than pitch, that is, literal imitation of a melody, produces *canon,* a type of polyphonic writing with
which we are already familiar (see p. 46). Sixteenth-century composers utilized canonic devices with considerable frequency, occasionally carrying them to extremes more gratifying to the eye than to the
ear. The peculiar delight of composing intricate canons has attracted
composers of all periods from the fifteenth century up to the present.[2]

Polyphonic compositions could be built around a *cantus firmus,* a pre-
existent melody. The *cantus firmus,* as its name indicates, a fixed
melody, would be assigned to one voice while the others wove a polyphonic texture about it. *Canti firmi* might be either Gregorian melodies, melodies from other polyphonic works, scale fragments, or
secular tunes. One of the most frequently employed secular melodies
was an old French song, *L'homme Armé (The Armed Man).* There
are over thirty polyphonic Masses that employ this tune as a *cantus
firmus.*

The prevailing forms of sacred music of the period were the *Mass*
and the *motet*. The former, as has already been indicated (p. 41),
was on a setting of the *Ordinary*. The motet, on the other hand, was
a short composition utilizing a text almost always in Latin and usually
a Biblical extract. The term "motet" is an old one with a variety of

[2] For the curious, enigmatical canons of the late fifteenth century see the article "Inscription"
in *Grove's Dictionary of Music and Musicians* (New York, 1927).

Ex. 1

implications, both sacred and secular, and only the sixteenth-century aspects of it can be discussed here.

The motet, which reached its greatest height in the works of Lassus, had a form determined by its text. The principle of design was fairly consistent: the text was broken up into its constituent phrases and each phrase was developed musically according to the implications of its words. The result was a carefully joined series of polyphonic units of varying degrees of textural complexity, tempo, and mood. Illustrations by musical means of pictorial words and words expressing emotion are common in the motet.

The secular equivalent of the motet was the *madrigal,* again a form that can be described here only in its sixteenth-century manifestations. It differs from the motet in these respects: (1) its text is in the vernacular; (2) it was sung by amateurs, usually members of the upper classes, and for their own pleasure in performance; that is, it was a form of vocal chamber music. This is our first contact with music of this type, music designed for its performers and not for listeners. This does not imply that listeners cannot enjoy rendition of music of this sort. But it does mean that like spectators at baseball or football games, they must know enough of the mechanism of the proceedings to identify themselves with the players; (3) homophonic textures (see page 48) will often be encountered; (4) the expressive power of dissonant chords were utilized more frequently than in sacred music.

Although the madrigal arose in Italy and reached an amazingly high degree of perfection in that land, it may be observed in what is often held to be its finest flower in Elizabethan England, where the cultivation of this engaging type of amateur music represented but one of the many facets of the rich cultural life of a brilliant period in English history.

The young gallant of Elizabethan England, like his Continental counterpart, found it incumbent upon himself to be a master of many arts—fencing, courting, equestrianism, verse-making, and the singing or playing of music. This amateur aspect of Elizabethan music-making cannot be too strongly emphasized. A visitor to a cultured Elizabethan household was not considered a person of breeding unless he could take his part in an after-dinner session of madrigal singing.

English interest in the madrigal had been stirred up by the publication in London in 1588 of *Musica Transalpina,* a collection of madrigals by prominent Italians. English composers adopted the form with enthusiasm, availed themselves of the rich poetic resources around them, and before long gave the madrigal a distinctly English character.

Following the prevailing musical taste of their times, the English composers found effective musical illustrations for the descriptive words or phrases in their texts. And they were particularly adept at utilizing dissonant chords to underscore important words. The contemporary emphasis on expression is best described by Thomas Morley, himself a distinguished composer of madrigals. Writing in his *A Plaine and Easie Introduction to Practicall Musicke* [3] (1597), he says of the form: "As for the musick it is next unto the Motet, the most artificiall [that is, full of artifice] and to men of understanding most delightfull. If therefore you will compose in this kind you must possesse your selfe with an amorus humor . . . so that you must in your musicke be wavering like the wind, sometime wanton, sometime drooping, sometime grave and staide, otherwhile effeminat . . . and the more varietie you shew the better shal you please."

Some of the outstanding English madrigal composers were William Byrd (1543-1623), Thomas Weelkes (c. 1575-1623), John Wilbye (1574-1638), held to be the greatest of the school, Orlando Gibbons (1583-1625), and the Thomas Morley (1558-1603) whose famous treatise has been quoted above.

Suggested Readings

Gustave Reese, *Music in the Renaissance,* now in preparation for the Norton History of Music series will be the best source for detailed information on the material discussed in this chapter. Guides to the technical aspects of sixteenth-century polyphony are Arthur Merritt, *Sixteenth Century Polyphony* (Cambridge, 1939) and Reginald Morris, *Contrapuntal Technique in the 16th Century* (London, 1922). The great three-volume work of Albert Einstein, *The Italian Madrigal* (Princeton, 1949), is a rich cultural history. Canon E. H. Fellowes, *The English Madrigal* (London, 1935) and Morrison Boyd, *Elizabethan Music and Music Criticism* (Philadelphia, 1940) are to be highly recommended. The texts used for the entire corpus of English madrigals have been assembled by Canon Fellowes in his *English Madrigal Verse* (London, 1929). Bruce Pattison, *Music and Poetry of the English Renaissance* (London, 1948) is a rich collection

[3] Reprinted in facsimile by the Shakespeare Association, London, 1937. A modernized version under the title *A Plain and Easy Introduction to the Skill of Music,* edited by R. Alec Harman, is also available (London, 1950).

of colorful material on music in the sixteenth century, the relationship of poetry and music, literary and musical forms, and so on. Although no English biography of Lassus is available, there is a lengthy article on him in *Grove's Dictionary of Music and Musicians* (New York, 1927). Palestrina's life and music are discussed in readable fashion in Henry Coates, *Palestrina* (New York, 1938).

Chapter VII

FUNDAMENTAL MUSICAL CONCEPTS: FORM

INDIVIDUAL tones have been likened to the letters of the alphabet. We have also observed how these tones may be grouped in some orderly manner to produce melodies. In examining the structure of melody, further analogies with the structure of language may be observed. It will be recalled that letters are grouped into words, words into phrases, phrases into clauses or sentences, and the latter into paragraphs. Paragraphs may be grouped into chapters and a series of chapters into a complete book. Analogous procedures may be observed in the composition of musical works.

The Motive, the Phrase, and the Sentence

The smallest meaningful unit of musical thought is the *motive*— a compact group of notes having a pattern sufficiently distinctive to differentiate it from other groups. A few well known motives will illustrate the meaning of the term:

Ex. 1. Beethoven—Symphony No. 5— First Movement.

Ex. 2. Beethoven—Symphony No. 9— Second Movement.

Ex. 3. Wagner—*Die Walküre.*

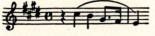

Ex. 4.   Franck—Symphony in D minor—
              First Movement.

A musical theme may consist of several motives. The opening melody of the Sixth Symphony (*Pastoral Symphony*) of Beethoven, for example, contains five motives:

Ex. 5

Later detached from the melody in which they first appear, these musical units are utilized by Beethoven in various ways, typical examples of which are:

Motive 1

Motive 2

Motive 3

Motive 4

Motive 5

The *phrase,* the next larger musical unit, consists of either repetitions of the same motive, or of several motives. It is analogous to the phrase in language, which is composed of several words comprising a unit of thought. Musical phrases, like written or spoken ones, have a measure of self-subsistence, but they lack complete sense until they are arranged in a *sentence* or period. The more conventional musical phrase is four measures long, and the more conventional musical sentence consists of two or more musical phrases.

The following excerpts will serve to illustrate the construction of the musical sentence:

Ex. 6.   Smith—*The Star-Spangled Banner.*

Ex. 7.   Foster—*The Old Folks at Home.*

Ex. 8.   Beethoven—Sonata, Opus 13 (*Pathétique*)—Second Movement.

Ex. 9.   Beethoven—Symphony No. 9—Fourth Movement.

Cadences

Each phrase in the above sentences concludes with a *cadence.* The cadences of a musical composition may be likened to the pauses, to the rising and falling of the voice, in spoken language. They indicate the completion of some unit of the structure and are powerful factors in the establishment of tonality. Cadences vary in conclusiveness. The more common cadences are called the *perfect cadence,* the *plagal cadence,* the *half-cadence* and the *deceptive cadence.*

The *perfect cadence* is analogous to the fall of the voice at a period. A typical example is:

Ex. 10

Almost every musical composition ends with a perfect cadence, additional examples of which will be found at the conclusion of the sentences quoted in Examples 6–9. The perfect cadence is produced by following the chord based on the fifth degree of the scale, the dominant, with one based on the first degree, the tonic.

The *plagal cadence* is produced by following the chord based on the fourth degree of the scale, the subdominant, with the chord based on the tonic:

Ex. 11

This cadence, while just as conclusive as the perfect cadence, has an atmosphere of dignity and impressiveness. It is almost invariably used for the *Amen* after hymns. An excellent instance of the use of the plagal cadence is found at the close of Wagner's Prelude to *Lohengrin*:

Ex. 12

The *half-cadence* is analogous to the fall of the voice at a semicolon. It may be produced by following any chord with one based on the dominant:

Ex. 13
(a)

or

(b)

The *deceptive cadence,* also called the interrupted cadence, is produced when the chord based on the dominant is followed not by the awaited chord based on the tonic, but rather by a wholly unexpected chord; in fact, the deceptive cadence is not a cadence at all in that it wholly negates any feeling of conclusiveness. The effect of the deceptive cadence is always one of surprise, for the expected conclusion fails to materialize. The Prelude in E-flat minor from Part One of *The Well-Tempered Clavier* of Bach possesses two dramatic deceptive cadences:

Ex. 14
(a)

instead of:

(b)

and

Ex. 15
(a)

instead of:

(b)

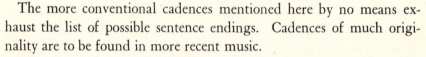

The more conventional cadences mentioned here by no means exhaust the list of possible sentence endings. Cadences of much originality are to be found in more recent music.

The sentences quoted in Examples 6–9 are all eight measures long, divided into two phrases of four measures each. The structure of musical works would be uninteresting, however, if all sentences were so constructed. Many other arrangements are not only feasible but extraordinarily common. Phrases may be shortened, extended, or overlapped without doing violence to our feeling for balance and symmetry.

Musical Forms

The term *form* permits of two broad interpretations, the first of which is essentially subjective in nature. We say that an art work possesses form when the relationships and arrangement of its component parts give rise to a feeling of unity and proportion. A musical composition thus possesses form when the ear perceives it as a unified and well-proportioned structure in sound. The first interpretation of form is therefore the concern of aesthetics.

The second interpretation of form is essentially objective in that it represents a system of classification of the methods employed by composers. If we speak of the *Sonata,* the *Concerto,* the *Overture* as encountered early in the nineteenth century in the works of Beethoven, we deal with a large number of highly individual compositions possessing many common characteristics of form. Thus a study of musical forms can be used to furnish a statistical account of the implications of certain titles at certain specific epochs. One can, for example, predict with considerable accuracy the form of a composition that Haydn or Mozart would label *Minuet*. But the forms employed by composers should not be regarded as rigid molds for the mass production of musical works. No great composer has meekly accepted the prevailing forms of his day as invariable codes of procedure to which he was compelled to adhere.

A great many compositions cannot be discussed in terms of traditional designations of form. That is, many works have a thoroughly satisfying formal structure that is unique and without any relationship to a conventional form. Many of the organ preludes of Bach, the Third Act Preludes of Wagner's operas, the tone poems of Richard Strauss, and the piano pieces of Debussy, for example, have forms which can only be described as *sui generis*.

It is essential to distinguish between *form* and *style* in music. Strictly speaking, the form of a composition is only the sequence and relationship of its various parts. Thus a minuet of Haydn and the chorus of a contemporary fox trot may have identical forms but differ vastly in style. Actually a large number of musical labels are much more descriptive of style than they are of form. Such titles as *motet, prelude, fugue,* will deal purely with the style of a composition; while terms such as *sarabande, courante,* and *gigue* will usually include works having the same form but varying styles. The medium for which a composition is written—for example, string quartet or symphony orchestra; its texture—homophonic or polyphonic; its place of performance—for instance, the concert hall or the choir loft; its function; its national origin; the personal style of its composer; all these ingredients and many others enter into a discussion of the style of a composition as apart from its formal patterns.

Recognition of the form of a composition demands perception of the identities and diversities of its constituent parts, for musical form is the product of repetition and contrast. Every element of music mentioned in Chapters III and V—melody, rhythm, and harmony—may be involved in the creation of these identities or diversities. The ear also demands that the various constituent parts of a composition possess some symmetry in time, that is to say, durational balance.

The Two-Part Form

The simplest musical form consists of two complete sentences, a structure that divides naturally into two parts and is consequently called a *binary form,* or a *two-part form.* This form is to be found in many folk songs, hymns, and shorter piano pieces. A beautiful example is the folk-like song of Brahms—*Wiegenlied* (Lullaby):

Ex. 16

This melody consists of two sentences, each eight measures in length. Employing letters to designate the two sentences, its form may be schematically represented as A B.

Both halves of a two-part form may be considerably extended; that is, they may consist of several sentences. The perfect balance exhibited by the example quoted will not be retained invariably, nor will the second part always remain in the same key. But no matter how extended or complex the two sections may become, the structure consists of two distinct parts. Many examples of extended pieces in two-part form are to be found in the clavier suites of J. S. Bach.

The Three-Part Form

From the theoretical standpoint the number of musical forms is an infinite one. It can be shown, however, that one principle of construction has been employed more frequently than any other. This principle may be set forth as: *Statement—Digression—Restatement.* The form itself is called *three-part form, ternary form,* or *three-part song-form.*

The nature of this fundamental form may well be demonstrated by the familiar *Drink to Me Only With Thine Eyes:*

Ex. 17

The song consists of only two phrases; the first is heard three times, the second once. Using letters to represent these phrases the form of this song may be given as A A B A, or in semi-musical notation, A:||B A, signifying Statement (repeated)—Digression—Restatement. *Drink to Me Only With Thine Eyes* is, of course, a very elementary example of three-part form. In more extended works, the B section presents a more vivid contrast than that found in the simple example quoted above. Such contrast may be obtained by change of tonality, rhythm, or tempo, or by employment of new thematic material. Nor is the first part always repeated literally.

Further instances of the three-part form are legion in number. Detailed descriptions of other works employing the form will be discussed as they appear in the historical development of music. One of the surest routes to a rich appreciation of music is through a study of form. No opportunity for analysis of any work should be overlooked, though such analysis should at first be conducted along broad lines. Intelligent listening to folk songs, hymns, and short piano pieces will create an excellent background for the perception of the more subtle identities and diversities to be found in the larger forms. Much modern dance music is quite regular in design, and the average current song hit affords an easy study of the first principles of musical form.

SUGGESTED READINGS

The number of texts on musical form that can be easily read by a non-professional is small in number. The student who is familiar with the notation of music can find valuable material in Morris, *The Structure of Music* (London, 1940), Murphy, *Form in Music for the Listener* (published by the Radio Corporation of America, RCA Victor Division, Camden, 1945) and George Wedge, *The Gist of Music* (New York, 1936).

Chapter VIII

THE BAROQUE EPOCH

ALMOST all the characteristic features of the music commonly heard today, that is, the music of the last two centuries, have their origins in the remarkable development of musical styles which took place in the seventeenth century.

The principal impetus to the formulation of these new methods was the birth and subsequent intense cultivation of the opera. Following the opening of public opera houses, admission-paying audiences came into being and the secularization of music was greatly accelerated. With its stress on the solo voice, the opera demanded a new style—homophony with its emphasis on melody supported by chords as opposed to the equality of parts of earlier polyphonic music. And with the recognition of the function of chords as entities rather than as the by-products of polyphony, a rapid development of harmony as a means of musical expression took place, particularly in the use of dissonant chords as media for the intensification of words.

Instruments of various types were employed for the early operas, and from the various experimental groupings of them arose our modern orchestra, an aggregation of players with a name that indicates its origin in the theater. The use of the orchestra for dramatic purposes stimulated the development of instruments and of characteristic instrumental tone colors as, for example, in the exploitation of trumpets for martial scenes.

The increased use of instruments resulted in a growing awareness of intrinsic instrumental idioms. Music was written specifically in terms of the capabilities of various instruments, particularly the violin and the keyboard instruments. Differences between vocal and instrumental capacities were not only recognized but were utilized to produce one of the characteristic types of the baroque period, the *concerto,* a style that throughout its long history has capitalized on contrast of sonorities.

To the orchestra also fell the task of supplying incidental music before and during the opera, as well as music for ballet. In many operas, notably those by French and English composers, a considerable amount of this purely instrumental music was inserted. And in their solutions of the problems involved in writing instrumental pieces whose form depended on purely musical considerations without the organizing aid of a text, these composers laid the foundations for what later became one of the most significant of musical forms—the symphony.

The musical methods and the instrumental media mentioned above were conceived by the composers who used them as a means of expression, particularly when associated with words. Hence the music of the period places emphasis on movement and surprise and avoids the complacency of obvious symmetry. Its melodic lines are often richly ornamented, its harmonies striking, its emotional tensions strong, its often pictorial aims brilliantly achieved.

New musical styles come into being in the church as well as in the theater. Characteristic forms and idioms were developed for the organ, an instrument whose greatest music dates from this period. Italian innovations were assiduously cultivated and carried to high levels of perfection by Dutch and German organists, the latter making extensive use of the great number of *chorales* (congregational hymns) brought into being by the spiritual impetus of the Reformation.

Within the confines of palace and house and with some frequency in the church as well, chamber music, vocal or instrumental, with a keyboard instrument as an indispensable adjunct, was ardently cultivated, with the resultant creation of new forms. The *sonata* is another product of this era.

The period from about 1600, the end of the High Renaissance, to about 1750, the year in which J. S. Bach died, is generally referred to today as the "Baroque" period. The term "baroque" itself is of uncertain origin. Contemporary scholarship holds it to be derived from a meaningless mnemonic device of formal logic. At first the word was used depreciatively for some of the more bizarre styles of architecture, sculpture, and painting that developed in Italy around 1600 and spread all over Europe. Today the term is used almost universally by cultural historians to describe the salient features of seventeenth-century civilization.

The unique and immense baroque contribution of musical materials to posterity can be discussed here only in terms of its culmination in the works of two composers, Johann Sebastian Bach and George Frideric Handel. It should be borne in mind that many illustrious names and a great catalogue of distinguished music preface this climax. The music of Bach and Handel typify the baroque style only at its most fully developed level, a stage that was reached after the participation of many composers in a century-and-a-half-long quest for suitable methods of musical expression. But in the works of Bach and Handel we shall encounter almost every form and every idiom of the period.

SUGGESTED READINGS

The first and only English book devoted to baroque music is the basic work of Manfred Bukofzer—*Music in the Baroque Era* (New York, 1947). Another significant contribution, Susanne Clercx—*Le Baroque et la musique, Essai d'esthétique musicale* (Brussels, 1948), awaits translation into English. A lack of command of German should not deter the student from examining Robert Haas—*Die Musik des Barocks,* (Wildpark-Potsdam, 1929) a volume in the *Handbuch der Musikwissenschaft,* edited by Ernst Bücken—for the work is richly illustrated with all manner of contemporary material. For the beginnings of opera see Donald J. Grout, *A Short History of Opera* (New York, 1947).

Only a handful of the outstanding baroque composers who preceded Bach and Handel are discussed in books in the English language. Among the more valuable treatises may be mentioned: Henri Prunières, *Monteverdi, His Life and Work* (New York, 1926); Leo Schrade, *Monteverdi, Creator of Modern Music* (New York, 1950); J. A. Westrup, *Purcell* (London, 1937); Edward J. Dent, *Alessandro Scarlatti* (London, 1905); and the same author's *Foundations of English Opera* (Cambridge, 1928).

Chapter IX

THE CULMINATION OF THE BAROQUE: JOHANN SEBASTIAN BACH

JOHANN SEBASTIAN BACH, the greatest of a line of over fifty Thuringian musicians bearing this family name, was born in Eisenach on the 21st of March, 1685. Left an orphan at the age of ten, he was taken into the family of an older brother who served not only as a foster parent, but also as his instructor in music. Like most of the musicians of this period, Bach became an expert performer not only on the organ and the clavier (a generic name which includes the various keyboard instruments of the period), but also on the violin. Bach's academic education consisted of ten years of schooling, upon the completion of which, at the age of eighteen, he held posts as organist in two small German towns, Arnstadt and Mühlhausen. In the former place he seems to have drawn the wrath of the church officials upon himself because of the "strange harmonies" that he introduced into his organ playing.

Before proceeding to describe the three important posts that Bach held during his lifetime, the position of the musician during this period must be made clear: he was regarded merely as an employee whose duty it was not only to perform music, but also to create it. The music so created usually remained the property of his employer. Musicians were expected to furnish new music for all occasions, and such inspiration as might accompany the composition of a new work was entirely incidental. Writing for small courts rather than for a large public, composers wrote only such music as was demanded of them. Music was a commodity supplied by the court composer in precisely the same manner that food was supplied to the princely table by the cook.

Wilhelm Ernst, Duke of Saxe-Weimar, took Bach into his service as court organist and chamber musician in 1708. Since the Duke was an intensely religious man, Bach's duties were confined entirely to the services held in the ducal chapel; and most of his major works for organ and a few cantatas were composed during this nine-year sojourn in Weimar. Failure to receive an expected promotion to the post of Kapellmeister caused Bach to resign, and his audacity in demanding his release from ducal service earned him one month's arrest.

From 1717 to 1723 Bach was at Anhalt-Cöthen at the court of Prince Leopold, a young man fond of chamber music but not at all concerned with religious music. Accordingly, almost all of Bach's secular works were composed while he was in the service of this nobleman.

Chiefly because of a desire to give his numerous progeny the educational advantages of a large city, Bach accepted in 1723 his third and last post, that of Cantor of St. Thomas' Church in Leipzig. Besides being responsible for all the music required by the four churches included in the parish of St. Thomas', Bach was charged with the musical instruction of the choirboys in the church school. The products of his Leipzig period include the greater part of the choral music and some works for organ and clavier. He died on July 28, 1750.

Bach was recognized in his day mainly as a performer on the organ. Most of his compositions remained unprinted during his lifetime, and many have been lost. Felix Mendelssohn, who conducted the *St. Matthew Passion* in Berlin in 1829—probably the first performance of the work after the death of the composer—started the movement that has culminated today in world-wide recognition of Bach's singular genius.

With the exception of the opera, there is hardly an aspect of the music of the seventeenth and eighteenth centuries with which Bach did not concern himself. All of the numerous forms in which he wrote were brought to such heights by him that they overshadow entirely the works of his contemporaries. Bach has had no successors, no imitators. Such was the unique quality of his inspiration that, like almost every other genius in the history of art, he founded no school.

The Keyboard Stringed Instruments of Bach's Day

Before passing on to a discussion of the forms used by Bach, the various keyboard stringed instruments in use during his lifetime must

JOHANN SEBASTIAN BACH

be described. These instruments can be divided into two classes: (a) those whose strings were struck, and (b) those whose strings were plucked.

The first class is represented by the *clavichord,* an instrument that at Bach's time had a range of about four octaves:

The striking mechanism consisted of brass tangents which were placed in the ends of the key-levers. When a key was depressed, its tangent struck the wire string and set it in vibration. A peculiar feature of the clavichord, however, was the fact that the tangent remained in contact with the wire as long as the key was depressed, and consequently determined its pitch. A much more important consequence of this continued contact of tangent and string was the degree of control exercised by the player over both the dynamic value and the quality of the sound produced. Although the clavichord produced a tone that was somewhat thin and lacking in brilliance, it possessed a much greater expressive power than any other keyboard instrument of its day. Its responsiveness caused Bach to prefer it for certain types of music.

To the second class belongs an instrument with several names. The English knew it as the *harpsichord,* the French as the *clavecin,* the Germans as the *Flügel,* the Italians as the *clavicembalo* or *cembalo.* Bach usually used the Italian term *cembalo.* The harpsichord was wing-shaped, resembling the form of a modern grand piano. This accounts for the German name *Flügel* (wing), a designation still employed in Germany for the grand piano. The strings of the harpsichord were actuated by plectra, fashioned from either crow quills or pieces of hard leather, and placed in short upright pieces of wood known as jacks, fastened to the ends of the key-levers. When the key was depressed, the jack was forced upward and the plectrum twanged the string. Harpsichords were sometimes provided with two keyboards (manuals) producing differing tone colors. The instrument also possessed couplers, mechanical devices that caused corresponding notes on a different manual or in a different octave to sound simultaneously. By means of the two manuals and the couplers, players could obtain a degree of dynamic alteration that was limited in scope and confined largely to contrasts between the larger divisions of a work. The harpsichord's deficiencies in nuance were amply atoned for by its preciseness, brilliance, and ability to produce varied tone colors.

The harpsichord should not be regarded as a crude ancestor of the modern piano. It reached a high plane of mechanical perfection during Bach's lifetime, and it was not until the beginning of the nineteenth century that it was supplanted completely by the piano. While the piano may have ousted the harpsichord, it has not taken its place entirely; and modern times have witnessed a strong revival of interest in this instrument.[1] It has even been used in "popular" music, e.g., Artie Shaw's *Gramercy Five* recordings.

Bach became acquainted with one of the precursors of the modern piano when he visited King Frederick the Great in 1747; but he found the tone of this as yet unperfected instrument unpleasant. It is difficult to generalize about the performance of Bach's harpsichord and clavichord works on the modern piano. Many of the clavichord works may be benefited by the transference; certain harpsichord pieces which demand the two keyboards of the older instrument lose both clarity and vivid contrasts in tone color.

The German word *Clavier* is a general term which embraces all of the keyboard stringed instruments—clavichord, harpsichord, and piano. In order to avoid confusion the common practice of designating compositions for these instruments as clavier music will be followed.

CLAVIER MUSIC

Reference has already been made to music designed primarily for the pleasure of those who recreate it in performance (page 60). Bach himself has given us a characteristic description of such music when, in publishing his seven clavier *Partitas,* he gives their purpose as: *denen Liebhabern zur Gemüts-ergötzung* ("for the delectation of amateurs"). Although much of the instrumental music of Bach is performed publicly today, it must always be borne in mind that the greater part of it, his church music being the outstanding exception, was designed for intimate private performance either with no audience at all or at most a few listeners seated close to the player or players.

---

[1] There are now (1950) two American craftsmen engaged in the manufacture of harpsichords and clavichords—John Challis (Detroit) and Julius Wahl (Los Angeles).

The Suites

We encounter one of the most typical of the eighteenth century in-strumental forms in Bach's six *French Suites* and six *English Suites* written at Anhalt-Cöthen, and in the seven *Partitas* written at Leipzig. Various explanations have been set forth concerning the origin of the terms *English* and *French* as applied to these clavier suites. None is satisfactory, however, and the question is only of academic interest.

A well-marked differentiation between vocal and instrumental idi-oms was not often found in the music of the sixteenth century, the brilliant period whose vocal polyphonic music we have already dis-cussed; and compositions often bore the indication, "Apt for voices or viols." Thus many of the first attempts at instrumental music were merely transferences to instruments of music conceived along vocal lines. Composers of instrumental music soon found better models in dances with their well-defined rhythms and symmetrical construction. Although composers retained the titles and rhythmic characteristics of these dances, the artistic manner in which they treated them soon lifted them out of the category of mere dance music and made of them self-sufficient media of artistic expression. Pieces so composed are therefore better described as idealized dances or pieces in dance forms.

An important step in the development of modern instrumental music was taken in the early part of the seventeenth century when composers discovered that they might construct larger instrumental works by ar-ranging these pieces in a well-contrasted series. For such a series of pieces the designation *suite* gradually came into use. The national origin of the term serves to indicate the important part played by France in the development of this form. The dances of many other European countries were taken up and cultivated by the French, only to be exported later on with Gallicized names, such as *allemande, polonaise, anglaise,* and so forth. Other designations in use for a series of pieces in dance forms were *Lessons* or *Suite of Lessons* in England, *Ordre* in France, and *Partita* in Italy and Germany.

The only uniform characteristic of the suite of Bach's day was that all of the pieces comprising it were usually in the same key. Although the conventions with regard to the nature and number of the pieces were not particularly rigid, the following forms usually appeared in the order given: *allemande, courante, sarabande, gigue.* But many other forms were introduced at will and placed between the *sarabande* and the *gigue.* It is important to notice that almost all the movements of Bach's suites are in two-part form, each of them divided into two nearly equal parts. Commencing in the tonic key, the first half gradually modulates and comes to a well-defined point of rest with a perfect cadence, usually in the key of the dominant; the second half commences in the key of the dominant and gradually returns to the tonic. There is usually a marked degree of correspondence between the opening and closing measures of each half.

French Suite No. VI, in E Major

The sixth of Bach's French Suites will serve as a typical example of the suite form. The work consists of eight movements, all of which are in the tonality of E major. Bach retains the conventional *allemande-courante-sarabande* sequence and inserts four light, gay movements before the final *gigue.*

The *allemande* is in quadruple rhythm. Commencing with an up-beat, that is, an unaccented note or group of notes leading up to a strong beat, it is moderate in speed and exhibits an easy flow:

Ex. 1   1. Allemande.

The *corrente* is a lively animated movement in triple rhythm.[2] Like its predecessor, it also commences with an up-beat:

Ex. 2   2. Corrente.

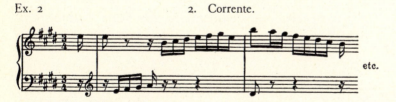

[2] The French *courante* is characterized by shifts of rhythm from triple to duple and a polyphonic texture. It is often confused with the *corrente,* which is of Italian origin. Either form might appear after the *allemande.*

The *sarabande,* in contrast with the two movements that have preceded it, is a slow, dignified, inherently serious dance. It is in triple rhythm often characterized by a tendency to accentuate the second beat:

Ex. 3   3. Sarabande.

The *gavotte* is a moderately fast dance in quadruple rhythm. It almost always commences on the third beat:

Ex. 4   4. Gavotte.

The *polonaise,* as treated by Bach, is a simple, unpretentious movement in triple rhythm. Despite its name, the Bach form shows no marked Polish tendencies and should not be confused with the *polonaise* as found in the works of Chopin:

Ex. 5   5. Polonaise.

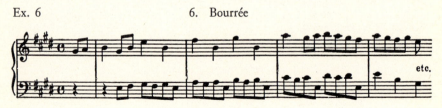

The *bourrée* is a lively, animated dance in quadruple rhythm, occasionally in duple:

Ex. 6   6. Bourrée

The *minuet* of Bach's time was a graceful, courtly dance in a moderately fast triple rhythm. The minuet possesses special interest inasmuch as it was the only element of the suite to become a member of that series of movements of later development that comprise the sonata and the symphony. Like the *polonaise,* the minuet took on different characteristics in the hands of later composers such as Haydn and Mozart:

Ex. 7   7. Minuet.

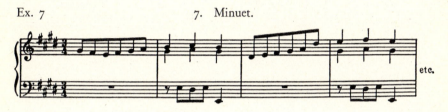

The *gigue,* the final movement of the suite, is a lively, rollicking dance employing triple rhythm or some multiple of it, that is, $\frac{3}{8}$, $\frac{6}{8}$, or $\frac{12}{8}$. The *gigue* is often written in a polyphonic manner with considerable imitation in the various parts.

Ex. 8   8. Gigue.

Listening to a suite such as the one just discussed should serve to contradict irrefutably the old belief that the music of Bach is cold, impersonal, and mathematical. The clavier suites demonstrate, above all, Bach's ability to arrive at the true nature of these apparently stiff dance forms and, within their limitations, to create the profundities of the *sarabandes* and the gay, witty repartee of the *gigues*.

The first *Passepied* (a graceful dance in triple rhythm, commencing on the third beat) of Bach's fifth English Suite is written not in the usual two-part form, but in *rondo* form. The arrangement of the thematic material of the rondo (French *rondeau*) can be represented schematically as follows: A B A C A D A. The plan of the rondo is thus merely an extension of the principle of construction shown by three-part form (statement—digression—restatement) to include several digressions each followed by a return to the principal idea, often called the *refrain*. The digressions are written in a contrasting style and are usually called *episodes*. The *Rondeau* of Bach's second Partita is an excellent example of this procedure. The rondo scheme might be applied to many dance forms, and pieces so written bore the designation *en rondeau* in addition to their usual title; for instance, *Minuet en rondeau* and *Passepied en rondeau*. The rondo of Bach and his contemporaries should not be confused with the form as remodeled and made into a movement of the sonata by Haydn, Mozart, and Beethoven.

Not all of the movements found in Bach's clavier suites are dancelike. The second French Suite contains an *Air;* all six English Suites and the seven Partitas commence with prefatory pieces having titles such as *Prélude, Sinfonie,* and *Fantaisie.* The latter pieces usually follow no set form. Although their music has been set down for the player, they are designed to produce an effect of improvisation.

In his third and sixth English Suites Bach writes a pair of gavottes to be played in this order: Gavotte I—Gavotte II—Gavotte I. In this way two two-part forms were arranged so as to produce a three-part form. Inasmuch as Gavotte I was repeated literally, Bach followed the custom of merely writing *Da capo* at the end of Gavotte II. This Italian designation meaning "from the beginning" was an indication to the player to return to the beginning and play the first gavotte once more. *Bourrées* and *minuets* are also found grouped in this manner. It often happened that the second of such a pair of minuets was written in three-part harmony, thereby causing the second minuet to be called a *Trio.* The custom of writing this second minuet in three voices died out with Bach, but the name *Trio* has persisted as a designation for the middle section of such three-part forms as the minuet, the march, and the scherzo.

The term *suite* can be said to refer to a definite form—a series of idealized dances—only in so far as it is restricted to the works of seventeenth and eighteenth century composers. Later composers have used the term with great freedom, and it is frequently used as a designation for works such as the following:

1. A series of extracts from the incidental music written for a drama:

Bizet—Suite from *L'Arlésienne* (Daudet)
Grieg—Suite from *Peer Gynt* (Ibsen)

2. A series of extracts from the music for an opera or ballet:

Bizet—Suite from *Carmen*
Tschaikovsky—Suite from *The Nutcracker*

3. A series of narrative or descriptive pieces:

Rimsky-Korsakoff—*Scheherazade*
John Alden Carpenter—*Adventures in a Perambulator*

The Inventions

Bach gave the name *Inventions* to a collection of fifteen short two-part (two-voiced) clavier pieces that he wrote as models for young musicians. A corresponding set of fifteen pieces in three parts he called *Symphonies,* an illustration of the loose way in which the term *symphony* was used for instrumental music during the seventeenth and eighteenth centuries. The Symphonies are now universally known as the Three-Part Inventions. The inscription with which Bach prefaced the collection of Inventions describes them for us: "A sincere guide wherein lovers of the clavier and especially those anxious to learn are shown a clear method for playing with facility in two parts, and, after suitable progress, in three parts; and wherein they may also learn how not only to create good ideas (*inventiones*), but also to develop them well and above all attain a *cantabile* (singing) style in playing and acquire a strong predilection for composition." The mention of *cantabile* playing in this preface indicates that the Inventions were written for the clavichord. The Inventions are *études,* pieces designed as exercises for the development of technique. But as the composer tells us, these études are also models of the art of composition, having as an additional purpose the development of artistic discernment. The Inventions are short pieces written in a polyphonic style, but the contrapuntal ingenuity displayed in them is unobtrusive. Many of them possess the freshness and spontaneity of improvisation.

The Well-Tempered Clavier

Bach gave the title *Das wohltemperirte Clavier* (*The Well-Tempered Clavier*) to a series of twenty-four preludes and fugues, in each of the twenty-four major and minor keys, which he completed at Anhalt-Cöthen in 1722. A second set of twenty-four was composed at Leipzig twenty-two years later, and the two sets are now referred to as Part I and Part II. Although Bach's title is often translated into English as *The Well-Tempered Clavichord,* the specific keyboard instrument he had in mind remains a matter of scholarly dispute. While many of the pieces seem to have been conceived for the clavichord, there is a significant number that would appear to demand the harpsichord. Like the Inventions, the forty-eight preludes and fugues of *The Well-Tempered Clavier* were designed for "the use and benefit of young musicians who are anxious to learn."

In describing the keyboard instrument on which these works were to be played as "well-tempered" the composer was referring to the system in which its strings were tuned. A tempered or well-tempered scale is one whose pitches are so regulated as to permit their forming a part of the scale of any key. It is the use of this system of tuning which enables the notes B-sharp, C-natural and D-double flat, for example, to be sounded by one and the same string instead of by the three different strings theoretically necessary. In the tempered system of tuning, the octave is divided into twelve equidistant semitones; and, while as a result of this, certain tones are somewhat higher and others lower than their acoustically correct values, the deviations are not appreciable to most ears. Bach was not the inventor of this system of tuning, but inasmuch as *The Well-Tempered Clavier* could only be performed on an instrument that was tuned to it, his work served as a strong incentive to its ultimate universal adoption.

The Prelude

The term *prelude* is one of the most loosely used designations in the entire vocabulary of music. Composers have employed this title in many ways; it would be impossible to coin a definition that would cover a Bach prelude, a Chopin prelude, and a prelude to a Wagner music drama. Discussion of the term must therefore be restricted to a particular composer's concept of it.

As used by Bach, the label *prelude* describes a manner of writing rather than a set form. The general style of the preludes of *The Well-Tempered Clavier* is one of improvisation. They may be brilliant or sombre, impulsive or restrained; some are rhapsodic songs in a homophonic style, others are worked out along polyphonic lines. Each of the forty-eight preludes is a law unto itself. All the preludes are coupled to fugues in the same key; but despite the implications of their title, they are not merely prefaces to the fugues. The preludes are complete in themselves and might conceivably be played as independent pieces.

A Bach *Prelude and Fugue* is therefore a work whose two movements may be regarded as compeers, contrasting in mood and style, but joined through the use of a common key.

The Fugue

The chief characteristics of a *fugue* consists in the polyphonic elaboration of a melodic idea, called the *fugue-subject,* by several voices, fixed in number for a given work. Fugues may be written for instruments or for voices. A vocal terminology is used in either case and the various parts are always referred to as "voices." The constituent parts of a four-voiced fugue, for example, would be labeled: Soprano, Alto, Tenor and Bass.

The interplay of the voices in a rapid fugue will often give the effect of pursuit, whence the use of a word derived from the Latin *fuga* (flight) as a title; but fugues may be written in slow tempi as well, and the origin of the term should, therefore, not be taken too literally. From the standpoint of the listener, a fugue comprises two divisions—the *exposition* and the *development.*

The exposition consists of successive presentations of the fugue-subject by each voice in turn. The order of entry of the voices is not subject to any fixed rule. The compact exposition of the Fugue in C major, Part I, No. I, of *The Well-Tempered Clavier* will serve as an example:

Ex. 9

(*Continued on following page*)

Ex. 9 (*continued*)

In this particular fugue the subject is given out by the alto voice. At the conclusion of this enunciation of the subject, the soprano voice presents it, but in the key of the dominant. This second entry is called the *answer,* though in truth this second appearance of the subject is not to be construed as only a reply to the first. While the soprano gives out the subject, the alto voice continues with a new and subordinate melody in contrapuntal combination with it. In some fugues this new melody attains a degree of importance and is then known as the *counter-subject.* Similarly, when the subject is announced for the third time in the tenor voice, the two upper voices continue in contrapuntal combination. The same procedure is followed when the fourth and last voice, the bass, enters. There are several features of the exposition worth pointing out:

1. The fugue-subject has appeared in all the voices and has therefore been heard as many times as there are voices.

2. The voices enter successively and at different pitches; the effect is thus cumulative.

3. The exposition is the most regular part of the fugue—the only part that can be described with some degree of statistical accuracy.

4. For the listener the most important section of the work is the exposition; and to fail to apprehend its content is like missing the first act of a play—one is ignorant of the situation.

In a few fugues the exposition is followed by one or more re-entries of the subject; if these entries occur in all the voices they constitute what is called a *counter-exposition*. Counter-expositions are to be found in Fugues I and IX of *The Well-Tempered Clavier,* Part I.

The succeeding section of a fugue is called the *development* and, as its name implies, is that part of the fugue in which the composer reveals the potentialities of the subject in any manner his imagination may suggest and his contrapuntal technique permit. In writing the development the composer is governed by no rigid conventions; it is evident, however, that the process of development must conform to the inexorable demand that every art work possess an organic unity. The development of the fugue consists of numerous entries of the subject in various tonalities, and in many cases with significant melodic and rhythmic alterations. The various entries are separated from each other by *episodes*—truce-like sections of great psychological effectiveness, in which the subject as an entity temporarily drops out of sight. The successive entries of the subject and the intervening episodes thus constitute an elaborate scheme of repetition and contrast.

There are three conventional methods of altering the subject during the course of the development. These procedures are called *inversion, augmentation,* and *diminution.* In inversion, the fugue-subject is turned upside down; that is, the directions of the constituent intervals are reversed, upward movement becoming downward and vice versa; for example, Bach—*The Well-Tempered Clavier,* Part I, Fugue No. VI:

Ex. 10
(a)   Subject.

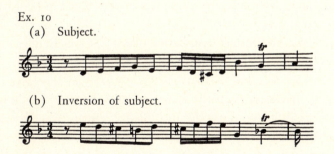

(b)   Inversion of subject.

Augmentation is a process of enlargement; that is, the lengths of all the constituent notes are multiplied, usually by two. Inasmuch as the relative time values remain undisturbed, the contours of the subject remain unaltered; for example, Bach—*The Well-Tempered Clavier,* Part I, Fugue No. VIII:

Ex. 11
  (a) Subject.

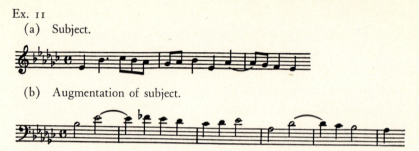

  (b) Augmentation of subject.

Diminution is the converse of augmentation; the notes of the subject are now decreased in value, producing an effect akin to compression; for example, Bach—*The Well-Tempered Clavier,* Part II, Fugue No. IX:

Ex. 12
  (a) Subject.

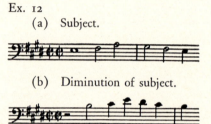

  (b) Diminution of subject.

Another method of elaboration of the subject is a device called *stretto,* a procedure wherein the entries of the subject overlap; that is, the subject is announced in one voice before the completion of the previous entry. The various voices apparently pile up on each other in a well-planned confusion productive of telling emotional effect. It cannot be too strongly emphasized that the fugal devices herein described do not exhaust the possible methods of development and that all, some, or none of them may be found in any given fugue. The fugue concludes with the *coda* (Italian for "tail") in which the subject, after all its tonal wanderings, finally returns to the home key— the original tonality. In many fugues, this return of the subject to its tonic will have about it an air of conquest and victory, much as if the subject were expansively proclaiming its triumph over the vicissitudes of the development.

The *sine qua non* for proper appreciation of a fugue is the ability to recognize the subject in its numerous repetitions, no matter how it may be disguised or transformed. This ability can be achieved only by concentration on the part of the listener. An excellent preliminary step in the acquisition of this habit is to count the entries of the subject.

There is a widely prevalent belief that the fugue is an essentially intellectual musical form, devoid of emotional appeal. The mechanism of the fugue is such that it can be used by composers who possess craftsmanship but lack inspiration. On the other hand, this same mechanism may be made to serve as a means of artistic communication which is not only forceful and direct but, as the fugues of Bach so well demonstrate, also capable of expressing many shades of human emotion.[3]

The possibilities of polyphonic elaboration inherent in the fugal style have caused many composers to employ it for portions of larger works. A section so written is called a *fugato;* it often embodies only the exposition of a fugue. Examples are to be found in works far removed from Bach, such as many of the symphonies of Beethoven, the overture to Smetana's opera *The Bartered Bride,* the prelude to the third act of Wagner's opera *Die Meistersinger von Nürnberg, Through the Looking Glass* of Deems Taylor, and many others.

Like the Inventions, the preludes and fugues of *The Well-Tempered Clavier* show amazing variety not only in the character of their thematic material, but also in the method in which this material is employed. While the composition of all of these works demanded great contrapuntal skill, they give the listener the impression of being essentially improvisational music. But free as the flow of Bach's fancy may seem, closer examination will show that his works are the product of splendid musical logic. Even his ostensibly theoretical treatise, *Die Kunst der Fuge* (*The Art of Fugue*), a collection of seventeen fugues and four canons on the same fugue-subject, possesses an expressive power that wholly overshadows the didactic aim of the work.

The Chromatic Fantasia and Fugue is one of Bach's larger works for the clavier and one of the few not part of a collection. Written

[3] Within certain limits the fugue can even be used for descriptive purposes. An American composer, Philip James, concludes his *Suite for String Orchestra* (1934) with a fugue depicting a scene in a university classroom. The professor, impersonated by the eminently respectable double bass, announces the topic of the day. This is taken up joyfully by the students in the fugal exposition; the discussion is described in the development; and the jolly coda is rudely terminated by strident chords suggesting the closing bell.

in a majestic style with a long and impulsive fantasia, it closely ap-
proaches the idiom of the larger organ compositions. The chromatic
style of the fantasia gives the work its name. The expressive fugue-
subject is:

Ex. 13

One of Bach's most brilliant pieces for the clavier, this work was
among his first compositions to win popularity.

The *Italian Concerto,* written for the harpsichord, bears a title
illustrative of the loose way in which musical works were labeled
during the eighteenth century. The title that Bach bestowed upon
this harpsichord piece was *Concerto, after the Italian Manner.* The
designation "concerto" derives from the practice then current in Germany of writing works for clavier solo in the style of the Italian
concertos for violin and orchestra. This also explains "after the
Italian Manner." The contrasts of *tutti* and *solo* which characterized
the orchestral concerto [4] are realized in these solo concertos for harpsichord through changes of manuals. The *Italian Concerto* with its
three movements strongly prefigures the sonata form that was to
occupy the center of the musical stage after the death of Bach.

Organ Music

The organ works of Bach may be divided into two groups: (1) the
larger works such as the Preludes and Fugues, Toccatas and Fugues,
Fantasias and Fugues; and (2) the shorter, more intimate Chorale-
Preludes. Bach's organ works form only a small part of his total
creative accomplishment [5]; but they constitute the very foundation of
the repertory of the modern organist.

Like the keyboard instruments already mentioned, the organ of
Bach's day differed radically from its present-day counterpart. It was
a small instrument with two, occasionally three, manuals in addition to
the usual pedals. The number of stops was also limited to a maxi-

[4] See page 101.
[5] Four of the sixty volumes of the complete edition issued by the Bach Gesellschaft.

mum of about thirty-five. There was no mechanism for permitting gradual adjustment of volume, that is, swelling or decreasing of tone was impossible, exactly as was the case with the harpsichord; and tonal changes were limited to abrupt contrasts. A very low wind pressure served to make the pipes sound. The tone of the instrument was clear and transparent, and its prevailing lightness of color made it an admirable medium for the reproduction of polyphonic textures. Under the name "Praetorius Organ," after the German writer Michael Praetorius (1571-1621), who wrote an important treatise on the music and the instruments of his day, or under the title "Baroque Organ," referring to its period, it has been reconstructed by contemporary organ builders. One of the best known of these instruments is located in the Germanic Museum of Harvard University. Like the other keyboard music of Bach, the organ works appear to their best advantage when performed on the instrument for whose idiom they were created.

Bach wrote some of his most majestic instrumental music for the organ. It was, it should be recalled, the instrument that he himself played, and unlike the uncertain orchestral resources of which he could avail himself, it offered him a reliable medium for the performance of larger instrumental works. It is interesting to note that although Bach was the greatest organ virtuoso of his day, if not of all time, only a very small proportion of the works that he composed for this instrument falls into the category of music that exists simply to allow a performer to demonstrate his mechanical dexterity. The organ works of Bach are difficult, but the difficulties are incidental to a higher musical purpose and are not merely quasi-artistic hurdles.

Most of the fugues for organ are monumental works based on subjects of much originality, treated in a manner from which a dramatic style is seldom absent. Bach exploits to the full the organ's ability to provide effective contrasts and thrilling climaxes.

Like the fugues, whatever differences exist between the organ preludes and the clavier preludes have their origin in the nature of the instrument for which the works were designed. Two other forms, the *fantasia* and the *toccata,* are also found in combination with the organ fugues.

The term *fantasia,* like the term *prelude,* has had a somewhat checkered career in the service of the world's great composers. As employed by Bach, it is a freely constructed work giving the impression of being an extemporization. It usually differs from the prelude in that it displays a variety of moods and styles. One of Bach's finest fantasias is to be found in the Fantasia and Fugue in G minor, one of the most famous of Bach's organ works. The fugue subject is:

Ex. 14

The *toccata* derives its name from the Italian *toccare* (to touch). The toccata is a "touch piece," brilliant in style, rapid in tempo, and abounding in spectacular effects. Like the fantasia, it is cast in the free style of improvisation. Its original purpose was merely to serve as a vehicle for virtuoso display, but in the hands of Bach the form was elevated to a position of true musical value. A typical Bach toccata is the celebrated one in F major:

Ex. 15

It is difficult to generalize about these monumental compositions. To a great majority of individuals they remain almost unknown because of the infrequency or inaccessability of performances on the instrument for which they were composed. Such is their musical worth, however, that other musicians have not been content to allow them to remain the exclusive property of organists. Pianists have adapted several of them for their instrument: notable arrangements have been made by Liszt, Tausig, von Bülow, and Busoni. Many have also been arranged for orchestra, occasionally with questionable results. Among those who have made orchestral transcriptions of Bach's organ works may be listed the composers Sir Edward Elgar, Ottorino Respighi, and Arnold Schoenberg, and the conductors Leopold Stokowski and Sir Henry Wood. But as attractive as these arrangements may be, it is essential that the works in question be heard in their original idiom.

PASSACAGLIA AND FUGUE IN C MINOR

As one of Bach's most important organ works, the Passacaglia and Fugue in C minor merits detailed discussion. The *passacaglia* is descended from a slow Spanish or Italian dance in which a short bass melody was repeated incessantly. Although the passacaglia is almost identical with the *chaconne,* theorists have attempted to establish a difference between the two forms by stating that the theme of the passacaglia remains continually in the bass, while that of the chaconne may wander into the upper voices. Composers, however, do not seem to have been guided by consideration for such niceties of definition; Bach in his Passacaglia has not hesitated to introduce the theme in the upper voices.[6]

In the passacaglia we encounter a new application of the basic principles of musical form as displayed by works that are classified as *variations.* Variations are a series of melodic, harmonic, or rhythmic transformations of some self-contained theme; these transformations may follow each other without pause, or they may be in themselves self-contained pieces terminating with a full close. The variation form thus satisfies in a very simple manner our desire for repetition and contrast in a musical composition. Variations are often grouped in order of complexity and brilliance, thus producing an additional effect of organic growth. There are many different types of variations. These will be described as we encounter them in the works of the great composers.

The passacaglia is a variation form characterized by the use of a short bass phrase as its theme, and by the construction of numerous variations above successive repetitions of this phrase. A phrase so employed is often called a *ground,* a *ground bass,* or *basso ostinato* (Italian for "persistent bass"). In many passacaglias the ground bass remains substantially unaltered; but in some instances it may be in-

---

[6] Bach was above all a practical musician. The description of him to be found in an obituary notice published by a Leipzig musical society includes the following: "Our late friend Bach never entered into deep theoretical discussions about music, and was all the more proficient in art." (Bernhard Friedrich Richter, "Der Nekrolog auf Sebastian Bach von Jahre 1754." *Bach-Jahrbuch* 1920.)

verted, or broken up into smaller figures, or placed in an upper voice.

Bach's Passacaglia utilizes a solemn ground bass of eight measures, borrowed from a composition by a French organist, André Raison:

Ex. 16

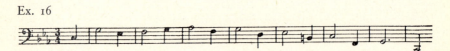

On this melody Bach proceeds to construct twenty variations. Two variations are quoted here to demonstrate the technique that he has employed:

Ex. 17
   (a) Variation I.

The variations follow each other without pause and with continually increasing complexity. By the end of the twentieth variation, the listener might suspect that the possibilities of the ground bass have been exhausted; but Bach, in very dramatic fashion, takes its first four measures, alters them slightly and combines them with a new theme:

and proceeds to cap this magnificent tonal structure with a tremendous *double fugue.*[7]

The Chorale-Preludes

The larger organ works represent Bach, the organ virtuoso, who delights in the creation of towering edifices in sound. There is, however, another aspect of his creativeness—his ability to frame the hymns of the Lutheran Church in imaginative musical settings.

The expressive congregational hymns of the German Lutheran Church are known as *chorales*. To aid in the work of the Reformation, Luther himself wrote the melodies for eight chorales as well as texts for many melodies already in existence. In attempting to understand the nature of the *chorale-prelude*, it must be borne in mind that the chorales were sung by the entire congregation in its native tongue. The beautiful melodies of the chorales as well as their fervid texts were therefore known to all and could be employed by the organist in a manner which his listeners would find meaningful. For Bach's congregation, therefore, the chorale-prelude was nothing more or less than a variation on a well-known melody.

During the principal service of worship of the Lutheran Church it was customary for the organist to play a prelude, i.e., a variation, on the appointed chorale before the congregation sang it. Hence the name *chorale-prelude (Chorale-Vorspiel)* for a form which may be defined as a free variation for organ on the melody of a chorale. Examination of Bach's chorale-preludes will show that the composer has utilized his harmonic and contrapuntal technique as well as his melodic invention in the creation of what are essentially new versions of the chorales, versions that are sensitive interpretations of a highly subjective nature. Furthermore, it will be found that Bach derived his inspiration for many of these settings from the chorale texts. True

---

[7] A *double fugue* is a fugue on two subjects. In this particular double fugue, the subjects are announced simultaneously and remain inseparable throughout.

appreciation of the chorale-preludes demands possession of the self-same equipment as that of the parishioners of Bach's church, namely, a knowledge of both the text and the melody of the chorale on which the chorale-prelude is based.[8]

Of the several diverse styles employed by Bach in his treatment of the chorale melodies, the simplest and at the same time most effective may be described as follows: the melody of the chorale is preserved almost intact and appears in the soprano voice; to this melody are added new melodies of a descriptive or symbolic nature, inspired by the text of the chorale.

CHORALE-PRELUDE—"ICH RUF' ZU DIR, HERR JESU CHRIST"

A typical example of such a setting is the prelude on the chorale *Ich ruf' zu dir, Herr Jesu Christ* (I cry to Thee, Lord Jesus Christ) from the collection of forty-five chorale-preludes called by Bach *Orgelbüchlein* (Little Organ Book).[9] The original melody of this chorale is:

(*Prose translation of the text:* I cry to Thee, Lord Jesus Christ, hear my plaint, I pray! Incline Thy Grace to me at this moment, do not let me lose heart! Grant me the True Faith, O Lord, to live for Thee, to help my neighbor and to keep Thy Word holy.)

[8] All of the ninety-odd chorales which served Bach as the source for his one hundred forty-three chorale-preludes are to be found in Vol. XX of the Novello edition of his organ works.

[9] There is no better key to the musical language of Bach than a study of the imaginative musical miniatures comprising the *Orgelbüchlein;* nor is there any better way to approach Bach than by actual performance of them. They can be played on the piano with pleasure and profit by dividing the three staves employed for organ music between two players in an impromptu piano duet. An excellent American edition of the *Orgelbüchlein,* edited by Albert Riemenschneider and published under the title *The Liturgical Year,* includes not only the chorale-preludes, but also the equally important chorales as well as translations of their texts.

In the chorale-prelude that Bach writes on this melody the following occurs: (1) The melody, slightly changed and embellished but entirely recognizable, appears in the topmost voice; (2) the note of fervid supplication expressed by the text of the chorale is illustrated musically by two persistent figures, an undulating melody in the middle voice and a pulsating motive in the bass. The nature of Bach's interpretation of the chorale text must have been instantaneously apparent to his congregation.

Ex. 20

ORCHESTRAL MUSIC

The orchestral music of Bach may be conveniently classified as follows: (1) the four orchestral suites, (2) the six Brandenburg concertos, and (3) the concertos for violin, or for clavier, and orchestra. The infrequency of performance of many of these works should not be construed as in any way indicative of their artistic worth as compared to that of the relatively few Bach compositions which have been singled out for regular presentation. There is an enormous amount of truly inspired music by Bach which is heard all too seldom.

Although these compositions are classified as orchestral music today, the designation is something of a misnomer for, according to modern usage, the term implies music to be played by a symphony orchestra at a public concert.

Bach took but little interest in the attempts which were made during his lifetime to establish public concerts in Leipzig. It was not until 1781, thirty-one years after his death, that a series of regular public concerts was started in that city. During the greater part of Bach's lifetime the art of music as practiced by professional musicians was restricted to the church, the opera house, and the salons of the nobility.   Various musical activities were also undertaken by the *Collegia musica,* organizations composed of amateur performers.   Bach's orchestral works therefore fall into the category of chamber music—music to be played in the salon or drawing room.   At Anhalt-Cöthen, where much of his orchestral music was composed, performances were given by an orchestra of sixteen players for the delectation of Prince Leopold and his guests.   In Leipzig Bach was director of the *Collegium musicum* of the University for seven years, and both he and his two sons, Karl Philipp Emanuel and Wilhelm Friedemann, frequently took part in its activities.

All of the music of this period which was written for combinations of instruments, or of instruments and voices, demanded harmonic completion by an accompanying harpsichordist or organist playing a part called either *basso continuo, continuo,* or, in its conventional translation, *thorough-bass.*   The harpsichordist not only served as a sort of leader for the other performers, but also "filled in" the harmonic structure of the work from a description of it written in a musical shorthand and called a *figured bass.*   This figured bass consisted of the bass forming the harmonic substructure and numbers describing the chords to be constructed upon it.   The method of elaboration of the figured bass was left to the discretion of the harpichordist, who extemporized his part from this shorthand version of the required chords.   This filling in of the harmonies is an absolute prerequisite for correct performance of the concerted music of Bach's day.   Omission of it will give the listener a thoroughly inadequate, often grotesque, idea of a particular work.   It was not until the time of Joseph Haydn that instrumental music finally dispensed with the use of the continuo as an agency for harmonic "filling in."

The Orchestral Suites

Of the four orchestral suites only two are heard today, the second, in B minor, for flute, strings, and continuo, and the third, in D major, for trumpets, oboes, kettledrums, strings, and continuo.   In each of these four works we find a long preparatory piece called an *overture* [10] written in a form that had become a convention in the works of French operatic composers.   This so-called French overture is another

---

[10] Bach called his four orchestral suites "overtures."

addition to our collection of three-part (A B A) forms. The first section is slow, dignified, and majestic in character and almost invariably employs dotted rhythmic figures of this type:

$$\text{♫. ♫. ♫}$$

It is followed by a lively fugue. The third section may either be a literal repetition of the first, or a slightly altered version.

The other numbers of the suite are all pieces in dance form with the exception of the celebrated "Air" for strings from the third suite. An inartistic arrangement of this Air as a G-string solo for violin with piano accompaniment was made over a century after the composer's death, and Bach's work is therefore erroneously known as the "Air for the G-string." In the orchestral suites, the conventional *Allemande* and *Courante* have been supplanted by other dance forms. The second suite, for example, contains a *Polonaise* and a *Badinerie* (French for "fooling," "trifling").

The Concertos

The remaining orchestral works of Bach are examples of another important instrumental form of the early eighteenth century—the *concerto*. The name *concerto* or *concerto grosso* was given during Bach's time to a composition for many players in which certain passages were played by all of the instrumentalists while others were assigned either to a solo performer or to a small group of solo performers. The larger group consisted almost exclusively of performers on string instruments and was known as the *ripieno* or *concerto grosso* (large concerto). The smaller group was called the *concertino* (little concerto), and often consisted of two violins and a violoncello; the solo performers were usually violinists.

The preponderance of string instruments is a direct result of the high degree of perfection which they had already attained. It is interesting to observe that Bach was one of the first composers to write concertos in which the harpsichord was used either as a solo instrument or as a member of the concertino.

No strict demarcation can be made between the concerto and the concerto grosso of the early eighteenth century. The former term, preferred by Bach, was more inclusive; the latter was apparently reserved for works with a concertino of three or more instruments. There is, however, a marked difference between the concerto of Bach and his age and the better-known concerto of Mozart and his contemporaries and successors. Of the earlier type, which is now being discussed, the most celebrated masters were the Italians, Arcangelo Corelli (1653-1713) and Antonio Vivaldi, (c. 1678-1741), Bach, and his great contemporary, Handel. Corelli is known today largely for his Concerto Grosso in G minor (No. 8), described by the composer as "written for Christmas Eve," and now called the Christmas Concerto. It was Corelli who first demonstrated the effectiveness of a concertino composed of two violins and violoncello. Vivaldi, some of whose concerti grossi were transcribed for either organ or harpsichord by Bach, composed many brilliant solo concertos for violin, several of which bear fanciful titles such as *La caccia* (The Hunt) and *La tempesta di mare* (The Storm at Sea).

Before proceeding to a discussion of Bach's concertos, it should be observed that the underlying principle of the early eighteenth-century concerto was that of contrast between passages alternately delivered by groups differing in strength and in tone-color. Although those passages that were allotted to the solo performers were frequently more difficult than those assigned to the ripieno, the concerto of the period was more than simply a medium for the display of virtuosity.

A number of solo concertos by Bach may be heard today. Of these, the best known are the concertos in A minor and in E major for solo violin, the concerto in D minor for two violins, and the concerto in D minor for clavier. There are also two concertos for two pianos, two for three pianos, and a concerto for four pianos. The last was transcribed from a work by Bach's model in concerto composition, Vivaldi.

Many of the clavier concertos are transcriptions of violin concertos whose original scores have been lost. Bach probably made these occasionally ineffective transcriptions for performance at the meetings of the *Collegium Musicum* of the University of Leipzig.

It has already been observed in the suite and in the prelude and fugue, for example, that large musical works are frequently constructed by arranging in series a number of shorter works which are entities in themselves. From a theoretical standpoint the individual

movements of most of the larger works written before the advent of
Beethoven may be regarded as independent; the only objective demonstration of their affinity consists in pointing out their common source
and their ties of tonality.   But independent as individual movements
may be, they are only parts of a larger artistic whole, a unique fed-
eration in which the degree of autonomy enjoyed by the members is
somewhat limited.   Composers have on occasion not been loath to
revamp a movement from some earlier work and to insert it in some
new composition.   In this respect Bach was a chronic offender, a cir-
cumstance which is easily understood when one recalls his obligation
to supply music for so many diverse occasions.

Most of Bach's concertos consist of three movements, the first and
last of which are in a fast tempo.   Both the first and the last movements are in the same key, and it is by this key that the concerto is
designated.   The middle movement offers a contrast in style and in
tonality; it is slow and serious in vein and is in a related key.   The
usual characteristics of the individual movements that comprise a Bach
concerto are described below.

The first and the last movements consist of passages delivered alternately by the soloist or soloists and the ripieno.   A passage played
by all the instruments is called a *tutti* (Italian for "all"); similarly a
passage for the soloist is called a *solo*.   In the solo sections the ripieno
merely furnishes a discreetly coöperative background which is, however, more than a mere accompaniment.   In many concertos there is
a strong division of thematic material between the tutti and the solo
parts.   In others, however, the solo episodes are based on motives derived from the tutti.   The tutti section will reappear from time to
time much like a refrain, hence the name often given to it, *ritornello*
(Italian for "refrain").   These successive reappearances of the ritornello
can be likened in many respects to the behavior of the subject in a
fugue; the solo episodes are also analogous to the episodes of a fugal
development.   In some of the finest of Bach's concertos the fast movements open and close with powerful tuttis.

The slow middle movements of Bach concertos are wonderful demonstrations of his genius.   They are constructed in a manner that,
while extremely simple, is extraordinarily effective.   Bach habitually
built these movements on an expressive bass melody akin to a ground

bass, but modulating freely. Over this bass the solo instrument sings an elaborate melody in a rhapsodic manner.

No technical description, however, does justice to the vitality and robustness of the Bach concertos. The concerto is a form which Bach seems to have handled with great zest, never losing sight of the friendly struggle which the etymology of the term implied (Latin *concertare*— to compete). A Bach concerto is a group effort on the part of several performers, each of whom is entrusted with an important part in the lively contrapuntal interplay.

CONCERTO FOR VIOLIN IN E MAJOR

As a typical work in this form we may investigate briefly Bach's Concerto for Violin in E major. The first movement begins with this animated tutti:

Ex. 21

The solo episodes consist of very elaborate passages for the violin. It will be noticed, however, that a motive drawn from the ritornello, that is, its first three notes, appears in all of the episodes.

The middle movement, in the related key of C-sharp minor, is built on a profound bass melody:

Ex. 22

The final movement is an interesting combination of the rondo [11] and the concerto forms. The ritornello:

Ex. 23

is heard five times, each time in the same key. Between these appearances of the ritornello four different episodes are to be found. The organization of this movement may thus be represented schematically as A B A C A D A E A. All of these divisions are sixteen measures long with the exception of E, which is enlarged to thirty-two measures.

The six *Brandenburg Concertos,* which take their name from their dedication to Christian Ludwig, Margrave of Brandenburg, are really concerti grossi. They demonstrate, above all, Bach's ability to take the conventional forms of his day and bring them to a state of perfection in which they not only outstripped the works of all his predecessors and contemporaries, but also brought the form in question to its zenith for all time. Retaining the fundamental idea of contrast between tutti and soli, these concerti grossi possess a wealth of polyphonic texture and dramatic development. Bach has not been content merely to employ string instruments for the concertino; he introduces such groupings as trumpet, flute, oboe, and violin (Concerto No. II), violin and two flutes (Concerto No. IV), or violin, flute and clavier (Concerto No. V). With the exception of the first concerto, which contains some dances usually associated with the suite, and the third, which consists of two fast movements joined by two chords, the order and character of the movements of the Brandenburg concertos are in accordance with the convention of the period.

Other Instrumental Music

No discussion of Bach's instrumental music is complete without mention of the six sonatas for unaccompanied violin. The most celebrated single movement from these sonatas is the great *Chaconne* with its sixty-two variations on the bass of this four-measure theme: [12]

Ex. 24

The *Chaconne* is a worthy compeer of the great organ works. It, too, has been transcribed for piano solo. Bach has also written six suites for unaccompanied cello as well as several sonatas for flute and clavier, and for violin and clavier.

[12] See the discussion of the passacaglia, page 95.

Choral Music

Bach's choral music constitutes the major part of his creative accomplishment. It was in music of this type that he reached his greatest heights of inspiration. With the exception of a few secular works, all his choral music is liturgical and was written to be used in the various Lutheran churches for whose services he was expected to supply the music.

We may thus include these works in the category of functional music—music written for some specific occasion. A knowledge of the circumstances which brought these works forth will therefore be of aid in the understanding and appreciation of them. The more important choral works are: (1) the church cantatas (2) the *St. John Passion,* (3) the *St. Matthew Passion,* and (4) the *Mass in B minor.*

The chorale plays an important part in all of Bach's sacred works based on German texts. These devout and expressive hymns sung in the vernacular in the Lutheran Church had a strong attraction for Bach. He created inspired interpretations of them in his chorale-preludes and used them freely in his larger choral works. He himself wrote only a few original chorale melodies. His great contribution consists of the new harmonic settings that he devised for these traditional melodies, transformations that add immeasurably to their expressiveness.

The Church Cantatas

The term *cantata* (Italian *cantare*—to sing) was initially used to differentiate a work designed to be sung from the *sonata* (Italian *suonare*—to play), a work to be played. The long history of this form which, like all the others treated by Bach, reached its high point in his work, need not concern us here. The church cantata will be discussed in this section solely as treated by Bach; for, while he was far from being the only German composer to write church cantatas, his works in this form are practically the only ones performed today.

The cantata was one of the musical parts of the principal service, the service for Sundays and holidays, of the Lutheran Church. The liturgical usage of St. Thomas' Church in Leipzig, for example, specified fifty-nine annual occasions for which Bach had to supply music

—either works from his own pen, or such works as were already in the church library, or which could be obtained from other composers. For these fifty-nine occasions Bach composed sets of works for five full years—two hundred and ninety-five cantatas, of which about one hundred and ninety-five have been preserved.

In the Leipzig service the cantata not only followed the reading of the appointed Gospel, but was in itself a setting of a text based on selfsame Gospel extract. It usually comprised several numbers for chorus, soloists, and orchestra. In Bach's hands it was primarily a descriptive work, in which the composer strove continually to drive home to the listener the implications of the Gospel text, as he saw them. The vividness of presentation, both vocal and instrumental, and the mastery of combination of word and tone that the cantatas display place them on the same dramatic plane as the music-dramas of Wagner. They represent, in their multiplicity of moods and in the wealth of subjects they portray, the most intimate, the most personal of all of Bach's works. They reveal for us his theology, his world outlook, his faith. The great Bach critic and world-famous theologian, Albert Schweitzer, has aptly observed: "In comparison with the cantatas, everything else that Bach has done appears as hardly more than a supplement." [13]

The texts of most of the cantatas were supplied to Bach by various writers in Weimar and Leipzig. Over thirty were written by the composer himself. They consisted of verses based on the Gospel for the day and usually divided into six or seven numbers suitable for choruses, recitatives,[14] arias, duets, and so forth. There was no prescribed order. Most of the cantatas opened with a chorus of large dimensions followed by recitatives and arias, and usually closed with a chorale, in the singing of which the congregation joined. They ranged in duration from twenty minutes to half an hour.

The resources available to Bach for the production of these works were indeed pathetic, and it is not surprising that the cantatas apparently made no impression when they were performed. Bach had to content himself with a chorus of about seventeen voices and an orchestra of about twelve players, many of whom were poor perform-

---

[13] Albert Schweitzer, *J. S. Bach* (New York, 1923), Vol. I, page 264.
[14] See page 109.

ers. Only one of the cantatas was printed during Bach's lifetime; [15] and it was not until 1821, seventy-one years after Bach's death, that publication and dissemination of these musical treasures were begun.

Inasmuch as the available recordings of representative cantatas are either incomplete or inadequate, and since opportunities for hearing these magnificent works are rare indeed, no cantata can be singled out for discussion here. The neglect which continues to be the lot of these masterpieces is most unfortunate. Until such time as they achieve their due measure of public performance, Bach will remain a composer of whom our picture is woefully incomplete.

The Secular Cantatas

For weddings, ceremonies honoring university professors, civic ceremonials, and various functions in honor of visiting royalty, Bach composed some twenty secular cantatas. Of these, three have become well-known to modern audiences: *The Contest between Phoebus and Pan* (*Der Streit zwischen Phoebus und Pan*); the *Coffee Cantata* (*Schweiget stille, plaudert nicht*); and the *Peasant Cantata* (*Mer han en neue Oberkeet*). The last two works are examples of the comparatively unknown aspect of Bach as a humorist in music. The *Coffee Cantata* deals with the comical situation that develops when a father tries to break his daughter of the habit of drinking coffee.[16] The *Peasant Cantata* was written to felicitate an official of the city of Leipzig on his acquisition of some land. After the villagers have congratulated their new master they retire to the inn for free beer. For this work Bach writes an overture employing peasant tunes and finishing with a waltz. The text must have appealed strongly to Bach, for the entire *Peasant Cantata* is filled with jolly tunes of a rustic nature.

Passion Music

The *Passion,* one of the oldest of musical forms, arose from the practice of reading publicly during Holy Week those sections of the Gospel dealing with the sufferings and crucifixion of Jesus. In its aim to dramatize biblical events for the laity, the Passion claims relationship to the medieval mystery play.

As brought to its highest point of development by Bach, the Passion

---

[15] An early cantata, written in 1708 for the inauguration of a *Bürgermeister*.
[16] See C. v. d. Borren, "Tobacco and Coffee in Music," *The Musical Quarterly*, July, 1932.

consists of a setting for soloists, chorus, orchestra, and organ of a text based on the portions of the Gospels describing the agony and sufferings of Jesus.[17]   It was performed in the church as part of the vesper service for Good Friday, the anniversary of the Crucifixion.   Bach is said to have composed four Passions, of which two, the *St. John Passion* and the *St. Matthew Passion,* have survived in their entirety.

Of these two settings of the Passion, that according to St. Matthew, composed in 1729, is universally regarded as the finer.   It is a work similar in spirit to the cantatas and possessing the same fundamental aim: a vivid presentation of a text based on the Scripture lesson for the day, in this instance one of sadness and suffering.

The text of the *St. Matthew Passion* consists of (1) rhymed paraphrases of excerpts from the Gospel, and (2) verses of a devotional or commentative nature interpolated at salient points in the unfolding of the narrative.   Of the several soloists, the most important is the "Evangelist" to whom the greater part of the Biblical text is entrusted. Other soloists either portray characters such as Jesus and Pontius Pilate, or sing the commentative verses.   The chorus has the same duality of function: it participates as a dramatic protagonist, for example, the crowd at the trial before Pontius Pilate; or it serves as a medium for the expression of devotional commentary.   The whole is arranged in a series of scenes consisting of recitatives, arias, duets, and choruses.   Of these types of vocal expression, only the first demands explanation.

The *recitative* (Latin *recitare*—to recite) is a musical setting of a text in either prose or verse, the words of which are not sung but rather declaimed.   The performer is usually not held to any predetermined rhythm; music serves here as an agency to heighten the declamatory accents of speech.   In the simpler styles of recitative the accompaniment consists of a succession of supporting chords.   During Bach's day these were usually played from a figured bass by the organ, assisted by a violoncello and a double bass.   In the *St. Matthew Passion* the recitatives of Jesus are always declaimed to a soft, limpid accompaniment played by all the strings.

The musical idiom of the *St. Matthew Passion* is one of intense piety and devotion.   In this work, as in the cantatas, we find many examples of Bach's ability to characterize and to depict in a manner

[17] St. Matthew xxvi-xxvii, St. Luke xxii-xxiii, St. Mark xiv-xv, St. John xviii-xix.

remarkable even today. One of the finest examples of this art of tonal painting is the aria for soprano, *Aus Liebe will mein Heiland sterben,* which forms a part of the trial scene. The combination of dramatic and devotional elements in the *St. Matthew Passion* can be shown by the recitatives which precede this aria. These, in translation, are:

The Evangelist: (as narrator)	The Governor said:
Pilate: (as participant)	What evil hath He done?
Soprano: (as devout commentator)	He hath done good to us all. He gave the blind their sight, He made the lame walk; He spoke His Father's Word to us, He drove the devil away; He consoled the downcast; He lifted up the sinful and embraced them; nought but this did my Jesus do.

The aria which follows these recitatives is a setting of this text:

> Aus Liebe will mein Heiland sterben,
> Von einer Sünde weiss er nichts.
> Dass das ewige Verderben
> Und die Strafe des Gerichts
> Nicht auf meiner Seele bliebe,
> Aus Liebe will mein Heiland sterben, *etc.*

(*Prose translation*: For love would my Saviour die, He knows nought of sin. So that eternal ruin and the punishment of the Last Judgment do not rest on my soul, for love would my Saviour die.)

Bach describes the innocent Jesus in the instrumental introduction to the aria. He employs only three instruments, a flute and two oboes da caccia (obsolete instruments closely related to the modern English horn) in the presentation of this gentle melody:

Ex. 25

The vocal soloist then enters as a fourth voice in the plaintive discourse. The aria is cast in Da Capo form,[18] the instrumental introduction being repeated.

18 See page 84.

The *St. Matthew Passion* also contains many magnificent choruses. Outstanding among them are the opening movement depicting Christ on the road to Calvary, and the final movement in which the chorus cries down to Christ in His tomb. This last chorus is one of the world's great masterpieces of devotional music.

In the *St. Matthew Passion* Bach again makes effective use of the Lutheran chorale. One of the most moving of these chorale interpolations occurs in the prison (Praetorium) scene (St. Matthew xxvii). The Evangelist has declaimed "and they spat upon Him, and took the reed and smote Him on the head." Bach then introduces this chorale, one of his numerous harmonizations of a melody that, although completely secular in origin, had taken on a funereal character:

Ex. 26

O Haupt voll Blut und Wun - den, voll Schmerz und voll - er Hohn!
O Haupt, zu Spott ge - bun den mit ei - ner Dor - nen - kron!

O Haupt, sonst schön ge - zie - ret mit höch-ster Ehr' und Zier, Jetzt

a - ber hoch schimp - fi - ret: ge - grü - sset seist du mir!

(*Prose translation of the text:* O Head covered with blood and wounds, O Head tortured and despised! O Head mocked by a crown of thorns! O Head once adorned with highest honor, and now abused: I bow before Thee!)

The Mass in B minor

Bach's Mass in B minor is only one of thousands of musical settings of a text that has attracted composers since its final formulation as part of the liturgy of the Roman Catholic Church in 1014. The various parts of the Mass and the musical implication of the term have been discussed on page 41.

The question immediately arises: What caused Bach, a Lutheran, to set a text so closely identified with the Catholic Church? This is easily answered. The Lutheran Church had preserved many of the elements of the Catholic ritual, and while the Ordinary of the Mass was not utilized as an entity, each of its five parts might be heard at different times during the church year. The so-called Lutheran Mass, for example, was composed of the *Kyrie* and *Gloria*. In 1733, Bach forwarded such a *Kyrie* and *Gloria* to his sovereign Augustus III, Elector of Saxony and a Roman Catholic. A petition asking that he be appointed Court Composer accompanied the music. The title was conferred upon Bach in 1736; but there is no record of any Dresden performance of the Lutheran Mass.

Bach's nature was apparently such as to compel him to complete a work. Movements were added to this Lutheran Mass, so that by 1737 an entire Roman Catholic Mass had been created. Eight movements, which include some of the most beautiful sections of the entire Mass, were adapted from existing cantatas.

Bach's setting of the Mass is scored for chorus, soloists, and orchestra. It consists of twenty-four movements of which fifteen are choruses, six are arias, and three duets. Bach conforms to Catholic tradition in not admitting recitative. The comparatively large orchestra comprises strings, two flutes, two oboes, two oboes d'amore (obsolete lower-pitched relatives of the oboe), two bassoons, one horn, three trumpets, timpani, and the indispensable continuo.[19] (Not all of these instruments are used in every movement.) The designation Mass in B minor indicates that B minor is the basic tonality; but the work does not remain in this key throughout, and use is made of the more closely related keys. Only five of the twenty-four movements are in the key by which the Mass is known.

[19] See page 100.

Although the Mass in B minor was inspired by a liturgical text, it cannot in any sense be regarded as liturgical music except insofar as portions of it are suitable for the rites of the Lutheran Church. Its length alone renders it unusable in the church from whose ritual its text was borrowed.

The idiom of the Mass in B minor is precisely like that of the cantatas and the *St. Matthew Passion*. In this work we find the same grasp of the implications of the text combined with an ability to give utterance to this interpretation by means of realistic music.

In his setting of this ancient text Bach has revealed his own innermost faith. A beautiful illustration of the intensely subjective nature of the Mass is afforded by the vast opening movement *Kyrie eleison* (Lord, have mercy upon us), almost the whole of which consists of a fugal elaboration by voices and instruments of this supplicatory theme:

Ex. 27

SUGGESTED READINGS

The outstanding authority on Bach was the late Professor Charles Sanford Terry of the University of Aberdeen, and his *Bach, A Biography* (London, 1933), is the best work dealing exclusively with the composer's life. His *The Music of Bach* (London, 1933) is, similarly, the best short guide to the more important works. Professor Terry also made a study of the liturgy of Bach's day and combined this with English translations of all the cantata texts in his *Joh. Seb. Bach Cantata Texts, Sacred and Secular* (London, 1926). *The Musical Pilgrim,* a series of handbooks on musical classics published by the Oxford University Press of London contains four works by Professor Terry, The *Magnificat,* The *Mass in B Minor,* The *Passions,* The *Cantatas.*

Bach's art, notably his pictorialism, is critically treated in the celebrated two-volume work of the Alsatian organist, theologian, medical missionary and philosopher Albert Schweitzer, *J. S. Bach* (New York, 1923). David and Mendel, *The Bach Reader* (New York, 1945), is an engaging biography of Bach set forth in letters and documents. Section Seven of this work, "The Rediscovery of Bach," should prove exceptionally interesting to the student. The three-volume work of Spitta, *The Life of Bach* (London, 1899), tends to be verbose but contains much that is unavailable in other works on the composer.

Chapter X

THE CULMINATION OF THE BAROQUE:
GEORGE FRIDERIC HANDEL

O F THE numerous significant contemporaries of Bach, the most outstanding was George Frideric Handel,[1] born only a few weeks before Bach on February 23, 1685, in the town of Halle, not far distant from Eisenach. Both the careers and creative accomplishments of these men stand in sharp contrast to each other. Handel seems to have been ignorant of Bach's attainments, but he cannot be reproached for this inasmuch as Bach was an obscure cantor in a provincial city. Bach, on the other hand, always the zealous student of the works of other composers, studied some of Handel's compositions, as copies of them in his own hand attest. The two men never met.

Unlike Bach, Handel could claim no musical heritage; no traces of any musical proclivities are to be found in his ancestry. His father was a barber-surgeon, the stern head of a typical German middle-class family, who desired nothing more of his son than that he also embark upon some respectable professional career.

The father's hopes received their first jolt when his son gave evidence of marked musical talent; and it was only at the insistence of a local ruler, the Duke of Weissenfels, that Handel was permitted to receive systematic musical instruction. The lad was placed under the tutelage of Zachow, the organist of the Liebfrauenkirche in Halle, and received from him a thorough grounding in the technique of composition as well as training in playing the violin, the oboe, the clavier, and the organ. Handel developed rapidly as a virtuoso performer on the harpsichord, and even made two trips to Berlin to appear as a prodigy before the Prussian court. Inasmuch as Handel's father had

[1] The original German form is *Händel;* this has now been Anglicized as *Handel.*

GEORGE FRIDERIC HANDEL

planned a legal career for him, none of this musical activity was allowed to interfere with his academic training. He was graduated from the local *Gymnasium* and in 1702 he enrolled as a student at the University of Halle. In the same year he was given the post of organist at the Domkirche (Cathedral) in Halle. But Handel was not attracted by the prospect of life in a smug commercial town, and in 1703 he resigned from both the University and the Domkirche. The prime cause for this decision was the attraction exercised upon him by the glamorous musical life of Hamburg, and it was to this thriving seaport that he now betook himself.

Hamburg was at that time the leading musical center of Germany. Bach had visited it in the previous year to hear the playing of its famous organist, Johann Adam Reincken (1623-1722). But Handel had been attracted not by the music to be heard in Hamburg's churches, but rather by the productions of its celebrated opera house then at the height of its fame. He quickly found a place for himself in the opera orchestra. His initial engagement was as a violinist, but his talents were such as to win him promotion to the position of harpsichordist, a post of great importance. It was at Hamburg that works from Handel's pen were first heard by a large public. These were a *St. John Passion* and four operas. One of these operas, *Almira,* was successful enough to warrant its being performed over twenty times in one season. But Handel was drawn to yet another focal point of musical life, Italy, and toward the end of 1706 he left Hamburg.

The years which Handel spent in Italy were profitable indeed. Here he came into close contact with the oratorios of Giacomo Carissimi (1604-1674), and became personally acquainted with the great opera composer Alessandro Scarlatti (1659-1725) and his son, the harpsichordist, Domenico Scarlatti (1685-1757), as well as with an important figure in the development of violin music and the concerto grosso— Arcangelo Corelli.[2] The talented Handel was enthusiastically fêted by the art-loving princes of Italy. He also wrote two operas for Italian theaters. One of these, *Agrippina,* was given twenty-seven successive performances. The three years that Handel spent in Italy were filled with such triumphs that, although only a young man of twenty-five, he had already become famous.

[2] See page 102.

He left Italy to assume the post of Kapellmeister at the court of the Elector George of Hanover. A short time after entering the Elector's service, Handel received permission to visit London. This journey proved to be a turning point in his life. Opera in Italian had become firmly established in the English capital, and a magnificent opportunity now presented itself to a composer of Handel's attainments. Shortly after his arrival in London he was introduced to the manager of the Haymarket Theater. Within fourteen days he had composed the music for *Rinaldo,* performed on February 24, 1711, to great acclaim.

Handel's first stay in London was cut short by his obligation to Hanover. But Hanover had no operatic performances at the time, and the autumn of 1712 found Handel back in London composing more operas. From 1712 until his death, England was his home; he became a naturalized British subject in 1726. The Elector of Hanover, from whose service Handel had been playing truant, became George I of England in 1714. Handel was forgiven by the king, a pension was conferred upon him, and he was appointed music master to the two princesses. In the meanwhile opera had fallen into desuetude in London, and for a period of time Handel served as music director to the Duke of Chandos.

In 1719 a new operatic venture, the Royal Academy of Music, was started in London. Handel turned out opera after opera for this institution until its bankruptcy in 1728. An important factor in the downfall of the Royal Academy was the popularity of *The Beggar's Opera* of Gay and Pepusch, a parodic and somewhat licentious work, the music of which was largely a compilation of popular songs coupled with several purloinings from the works of England's greatest composer, Henry Purcell (1659-1695), and from Handel.

Handel resumed the composition of operas in 1730 and continued to produce works in this form until 1741, although the enormous expenses and the dwindling proceeds from operatic performances had forced him into bankruptcy in 1737. A curious combination of events served to turn his attention to another type of dramatic music, a form in which he scored his greatest triumphs—the *oratorio.* While in the service of the Duke of Chandos, Handel had composed a masque, *Haman and Mordecai,* for presentation in the Duke's private theater. In 1732 he proposed to mount this twelve-year-old work at one of the

London theaters.   This plan to present Biblical incidents on a public stage met with much opposition and the Bishop of London banned the performance.   The stubborn Handel added a few scenes to the masque, changed its name to *Esther,* and performed it as *The Story of Esther, An Oratorio in English.*   A note in the advertisement announcing the performance read as follows: "There will be no action on the stage, but the House will be fitted up in a decent manner for the Audience." [3]

The success of this presentation served to awaken Handel's interest in the artistic potentialities of the oratorio, and a notable series of works in this form now commenced to flow from his facile pen. They met with varying sorts of receptions, and the composer's status in the musical life of London remained uncertain until the triumphant performance of his oratorio *Judas Maccabaeus* in 1747.   From this time on he was the undisputed master of English music.   No other composer arose to contest his supremacy.   He became totally blind in 1753; but this neither prevented his appearing in public as organ soloist at performances of his oratorios nor kept him from composing.   A musical secretary, Christopher Smith, took down his last works as he dictated them.   Handel died in 1759.   The choice of Westminster Abbey for his final resting place indicates the esteem in which the British held this remarkable foreigner.

The list of compositions by Handel includes forty-six operas, thirty-two oratorios, and many instrumental works, of which the more important are the *Water Music* for orchestra, the concerti grossi for strings, the organ concertos, a few harpsichord pieces, and the sonatas for violin and clavier.   But Handel has shared the fate of his contemporary, Bach: only a small fraction of his creative accomplishment is known to the musical public of today.

The Early Opera

The opera, a form which Handel so assiduously cultivated, had been in existence less than a hundred years when he was born.   It owed its origin to one of the characteristic aspects of the Italian Renaissance— interest in the civilization of ancient Greece.   Between 1580 and 1589 a group of Florentine gentlemen met regularly at the home of Count

[3] Newman Flower—*George Frideric Handel* (Boston, 1923), page 196.

Giovanni Bardi, an accomplished scholar and mathematician. In their discussions, which were concerned with the nature of Greek drama, the Florentines maintained that the dramas of classical antiquity were sung in a declamatory manner and that the style of Greek music was more fitted for dramatic expression than the complex polyphony of the sixteenth century. In an endeavor to restore what they deemed to be the style of Greek drama, this group of Florentine gentlemen created the opera. The earliest operas were plays whose texts were declaimed in a recitative-like style to the accompaniment of a few string instruments. While these earliest operas would hardly be interesting to modern ears, their advent marked a well-defined turning point in the history of music. Through their emphasis on one voice, they served to accelerate the development of a homophonic style, and, through their significant employment of instruments, to aid in the formulation and growth of the orchestra. But above all it should be observed that the first operas were conceived primarily as dramatic works, in which music was regarded merely as a medium for heightening the effectiveness of dramatic poetry. The earliest opera that has been preserved is the *Euridice* of Jacopo Peri, performed in 1600. The new form immediately found many adherents. The first truly great opera composer was Claudio Monteverdi (1567-1643), whose *Arianna* (Ariadne) given at Mantua in 1608 contains the celebrated "Lament."

The first public opera house was opened in Venice in 1637, less than fifty years before Handel's birth. It was not long before the initial dramatic purpose of the opera was obscured by the various extravagances that the populace came to demand from it. Works were performed with magnificent settings and spectacular stage effects which frequently included wild animals, representations of storms, and aerial flights. The stage machinist often outranked the composer. The dramatic recitative gradually disappeared, and in the works of Monteverdi's pupil, Francesco Cavalli (1602-1676), and those of Marc' Antonio Cesti (1623-1669), tuneful melodies written in a popular vein became an important feature of the opera. The rapidly increasing musical public soon developed an appreciation of fine singing and was prompt to bestow its patronage upon its favorite performers. These favorites, on the other hand, were not loath to make capital of their attainments. Fabulous fees were earned by them and such was their position that they tyrannized managers and composers with impunity. Our modern "star" system with all its abuses probably traces its history back to the early days of opera.

The diverse trends of early Italian opera are summed up in the work of Alessandro Scarlatti (1659-1725), with whose compositions Handel was familiar. Scarlatti, composing for the royal opera at Naples, introduced several devices into the Italian opera of the eighteenth century, which through persistent use in his own works became established conventions. Of these the most important were: (1) the Da Capo form (A B A) as a pattern for the organization of arias; (2) the employment of a series of three instrumental movements as an introduction to an opera. The Da Capo form [4] became a somewhat deadly stereotype. The three short instrumental movements were called by Scarlatti *Sinfonia*. The first movement was fast, the second slow, the third again fast. It is from this Italian type of introductory piece (overture) that our modern symphony evolved.

Handel's Operas

Handel was the direct successor of Scarlatti. All his operas employed Italian texts and followed the Italian tradition. The libretti of these works were usually based on classical history or medieval romance. Typical operas were *Rinaldo, Flavio, Giulio Cesare, Orlando,* and *Alcina.* The literary value of most of the texts was almost negligible. The cast was usually confined to a few characters, and the chorus played a very unimportant part. The male parts were sung almost exclusively by *castrati,* male sopranos, the pitch of whose voices had been preserved from boyhood by a brutal and dangerous operation. Solo music predominated, and a Handel opera might well be described as a series of recitatives and arias, designed to permit singers to display their ability and at the same time to regale the audience with attractive melodies. Handel strove to make his musical settings as faithful to their texts as the conventions of his epoch allowed and a surprising degree of dramatic verisimilitude may often be found in them. Original and effective passages were also entrusted to the orchestra. But the Handel operas are primarily collections of beautiful melodies of all shades and types. The conventions which governed the

[4] See page 84.

composition of these works have stood in the way of their performance today. The male parts in particular present difficult problems.

The most widely known piece of music by Handel, the celebrated
Largo,[5] is operatic in origin. Thoroughly typical in its breadth, it was
originally an aria (*Ombra mai fù*) in the humorous opera *Serse*
(Xerxes), sung by King Xerxes as he thanks a plane tree for its wel-
come shade. Many of the present-day transcriptions of this simple
melody amply merit the condemnation "monstrous perversion" meted
out to them by a great American critic, Philip Hale (1854-1934).

The Oratorio

The Handelian *oratorio* may be defined as an extensive setting for
solo voices, chorus, and orchestra, of a text derived from or based on
the Bible.[6] It is performed without scenery, costumes, or action. The
earliest oratorios were descended from the allegorical mystery plays
which were presented in the church. With the advent of the opera
toward the end of the Renaissance, these plays became to all intents and
purposes sacred operas, produced in the church with orchestra, action,
and costume. The name given these works was in reality the name
of the chapel in the church in which they were performed, the *oratorio* (oratory). As already stated, the operas of Handel were written
with due deference to the conventions established by his predecessors;
his oratorios, on the other hand, while showing some influence of the
early Italian composers, are far removed from all other earlier works
in this category. The oratorio, in the modern sense of the word, is
largely Handel's own creation.

The Handel oratorio, unlike the Bach cantata, was not part of a
liturgy. It was designed for performance on the stage of the theater
and not in the choir loft; it was written for an audience and not a
congregation. Its text, written in the English language and based on
familiar selections from the Scriptures, was infinitely superior to the
stilted and artificial libretto of the opera. The members of the chorus,
with the music before their eyes, were freed from the necessity of
memorizing their parts and could therefore be utilized in a manner

---

[5] See page 32.
[6] An oratorio may occasionally employ a text of secular origin and then be designated as a
"secular oratorio."

so effective as to compensate amply for the absence of action, scenery, and costume. The raising of the chorus to the role of principal dramatic protagonist constitutes Handel's most significant contribution to the oratorio. The other features of the Handel oratorio are shared by his operas—the profusion of expressive melodies, the ability to make a text dramatically effective by simple means. As has been observed, the Handel oratorio is an "entertainment." Although based on Holy Writ, these Handel oratorios cannot be considered truly religious music. They were designed not to stimulate piety and devotion, but rather to furnish a full evening of vocal music utilizing the dramatic potentialities of Biblical episodes. No matter what type of text he employed, Handel remained an eminently practical composer of music for the theater, and like most theatrical composers, he always had his audience in mind. His oratorios, like his operas, are conceived along broad lines such as would be easily appreciated by the public. In this respect he and Bach represent opposite poles of musical thinking.

MESSIAH

Of Handel's oratorios the better known are *Israel in Egypt, Samson, Judas Maccabaeus,* and *Messiah.* The last-named work is performed with great frequency today by choral bodies everywhere, with consequent neglect of the other oratorios. The unique appeal of *Messiah* has been responsible for the continued existence of many choral organizations, for the character of the music has always served to attract both participants and auditors.

Handel composed *Messiah* in 1741 in the incredibly brief space of twenty-four days. His fertility was extraordinary, even for an epoch in which composers were expected to toss off music for any occasion at a moment's notice. The work had its first performance in Dublin in 1742. It was given in London the following year; but it met with such a storm of protest from the clergy that Handel was forced to advertise it without its name, as "A Sacred Oratorio." It was not until 1750 that *Messiah* was accepted by Londoners. Since that date it has probably been sung more often than any other large choral work.

The text of *Messiah* was compiled by a British literary dilettante, Charles Jennens. It consists of a series of Biblical excerpts telling of the second coming of the Redeemer, drawn from the Psalms, the

Prophets, and the Gospels. These excerpts are arranged as a series of episodes that possess little dramatic continuity. This lack of dramatic continuity is unique to *Messiah* and is not characteristic of Handel's other oratorios. In fact, great a work as *Messiah* may be, it is not a representative Handel composition in this category.

The orchestra that Handel demanded for *Messiah* consisted largely of strings; wood-wind and brass instruments found only occasional employment. As in the choral works of Bach, many of the recitatives were accompanied from a figured bass. The organ was also utilized, either for the accompaniment of recitatives or to lend support in the choral numbers. *Messiah* contains two celebrated purely instrumental movements—the overture and a "Pastoral Symphony." The overture follows the customary French pattern,[7] but without repetition of the opening *Grave*. Its concise fugue is based on this robust subject:

Ex. 1

Like all the overtures written at this time, the overture to *Messiah* bears no dramatic relationship to the work that it prefaces. The "Pastoral Symphony" is played by the orchestra immediately before the recitative for soprano: "There were shepherds abiding in the field, keeping watch over their flocks by night." The title "Symphony" was used freely for instrumental music at this time and should not be interpreted in the more modern sense. The "Pastoral Symphony" is a charming orchestral intermezzo which in its use of $\frac{12}{8}$ rhythm and its drone-bass recalls the tunes played by Italian shepherds, tunes Handel must have heard during his stay in Italy.

Messiah is replete with beautiful arias, of which the greater number are happy fusions of Handel's melodic and dramatic gifts. Two of the more outstanding arias are the solo for the bass, "The people that walked in darkness," and the solo for the alto, "He shall feed His flock like a shepherd." In the former aria Handel creates an atmosphere appropriate to the text by having the strings play the following groping figure in unison with the voice:

[7] See page 100.

Ex. 2

The peo-ple that walk-ed in dark · ness, that walk-ed in dark · ness.

The alto aria describes the Lord as the Protector of His flock by means of this expressive melody written in the manner of a *pastorale:*

Ex. 3

He shall feed His flock like a shep - - herd,

The choral writing, in four parts throughout the work, reveals Handel as a consummate master of vocal idiom. The choral numbers abound in passages that, although difficult, are nevertheless thoroughly vocal in style and offer no insurmountable obstacles to executants of only moderate attainments. Hence *Messiah* is invariably performed with gusto by amateur choral groups. The choruses vary from the simple massive style of, for example, "Surely He hath borne our griefs":

Ex. 4

Sure · ly,   sure · ly,   He hath borne our griefs, and car - ried our sor - rows,

(The vigorous orchestral part is not shown.)

to the expressive polyphony of the fugal chorus, "And with His stripes we are healed." constructed on this dramatic subject:

Ex. 5

King George II rose from his seat when he heard the imposing "Halle-lujah" chorus, thereby establishing a custom that has now become universal.

Messiah has been subjected to all manner of editions, accretions, re-visions, and cuts since its first performances. Well-intentioned as some of these alterations may have been, notably the "additional accompani-ments" supplied by Mozart for a performance in Vienna in 1789, they have served merely to deface and deform Handel's music. In some instances these changes have resulted in a complete negation of the composer's intentions. It is only recently and thanks to the industry of an American Handel authority, Dr. Jacob Maurice Coopersmith, that Handel's original score has been made available to choral societies.

Contemporary performances by large mixed choruses should not be regarded as the embodiment of Handel's intentions. The choruses that he utilized for the production of his oratorios were fairly small and were composed entirely of men and boys. (Women appeared as soloists.) The tradition of performing *Messiah* with gigantic forces seems to have begun in 1784 with the twenty-fifth anniversary of Handel's death. During the "Handel Commemoration" held in that year in Westminster, *Messiah* was given by an ensemble of 525 voices and instruments.

Instrumental Music

Handel's best-known instrumental work is a set of variations that ends a harpsichord suite in E major (No. V). The five essentially simple variations are based on a broad, robust theme called "The Harmonious Blacksmith." The misleading title was not given to the music by Handel, and it did not make its appearance in association with his work until long after his death. The set of twelve concerti grossi for string orchestra was composed in 1739. As usual Handel composed these works with amazing facility; so quickly did his crea-tive processes operate that the composition of each concerto grosso consumed about a day. The concertino employed for these works consists of two violins and cello, an indication of Handel's familiarity with the works of Italian masters, notably Corelli. The number of movements to be found varies, and dance forms such as the sarabande and the minuet make their appearance. The twelve concerti grossi are not of equal worth; several betray the haste with which they were composed, others bear the stamp of genius. The style of these works differs markedly from the Brandenburg concertos of Bach. The Handel movements give a continual impression of improvisation, and more than one movement that starts out as a fugue tarries joyfully by the wayside as its composer toys with his material in brilliant fashion.

For a concert on the river Thames given for King George I in 1717 Handel composed what is now called the *Water Music*. This consisted of twenty-five pieces that were rendered by an orchestra of fifty musicians playing on a barge adjoining that of the King. There is a traditional tale to the effect that King George had been angry with Handel as a result of the latter's failure to return to Hanover; but, deeply impressed by the wonderful music that reached the Royal Barge, he summoned Handel and bestowed his forgiveness upon him. Attractive as this anecdote may be, its veracity is open to question. Extracts from the *Water Music* are played today in an unnecessarily modernized version. A lovely "Air" and a vigorous "Hornpipe" are notable features of the score.

Of the world's great composers, Handel spoke in the simplest and most direct musical language. It is indeed regrettable that so few of his many masterpieces are well known.

Suggested Readings

The best available English biographies of Handel are: Flower, *George Frederic Handel,* rev. enl. ed. (New York, 1948), and Weinstock, *Handel* (New York, 1946), both of which contain much valuable material but suffer from various inadequacies and omissions. Myers, *Handel's Messiah, A Touchstone of Taste* (New York, 1948), is an engagingly written and well-documented account of the history of this important work. Herbage, *Messiah* (New York, 1948), is entirely reliable and is enlivened by many excellent illustrations.

Chapter XI

CHRISTOPH WILLIBALD GLUCK

THE VARIOUS abuses that had crept into the opera have been described in the previous chapter.[1] Handel accepted these abuses and later turned his attention to the oratorio. While the artificialities of the opera had been the object of many bitter and satirical literary attacks, it was not until three years after the death of Handel that an attempt was made to return to the principles of dramatic propriety laid down by the Florentine composers who had brought the opera into being. The epoch-making opera was *Orfeo ed Euridice* (Orpheus and Eurydice), composed by Christoph Willibald Gluck and produced in Vienna in 1762. It is the oldest opera to retain a firm place in the repertory of the world's great opera houses.

Gluck was the son of a gamekeeper on the Bavarian estate of Prince Eugene Lobkowitz, a music-loving nobleman whose son later became one of the important benefactors of Beethoven. He was born in the small town of Erasbach in the Upper Palatinate in 1714. Most of his early musical education was acquired at a Jesuit school in Bohemia, and he became tolerably proficient as a vocalist and as a performer on the violin and the violoncello. In 1736 he went to Vienna, and through his association with the Lobkowitz family met a wealthy musical amateur, Prince Melzi, who defrayed the cost of further musical study in Italy. Seven operas were composed by Gluck for Italian audiences, and he met with a success sufficient to warrant his traveling to London in 1745. His attempts at operatic production in London were utter failures, however, and Gluck returned to Vienna and devoted himself to supplying conventional Italian operas for the court theater.

[1] See page 119.

CHRISTOPH WILLIBALD GLUCK

The break with the old tradition occurred with the mounting of *Orfeo ed Euridice* in 1762; this was followed by the equally daring *Alceste* in 1767. An attaché of the French embassy in Vienna now became interested in Gluck and his operatic theories, and prevailed upon him to set to music the *Iphigénie en Aulide* of Racine. The composer was called to Paris to superintend the first performance of his work, and *Iphigénie* was presented there in 1774. The partisans of the old-style Italian opera were outraged by the success of this new-comer, and rallied around the now forgotten Italian composer Niccola Piccinni. The acrimonious squabble that ensued between the Gluck-ists and Piccinnists assumed the dimensions of warfare. The Gluckists emerged victorious, and after the successful presentation of his *Iphigénie en Tauride* Gluck returned to Vienna where he passed his last years in ease and comfort. He died in 1787. He had been made a member of the Order of the Golden Spur by Pope Benedict XIV in 1756, and from that time on had always called himself "Chevalier (or Ritter) von Gluck."

Gluck's Reform of the Opera

Gluck was a reformer and possessed a true reformer's temperament. He was unyielding in his belief that the prime purpose of the opera was a dramatic one, and that every aspect of the opera was to be sub-ordinated to the accomplishment of this goal. Gluck's ideas were not new; but he was the first individual with the courage and the energy to bring them to fruition. Like all reformers, he was intolerant and often tyrannical. As a conductor of his own works he was merciless with singers, dancers, stage-machinists, and scene-painters. He was one of the first of the world's great orchestral conductors. Nor did he hesitate to resort to the pen in defense of his ideas. His opera *Alceste* is prefaced by this *credo*:

When I undertook to set this poem, it was my design to divest the music entirely of all those abuses with which the vanity of singers, or the too great complacency of composers, has so long disfigured the Italian opera, and ren-dered the most beautiful and magnificent of all public exhibitions, the most tiresome and ridiculous. It was my intention to confine music to its true dra-matic province, of assisting poetical expression, and of augmenting the interest of the story without interrupting the action, or chilling it with useless and superfluous ornaments; for the office of music, when joined to poetry, seemed to me, to resemble that of coloring in a correct and well-disposed design, where the lights and shades only seem to animate the figures, without altering their outlines.

I determined therefore not to stop a singer, in the heat of a spirited dialogue, for a tedious *ritornell;* nor to impede the progress of passion, by lengthening a single syllable of a favorite word, merely to display agility of voice; and I was equally inflexible in my resolution, not to employ the orchestra to so poor a purpose, as that of giving time for the recovery of breath, sufficient for a long and unmeaning cadence.

I never thought it necessary to hurry through the second part of an aria though the most impassioned and important, in order to repeat the words of the first part, regularly four times; or to finish the aria, where the sense is unfinished, in order to give the singer an opportunity to show that he has the impertinent power of varying passages, and disguising them, till they shall be no longer known to the composer himself; in short, I tried to banish all those vices of the musical drama, against which, good sense and reason have so long protested in vain.

I thought that the overture ought to prepare the audience for the action of the work, and serve as a kind of argument to it; that the instrumental accompaniment should be regulated by the interest of the drama and not leave a void between the aria and recitative of a dialogue; that they should neither break into the sense and connection of a period, nor wantonly interrupt the energy or heat of the action.

And lastly, it was my opinion, that my first and chief care, as a dramatic composer, was to aim at a noble simplicity; and I have accordingly shunned all parade of unnatural difficulty, in favor of clearness; nor have I sought or studied novelty, if it did not arise naturally from the situation of the character, and poetical expression; and there is no rule of composition, which I have not thought it my duty to sacrifice, in order to favor passion and produce effects.

Gluck commenced his operatic reform with an examination of the conventional libretto. Here he was fortunate to have the association of an Italian man of letters, Ranieri Calzabigi. In *Orfeo* and *Alceste* they produced jointly libretti of classical simplicity from which the traditional intrigues and counterplots were entirely excised. The old laws governing the number of characters and types and sequence of arias were completely disregarded.

The musical setting of these simple texts aimed continually at dramatic truth. Such stereotypes as the Da Capo aria were dispensed with. Singers were afforded no opportunity whatsoever for vocal acrobatics, and were permitted to take no liberties with the composer's music. Arias were simple and comparatively short, and evolved naturally from the drama. Recitatives were conceived not as dull interludes between arias, but rather as highly realistic declamatory passages, accompanied by full orchestra rather than by the harpsichord. The chorus took on a wholly new importance in the unfolding of the drama, and such a work as *Orfeo* may well be described as a choral opera. Gluck was superb in the writing of pathetic music. No finer example can be given than the celebrated lament of Orpheus for his dead Eurydice:

Ex. 1

Che fa - rò senza Eur - i - di - ce! dove an - drò senza il mio ben?

(*Translation:* What shall I do without Eurydice! Where shall I go without my beloved?)

Of equal importance was Gluck's concept of the role of the orchestra. The orchestra plays no subordinate part in his operas. As Gluck himself has written in the above-quoted preface to his *Alceste,* he considered the overture to be in the nature of an introduction to the opera; his overture to *Iphigénie en Aulide* is one of the world's great pieces of dramatic music. Gluck banished the harpsichord from the opera orchestra, and with it went the older custom of "filling in" the orchestral harmonies from a figured bass.[2] Gluck was also one of the first composers of dramatic music to utilize the possibilities of dramatic expression latent in the various orchestral timbres. His works abound in usages of the orchestral instruments that were highly original in their day. Berlioz in his *Treatise on Instrumentation* (1844) quoted many examples from Gluck's operas. The scores of Gluck ushered many instruments into a permanent place in the modern orchestra—the piccolo, the harp, the trombones, the bass drum, the cymbals, the side-drum, and the triangle. Gluck was not only a reformer of the opera; he was also one of the first great masters of orchestration.

The reforms which Gluck advocated and whose artistic validity he so successfully demonstrated in his own works were short-lived and did not take firm hold until almost a hundred years after the composition of *Orfeo,* when another reformer, Richard Wagner, took up the cudgels in defense of dramatic truth in opera.

Only two works of Gluck may be heard today: the opera *Orfeo* and the celebrated overture to the opera *Iphigénie en Aulide* (Iphi-

[2] See page 100.

genia in Aulis). The latter work is always performed with a concert-ending written for it by Richard Wagner. (In the opera the overture proceeds without pause into the opening scene.) It is a perfect example of the nobility, the grandeur, and the classically restrained pathos of Gluck's style.

SUGGESTED READINGS

The best single volume on Gluck and his works is Alfred Einstein, *Gluck* (New York, 1936). Another work of the same type is Martin Cooper, *Gluck* (New York, 1935). The article on Gluck by Donald Francis Tovey in *The Heritage of Music,* Pt. II (London, 1924), is an excellent commentary. The chapter on the operas of Gluck in Vol. I of Grout, *A Short History of Opera* (New York, 1947), should also be consulted. The peculiar history of Gluck's masterpiece is treated in Alfred Loewenberg, "Gluck's Orfeo on the Stage," *The Musical Quarterly,* July, 1940.

Chapter XII

THE VIENNESE SCHOOL: JOSEPH HAYDN

DURING the second half of the eighteenth century there occurred what may well be called a revolution in the art of music. The forms and the styles employed by Bach and Handel gradually disappeared and new forms and a new style, both of which had been slowly evolving from the opera, commenced to dominate the musical scene.

This revolution in the art of music coincided with other revolutions, political and economic. The French Revolution (1789-1799), the American Revolution (1775-1783), and the Napoleonic Wars (1804-1815) brought forth new nations and established new political ideas. The invention of the steam engine, the spinning jenny, the cotton gin, the steamboat, and the locomotive altered the entire course of civilization. Equally significant activity was to be found in the sphere of arts and letters. In Germany Lessing (1729-1781), Schiller (1759-1805), and Goethe (1749-1832) were creating the great classics of their national literature; in England the celebrated literary figures were the poets Burns (1759-1796), Blake (1757-1827), Coleridge (1772-1834), Wordsworth (1770-1850), Shelley (1792-1822), and the playwright Sheridan (1751-1816). England's greatest painters were also active at this time—Gainsborough (1727-1788), Reynolds (1723-1792), Turner (1775-1851), and Constable (1776-1837).

The forms whose cultivation brought about the revolution in music were the symphony and its related types—the sonata, the string quartet, the overture, and the concerto; and the new style was a homophonic one with a strong emphasis on melody. Simultaneously, public orchestral concerts commenced to flourish; orchestras composed of both professionals and amateurs were formed in many of the towns

JOSEPH HAYDN

and cities of Germany; and orchestras and wind bands were maintained by many members of the nobility. The piano came to the fore as a keyboard instrument, displacing the clavichord and the harpsichord; the virtuoso performer appeared on the scene. In the midst of all this activity most of the few works of Bach that had been published seem to have been entirely forgotten. While some of the composers of the period were acquainted with his music and had occasionally expressed some admiration for it, no strong influences can be traced. Polyphony had reached its second high point in the compositions of Bach. Thenceforth a new idiom was to become paramount.

With the mechanical perfection of instruments, instrumental music now came into its own, and the orchestra evolved from a miscellaneous collection of instruments into a well-defined body; but interest in the opera was by no means dormant, and hundreds of operas were written and produced.

Precisely as Bach and Handel were not pioneers but rather individuals who utilized to the full the rich heritage left to them by the efforts of hundreds of predecessors, so the great instrumental composers of this period, Haydn, Mozart, and Beethoven, were indebted to a great number of composers of lesser talent who had conducted the preliminary explorations for them. Their works were rather the culmination of a movement than the movement itself.

The activity of these composers was confined for the most part to Vienna and its vicinity and while no one of them was actually born there, they are frequently referred to as the "Viennese School" and their epoch as the "Viennese Period," one of the most significant periods in the development of modern instrumental music. Ostensibly the chronological limits of the period would extend from the birth of Haydn (1732) to the death of Beethoven (1827). In truth, however, it was not until 1781 that Haydn gave the world his Opus 33, six quartets which mark his maturity as a composer.

Vienna at the Close of the 18th Century

Vienna, at that time the third largest city in Europe (population in 1800: 231,050), was the capital of a large and heterogeneous empire containing many racial groups. Strategically located on the Danube and long the seat of the Holy Roman Empire, the city was an impor-

tant commercial and political center. The Hapsburgs and many of
the nobles attached to their court had huge and luxurious palaces
within the city walls. A strict censorship was in operation to prevent
the infiltration of "revolutionary" ideas engendered by the French
Revolution.

Vienna had long been famous as a center of musical activity. The
principal feature of its musical life, however, was the number of private orchestras maintained by members of the nobility. These orchestras were composed of musicians who not only wore the livery of their
princely employer but also performed other household duties. It was
customary for the director of the orchestra, the Kapellmeister, to compose music for it; and all music so composed was the property of the
individual in whose employ the Kapellmeister was, unless express permission could be obtained for its sale to some other private individual
or to a publisher.

Musical tastes were exactly the reverse of those of today—the Viennese nobles demanded a continuous supply of *new* music. Inasmuch
as their private concerts were quite long, there was a tremendous demand for new works. Curious ways of securing music prevailed.
Princes would frequently commission composers to supply their establishments with music and would order their musical needs in batches,
usually dozens or half-dozens; so that we find Haydn, for example,
writing six symphonies for some concerts in Paris, or six quartets for
a wealthy Viennese wholesale merchant who was eager to have some
Haydn quartets for the delectation of prospective purchasers of his
goods.

While these proprietary rights of the nobles to the music produced
by their various Kapellmeisters may seem a bit odd today, it must be
borne in mind that the system was not without its benefits and advantages. The incentive to musical creativeness afforded by the incessant demand for new music greatly accelerated the progress of the
art; and the composer of the period was liberally compensated for
whatever social inferiority he was made to feel by having the pleasure
of knowing that everything that he wrote would be performed, usually
before select and discriminating audiences.

Music-making, however, was not confined entirely to professionals.
Many members of the nobility were themselves competent instru-

mentalists or vocalists, and frequently participated in the musical events that were given at their palaces. The middle classes were also extremely musical, and orchestras composed almost entirely of amateurs gave concerts at the homes of the more prosperous merchants.

JOSEPH HAYDN

The first composer to play an important part in all this activity was (Franz) Joseph Haydn. He was born in 1732, in the small village of Rohrau, in Lower Austria. His musical aptitudes as a small boy caused his parents to send him to school at the not far distant town of Hainburg, where he received instructions in voice, clavier, and violin. His fine singing ultimately won for him a place in the choir of the famous cathedral of St. Stephen's in Vienna. During the nine years that Haydn served as choirboy at St. Stephen's his academic studies included reading and writing, religion, and Latin; his musical studies, clavier, violin, and singing, and a scant amount of harmony and counterpoint. When his voice broke St. Stephen's had no further use for him and he was dismissed in 1749. Occupying a drafty garret and possessing only an old decrepit clavichord, the penniless youth eked out an existence by playing the violin in the nocturnal serenades then so popular in Vienna, and by giving lessons. The most important aspect of this period in Haydn's life was the rigorous discipline of self-instruction which he imposed upon himself. The guides whom he took for himself were Karl Philipp Emanuel Bach, the famous son of the great Leipzig cantor, whose sonatas for clavier he studied assiduously, and Johann Joseph Fux, to whose theoretical work, *Gradus ad Parnassum,* Haydn applied himself with great thoroughness. Like almost every other composer of genius, Haydn was practically self-taught.

After making the acquaintance of several of the important musical personages of Vienna and for a time holding the post of music director at the court of Count Morzin at Pilsen, in Bohemia, Haydn was engaged as assistant Kapellmeister at the palace of Prince Paul Esterhazy (1761). The Prince maintained an excellent orchestra of fourteen performers at his estate at Eisenstadt, not far from Vienna.

The contract that Haydn signed when he entered into the service of the Esterhazy family gives us an excellent description of the status of the musician at that time. Haydn agreed to take charge of the music, conduct himself in a sober manner, see that the musicians appeared in white hose and with their wigs thoroughly powdered, preserve peace among the musicians, "compose such music as His Highness shall order, divulge these new compositions to no one—and compose nothing for anybody without His Highness' knowledge and gracious permission." He agreed, furthermore, to take zealous care of the musical instruments, instruct the singers, play upon the various instruments of which he had command, and so on.[1]

Prince Paul died in 1762 and was succeeded by his brother, Prince Nicholas, who gave Haydn full direction of his musical forces in 1766. Prince Nicholas, an enthusiastic patron of music, was very kind to Haydn and valued his musical gifts highly. The situation was a fortunate one for the composer as is shown by the great number of works composed while Haydn was in the employ of the Esterhazy family. His name now began to be known in all of the musical circles of Europe. His works were brought out by various publishers, and commissions for new compositions came from places as far away as Paris and London. Two Haydn symphonies were performed at an orchestral concert given in New York City on April 27, 1782. On one of his sojourns in Vienna, Haydn came in contact with Mozart. The fast friendship that was formed between the older master and his youthful contemporary was interrupted by the untimely death of Mozart in 1791.

On the death of Prince Nicholas in 1790, Haydn accepted an invitation to appear at a series of concerts in London under the management of the violinist-impresario, Salomon. His fame had preceded him to England, and he was received there with much enthusiasm; all his concerts were heavily patronized, dinners were given in his honor, and Oxford University bestowed upon him the degree of Doctor of Music. Haydn returned to Vienna in 1792, but he went back to London for another series of equally successful concerts in 1794. For these London performances he composed twelve new symphonies. Returning to Vienna in 1795, he commenced the composition of an oratorio, *The Creation*. The first performance (1798) of this work was a great personal triumph. All the nobility of Vienna were present

[1] C. F. Pohl—*Joseph Haydn* (Leipzig, 1878), Vol. l., pages 391-394.

and the composer was the object of universal acclaim. The next oratorio to appear was *The Seasons* (1801). The closing years of Haydn's
life were spent in retirement in Vienna. Musicians came from far
and wide to visit him. He was made an honorary citizen of the city,
had many medals and decorations bestowed upon him, and was
elected to membership in many honorary societies. He died of old
age in 1809.

Haydn was a gentle, kindly individual who won for himself the
affection and esteem of all with whom he came in contact. He was
almost universally known as "Papa Haydn." A pious Catholic, he
maintained that his mission as a composer was merely to utilize to the
full the gifts that God had given him.

Despite his devout nature, the more important works of Haydn were
not his masses and sacred music, but rather his instrumental music, particularly his symphonies and string quartets. Of the tremendous quantity of music Haydn wrote—seven hundred instrumental works alone,
including at least one hundred and four symphonies and eighty-three
string quartets—a comparatively small fraction is played today. Only
a few symphonies and about a dozen string quartets are heard with
any degree of frequency; and all these are works written in Haydn's
later years.

The Historical Importance of Haydn

Historically Haydn is of tremendous importance. He has even
been called "the father of the symphony," and "the father of the
string quartet"; but these appellations, complimentary as they are,
must be regarded as exaggerations. Both the symphony and the string
quartet had existed long before Haydn. Nor did he invent any new
forms. The true significance of Haydn lies in the fact that he crys-
tallized these forms for all time, and by continually employing them,
demonstrated their musical potentialities to the world.

Haydn was predominantly a composer of instrumental music, and
his idiom, as opposed to that of Bach, was essentially a homophonic
one. The outstanding characteristic of Haydn's music is the wealth
of fresh and sparkling melody to be found in it—melody intrinsically
instrumental in style. The composer also manifested a fondness for
themes that are folk-like in character, occasionally even going so far

as to employ actual dance tunes.   Throughout all his music, however, there is a trend towards expressive melody—melody which may be gay and sprightly and occasionally almost naive, as in some of the symphonies, or profound and meditative, as in the slow movements of many of the string quartets.   It is wholly erroneous to believe that Haydn wrote only "pleasant" music or that his own personality found no expression in his compositions.

One of the great contributions of Haydn was the standardization of the instrumentation of the orchestra.   The one hundred and four symphonies of Haydn demonstrated the possibilities of the combination of instruments that he had chosen; and this particular orchestral grouping has remained substantially unaltered to the present day. Later composers have merely added more instruments.   This "classical" orchestra was composed of the usual strings; a wood-wind section of six players: two flutes, two oboes, and two bassoons; a brass section of four, all *natural* instruments: two horns and two trumpets; and a pair of kettledrums; clarinets are found only in the last symphonies. Haydn handled this comparatively small orchestra with consummate skill and with a fine appreciation for the idiom and tone color of each particular instrument.

Haydn not only wrote for the orchestra with due regard for its coloristic possibilities, but also employed a harmonic idiom which was full and complete in itself so that it became unnecessary to employ a harpsichord to "fill in" the gaps caused by poverty of harmonic texture. Haydn's symphonies mark the disappearance of the harpsichord as a sort of crutch to support the harmonic structure.

The Sonata Form

The form which Haydn brought to its full definition appears under various names, depending entirely on the instruments or instrumental combination for which it is employed.   For a solo instrument or for two instruments in combination, such as the piano and the violin, the term *sonata* is used; for the usual group of strings—two violins, viola, and violoncello—*string quartet* serves as the designation, while the name *symphony* is given to works for orchestra alone, and the title *concerto* to a composition for orchestra and solo instrument (or instruments).   No matter what the instrumental combination may be, the form is substantially the same. The evolution of the symphony from the early opera overture need not concern us here.

The sonata (or string quartet, or symphony) is an instrumental work, usually in three [2] or four movements, the first movement of which is in the so-called "sonata form." Inasmuch as this form is invariably associated with the first movement, it is sometimes known as sonata first-movement form; and since the first movement is frequently in a fast tempo, it may occasionally be called sonata-allegro form.

The four movements of a typical Haydn symphony usually are:

I. A short, slow introduction followed without pause by a fast movement in sonata form.

II. A slow movement—either a set of variations or a song-like movement in three-part form.

III. A minuet.

IV. A fast movement in sonata form (occasionally in rondo form). The first and last movements are usually in the same tonality, and it is this tonality by which the symphony is known. The second and third movements are usually in tonalities closely related to that of the first movement.

The sonata first-movement form may be schematically represented as follows:

A. EXPOSITION
  1. First Group
      One theme, or several themes, in the tonic key.
  2. Second Group
      One theme, or several themes, in a closely related key, usually that of the dominant. Frequently closes with some allusion to the first theme of the first group.
  The entire exposition is often repeated.

B. DEVELOPMENT
      Free development of the subject matter of the exposition. Modulation into remote keys with ultimate return to the tonic, leading to the—

C. RECAPITULATION
      Repetition of the entire exposition, the second group now not in the key of the dominant, but in that of the tonic.

[2] If a work is in three movements, as often happens in the solo sonata, the middle movement may be either a slow movement or a minuet.

D. Coda

> May be a short and cursory conclusion or be quite extended and even partake of the nature of a second development.   Brings the movement to a conclusion.

It should be borne in mind that the above scheme is merely an ideal form, a statistical representation.   Few movements follow this form literally.   It is, however, the basic skeleton upon which great composers have created hundreds of sonatas, symphonies, string quartets, and so forth.

The most striking characteristics of the sonata first-movement form are the division of the exposition into two sections in two different keys, and the presentation of at least two, and frequently more, themes. It is this plurality of thematic material that sets the sonata apart from the fugue and that makes the sonata form such an ideal method of presentation of musical thought.   Besides the inevitable contrasts of key, contrasts of style between the various groups of themes may occasionally occur.   The first group, for instance, may open with a theme of a forceful and dynamic nature, while the second group may commence with a theme which is lyrical or song-like.   The end of the second group, that is, the close of the exposition, is usually vigorous and conclusive, and often contains allusions to the opening theme of the first group.

It is in the development section that the musicianship and imagination of the composer make themselves manifest.   The composer may choose to work with only one, some, or all of the themes presented in the exposition.   Restrained by no convention except that of good taste, he is free to do as he pleases with his subject matter.   Needless to say, appreciation of the development presupposes a knowledge on the part of the listener of the thematic content of the exposition.   The manner in which the development is joined to the recapitulation is always an interesting detail of any movement in sonata form.

The term *recapitulation* is somewhat of a misnomer, for this section is largely a restatement of the exposition and not a summation of the movement.   The French designation *réexposition* is more accurate.   To avoid the monotony of literal repetition of the exposition, however, composers have frequently made certain changes in harmonization or instrumentation.   Since the recapitulation remains in the tonic key, the transition section joining the first and second groups affords composers their best opportunity to avoid obvious restatement.

The coda is the true summing-up or epilogue of the movement. It varies in length and importance, depending on the composer. Those of Haydn and Mozart are usually short, while those of Beethoven are often quite extensive.

It may also be observed that sonata first-movement form has the essential characteristics of three-part form (see p. 70): the Exposition-Development-Recapitulation sequence approximates the Statement-Digression-Restatement feature of three-part form, while the coda serves to give a satisfying conclusion to the whole.

SYMPHONY NO. 94 IN G MAJOR ("THE SURPRISE")

As a typical example we may take one of the most celebrated of the Haydn symphonies—the Symphony in G major (No. 6 in the old catalogue of the publishers Breitkopf and Härtel, No. 94 in the new and correct numbering). This work, written for the first series of London concerts, bears the title *The Surprise* because of a wholly unexpected loud chord that appears in the second movement. All the names attached to Haydn symphonies, such as *The Clock, The Bear, The Hen,* and so forth, were given to the works not by Haydn himself but by well-meaning admirers.

The symphony opens with a slow and somewhat solemn introduction of sixteen measures:

Ex. 1

The first group of the first movement proper presents the following sprightly and thoroughly typical themes:

Ex. 2

This leads to the key of the dominant and to the second group, which commences with a dance-like theme shown on page 144.

Ex. 3

and also includes this rustic melody:

Ex. 4

The brief and compact development begins with motives from Example 2. The recapitulation presents no striking points of departure. The coda commences with this pleasant allusion to the principal subject given out by a solo flute:

Ex. 5

The second movement of a Haydn symphony is frequently a theme and variations, although occasionally the movement may be in three-part form. The presence of a variation form in the symphony or sonata can be traced back to the practices of the suite. Using the *Surprise* Symphony again as an example, we find a theme consisting of an extremely simple, almost child-like melody[3] commencing as follows:

Ex. 6

This is then repeated very softly only to be interrupted by the loud chord which has given the symphony its name.[4] On this theme

[3] It is claimed that Haydn borrowed this theme from a German folk song. See Ernst F. Schmid—*Joseph Haydn, Ein Buch von Vorfahren und Heimat des Meisters* (Kassel, 1934).

[4] There is a widely prevalent story to the effect that Haydn inserted this chord to awaken sleeping members of the audience. This symphony was written for London and was per-

Haydn proceeds to construct variations of much charm and originality. The third variation

Ex. 7

in which the theme is entrusted to the oboe, and the fourth, in which it is given out by the strings and combined with two new melodies in the flute and oboe, are excellent examples of Haydn's command of the orchestra.

Ex. 8

The third movement of a Haydn symphony is almost invariably a minuet—the sole dance form to survive from the suite. The minuet is in triple rhythm and is performed in a moderate tempo. As found in the symphony it is a three-part form, another ABA. The B section, which is usually in another key, is called the *Trio.*[5] The fresh and lively minuets to be found in the Haydn symphonies represent one of the most characteristic features of his art. That of the *Surprise* Symphony opens with this robust figure:

Ex. 9

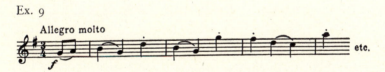

The Trio, in this instance in the same key, affords an effective contrast:

Ex. 10

formed before audiences so enthusiastic and so appreciative that second movements of symphonies frequently had to be repeated. We may interpret the loud chord merely as a bit of pleasantry on Haydn's part.

[5] For the origin of this term see page 84.

The fourth movement of a Haydn symphony is usually a fast, breezy affair. The last movement of the *Surprise* Symphony is in sonata form and commences with this lively theme:

Ex. 11

The second group begins with this laconic subject:

Ex. 12

The development is a masterpiece of terseness and condensation. Almost every symphony of Haydn is brought to a close by a brisk, sparkling movement of this type.

The four movements of the Haydn symphony have no relationship other than that of key. It was not until Beethoven that the four movements of the symphony were fused into one organic whole.

Of the one hundred and four symphonies which Haydn composed, the following, all late works, and with one exception composed for his London concerts, are likely to be heard today:

1. Symphony in G major, No. 88 (Breitkopf u. Härtel old No. 13), composed for the *Concerts Spirituels* in Paris

2. Symphony in G major (*The Surprise*), No. 94 (Breitkopf u. Härtel old No. 6)

3. Symphony in D major (*The Clock*), No. 101 (Breitkopf u. Härtel old No. 4)

4. Symphony in E-flat major (*The Drum-roll*), No. 103 (Breitkopf u. Härtel old No. 1)

5. Symphony in D major (*London*), No. 104 (Breitkopf u. Härtel old No. 2).

THE STRING QUARTETS

The string quartet, like the symphony, had been in existence long before the time of Haydn. But little music of consequence had been written for it and, as an instrumental medium, it had frequently been associated with nocturnal serenades. (Haydn called his earliest quartets *divertimenti.*)   It was his set of six quartets, Opus 33, published in 1781, which established the form on the high artistic level to which it has since adhered.

To the string quartet Haydn brought the same sense of instrumental color and the same power of development that had made his symphonies so outstanding.   Writing for the string quartet demands an intimate knowledge of the innate idiom of string instruments.   Each of the four parts must have equal musical interest; no one may be allowed to dominate the others.   Goethe happily described the string quartet as "the serious conversation of four individuals."   It was Haydn who established the principles of writing for this combination of instruments.   Every contemporary musician praised his quartets highly; and Mozart said, "I learned string-quartet writing from him."

It is in his string quartets that we find the true Haydn.   The intimate nature of this medium as compared to the symphony gave him opportunity to express his own most personal emotions.   Particularly is this true in the slow movements.   Here Haydn seldom employs the variation form, but rather writes slow song-like movements of great profundity and intensity.

The string quartet employs the same form as does the sonata or symphony.   Occasionally the positions of the slow movement and the minuet are reversed; that is, the second movement will be a minuet and the third a slow movement.

Two quartets, the Opus 33, No. 3, in C major and the Opus 74, No. 3, in G minor, will serve as typical examples.

STRING QUARTET IN C MAJOR, OPUS 33, NO. 3

The String Quartet, Opus 33, No. 3, is one of a set of six dedicated to the Archduke Paul of Russia.   An interesting feature of this set is the appearance in each quartet of a movement marked *scherzando* (Italian for "humorously")—the forerunner of the *scherzo* of Beethoven.   The Opus 33, No. 3 quartet is filled with figures which suggest the sounds of birds, and consequently it has been given the name "Bird Quartet" (*Vogelquartett*) though, to be sure, Haydn had no such descriptive intent.

The first movement opens, after a preliminary measure, with the theme shown on the following page:

Ex. 13

The second group, in G major, begins with some pleasant twitter:

Ex. 14

The second movement, marked *Scherzando,* is an ABA form, and has an interesting middle section, a duet for the two violins.

The third movement, a slow movement, is one of the few Haydn slow movements written in sonata form.

The last movement is in rondo form, which is frequently used for last movements by the Viennese School. The designation "rondo" has been freely and, on occasion, misleadingly used by composers. Many types of rondo exist, but a thorough explanation of the form is beyond the scope of this volume. As used by the Viennese masters the rondo is a fast movement, usually witty and epigrammatic. It is characterized by the successive reappearance between digressions, or episodes, of the rondo subject.[6] For the last movement of this quartet Haydn employs a combination which may be graphically represented as follows:

A   —   B   —C(Development)—A—B—A—Coda.
(Tonic)   (Relative minor)   (Tonic)

The rondo theme, A, is:

Ex. 15

Theme B is:

Ex. 16

[6] See page 83.

STRING QUARTET IN G MINOR, OPUS 74, NO. 3

The Quartet in G minor, Opus 74, No. 3, was written in 1792, when Haydn had returned to Vienna after his first series of concerts in London. Like the Quartet in C major, Opus 33, No. 3, it too has certain characteristics that have caused a name to be attached to it. This particular quartet is usually called the "Horseman Quartet" (*Reiterquartett*) because of certain jogging figures which appear in the first and last movements; but again it must be borne in mind that this appellation was not bestowed upon the work by Haydn.

The figures which have given the quartet its name are heard at the beginning of the first movement:

Ex. 17

After two measures of silence, this expressive subject follows:

Ex. 18

The second group strikes a cheerful note with this exuberant theme:

Ex. 19

The development is an elaboration of the themes set forth in Examples 17 and 18. The coda is unusually short.

The outstanding feature of each of the late Haydn quartets is the slow movement, and the slow movement of this quartet is no exception. Haydn has chosen to write it in a very remote tonality, E major, thereby anticipating the methods of Beethoven. Like most of the slow movements of the Haydn quartets, this movement is in three-part form, the A section of which is varied and embellished on repetition. The thematic material of both sections is profound and reflective:

Ex. 20

(a)

(b)

The minuet is in the usual cheerful vein. The fourth movement, in sonata form, commences with a capricious subject whose characteristic features are sudden alterations between forte and piano, and jogging after-beats:

Ex. 21

The second group establishes a more confident mood with one of Haydn's most optimistic melodies:

Ex. 22

The development disports itself with the theme of Example 21. The coda is a humorous trifle into which this motive from Example 21 insists on intruding:

Ex. 23

CHORAL MUSIC

Haydn's two oratorios, *The Creation* and *The Seasons,* for a long time rivalled those of Handel in popularity, but they are performed comparatively seldom today. The first of these two works is not without historical significance. As Arnold Schering has pointed out,[7] *The Creation* was one of the great moving forces which brought our modern concert life into being; a desire to perform this celebrated work was responsible for the formation of choruses and orchestras in many of the smaller cities and towns of Europe. While a few of the choruses and arias in these oratorios merit praise, and although the orchestral writing is masterful and ingenious, lack of a dramatic sense prevented Haydn from becoming a great writer of choral music. In the field of the oratorio he is definitely overshadowed by Handel, a hearing of whose works in London had prompted Haydn to compose in the same form.

The composition of Haydn that is best known and most often performed is neither a symphony nor a string quartet, but a simple heartfelt song, *Gott erhalte Franz, den Kaiser,* composed for the birthday celebration of Kaiser Franz II in 1797. So enthusiastically was the song received that it became a national hymn spontaneously. Haydn, who played the hymn almost daily, always spoke of it as his favorite work and used it as a theme for the set of variations which comprise the second movement of the Quartet in C major, Opus 76, No. 3, known consequently as the *Emperor* Quartet (*Kaiserquartett*). This beautiful melody has not remained the exclusive property of Austria. In 1841 a German poet, Hoffmann von Fallersleben, wrote the text, *Deutschland, Deutschland über alles* to be used with Haydn's melody, thereby creating what is now one of the national hymns of Germany. The melody has also been employed for church hymns and is to be found in combination with various texts in the church hymnals of England and America.

[7] *Geschichte des Oratoriums* (Leipzig, 1911), p. 386.

Suggested Readings

The best work on Haydn in English is Geiringer, *Haydn, A Creative Life in Music* (New York, 1946). H. E. Jacob, *Joseph Haydn, His Art, Times and Glory* (New York, 1950) is an eminently readable work marred by a few questionable passages. The most detailed treatment, the three volume Pohl-Botstiber, *Joseph Haydn* (Leipzig, 1878-1927), remains untranslated from the German. M. Brenet, *Haydn* (London, 1926), is a concise account. The *Musical Quarterly* for April 1932 is given over entirely to articles on Haydn, of which the essay "Haydn in England" is especially interesting.

An illuminating study of the string quartets is to be found in the compendious article on Haydn contributed by Sir Donald Francis Tovey to *Cobbett's Cyclopedic Survey of Chamber Music* (London, 1929). Volume I of the same writer's *Essays in Musical Analysis* (London, 1935) contains lively analyses of the better known Haydn symphonies.

Chapter XIII

THE VIENNESE SCHOOL:
WOLFGANG AMADEUS MOZART

WOLFGANG Amadeus Mozart, like Haydn, was not a native of Vienna. He was born in Salzburg on January 27, 1756, the son of Leopold Mozart, vice-Kapellmeister and court-composer to the Archbishop of Salzburg. Although Mozart was twenty-four years younger than Haydn, the two men must be regarded as contemporaries; and it should be observed that the majority of the works of Haydn which are heard today are of later origin than those of Mozart.

The phenomenal musical capacities of Mozart made themselves manifest when he was very young. He played the harpsichord when only three years old, and by his fifth year he was already composing short pieces. His studies in clavier, violin, and composition were all carried out under the direction of his able and sympathetic father. Mozart's sister Marianne was also a proficient harpsichordist, and in 1763 the father took the two child prodigies on a tour of the principal European cities. The travelers spent much time in Paris and in London. Fourteen days were spent at Versailles where the young Wolfgang amazed the members of the court by his performances on the harpsichord, the violin, and the organ, by his ability to accompany songs and transpose them at sight and, above all, by his skill at improvisation. While there Mozart composed a violin concerto for the Princess Adelaide. The London appearances were also highly sensational.

The Mozart family returned to Salzburg in 1766, but two years later father and son set out on another series of artistic journeys, this time in Italy. The Italian tours were another succession of triumphs. The younger Mozart was fêted everywhere and honors were heaped upon him. It was during this Italian trip that the boy accomplished his celebrated feat of writing down from memory the *Miserere* of Gregorio Allegri, a work for nine voices in two choirs, after having

WOLFGANG AMADEUS MOZART

(An unfinished painting by his brother-in-law, Joseph Lange)

heard it sung only once at the Sistine Chapel in Rome. Up to the year 1773 the account of the life of Mozart is largely the chronicle of his travels, of his meetings with the important musicians of the day, and of his achievements as a performer and a composer.

In taking his son on a tour of the larger European cities, Mozart's father had as his prime purpose the publicizing of the boy's name and talents so that, when he became of age, he might be offered an appointment commensurate with his gifts. In this the father was unsuccessful. To make matters worse, the new Archbishop of Salzburg, Hieronymus, was unimpressed with Mozart's abilities, and, following the custom of the times, was partial to Italian musicians. The Archbishop was an efficient though despotic administrator, who regarded the Mozarts merely as names on a payroll. Father and son, now grown accustomed to acclaim and adulation, found his attitude unbearable and much hard feeling ensued. The Archbishop had appointed Mozart to the posts of concertmaster (principal violinist) and court organist, but the remuneration was small and the conditions of employment far from congenial. By 1781 the strained state of affairs developed into an open breach. Mozart petitioned for a discharge and was rudely dismissed from the Archbishop's service.

From 1781 till his death in 1791 Mozart was a free lance in Vienna. He earned a miserable living by giving lessons and appearing as composer and soloist at concerts managed by himself. Important compositions flowed from his pen in a steady stream, but the financial results were disappointing. The Austrian Emperor did go so far as to appoint Mozart *Kammerkompositeur* (chamber-composer); but the duties of this position were confined to the writing of dances for the Imperial masked balls, and the compensation was small. Continued overwork coupled with financial worry brought about Mozart's complete physical collapse, and he died in 1791 in his thirty-fifth year. He was given a third-class funeral and was buried in a potter's field.

Mozart was one of the most gifted composers that the world has ever known. Yet through an unfortunate combination of circumstances his extraordinary creative talent was cut off before it had blossomed into full flower. With few exceptions, the world's greatest musical works have been written by composers who were in their forties or fifties. Bach, Beethoven, and Wagner were creative artists

whose finest compositions were written in their later years. It is interesting to speculate, therefore, on what course of development the
art of music might have taken if Mozart had found a kindly and sympathetic master such as Prince Esterhazy, or if the Austrian Emperor
had offered him a post commensurate with his talents, or if he had
had the tenacity and aggressiveness of a Beethoven or a Wagner.

Some of the happier moments of Mozart's brief life were spent in
the company of Haydn. The two men had met in Vienna in 1781
and a fast friendship combined with a sincere mutual admiration
had resulted. The comments made by both of these great composers
about each other's works are touching indeed. Haydn, on hearing
some of Mozart's quartets performed, turned to the composer's proud
father and said: "I assure you before God, as an honorable man, your
son is the greatest composer that I know personally or by reputation;
he has taste and in addition the greatest knowledge of the technique
of composition." [1]   Mozart, in turn, inscribed this group of six quartets
with a heartfelt dedication to his "caro amico Haydn." [2]

Mozart was a short, slight individual whose head seemed too large
for his body and whose outward appearance would not have led
anyone to suspect his artistic capacities. He was exceptionally proud
of his small, ultra-refined hands. Socially, Mozart might have been
called "a good fellow"; he was fond of conversation, dancing, and
billiards. Despite the critical nature of his times, he seems to have
manifested no interest in politics; nor was he well read. He was
highly impractical, especially as far as his finances were concerned,
and this impracticality combined with his kindly disposition made
him an easy prey for designing friends. A pious Catholic, he had
always longed for a position in a church, and one of his greatest works
is his last composition, a *Requiem Mass*.

Characteristics of Mozart's Music

Unlike Haydn, Mozart was versatile in all types of composition, and
made significant contributions to the world's store of operas, orchestral
music, chamber music, and choral music. He was a composer whose
compositions flowed effortlessly from his pen. It was his custom to

[1] Pohl—*Joseph Haydn* (Leipzig, 1878), Vol. II, page 211.
[2] *Ibid.*, page 212.

work out the details of a composition mentally, and the actual writing, regarded by him as an unpleasant mechanical task, was frequently delayed to the last moment. He was one of the world's greatest masters of melody, yet he did not restrict himself to a homophonic style of writing and on occasion would write with great fluency in a complex polyphonic idiom.

Mozart's harmonic technique was singularly advanced for its time, and in many instances it defintiely anticipated nineteenth-century procedures. The following semitonal progression from the second movement of the Quartet in E-flat major, K. V. 428, is a fine example of the chromaticism to be found in Mozart's works, as well as a striking foreshadowing of a passage in Wagner's *Tristan und Isolde*:

Ex. 1
(a)

(b) Wagner—*Tristan und Isolde.*

The opening of the C major Quartet, K. V. 465, with its strongly dissonant A-natural in the first violin and its chromatic melodic progressions, represents a Mozart so far ahead of his age that some conservative musicians were moved to "correct" it:

Ex. 2

The formal perfection of Mozart's works has become proverbial; they are continually cited as true examples of classic art—works in which form and content are inseparably united and are co-existent. Mozart's compositions give no evidence of fussy overattention to detail; spontaneity is one of their chief characteristics. And the emotional content of Mozart's finer works will elude the casual listener. The unhappy circumstances of his life found but little reflection in his music; and while gaiety and vivacity characterize many of his compositions, it must be emphasized that passionate utterance was not foreign to Mozart's temperament and that he has, on occasion, spoken in tragic accents. Notable examples of this aspect of Mozart's art are the symphony in G minor, K. V. 550, and the quintet in G minor, K. V. 516.

Mozart's records of his productivity were fragmentary—it was not until the day of Beethoven that composers began to make systematic numbering of their works a regular practice. To eliminate confusion, a German scholar, Ludwig von Köchel, compiled a catalogue of Mozart's works in 1862, and they are now known by their numbers in this catalogue. The letters *K. V.* are the abbreviation of its German name, *Köchel Verzeichnis.* Over 600 works by Mozart are listed by Köchel.

Dramatic Music

It was but natural that the melodic attainments of Mozart should find their most congenial outlet in the opera. *Bastien und Bastienne,* his first important dramatic work, was composed in 1768 when he was only twelve years old. This charming little one-act pastoral opera is still an effective and thoroughly captivating stage piece. Mozart wrote twenty-two operas in all, of which the following, all written during the last decade of his life, are outstanding:

Die Entführung aus dem Serail (The Abduction from the Seraglio), 1782
Le Nozze di Figaro (The Marriage of Figaro), 1786
Don Giovanni (Don Juan), 1787
Così fan tutte (So Do They All), 1790
Die Zauberflöte (The Magic Flute), 1791

As the first and last titles on this list indicate, the distinction of having written the first great operas in the German language instead of the conventional Italian belongs to Mozart.

The texts for which Mozart composed music seem decidedly inferior when compared to those set by Gluck. If these operas seem vivid and effective on the stage today and if the characters in them appear genuine and valid, it is only because of Mozart's music. The operas of Mozart show a strong admixture of the Italian tradition, and unlike Gluck, Mozart has not hesitated to introduce so dramatically questionable a procedure as elaborate coloratura. With the exception of *Die Zauberflöte,* the chorus is either entirely absent or plays a very minor role. Mozart's outstanding virtue as a composer of operas was his ability to create convincing personalities by means of musical characterization. This characterization can be attributed to two of Mozart's unique faculties—his ability to write expressive melody, and his skill in treatment of the orchestra.

One of the finest examples of Mozart's skill at characterization is the page Cherubino of *Le Nozze di Figaro.* This adolescent, in the throes of his first love, sings an impassioned aria which tells of his new experiences, so pleasant and yet so distressing. Mozart's setting is an excellent description of Cherubino's agitation:

Ex. 3

(*Prose translation of the text:* I no longer know what I am or what I do; first I am hot as fire, then cold as ice. Every woman makes me blush, every woman makes my heart palpitate. Etc.)

The overtures to *Le Nozze di Figaro* and *Die Zauberflöte* are often played in the concert hall. The overture as written by Mozart and his operatic successors, Beethoven and von Weber, was an orchestral movement in sonata form, the exposition of which was not repeated. Mozart's overtures have a limited degree of musical affiliation with the works they preface.

CLAVIER MUSIC

The majority of Mozart's clavier works cannot be numbered among his great compositions. Most of them are early works, and many were written for students. One of the most popular of the seventeen clavier sonatas is the attractive one in A major, K. V. 331, of whose three movements not one is in sonata form. The first movement is a set of simple variations on this folk-like melody:

Ex. 4

The second movement is a minuet. The third, marked *Rondo alla Turca,* is an attempt to use the clavier to imitate the Turkish effects so common in the orchestral and operatic music of the period.

One of Mozart's greatest clavier works is the solemn Fantasia in C minor, K. V. 475, a late work which in many respects recalls the style of Bach. Its basic mood is established by the opening measures:

Ex. 5

Mozart later published this fantasia as an introduction to his great Sonata in C minor, K. V. 457.

CHAMBER MUSIC

The prolific Mozart composed a large amount of chamber music during his brief lifetime. Of this vast quantity of music the greater part consists of earlier works, many of which were written to order. The significant chamber-music compositions, all products of Mozart's maturity, are: the six quartets dedicated to Haydn (K. V. 387, 421,

428, 458, 464, 465); the three string quartets dedicated to King Friedrich Wilhelm II of Prussia (K. V. 575, 589, 590); and four string quintets (with second viola) (K. V. 515, 516, 593, 614). With the exception of the quartets dedicated to the King of Prussia, none of these works was commissioned and each may be considered the result of a genuinely artistic urge for expression. All were written after Mozart had made the acquaintance of Haydn, and show the influence of the older master. The later works have two striking features, an originality in harmonic method and a subjectivity in mood, which are comparable to the methods and idioms of composers of a much later period. A decided melancholia pervades most of them; and the Quintet in G minor, K. V. 516, in many respects Mozart's most profound composition, is surcharged with an emotional intensity and a spirit of tragic foreboding that place it in the same category as the last quartets of Beethoven. It seems worthy of note that all of the great Viennese masters preferred chamber music for the communication of their most personal utterances and that they all made important contributions to its literature.

The string quartets, together with the later symphonies, exhibit the most prominent characteristic of Mozart's instrumental style—the cantabile nature of his themes. His inexhaustible melodic invention found the limitations of instruments to be no barrier, and in writing for them he had no difficulty in making them sing with a fervor usually associated with the voice. Mozart does not reserve this song-like idiom for slow movements only, but introduces it in fast movements as well. This infusion of a cantabile style into the two fast movements of the string quartet and symphony was highly novel and constituted an important contribution to the development of these forms.

STRING QUARTET IN D MINOR, K. V. 421

The String Quartet in D minor, K. V. 421, the second of the Haydn group, serves as an excellent example of Mozart's accomplishments in the sphere of chamber music. The mood of the entire composition is established in the first few measures by one of Mozart's most moving subjects:

Ex. 6

A note of melancholy pervades the two subjects that comprise the second group:

Ex. 7
(a)

(b)

The development commences with a dramatically sudden modulation and contains some striking dissonances.

The second movement, an *Andante* in three-part form, offers only a change of key and of tempo; the melancholy mood remains. The first theme

Ex. 8

contains a short rhythmic motive (marked *m*) which pervades all but the middle section.

The *Minuet* is a fine study in contrasts: its main section is written in a thoroughly polyphonic style; the *Trio,* on the other hand, consists of a suave melody played by the first violin to a simple rhythmic accompaniment furnished by the rest of the quartet.

The last movement is a set of five variations on a dance-like theme:

Ex. 9

THE SYMPHONIES

Of the forty-nine symphonies which Mozart wrote, only four appear regularly in the repertory of modern symphony orchestras. These are:

The Symphony in D major, K. V. 385
The Symphony in E-flat major, K. V. 543
The Symphony in G minor, K. V. 550
The Symphony in C major, K. V. 551

The three last-named symphonies, written for a projected series of subscription concerts that never took place, were composed in 1788 within the space of six weeks. It should be noticed that all these symphonies antedate the well-known ones of Haydn.

The most important point of departure between the symphonies of Mozart and those of Haydn is to be found in the style of their thematic material. The Haydn themes are lively and fresh; those of Mozart are broad cantabile subjects from which a pathetic note is seldom absent. While Haydn occasionally builds his second group on themes similar in style to those heard in the first group, Mozart invariably secures an effective contrast between the two sections. Like the string quartet, the last symphonies contain many original harmonic progressions, particularly in the development sections. The orchestration of these works is masterly; the wind instruments, in particular, are treated with a thorough understanding of their capabilities. The texture of the symphonies, thanks to Mozart's polyphonic fluency, is always full and rich. The C major Symphony, for example, concludes with a celebrated movement which, although in sonata form, is worked out in a complex fugal manner and with a technical facility that enables the composer to accomplish the feat of combining in the coda all of the five themes he has employed during the course of the movement. This C major Symphony is often called the *Jupiter* Symphony. The origin of the name is not known.

SYMPHONY IN G MINOR, K. V. 550

The Symphony in G minor, K. V. 550, is the quintessence of all that is Mozartian. The cantabile first theme, of singular beauty and grace, and, like many of Mozart's melodies, characterized by a certain wistful quality, is announced by the violins in octaves over a restless rhythmic accompaniment in the violas. (The piano is quite incapable of reproducing the atmosphere of these initial measures.)

Ex. 10

The first three notes of this theme (marked *m*) constitute a motive that finds frequent employment throughout the movement. The second group, in the related key of B-flat major, presents a song-like subject, the chromaticism of which is typical:

Ex. 11

Toward the end of the exposition, motive *m* is again heard as a clarinet and a bassoon toss it back and forth; then the entire orchestra turns to the emphatic

Ex. 12

The exposition concludes with the usual stock cadences. By means of a few abrupt chords the tonal center of the work is shifted from G minor to the remote F-sharp minor. The composer then proceeds to develop the first theme (Example 10), which is thoroughly dismembered, carried through many keys, placed in various registers of the orchestra, and finally, by means of a beautiful chromatic passage in the wood winds based on motive *m,* allowed to merge into the comparative calm of the recapitulation. The coda is very brief.

The second movement, an *Andante,* is in sonata form. It abounds in chromatic progressions and colorful and original passages for the wood-wind instruments, and achieves a high degree of unity through Mozart's persistent use of a tiny motive composed of only two thirty-second notes which makes its first appearance in the seventh measure:

Ex. 13

The robust *Minuet* is another instance of Mozart's polyphonic facility. An unusual feature of this movement is the division of its main section into phrases that are three measures long instead of the conventional four:

Ex. 14

The graceful *Trio,* of charming rusticity, contains a prominent passage for the horns.[3]

The fourth movement, an *Allegro assai,* gets off to a cheerful start with:

Ex. 15

The second group, however, contains more than a hint of the melancholy mood of many of Mozart's last works:

Ex. 16

---

[3] Quoted on page 19.

The development is extremely energetic and replete with harmonic audacities. Mozart concentrates his efforts on the first theme (Example 15) with a tenacity which can be compared only with Beethoven's. The recapitulation is quite regular and the coda rather perfunctory.

THE CONCERTOS

The term *concerto* can be used to describe two types of works written for a solo instrument, or group of instruments, and orchestra. With the earlier form, the *concerto grosso,* whose formal design is based on the alternation of *tutti* and *soli* passages, we are already familiar. It will be recalled that concerti grossi were written predominantly for strings and that the form reached a high point in the works of Bach and Handel. It has been used but seldom since their day.

Mozart and his successors used the term *concerto* for a work that may be described as a symphony for a solo instrument and orchestra.

Form of the Mozart Concerto

The form of the concerto, as brought to a state of perfection by Mozart, differs from the symphony in the following respects:

1. The concerto has three movements instead of four.[4] The first movement is in sonata form. It will be recalled that the exposition of a symphony was usually repeated. In the concerto, instead of this literal repetition of the exposition, there are two expositions. The first of these expositions is usually entrusted to the orchestra alone, which represents the thematic material of the movement in a somewhat abridged manner and without any substantial degree of modulation. The second exposition, on the other hand, is written for both the solo instrument and the orchestra and follows the usual procedure in regard to arrangement of thematic material and distribution of keys. The second movement is slow, usually in three-part, variation, rondo, or sonata form; and the last is a lively movement in either sonata or rondo form. The double exposition, however, is confined to the first movement.

2. The cardinal principle of the concerto, contrast between dissimilar media, remains.[5] In the solo concerto of Mozart's day, that

---

[4] The Brahms Piano Concerto in B-flat major (1881) is in four movements.
[5] See page 102.

contrast is furnished by placing a single instrument in competition with a symphony orchestra. Alternation of *solo* and *tutti* passages still prevails. In short, the basic idiom of the concerto remains the same but now appears in a modification of sonata form, the thematic material of which is shared by the soloist and orchestra.

3. The solo part calls for a virtuoso performer: one of the incidental purposes of the concerto is to serve as a vehicle for the display of virtuosity.

4. A *cadenza* occurs in the first movement and often in the second and third as well. The cadenza is a brilliant unaccompanied passage for the soloist. Up to the time of Beethoven, the performer was expected to improvise the cadenza; Mozart in all his concertos merely indicated a pause for the orchestra at the point at which the cadenza was to be played. Nowadays cadenzas are no longer improvised; when presenting classical concertos, the performer plays one of his own choice which he has memorized beforehand. Cadenzas, written by Mozart for pupils or friends, are available for some of his concertos.

The peculiar nature of the concerto finds its explanation in the musical customs of the period in which it came to flower. The public concert was just starting to become a regular institution during Mozart's lifetime. He was in fact the first individual to play a piano concerto in public in Vienna (April 3, 1781).

Three things were demanded of the soloist at that time. He was naturally expected to be a finished performer. But the public also insisted that he be a composer as well, and when instrumentalists appeared in public they almost invariably played concertos of their own composition with an orchestra. The third faculty demanded was skill at improvisation. The performer was expected not only to extemporise the cadenzas for his concerto but also to regale his listeners with an elaborate series of improvisations on themes from some of his other works, or occasionally from those of other composers. The performance of concertos was the only way in which an instrumentalist might attract an audience to a public concert. (It was not until the day of Liszt that the solo recital came into vogue.) In his attempt to keep body and soul together, Mozart gave concerts in Vienna at which he appeared as soloist, playing a concerto freshly composed for each occasion. Between 1782 and 1786 he produced no less than fifteen concertos for the piano, an instrument that was then beginning to find widespread acceptance. His total production in this sphere included twenty-seven piano concertos and six violin concertos. The latter were composed in 1775-1776 while he was at Salzburg.

Several of the piano concertos composed for the Vienna concerts rank with Mozart's finest works. He himself was rather proud of them; and the audiences that heard them as they first came into the world under the fingers of their creator appreciated them thoroughly. These audiences were drawn exclusively from the ranks of the musically cultured upper classes, a social group whose taste finds a reflection in the compositions themselves. In a letter to his father, Mozart wrote: "The concertos are neither too easy nor too difficult; they are very brilliant and pleasant to the ear, without, however, lapsing into the superficial." [6] The piano concertos owe their effectiveness to Mozart's exquisite sense of form and to his skill in writing for both piano and orchestra. He has maintained in them a balance of importance between the solo instrument and the orchestra, which, while meeting the legitimate demands of the virtuoso performer, does not relegate the orchestra to the menial task of acting merely as accompaniment. Other notable features are the skilful manner in which the entrances of the solo instrument are brought about and the originality in utilizing the wood-wind instruments of the orchestra. The concertos, like the symphonies and the string quartets, contain a profusion of beautiful melodies.

PIANO CONCERTO IN D MINOR, K. V. 466

One of the finest of Mozart's creations in this form is the Piano Concerto in D minor, K. V. 466, composed in 1785. This work was a favorite of Beethoven, who played it in 1795 at a concert given for the benefit of Mozart's widow, and also wrote cadenzas for it. The first movement, an *Allegro,* commences with an orchestral exposition which, as was customary, is a purposely incomplete statement of the thematic material. The restless opening with its ominous bass figures casts a shadow over the entire movement:

[6] Jahn-Abert—*W. A. Mozart* (Leipzig, 1923), Vol. II, page 202.

Ex. 17

After the presentation of several expressive cantabile subjects, the first exposition is brought to an end by the entrance of the solo instrument, which introduces a new theme:

Ex. 18

Other themes make their first appearance in the course of the second exposition. The development commences with an orchestral tutti which after a *forte* statement of the theme quoted in Example 17 subsides to the level of a *piano* and ushers in the soloist. The development confines itself almost exclusively to the two themes quoted above. The manner in which they have been treated is significant: the first (Example 17) is given to the orchestra with rapid passages in the piano as embellishment; the second (Example 18) remains the exclusive property of the solo instrument and appears in three unaccompanied episodes of an improvisational character. The return to the recapitulation is brought about by a short and typically chromatic passage. Mozart has indicated that a cadenza be played just before the coda. The movement comes to a dramatic conclusion with a piano statement of the bass figures heard in the opening (Example 17). A strong resemblance may be observed between the mood of this first movement and that of another great Mozart work in D minor, the String Quartet, K. V. 421.

The second movement, in B-flat major and bearing the title *Romanza,* provides in its delightful artlessness an effective contrast to its more serious predecessor. The designation that Mozart has employed here is used by him and by later composers for instrumental pieces song-like in style and tenderly sentimental in character. The term indicates, therefore, more a style of writing than a specific form. In this instance the Romanza is cast in rondo form with one of Mozart's most attractive melodies serving as its *refrain:* [7]

Ex. 19

The prevailing calm of the movement is interrupted by a long and tempestuous episode in G minor.

Mozart calls the third movement a *Rondo;* but in this instance his use of the term, as is often the case, is more the result of its habitual use as a label for a last movement than an indication of a formal plan. In the strict sense this movement is not a rondo at all [8] but a brisk movement in sonata form, without optional repetition of the exposition and without a development section. To compensate for the lack of formal development, the thematic material is subjected to some elaboration in the recapitulation; and there is a coda whose length (sixty-three measures) and treatment of the subject matter are unusual for Mozart. The movement, which returns to D minor, commences with this epigrammatic theme given out by the solo instrument:

Ex. 20

The first group includes another subject, in a contrasting style though in the same key. It, too, is announced by the solo piano:

[7] See page 84.
[8] For the typical rondo of this period see page 148.

Ex. 21

But the most attractive feature of the entire movement is the appearance in the second group of a typically Mozartian melody which would be difficult indeed to surpass in gaiety and sparkle. Its first presentation is entrusted to the wood winds:

Ex. 22

The composer himself was apparently fascinated by this tune, for he has permitted it to play an important part in the coda, which forsakes D minor for the brighter realms of D major. No finer example of Mozart's ready wit can be found than this final treatment of the theme with its unexpected pirouette in the third and fourth measures, followed by a short fanfare in the trumpets and horns:

Ex. 23

The entire episode is a splendid instance of Mozart's skilful use of the orchestra.

SACRED MUSIC

The list of sixty-eight sacred works to be found in the Köchel catalogue includes twenty masses, portions of which are occasionally employed in church services today. Of the many shorter pieces of church music the *Ave verum corpus,* K. V. 618, is the best known. Mozart's crowning achievement in this sphere is his *Requiem Mass,* K. V. 626, in the composition of which he was engaged when he died.

Mozart undertook to make a setting of the *Missa pro defunctis,* the Mass for the Dead, as the result of a commission placed with him by a mysterious stranger who demanded that the composer complete the work by a certain date and under no circumstances attempt to ascertain the name of the individual who had ordered it. Mozart was in failing health at the time, and during the composition of the work was obsessed with the idea that he really was composing his own Requiem. He died before the work was finished and his widow, fearful lest the anonymous individual who had commissioned the score might take advantage of the situation, besought Mozart's pupil, Süssmayer, to complete it. Süssmayer had not only been in close contact with his master, but had a handwriting so similar to his as to confuse even experts. Süssmayer filled in the gaps, completed the instrumentation, and added three movements.

The identity of the individual who had ordered the Requiem was revealed after Mozart's death. He proved to be a Count von Walsegg, an amateur whose habit it was to purchase compositions, bind the composer to secrecy, and then palm them off as his own creations. In this instance, the Count had wished to have a Requiem Mass for performance in memory of his deceased wife.

The music of the *Requiem Mass* represents Mozart at the height of his powers. It emphasizes more than any other of his compositions the loss that the art of music sustained through his premature death. Throughout the work there is evidence of his study of the compositions of Bach and Handel. One of the subjects of the great double-fugue, *Kyrie eleison—Christe eleison,* seems to have been directly inspired by "And with His Stripes we are healed" from *Messiah.*[9]

Ex. 24

[9] Quoted on page 125.

Suggested Readings

The standard work on Mozart, the two-volume *W. A. Mozart,* by Hermann Abert (Leipzig, 1923), remains untranslated into English. An important five-volume work in French, Wyzewa and de Saint-Foix, *W. A. Mozart, sa vie et son œuvre* (Paris, 1936-46), is now being translated. Excellent one volume treatises on Mozart and his works are Einstein, *Mozart, His Character and Work* (New York, 1945), and Blom, *Mozart* (New York, 1944). The richly informative letters are available in Anderson, *Letters of Mozart and His Family* (London, 1938). Detailed information about the operas may be found in Dent, *Mozart's Operas* (London, 1947), and about the piano concertos in Girdlestone, *Mozart's Piano Concertos* (London, 1948), and Hutchings, *A Companion to Mozart's Piano Concertos* (London, 1948). The best discussion of the symphonies is de Saint-Foix, *The Symphonies of Mozart* (New York, 1949). The chamber music is discussed by H. Abert in *Cobbett's Cyclopedic Survey of Chamber Music* (London, 1929). The great index of Mozart's works, the celebrated *Verzeichnis* of Köchel appeared in a new edition prepared by Alfred Einstein (Leipzig, 1937); although it has since been reprinted in America it remains untranslated.

Chapter XIV

THE VIENNESE SCHOOL:
LUDWIG VAN BEETHOVEN

LUDWIG van Beethoven's compositions mark one of the most decided turning points in the evolution of the art of music. Appearing in Vienna at the close of the eighteenth century, Beethoven was not in any nobleman's service, and composed, for the most part, only such music as he was compelled to create through the force of his own unique personality. The infusion of his own ego into the traditional forms of his time paved the way for most of the music of the nineteenth century. It was Beethoven who sired the romantic movement in music.

Ludwig van Beethoven was, as the prefix *van* indicates, of Flemish ancestry. He was born on December 16, 1770, in the Rhine town of Bonn, the son of Johann van Beethoven, a tenor in the chapel choir of the Elector of Bonn. His musical gifts made themselves manifest during his early boyhood, and the father, seeing in the lad a second Mozart and hoping to reap financial gain thereby, cruelly forced him to practice an inordinate length of time, much to the neglect of his general education. His musical training was for a time under the supervision of his ne'er-do-well father and later under Tobias Pfeifer, a wandering actor-musician who boarded with the family. These youthful influences were of great significance in the formation of Beethoven's character. Maltreated and abused, with no one in whom he might confide or trust, it is small wonder that he felt himself isolated and excluded from the world. Deprived of the rudiments of a general education, suffering because of the social inferiority of his family and the degradation brought upon it by his drunkard father, Beethoven developed a character and personality for which artistic expression served as the sole means of relief. The few benevolent forces that operated upon Beethoven during his youth in Bonn were the chapel organist, Neefe, who gave him conscientious and sympathetic instruction, and the cultured von Breuning family, at whose home he was a frequent visitor. Eventually he became Neefe's assistant. In 1787 Beethoven journeyed to Vienna. He played before Mozart, who is said to have been impressed by his ability to extemporize, but the illness of his mother brought the youth back to Bonn before anything materialized from this artistic contact.

Two events, both of great importance in Beethoven's artistic development, occurred after his return to Bonn. The first was the beginning of his acquaintanceship with the young Count Ferdinand von Waldstein, the first of the many cultured, art-loving members of the nobility who through their interest and magnanimity aided in the unfolding of Beethoven's talents. The second was the formation in 1788 of an opera company at the Electoral Court. Beethoven became a member of the opera orchestra, playing the viola. The significance of this activity on his part cannot be overestimated. As a youth in his late 'teens, he was enabled to become intimately acquainted with the mechanism of the orchestra and, through participation in performance, to learn the important works of the time, notably the operas of Mozart. In July 1792 Haydn, returning from the first series of his London concerts, stopped at Bonn. Beethoven was introduced to him and showed him some of his compositions. It has often been surmised that Haydn invited him to be his pupil, although direct evidence is lacking. In November of the same year Beethoven again set out for Vienna, to remain there for the rest of his life.

After his arrival in the Austrian capital Beethoven immediately busied himself with study. His teachers were Haydn, with whom his relations were neither happy nor fruitful; Albrechtsberger, who gave him over two years of instruction in counterpoint; and Salieri, under whom he studied dramatic composition. Mozart had been dead for a year and the stage was now set for the appearance of a pianist of Beethoven's abilities. It was not long before his phenomenal pianistic talents were known to most of the nobility of Vienna. His services were much in demand and so rapidly did his fame increase that he appeared as soloist at several benefit concerts. During these early years

LUDWIG VAN BEETHOVEN

he also came in contact with other princely patrons and counselors—Prince Karl Lichnowsky, Baron van Swieten, and Prince Lobkowitz.

For some time Beethoven's proficiency as a pianist obscured public recognition of him as a creative artist. One of his first public successes as a composer was won by his Septet in E-flat major, Opus 20 (for violin, viola, cello, double bass, clarinet, bassoon, and horn), which with its piquant instrumentation and attractive melodies immediately became popular. On the same program on which the Septet was first performed publicly (there had been prior private performances at the Schwarzenberg Palace), the First Symphony also had its premiere (April 2, 1800). This work was not well received and, like some of the works that followed, was at first deemed eccentric and perverse by the Viennese. These initial condemnations, however, were almost invariably short-lived and were quickly supplanted by general approbation and enthusiasm.

The period 1799-1814 is an astounding record of artistic creativeness. During this comparatively short time Beethoven composed eight symphonies, three concertos for piano, a concerto for violin, seven sonatas for piano, eleven string quartets, much other chamber music, the opera *Leonore* (title later changed to *Fidelio*), and the music for Goethe's *Egmont,* as well as many shorter works. The Viennese public quickly came to appreciate the unique genius living in their midst; and at one time (1808-1809), when it seemed as if he might be lost to the city because of an offer of the post of Kapellmeister at the court of Jerome Bonaparte at Cassel, the Archduke Rudolph and the Princes Lobkowitz and Kinsky came forward and guaranteed him an annual income if he would remain. Unfortunately, the intrinsic value of this financial settlement was much reduced afterwards by monetary inflation. Nevertheless this magnanimous act is a clear indication of Beethoven's importance in the musical life of Vienna as well as of the artistic discernment of his patrons.

Beethoven's success, however, was marred by the greatest misfortune that could possibly befall a musician—deafness. The disease had made itself manifest as early as 1799, and in a most moving document, a letter to his brothers written in 1802,[1] Beethoven pathetically described

---

[1] This letter, known as the *Heiligenstadt Will,* may be found in Thayer's *Life of Beethoven,* Vol. 1, page 352.

his own despair at the life of isolation that lay before him. By 1814 the deafness had become so complete that he was prevented from making any further appearances as a soloist. At the first performance of the great Ninth Symphony in 1824, the composer, who sat on the stage, had to be turned around so that he might see the tumultuous applause that the second movement had brought forth.

Yet another cause for unhappiness was the composer's disappointment in love. Several ladies of the upper classes were the objects of his affection, but his uncouthness and personal unattractiveness coupled with the rigid class distinctions of the period caused his aspirations to end in bitter frustration.

A nephew, the son of his brother Kaspar, became his ward in 1815. Beethoven, seeking some outlet for the abundant store of affection pent up within him, lavished all manner of care and attention upon the unworthy youth. Much to his uncle's dismay he turned out to be a weak individual, unsuccessful even in an attempt to commit suicide.

Because of his deafness, Beethoven became quite detached from the active musical life of Vienna; but so great had his fame become that individuals came from far and wide to see him. Inasmuch as the composer could not hear, remarks had to be addressed to him in writing. Fortunately, these "conversation books" have been preserved. A commission to compose music even came from so distant a point as Boston, Massachusetts. The English piano manufacturer Broadwood presented Beethoven with one of his new grand pianos; another English admirer sent him a forty-volume set of the works of Handel.

All this attention, however, must be regarded as superficial. The last decade of Beethoven's life was spent in complete spiritual isolation. But this isolation bore magnificent artistic fruit—the *Missa Solemnis,* the Ninth Symphony, and the last string quartets—works that in their intense subjectivity, vastness of dimensions, and freedom from convention, present serious problems to the listener.

In December 1826 signs of dropsy made themselves manifest, and after much suffering Beethoven died on March 26, 1827. Twenty thousand persons gathered for his funeral.

In appearance Beethoven was a short, stocky individual with a swarthy face, ugly but expressive. The facial features that betrayed the artist underneath were the strong brow and the penetrating eyes. In dress

Beethoven often attempted to affect the grand manner, but carelessness in his attire, coupled with fantastic gestures, often caused onlookers to regard him as a curiosity.

One of the most important aspects of his personality was his intense and occasionally almost exaggerated love of freedom, which was combined with an exalted estimate of his own personal position. On more than one occasion he acted towards members of the nobility in a fashion which can only be described as boorish. An inordinate pride made him particularly sensitive to anything that might be construed as condescending or patronizing. His irascible nature, combined with a strong temper, kept him from forming any fast friendships. Many individuals clustered about him, yet none of them affected him vitally in any way. His love of nature was exceptionally strong and he spent much time in the country about Vienna. In a letter, Beethoven wrote: "No man can love the country as much as I do. Woods, trees and rocks supply the echo which man desires." [2] This appreciation of nature found musical expression in the *Pastoral* Symphony.

Almost all that we know about Beethoven's inner personality derives from his musical utterances. The deficiencies of his general education prevented his having any literary skill, and his letters are, as a whole, disappointing sources of information. He was a great admirer of the works of Goethe and Schiller, and no better proof can be given of his innate sensitivity to great literature than the music that he wrote for the former's tragedy, *Egmont*. But judged by the conventions of his time, Beethoven was not a cultured individual.

His compositions were the result of tremendous inner conflict and of great powers of concentration. It was the composer's custom to work out the subject matter and general plan for his works carefully over a long period of time before proceeding to their actual composition. The *Sketch Books,* in which Beethoven labored at the themes from which so many gigantic works were to grow, have been preserved. They serve not only as records of the various stages in the evolution of the great Beethoven melodies, but also as evidence of the searching self-criticism to which all of his compositions were subjected.

The key to the artistic and historical significance of Beethoven is to be found in his own personality. It was this personality that drove

[2] A. C. Kalischer, *Beethovens Sämtliche Briefe,* Vol. I, page 204.

him to speak as he did and, in so doing, to change the course of musical art. It is, however, fallacious to believe that his music is "personal" in the narrower sense. It is rather one man's expression of great universal concepts. One of the foremost of Beethoven's disciples and interpreters was Richard Wagner; and it was Wagner who has given us the tersest and, at the same time, most exact commentary on a work of Beethoven. After conducting the Third Symphony (the *Eroica*) in Switzerland, Wagner autographed a souvenir program. Writing out the opening theme of the symphony, Wagner added these words: *"So dachte B. über heroische Dinge!"* ("This was Beethoven's concept of the heroic!")

Most of Beethoven's works lack descriptive titles, but in many of them the listener is aware of a programmatic content. Beethoven himself has left us but few clues to the meanings of his works, yet by their very nature they have inspired a great mass of descriptive and interpretive commentary. Occasionally these commentaries, particularly those of Richard Wagner or of Romain Rolland, are provocative; but they serve more as revelations of the inner workings of the minds of their authors than of Beethoven.

It is difficult to speak of a specific Beethoven style, for one of the most prominent characteristics of his music is the unique quality of each work. While the external forms may frequently be similar, no two movements can be said to be alike.

Classification of Beethoven's Works

It is customary to divide the creative accomplishments of Beethoven into three groups and to assign a definite style to each. A knowledge of the style of each of these "periods" may prove helpful, provided that the lines of chronological demarcation are not drawn too rigidly. The "periods" should be considered merely as convenient groupings and not as successive metamorphoses of Beethoven as a composer. His development as a creative artist was continuous and the stamp of his genius is found on almost every work, no matter of what period. Unless they be done with caution and understanding, classifications of art works are destructive of their purpose—a better comprehension of the artist and his creations.

The first period, the "period of imitation," may be said to end with the Second Symphony (1802). This period may be described, with many reservations, as one in which Beethoven was under the influence of his great predecessors, Haydn and Mozart. The break with the traditions of the past commenced in 1803 with the Third Symphony. The second stage, or "period of realization," ends with the Piano Sonata in E minor, Opus 90 (1814). The last period, the "period of abstraction," commences chronologically with the Piano Sonata, Opus 101, in A major (1816); but its most typical works are the last string quartets (Opus 127, 130, 131, 132, 135), the Ninth Symphony, and the *Missa Solemnis*. In the last stage we find Beethoven deviating from traditional forms to an extreme degree. Everything is rendered subordinate to content. J. W. N. Sullivan has aptly remarked that "language . . . is poor in names for subjective states, and this poverty becomes particularly apparent when we try to describe such works of art as the late quartets." [3]

Beethoven and the Sonata Form

The majority of the works of Beethoven that are heard today are works of the second period, whose style may therefore be discussed in some detail.

Beethoven cast most of his musical expression in two forms—the sonata and the variation—and both were considerably altered by him in his search for adequate media of communication. Movements of sonatas, string quartets, symphonies, and so forth, were materially lengthened, development sections were considerably expanded and occasionally even contained new themes. The coda also took on added significance, frequently becoming so long and involved as to partake of the nature of a second development.

There is no better illustration of this expansion of the dimensions of the sonata form than the Third Symphony, written in 1804. Its performance lasts about fifty minutes as compared to the some twenty minutes required for the *Surprise* Symphony of Haydn, written in 1792.[4] But hand in hand with this expansion of dimensions goes a concentration on subject matter, so that developments become even more concise and direct. Entire movements may be based upon only

[3] J. W. N. Sullivan, *Beethoven, His Spiritual Development* (New York, 1927), page 226.
[4] Beethoven himself stated that this symphony was written "at greater length than usual."

one musical idea: for example, the first movement of the Fifth Symphony, dominated throughout by [musical notation]. The recapitulation often appears not as a mere repetition of the exposition, but rather as the culmination of the development. Beethoven also finds the old conventions of key relationship restrictive, and frequently indulges in considerable freedom in choice of tonalities for the internal divisions of movements as well as for the various movements of a given work.

One of Beethoven's great achievements was his development of the *scherzo* out of the old shell of the minuet. While preserving the outward form and rhythm of the older dance form, he greatly accelerated its pace, and made it into a vigorous and forceful, sometimes almost explosive, movement. The Beethoven scherzos are characterized by their overwhelming and inexhaustible energy, their sudden contrasts, their unexpected outbursts. In them are to be found some of the most striking examples of the composer's sense of humor. The term *scherzo* had been employed before Beethoven as a designation for a humorous piece (*scherzo,* Italian for "joke"); but the humor displayed by Beethoven in these movements is of far larger proportions.

The scherzo as employed by Beethoven is more a manner of expression than a form. The *Scherzo* of the Ninth Symphony, for example, is written in sonata form, while the *Scherzo* of the String Quartet in C-sharp minor, Opus 131 is written in duple rhythm. Beethoven himself was apparently conscious of this differentiation between an idiom and a conventional form. Many Beethoven movements which are universally referred to today as scherzos possess no titles other than the usual designations of speed.

One of the most important of Beethoven's innovations was his attempt to fuse the various movements of his larger works into one complete whole. The most striking instance is the String Quartet in C-Sharp Minor, Opus 131. Here seven movements are joined one to the other in an obligatory sequence. The third movement of the Fifth Symphony leads into the fourth and is later recalled. The last movement of the Ninth Symphony reviews themes from the preceding three.

The idiom of Beethoven is essentially homophonic.[5] Contrapuntal

[5] In the *Sketch Books* none of the themes is accompanied.

sections appear frequently and with a certain degree of effectiveness, particularly in the symphonies; but the part-writing is often labored and the listener easily perceives that as a writer of instrumental polyphony Beethoven must yield place to Bach and Mozart.

Use of the Variation Form

In his treatment of the variation form Beethoven again broke away from the conventions of the past. He was not content merely to utilize the obvious features of the theme as did his immediate predecessors; he minutely explored its every possibility and employed a rhythmic figure, a harmonic progression, a motive, or some other aspect as an idea on which to construct a variation. There are many magnificent sets of variations by Beethoven, his greatest work in this form being the Opus 120, a series of thirty-three variations on a theme of Diabelli for piano. More familiar variations are the thirty-two in C minor for piano (without opus number), the last movement of the Third Symphony, the second movement of the Fifth Symphony, and the last movement of the Ninth Symphony.

Beethoven's Humor

Within the works of Beethoven is to be found an infinite variety of moods, situations and conflicts, ranging from profound sorrow to the most rapturous exaltation, and often introducing an element of humor. Many of his compositions abound in boisterous outbursts akin to gigantic laughs. Beethoven himself described the mood that characterizes such movements as the finales of the Seventh Symphony and the Eighth Symphony as *aufgeknöpft* (unbridled).

Directions for Performance

Beethoven was one of the first composers to insert in his works meticulous and specific indications concerning dynamics, shading, and interpretation. He employed German as well as the conventional Italian terms and at no time hesitated to utilize any phrase which he deemed necessary for expressive performance. The second movement of the Quartet in E minor, Opus 59, No. 2, for example, is headed *Si tratta questo pezzo con molto di sentimento* (This piece is to be played with much feeling); and one of the variations in the Quartet in C-sharp minor, Opus 131, is marked *Lusinghiero* (in a coaxing manner). The *Missa Solemnis* bears the inscription *Vom Herzen, möge sie zu Herzen gehen* (From the heart, may it go to the heart).

Typical works from each category will now be examined, though it should be continually borne in mind that while each work is typical of Beethoven, it differs markedly from any of its fellows and can therefore be regarded as representative only in a limited sense.

Piano Music

Beethoven's works for piano solo include thirty-two sonatas, several sets of variations, and about one hundred shorter pieces, many in dance forms. All of these compositions must be regarded as chamber music, since they were designed for the intimate atmosphere of the salon and not for the concert hall. Whenever Beethoven appeared in public as a pianist he followed the custom of playing a concerto of his own composition with orchestra. Inasmuch as the piano was Beethoven's own instrument, it is but natural to conclude that his more intimate thoughts were confided to it. As a performer, Beethoven occupied a unique position in Vienna. His style differed markedly from the refined *galant* manner which the Viennese had so admired in the playing of Mozart. He strove continually to extract new and more powerful sonorities from the instrument; and his impetuous and fiery style of playing was often considered crude by contemporaries. But in improvisation he was universally regarded as a master. At no time did he allow the limitations of the instrument to hamper or confine him. Beethoven himself was a great virtuoso; but none of his piano music, difficult as some of it may be, was written to serve merely as a vehicle for feats of virtuosity.

SONATA IN F MINOR, OPUS 57

One of the best-known sonatas is the one in F minor, Opus 57, universally known as the *Appassionata*. This name, although far from misleading, was not given to the composition by Beethoven, but by the publisher Cranz. The work, completed in 1806, is in three movements, and is an excellent example of Beethoven's integration of several movements into a unified whole. The composer is said to have called it his greatest sonata.[6]

First movement—*Allegro assai; Più allegro* (F minor)

Preceded by no introduction, the first group commences with a portentous motive whose first two measures outline the chord of F minor:

Ex. 1

A short, repeated-note figure makes its appearance in the tenth measure:

Ex. 2

"Knocking" motives of this type are to be found in many of Beethoven's works—the Fifth Symphony, the Concerto for Violin, the Concerto for Piano in G major, the String Quartet in E-flat, Opus 74.

The second group commences in A-flat major with a short theme bearing a marked rhythmic resemblance to Example 1:

Ex. 3

(Continued on following page)

[6] According to his pupil, Carl Czerny. F. Kerst, *Die Erinnerungen an Beethoven* (Stuttgart, 1913), Vol. I, p. 55.

Ex. 3 (*continued*)

This gives way to yet another theme, a tempestuous motive beginning in A-flat minor:

Ex. 4

It will be observed that the fourth measure of this theme also contains a repeated-note figure. The development consists almost entirely of an intense working out of Example 1 and Example 3 and concludes with dramatic pronouncements of the "knocking" motive, Example 2. The recapitulation contains two notable features: (1) the return of Example 1 over a throbbing pedal leading up to (2), an emphatic statement of the same theme in F major with sudden alternations of *piano* and *fortissimo*. The "knocking" motive figures prominently in the transition section which leads to the lengthy coda. This concluding section is in reality a second development. The movement terminates with a last statement of Example 1 which finally disappears in a *pianissimo* chord of F minor.

Second Movement—*Andante con moto* (D-flat major)

This movement, comparatively short, serves as a breathing spell between the forceful outer movements. It consists of four essentially simple variations on this prayerful theme:

Ex. 5

A deceptive cadence at the close does not permit the movement to end but connects it directly to the last movement.

Third Movement—*Allegro ma non troppo; Presto* (F minor)

The quiet of the second movement is cut short by a trumpet-like figure:

Ex. 6

This is followed by a preparatory passage that eventually becomes the first theme of the first group:

Ex. 7

The second group, in C minor, commences with:

Ex. 8

The development, in addition to disclosing the potentialities of Example 7, introduces the entirely new theme shown in Example 9.

Ex. 9

Following the recapitulation, the coda introduces another new theme, a rapid march-like strain:

Ex. 10

which, however, finally yields precedence to the theme quoted in Example 7, with which the entire sonata is brought to an emphatic conclusion on reiterated chords of F minor.

THE SYMPHONIES

The nine symphonies of Beethoven are his best-known works. They form a considerable part of the orchestral repertory and are played with great frequency, yet without any diminution in their significance. Beethoven took the symphony at the point of development to which it had been brought by Haydn and Mozart, and made of it an art form in which he has never been surpassed.

Beethoven's innovations include not only the general alterations in form and style mentioned previously, but also a new and revolutionary concept of the orchestra, an instrumental medium with which he had become well acquainted during his period of service in the opera orchestra at Bonn. Utilizing for the most part the same orchestral equipment as did Haydn and Mozart, Beethoven employed the various instruments in a manner that was considered so unconventional and audacious at the time as to bring condemnation on his head. None of these new departures should be considered merely as innovations in instrumentation, for the musical thoughts which Beethoven wished to convey brought forth these instrumental settings as their natural means of expression. Among the more conspicuous new usages of the orchestra may be mentioned the novel employment of the hitherto fettered double bass, as in the Trio of the Scherzo of the Fifth Symphony and in the celebrated series of recitatives that open the fourth movement of the Ninth Symphony; the expressive writing for the horns in the Trio of the Scherzo of the *Eroica* Symphony; the elevation of the kettledrums to the point where they are actually entrusted with thematic material, as in the Eighth and Ninth Symphonies; and, in the Ninth Symphony, the introduction of the human voice.[7]

Three of the symphonies have programmatic connotations. The Third was originally dedicated to Napoleon; but when he elevated himself to the rank of Emperor in May, 1804, Beethoven angrily changed the title of his work to "Heroic Symphony, composed to celebrate the memory of a great man." Many individuals have attempted to elucidate in prose the contents of this great work, with results that have been none too happy.

The Sixth Symphony, the *Pastoral,* has a plentiful store of descriptive titles: "Awakening of Joyful Feelings on Arriving in the Country," "Scene by the Brook," "Joyful Gathering of the Country Folk," "Storm," "Shepherd's Song," "Glad and Grateful Feelings after the Storm." But lest the listener regard the work as mere musical photography, Beethoven places this caption on it: *Mehr Ausdruck der Empfindung als Malerei* (More an expression of feeling than tone-painting). The programmatic nature of the work greatly influenced subsequent composers such as Mendelssohn, Liszt, and Wagner, and for some time Beethoven was erroneously regarded as the father of modern program music.

The Ninth Symphony is dominated by a program that finds concrete expression in the last movement in which Schiller's ode, *An die Freude* (To Joy) is set for vocal quartet and chorus. One of the most significant features of this work is the manner in which themes from the first three movements are furtively recalled at the opening of the fourth movement and peremptorily dismissed by dramatic recitatives in the cellos and basses.

---

[7] Beethoven had used the chorus with orchestra and solo piano in his earlier Choral Fantasia, Opus 80. This work is now rarely heard.

The six remaining symphonies are devoid of specific programmatic connotations. That they do possess some definite programmatic content would appear undeniable, but the nature of this content must remain the subjective interpretation of the listener.

SYMPHONY NO. 5, IN C MINOR

The most famous Beethoven Symphony is the Fifth, in C minor, completed in 1807. It is doubtful if any other orchestral composition has been performed more often than this great work, whose message is such as to bear endless repetition.

First Movement—*Allegro con brio* (C minor)

The most striking feature of this movement is its relentless concentration on one motive, a terse repeated-note figure which is announced at the very beginning in an attention-arresting *fortissimo*:

Ex. 11

One need only compare the forceful opening of this symphony with that of the *Surprise* Symphony of Haydn [8] to realize how Beethoven was molding the symphony to suit his own needs of expression. His first biographer, Schindler, claims that the composer made this statement about the opening: "Thus Fate knocks on the door." But the veracity of Schindler is open to question. Repetitions of this motive culminate in two emphatic chords that bring about a modulation into E-flat major and pave the way for the entrance of the second group. This commences with an emphatic passage in the horns followed by a cantabile subject in the violins, which Beethoven has meticulously marked *dolce*:

Ex. 12

[8] See page 143.

It will be noticed that the repeated-note motive is heard in the horns and continues to hover in the cellos and basses (measures 7 and 8). The entire exposition is so brief and so terse that conductors usually exercise their option of repeating it.

The development contains an episode that illustrates one of Beethoven's characteristic procedures—the breaking up of a theme almost to the point of its complete demolition. Commencing with the first three measures of the second group (Ex. 12), into the last of which the trumpets insert an emphatically dissonant C,

Ex. 13

the composer proceeds to hack away until only these chords, given out in a hushed dialogue between strings and wood winds, remain:

Ex. 14

The development, as is usually the case in Beethoven's mature works, culminates in the recapitulation, the course of which is halted by the celebrated passage for solo oboe.[9] The coda not only proceeds to cast new light upon what has already been presented, but also contributes a new theme:

Ex. 15

Second Movement—*Andante con moto* (A-flat major)

This movement is a series of variations with many interpolated episodic passages. Beethoven has followed a procedure to which Haydn was partial—the use of two themes instead of one. The first

[9] Quoted on page 12.

theme, one of Beethoven's most beautiful melodies, is given out by the violas and cellos:

Ex. 16

The second theme makes a tentative first appearance in the clarinets and bassoons; but a modulation takes place en route, and it is transformed into a majestic tune solemnly intoned by the trumpets and horns:

Ex. 17

Beethoven's treatment of the variation form, as evidenced by this movement, again invites comparison with the methods of Haydn. The Beethoven variations lack a formal note; the composer has given his imagination free rein both in treatment of subject matter and coloristic use of the orchestra. Some of the passages in this movement which seem admirable to modern ears were once deemed to be errors on Beethoven's part. This is another movement upon which certain nineteenth-century pedants were tempted to lay a "correcting" hand.

Third Movement—*Allegro* (C minor)

This movement is a typical Beethoven scherzo, though not designated as such by the composer. In contrast to the two preceding movements, it commences in a subdued, almost mysterious manner, with this theme assigned to the cellos and basses playing at the level of a *pianissimo*:

Ex. 18

The mysterious atmosphere of these opening measures is suddenly dispelled by the horns, which blare out a repeated-note motive that can claim relationship to the one heard in the first movement:

Ex. 19

The *Trio,* written in a fugal style, is a fine example of that brand of musical humor that we associate with Beethoven. Cellos and basses perform lumbering acrobatics on:

Ex. 20

The return of the Scherzo is not the familiar *Da Capo,* but an entirely new treatment carefully marked by the composer *sempre pianissimo.* An air of expectancy is thus created and it develops that Beethoven has purposely avoided a literal repetition so that he may lead the Scherzo by means of a dramatic transition directly into the last movement. This union of two movements is another example of Beethoven's struggle to unify the hitherto independent movements of the symphony. A long period of suspense punctuated by a persistent repeated-note motive in the kettledrums culminates in the

Fourth Movement—*Allegro* (C major)

This movement is in sonata form and commences with a broad, triumphant phrase given out by the entire orchestra, to which trombones have been added for the first time in symphonic music:

Ex. 21

Example 22 cites another theme of the first group, one which will become prominent in the coda.

Ex. 22

The second group consists of two important themes, the first of which is:

Ex. 23

The short figure in half-notes, so unobtrusively presented by the cellos in the third measure of this example, assumes a very important rôle in the development, becoming, in fact, its most prominent feature. The other theme of the second group also employs repeated notes:

Ex. 24

The development carries the cello theme quoted in Example 23 through many keys and rises to an impressive climax that normally would lead to the recapitulation. But instead there is a hushed interpolation from the Scherzo, whose insistent "knocking" motives are finally dispelled when the entire orchestra commences the recapitulation with the melody quoted in Example 21. The brilliant coda reaches its high point with a canonic treatment of the opening theme of the movement:

Ex. 25

The close is an instance of another characteristic of Beethoven's style: the manner in which he emphasizes the tonality of a work. The last fifty-five measures of this movement never stray from C major, and the basic tonality is thus mercilessly impressed upon the listener with all the force that Beethoven can extract from his orchestra.

It should be observed that Beethoven was the first composer to write a last movement of this type. The concluding movement of this symphony is not merely a pleasant termination to a series of pieces in contrasted tempi, but rather a summation of the entire work, a finale in the true sense of the word.

The Concertos

In this category are to be found five concertos for piano,[10] one for violin, and a triple concerto for piano, violin and cello. The thematic content, loftiness of inspiration, and sympathetic treatment of the solo instrument which characterize these compositions have given them a position of great prominence in the literature of the concerto. In his treatment of the concerto form, Beethoven has again revised traditional concepts. These works are not compositions for a soloist accompanied by an orchestra, but are full-length symphonies in which a solo instrument is entrusted with a prominent part which at no time is more important than that of the orchestra. The Fourth and Fifth Piano Concertos (in G major and E-flat major respectively) introduce the solo instrument at the very beginning instead of at the commencement of the second exposition. In the latter work, known in the English-speaking countries as the *Emperor* Concerto,[11] Beethoven has done away with the custom of allowing the solo performer to improvise a cadenza. At the point in the first movement where the cadenza would normally appear he has inserted a specific prohibition of its introduction, and has written a rather brief passage for piano solo to take its place. Since the day of Beethoven no composer, with the exception of Brahms, has left the cadenza of his concertos to the discretion of a performer. In both of the above-mentioned works the second and third movements are joined, in an attempt at unification similar to that which has already been observed in the Piano Sonata in F minor and in the Fifth Symphony.

[10] An early piano concerto dating from Beethoven's fourteenth year was "reconstructed" from the composer's sketches in 1943.
[11] This title did not originate with Beethoven.

VIOLIN CONCERTO IN D MAJOR, OPUS 61

The Violin Concerto, universally acknowledged to be one of the greatest works for the instrument, was written in 1806 for one of Beethoven's friends, the Viennese violinist and conductor, Franz Clement. Beethoven, who always loved a joke, could not resist the temptation to make a pun on Clement's name and placed on the work the inscription, *"Concerto par Clemenza pour Clement."*

The first movement utilizes the traditional concerto form with its two expositions.[12] Like many other Beethoven movements it is permeated by a characteristic motive, in this instance a repeated-note figure. This makes its first appearance at the opening of the movement in a dramatically hushed passage for the kettledrum:

Ex. 26

Particularly effective quotation of this "knocking" motive occurs in the course of the development section, where it is relentlessly intoned by the brass instruments while the solo violin sings an impassioned melody.

Of the several themes of the second group, the most important is a simple scale-wise tune which, with the exception of its last presentation in the coda, appears in a major key and is then repeated in the minor. And, as is so frequently the case in Beethoven's works, the opening motive of the movement serves as its accompaniment:

Ex. 27

[12] See page 166.

Following the tradition of his period, Beethoven directs the performer to improvise a cadenza just before the coda. Today most violinists will play the cadenza composed by Joseph Joachim (1831-1907), a celebrated German violinist long active as soloist, teacher, and director of a famous string quartet. It was Joachim who restored what had become a neglected work to the repertory, when, as a thirteen-year-old boy, he played the Beethoven violin concerto in London at a concert conducted by Mendelssohn. (Joachim's name is also associated with a great violin concerto of another epoch, the one of his friend Brahms, dedicated to Joachim and given its first performance and supplied with cadenzas by him.)

The calm introspective second movement, a Larghetto in the key of G Major, has been aptly described as an instance of the "sublime inaction" [13] shown in some of the Beethoven slow movements.

A solemn theme given out by the muted strings serves as the material for a series of variations:

Ex. 28

Like the variations of the Fifth Symphony, discussed on page 192, this set also has a second theme, which in its broad melodic flow affords an excellent contrast to the halting rhythm of the principal theme:

Ex. 29

This second theme makes only two appearances, both of which are entrusted to the solo violin. Performance of a cadenza is indicated at the end of the movement and Beethoven directs that the soloist proceed without pause into the final *Rondo,* an *Allegro* in D Major.

For the last movement of his concertos Beethoven utilizes a form

[13] Tovey, *Essays in Musical Analysis* (London, 1936), Vol. III, p. 93.

that combines the elements of both the sonata and the rondo patterns. It may be represented schematically as follows:

I. First Group—Second Group—First Group—
     (Tonic)   (Related key)   (Tonic)
II. Development of previously stated material or introduction of new themes—
                               (Modulatory)
III. First Group—Second Group—First Group—
      (Tonic)   (Tonic)   (Tonic)
IV. Coda
     (Modulatory, but closing in tonic).

This sequence of formal elements may also be represented in this way: ABA—C—ABA—Coda. Beethoven, of course, does not adhere literally to the repetitions implied in this scheme. Interesting departures from it that do not radically affect the pattern are frequently met with. They afford much delight to the listener attentive enough to be aware of them.

The recurring theme of this brisk movement is a bright dance-like melody given out by the solo violin over a rudimentary bass:

Ex. 30

The second group concerns itself with a vigorous subject shared by orchestra and soloist:

Ex. 31

The middle section introduces a wistful song-like theme in a minor key:

Ex. 32

The various parts of this melody are first played by the solo violin and then repeated by the bassoon while the violin executes florid arabesques around them.

One of the most attractive features of this rondo, as is true in almost every Beethoven rondo, is the dramatic, suspense-creating manner in which the successive reappearances of the first theme are contrived.

Dramatic Music

Despite Beethoven's extraordinary powers of dramatic expression, he wrote only one opera, a work known today as *Fidelio*. His failure to write other operas may be attributed to his inability to find what he considered a suitable text. Many libretti were offered to him, and unfruitful discussions concerning possible opera texts took place with such literary figures as von Collin and Grillparzer; and like almost every other composer of the time, Beethoven considered the musical possibilities of Goethe's *Faust*.

The original title of the opera *Fidelio* was *Leonore*. Based on a melodramatic and somewhat obvious plot, the work deals with the last-minute rescue from death of an individual who had been illegally imprisoned—a favorite dramatic subject at the time. The first performance of the work in 1805 resulted in failure. After various deletions and revisions it was performed again the following year. Considerably altered and supplied with a new name and a new overture, it was revived as *Fidelio* in 1814 with much success.

Judging by *Fidelio,* it cannot truthfully be said that Beethoven was a great opera composer. The specific demands made by the libretto could only be met by him in such scenes as he found congenial to his own temperament. His opera remains an uneven work with many dramatic episodes that fail to give a unified impression.

Beethoven's dramatic instinct found free play when he was unencumbered by the exigencies of a libretto, that is, when he could express himself in a purely instrumental manner; and in so doing he created yet another great medium of musical communication, the dramatic overture. For the various performances of *Fidelio* no less than four overtures were composed. Three are known and numbered as *Leonore* overtures and the fourth as the *Fidelio* overture. Among the other overtures written by Beethoven for various dramatic works and festive occasions, two magnificent examples stand out: the overture for Heinrich von Collin's play *Coriolanus,* and that for Goethe's tragedy *Egmont.* For the latter play Beethoven also wrote some incidental music.

While Beethoven was not entirely successful in working out the details of a musical setting for a dramatic work, he showed a rare ability to extract from the libretto or play in hand the essence of its dramatic conflict, and to present this conflict in a musical condensation so vivid as to make the play that it preceded appear almost as an anti-climax.

OVERTURE TO "EGMONT"

Beethoven said that he wrote his overture and incidental music for Goethe's tragedy *Egmont* "purely out of love for the poet" [14]; but examination of the play will show that Beethoven himself must have been strongly drawn to the Dutch hero Egmont with his love of independence, his unlimited confidence in himself, and his general high-spiritedness. The essential conflict of the play, based on incidents which occurred during the Spanish rule in the Netherlands, is the struggle between liberalism and personal freedom as represented by Egmont, and reaction and tyranny as represented by the cruel and fanatical Alva, emissary of the King of Spain. Egmont was charged with treason and was executed at Alva's command on June 5, 1568.

Beethoven's overture is a powerful portrayal of Egmont, his aspirations, his failure, and his ultimate victory in death. The work is in three connected parts—a slow introduction, an *Allegro* in sonata form, and a brilliant coda. After a measure in which the note F is sounded by the entire orchestra, the strings emphatically announce an ominous theme:

Ex. 33

[14] Thayer-Krehbiel, *Life of Beethoven* (New York, 1921), Vol. I, page 192.

Plaintive answer is made by the wood winds. Another theme appears in the violins accompanied by a bass motive derived from the first two notes in the second measure of Example 33, also a "knocking" motive. After further repetition of this motive the tempo changes to an animated *Allegro,* the first subject of which is assigned to the cellos, with a significant concluding phrase in the first violins:

Ex. 34

This rises to a turbulent climax in which repeated-note motives play an important part. The second group commences with a dramatic dialogue between the strings and wood winds:

Ex. 35

The first two measures of this theme, it will be observed, are derived from the opening (Example 33). Here again we find a "knocking" motive.

The development confines itself almost exclusively to the theme quoted in Example 34, fragments of which are heard in the wood wind instruments, whose discourse is regularly interrupted by loud chords. The recapitulation exhibits no striking points of departure. The transition to the coda is based almost entirely on the repeated-note figure heard in Example 33, which is alternately hurled out defiantly by clarinets, bassoons, and horns, and played softly by the strings. A final *fortissimo* statement of this motive is followed by a pause from which these prayer-like chords emerge:

Ex. 36

Nothing could be simpler than the interpolation of this wood wind episode, yet it is one of the most moving passages that the composer ever penned. The triple *piano* that he has demanded is seldom realized in performance.

The coda bears one of Beethoven's most frequently employed designations—*Allegro con brio*. The key is now F major, and the atmosphere changes from one of oppression to one of victory and triumph. The thematic material of the coda is entirely new. The explanation of the mood of this conclusion is to be found in Goethe's play, at the end of which Egmont is led to his execution while a *Siegessymphonie* (Symphony of Victory) is played. The coda of the overture thus reappears at the conclusion of the play, not merely as a carrying out of Goethe's directions, but as a significant epilogue to the entire drama.

CHAMBER MUSIC

The chamber music of Beethoven includes ten sonatas for violin and piano, of which the Kreutzer Sonata (Opus 47) is the best known. Written in 1803 for the violinist, George Bridgetower, this work was published in 1805 with a dedication to another violinist, Rudolph Kreutzer, author of the famous etudes for his instrument. There are also five sonatas for cello and piano; eight piano trios; many pieces for miscellaneous combinations; and seventeen string quartets. Of these works the string quartets are the most important and form the very core of the literature for this particular instrumental combination. A knowledge of them is indispensable for a true appreciation of Beethoven.

Quartets composed of professional players often performed at the homes of Beethoven's patrons, and in his opportunities for hearing his works performed he enjoyed facilities which rivaled those of Haydn. As is the case with all the other musical media which he employed, Beethoven greatly enlarged the expressive possibilities of the string quartet. Nor did he permit the grandeur of his conceptions to be constrained by mere mechanical limitations; the last quartets, particularly, make severe demands on the players.

One of the most prominent of Beethoven's patrons was the Russian ambassador to Vienna, Count Rasoumovsky, to whom he dedicated the three quartets, Opus 59, and whose name they bear. As a complimentary gesture to his benefactor, Beethoven employed a Russian melody in a movement in each of the first two. These quartets, completed in 1807, mark a new departure in chamber music. Beethoven has done away with the old habit of composing quartets in batches of six; and after the Opus 59, he does not even write in groups of three, but regards each quartet as a distinct entity. An important feature of the Opus 59 quartets is their monumental size, an attribute that can be explained in terms of grandeur of conception, richness of development, and mastery of form. Hence it is difficult to regard the Opus 59 quartets as a "set" in the older sense of the term. These works are substantially longer than their predecessors, the Opus 18 quartets. The average length of a quartet from the latter group is twenty minutes; the first quartet of the Opus 59, however, consumes about forty-one minutes in performance. This lengthening of the traditional form can be attributed to Beethoven's need for an adequate medium of personal expression. The long movements that are encountered in his mature works are never diffuse; almost all exhibit that stupendous power of concentration which is so characteristic of his style.

STRING QUARTET IN E MINOR, OPUS 59, NO. 2

The first movement, in sonata form, opens with two emphatic chords followed by a measure of silence and a wistful melody:

Ex. 37

After brief manipulation of this material, including the impressive silences, another plaintive tune appears in the first group:

Ex. 38

The second group begins with another restrained melody:

Ex. 39

Towards the close of the exposition a series of syncopated chords played *pianissimo* presents a striking rhythmic pattern:

Ex. 40

A repetition of the exposition, while indicated by Beethoven, is seldom made by performers. With the exception of Example 39, all of the themes quoted above are exploited in the long and dramatic development, the end of which is marked by a powerful descending figure elaborated by trills and played by the four instruments in unison. The recapitulation offers no striking departures from its analogue, the exposition. The coda, of characteristic length, resumes the development of the thematic material and the movement closes with an impressive unison rendition of the melody quoted in Example 37 followed by three sombre chords.

The second movement of this quartet, one of the composer's most impressive utterances, is written in the intimate soul-revealing style that Beethoven reserved for his quartets. At its head there stands the characteristically Beethovenish direction to the performers already quoted on page 183: *"Si tratta questo pezzo con molto di sentimento."* But the music that Beethoven has written makes his request seem unnecessary. The movement commences with a contemplative melody of incomparable serenity:

Ex. 41

The second group introduces a fervid theme whose intensity is greatly increased through reversal of the usual positions of viola and cello and writing the latter above the former:

Ex. 42

The exposition comes to an end with an impassioned melody given out by the violins over a characteristic repeated-note motive in the viola and cello:

Ex. 43

The brief development is an intense working out of the motives quoted in Examples 41 and 43. The recapitulation is not a literal repetition of the exposition, but contains new figuration and important changes in instrumentation. The coda commences with a *fortissimo* statement of the opening theme, which soon gives place to the theme of Example 43 considerably expanded.

The third movement, which reverts to E minor, has only one caption, the tempo indication *Allegretto*. Although in a triple rhythm, it lacks the dynamic characteristics of a scherzo and is for the most part tender and wistful in character. The form of the movement is essentially an enlargement of the familiar three-part form associated with the minuet and its later development, the scherzo. Instead of bringing the work to a close after the first *Da Capo*, Beethoven here calls for additional repetitions, which result in the following sequence: Principal Section—Trio—Principal Section—Trio—Principal Section. (The most frequently heard example of this type of extension is found in the *Scherzo* of Beethoven's Seventh Symphony.)

The *Trio*, in E Major, employs a Russian folk-tune but manipulates it in a thoroughly Beethovenish manner. The melody has achieved perhaps greater fame through its more nationally idiomatic use in the great chorus heard in the Coronation Scene of Mussorgsky's opera, *Boris Godounoff*.[15]

The last movement, one of the most exciting in the entire string quartet literature, is cast in the sonata-rondo form that we have already encountered in the last movement of the Violin Concerto.[16]   But as is customary with Beethoven, the form is not adhered to literally. The deviation, in this instance, involves the omission of the first group after the development section and the beginning of the recapitulation directly with the second group.

The first group opens with a curious and effective oscillation in tonalities, for it shifts between C Major and E Minor:

Ex. 44

With the exception of the rather brief intrusions of the second group, the entire movement concerns itself with exploring the potentials of the several motives that make up this theme.

---

[15] See page 367.
[16] Quoted on page 198.

VOCAL MUSIC

Beethoven composed sixty-six songs, a few of which are heard today. One song of a religious character, *Die Ehre Gottes aus der Natur* (The Glory of God in Nature) has become well known in a choral arrangement which, however, is not the work of the composer.

An oratorio, *Christus am Ölberge* (The Mount of Olives), composed in 1801-1802, was somewhat popular during the composer's lifetime, but is seldom performed today. His great masterpiece of choral music is the *Missa Solemnis,* a setting of the Catholic Mass which, like that of Bach, extends far beyond the ritual of a church; and like Bach's Mass, Beethoven's setting is a confession of personal faith. So intense and so earnest was Beethoven in his desire to formulate his *credo* in tones that in this work, as in the choral parts of the Ninth Symphony, he has frequently disregarded the physical limitations of the human voice. But the strained character of the vocal writing does not impede the composer's fervidness of utterance, and a passage such as the *Dona Nobis Pacem* with its sound of distant trumpets may well be regarded as one of Beethoven's highest peaks of inspiration. At this point in the score Beethoven has revealingly written, *Bitte um innern und äussern Frieden* (Prayer for inner and outer peace).

SUGGESTED READINGS

The literature on Beethoven is being continually enriched by new publications. The standard biography is the three-volume treatise of A. W. Thayer, edited and revised by Henry Krehbiel, *The Life of Ludwig van Beethoven* (New York, 1921). This monumental piece of scholarship does not include critical examinations of the works. The two-volume *Beethoven Handbuch* by Theodor Frimmel (Leipzig, 1926), is an indispensable encyclopedia. The best single treatise on the career, the man, and his compositions is Paul Bekker, *Beethoven* (New York, 1925).

All the following works are valuable:

J. N. Burk, *The Life and Works of Beethoven* (New York, 1946).

Oscar Sonneck, *Beethoven, Impressions of Contemporaries* (New York, 1926).

Karl Kobald, *Beethoven, Seine Beziehungen zu Wiens Kunst, Kultur, Gesellschaft und Landschaft* (Vienna, 1927).

Romain Rolland, *Beethoven, The Creator* (New York, 1929).

J. W. N. Sullivan, *Beethoven, His Spiritual Development* (New York, 1927).

Donald F. Tovey, *Beethoven* (London, 1944).

Donald F. Tovey, *A Companion to Beethoven's Pianoforte Sonatas* (London, 1931).

Eric Blom, *Beethoven's Pianoforte Sonatas Discussed* (London, 1938).

George Grove, *Beethoven and his Nine Symphonies* (London, 1896).

Donald F. Tovey, *Essays in Musical Analysis,* Vols. I, II, III, IV, V (London, 1935-7).

Daniel Gregory Mason, *The Quartets of Beethoven* (New York, 1947).

Chapter XV

ROMANTICISM IN MUSIC

AT THE beginning of the nineteenth century a definite movement towards new modes of expression made itself manifest in all the arts. This trend has been called "the romantic movement," although the implications of the term "romantic" are somewhat vague. Examination of the works of the critical writers of this period will show that romanticism as an artistic tenet was expounded in various ways: Victor Hugo called it "liberalism in literature"; Heinrich Heine found in it "the reawakening of medieval poetry"; Jean-Jacques Rousseau emphasized the emotional individualism of the movement in these words: "I am different from all men I have seen. If I am not better at least I am different."

While it is customary to think of the terms *classic* and *romantic* as antonyms, closer consideration shows that, although certain generalizations can be made concerning each mode of expression, no hard and fast line of demarcation can be drawn between them. The "classical" style is characterized by its objectivity and by its emphasis on the universal, as opposed to the specific and particular. It is marked by mastery of form, clarity of presentation, and emotional restraint. Because of its objective nature, however, classical art tends to become stylized and encumbered with set forms and conventions.

The underlying spirit of romanticism, on the other hand, is one of discontent with the artistic formulae and conventions of its more immediate past. The romantic artists have, however, in their desire to find new modes of expression, created new forms that in their universality of acceptance have in turn become classic. The romantic spirit is essentially a progressive spirit and as such has always been present in all art epochs. Stendhal remarked that "all good art was romantic in its day," and numerous examples from such works as the cantatas of Bach or the string quartets of Haydn could be cited as proof. But what sets the romantic period apart is its self-consciousness, its ever-present sense of a break with the past. A romantic mode of expression was almost demanded of the artist; and literary critics insisted that it was his duty to seek out the strange and unusual, and to emphasize his own self, his own emotions, his own experiences. In artistic as well as in political thought the importance of the individual was stressed.

It is interesting to notice the emphasis placed on music in the literary discussions and in the critical essays of the period. Amidst the exaltation of personal feelings and sentiments, music is always described as "the language of the emotions." The romantic movement in literature, particularly in Germany, was to affect the progress of music in many ways. The poems of Goethe, Schiller, Heine, Eichendorff, and others prompted such composers as Schubert, Schumann, and Wolf to find musical settings for them; and Goethe's *Faust* served as an almost universal source of inspiration. In their love for the poetry of the Middle Ages, and in their interest in the great mass of German mythology and folk-lore with its elements of the fantastic and the supernatural as well as the picturesque and sentimental, such writers as Tieck, Schlegel, and the brothers Grimm were important factors in the development of the romantic opera. Composers shared with writers an enthusiasm for the works of Shakespeare. Outstanding instances are Mendelssohn's music for *A Midsummer Night's Dream* and Berlioz' symphony *Romeo and Juliet*.

The romantic movement in music also found inspiration in the subjectivity exhibited by the works of Beethoven, and it is the group of composers immediately following him who are conventionally designated as "The Romantic Composers." The outstanding ones were Franz Schubert, Felix Mendelssohn, Robert Schumann, Hector Berlioz, Carl Maria von Weber, Frédéric Chopin, Franz Liszt, and Richard Wagner. The musical aspects of romanticism are numerous and diverse, but several features stand out clearly and may be briefly surveyed.

Although all the romantic composers were ardent worshipers of Beethoven, the nature of their musical utterances made the sonata form seem unsuitable for their purposes. While many of them actually did compose sonatas, symphonies, and string quartets, in no instance did their mastery of these forms approach that of Beethoven. Their true significance lies in the wealth of new forms that they created: the many new types of shorter pieces for piano, the art-song, the longer programmatic orchestral forms, the romantic opera, and the music-drama. In the manner characteristic of the period, their expressions of subjective states are occasionally lacking in restraint and in some instances verge on the sentimental or the fantastic.

"Program music," music having a stated descriptive purpose, came to the fore during this epoch, and numerous works either bore poetic titles or were accompanied by detailed "programs." Poems inspired not only songs, but entire symphonic works. In much of this descriptive music no set form was employed, and the plan of a composition was determined purely by the nature of the poetic idea inspiring it.

Numerous improvements were made in the general design and mechanism of the piano, particularly by American manufacturers. Extension of the compass, acceleration of the action, introduction of steel strings, and perfection of the sounding-board greatly increased the sonority, dynamic range, and variety of tone-color of the instrument. Great piano virtuosi appeared on the scene, who, while not abjuring sensationalism, made significant contributions to the art of piano-playing. An important result of this improvement of the piano was the endowment of the instrument with a musical self-sufficiency. The manifold possibilities of the instrument, as unfolded by virtuosi, enabled the pianist to appear publicly as a solo performer without the assistance of an orchestra. The modern "piano recital" thus came into existence. The popularity of the piano as an instrument for public performance was paralleled by its widespread adoption as a domestic musical instrument in the households of the now emerging middle class. The nature of much romantic music, particularly of the shorter piano pieces, was such as to win for it ready popular acceptance. A growth of interest in music and an elevation in the general level of musical taste were also phenomena of the period.

Improvements in the wind instruments of the orchestra, particularly the addition of valves to the horn and the trumpet,[1] were followed by a keener interest in the expressive possibilities of orchestral tone-color,

[1] See page 18.

motivated, no doubt, by the desire to find new and effective ways of using instrumental music for descriptive and dramatic purposes. The orchestra was enlarged, instruments like the English horn, the bass-clarinet, the tuba, the harp, and so on, acquired full citizenship in it, and standards of orchestral playing were considerably raised.

It was during this period, too, that the art of orchestral conducting came to life. The new style of symphonic and operatic works made the presence of a conductor imperative, and his true function as an interpreter of orchestral music came to be realized. Composers such as Liszt, Berlioz, and Wagner were outstanding conductors of their day; and the latter two wrote fine treatises on the art.

Musicians also found it necessary to take to the pen in defense of their new ideas. Schumann founded and edited a critical musical magazine; von Weber and Liszt wrote numerous essays; while Berlioz was a regular contributor of *feuilletons* to the Paris papers and wrote extensively about his musical experiences. The most prolific literary musician was Wagner, with no less than ten volumes of prose works to his credit. All of this literary activity is a further indication of the self-consciousness that pervaded the romantic movement.

Suggested Readings

The penetrating treatise of Albert Einstein, *Music in the Romantic Era* (New York, 1947), is the best single volume on the subject. Particularly valuable is Part I of this work, "Antecedents, Concepts and Ideals." There is an excellent essay "The Music of the Nineteenth Century" in Cecil Grey, *A Survey of Contemporary Music* (London, 1927). French aspects of the romantic movement are discussed in Locke, *Music and The Romantic Movement in France* (London, 1920); Tiersot, *La Musique aux temps romantiques* (Paris, 1930); and Eckardt, *Die Musikanschauung der französischen Romantik* (Kassel, 1935).

Detailed treatment of certain aspects of the period are found in such works as Hutcheson, *The Literature of the Piano* (New York, 1948); Apel, *Masters of the Keyboard* (Cambridge, Mass., 1947); Graf, *Composer and Critic* (New York, 1946); Grout, *A Short History of the Opera* (New York, 1947); Harding, *A History of the Pianoforte* (Cambridge, 1933); Carse, *A History of Orchestration* (London, 1925); and the same author's *The Orchestra from Beethoven to Berlioz* (Cambridge, 1948).

Chapter XVI

FRANZ SCHUBERT

DURING the time that Beethoven was the dominant figure in
the musical life of Vienna, a shy and retiring individual living
obscurely in poor surroundings was composing literally hundreds of
works in a form upon which he was to leave as vital an impress as
Beethoven had on the symphony and string quartet. This younger
contemporary was Franz Schubert, and the form with which his
name is indissolubly connected is the song.

Franz Schubert, born in a suburb of Vienna on January 31, 1797,
was the son of a schoolmaster. His first lessons in music were received from members of his musically inclined family: his father
taught him to play the violin, an elder brother taught him the piano;
and a local choirmaster gave him vocal instruction. Like Haydn, the
young Schubert had a fine soprano voice that served as a stepping-
stone to his musical education.. But the lad was taken not into the
choir of St. Stephen's Cathedral, but into that of the Imperial Court
Chapel which, with the seminary associated with it, the *Konvikt,* offered
excellent opportunities for his musical development. Schubert not
only sang in the chapel choir, but also played violin and viola in the
student orchestra. Among the works performed by the youthful instrumentalists were symphonies of Haydn, Mozart, and Beethoven; and
while still a boy Schubert regarded the works of Beethoven with awe
and veneration. In addition to his studies at the school, Schubert received some instruction from the Imperial Kapellmeister, Salieri, who
many years before had given Beethoven lessons in dramatic composition.

At the behest of his father, whose opinions of a musical career were
none too high, Schubert entered a normal school in order to prepare

himself for a schoolteacher's post. When he had finished his period
of training he was given an appointment in his father's school. This
was the only regular post he ever held. But hand in hand with the
drudgery of the schoolmaster's lot went a vast amount of inspired
musical creation, and some of the world's greatest songs were composed during this period.

Three impetuous young men who had become enthusiastic over
Schubert's compositions finally prevailed upon him to drop his dull
position at the school and to join them in their somewhat bohemian
mode of life in Vienna. They also undertook to win some recognition for him by attempting to bring his compositions to the attention
of members of the upper classes and of various publishers.

Schubert now became a member of a group of writers, artists, and
poets who met frequently in the coffee-houses of Vienna. Among his
more celebrated associates at one time or another were the dramatist
Franz Grillparzer and the painter Moritz von Schwind. An influential singer, Johann Michael Vogl, was the first artist to realize the
worth of Schubert's songs, and the major portion of the limited recognition which Schubert received during his lifetime may be attributed
to Vogl's sympathetic rendering of them.

It was not until 1818 that any of Schubert's music was published;
none of the important songs appeared in print before 1821. His relations with his publishers were most unfortunate. Unlike Beethoven,
he lacked a strong belief in his own artistic superiority; and priceless
works were turned over by him for ridiculously small honoraria. Inasmuch as the income from the sale of his works was his principal
source of funds, the poverty in which he lived may well be imagined.

The blame for the neglect of Schubert cannot be squarely placed
on either the public or the publishers of his time. Unlike Mozart and
Beethoven, he was not a great virtuoso who could at once command
public attention. He lacked the polish and finesse of the former,
and the strong, indomitable will of the latter. Nor was he fortunate
enough to find a discerning prince to take him into his musical establishment and allow his creative gifts to flower unimpeded by pecuniary
worries. The song, the medium in which Schubert excelled, was as
yet confined to the salon, and no public recognition could be won
through works which were then regarded as belonging to the domain

FRANZ SCHUBERT

of chamber music. Schubert appeared before the Vienna public primarily as a composer of opera—a form in which his talents did not appear at their best. To make matters worse, the Viennese had become infatuated with the ingratiating operas of Rossini, and the dazzling virtuosity of the violinist, Paganini. While it is true that Schubert enjoyed a small measure of popularity during his lifetime, and that the solitary concert that he gave not long before his death was well attended, he never received even a fraction of the recognition and affection that the Viennese public had lavished upon Haydn and Beethoven.

The ultimate recognition of Schubert's genius took place long after his death. The great C major Symphony was discovered by Robert Schumann in a pile of old manuscripts in 1839, eleven years after Schubert's death. The celebrated torso now known as the *Unfinished* Symphony was not unearthed until 1865. The brilliant piano transcriptions of over fifty songs, which Franz Liszt made and performed at his concerts, served to popularize Schubert's name over the entire European continent.

The untimely death of Schubert in 1828, twenty months after the death of Beethoven, constituted a tragedy that in its artistic implications can be likened only to that of Mozart, with whose life that of Schubert exhibits many parallelisms. Like Mozart's, the brevity of Schubert's career is no index of his creative accomplishment. Within the comparatively short period in which he was engaged in composition, he composed about 600 songs, nine symphonies, much chamber music and a great quantity of music for piano, including twenty-one sonatas and characteristic shorter pieces such as the *Impromptus, Moments musicaux,* marches, and many works for piano duet. He also wrote two operas, some dramatic music, and much sacred music, including six masses. The sum total of his works, over twelve hundred, comprises what is beyond doubt one of the most extraordinary records of musical fertility.

The sheer volume of Schubert's output may be attributed to his regular habits of work: every morning was devoted entirely to creative activity. His method of composition was the exact opposite of Beethoven's: all of Schubert's works were conceived with slight effort, and with a spontaneity that is often astounding. Many of his famous masterpieces were dashed off at great speed; as many as six songs were composed in one morning. But hand in hand with this seemingly limitless flow of music there sometimes went a lack of self-criticism, a lack of concentration and sustained development, which resulted in prolixity and diffuseness, particularly in the instrumental compositions. What was a priceless virtue in the shorter works, such as the songs and the *Impromptus* for piano, became almost a fault in works calling for more extensive organization of material and attention to detail.

The major instrumental works of Schubert show the influence of Beethoven, whom he greatly admired, more in form than in spirit, for their style is predominantly lyrical. One need only recall the celebrated cello melody from the *Unfinished* Symphony:

Ex. 1

Even the scherzos of his works have essentially tuneful components. Two of Schubert's symphonies, No. 8 in B Minor, the *Unfinished,* and No. 9 in C Major (occasionally and erroneously designated as No. 7), are staples of the modern orchestral repertory. The compelling beauty of their thematic material and the originality of their orchestration more than atone for their diffuseness.

Some of Schubert's greatest instrumental essays are to be found in his chamber music. Among them may be listed the posthumous Quartet in D Minor, commonly known as *Death and the Maiden* (its second movement is a set of variations on the theme from Schubert's song *Der Tod und Das Mädchen*) and a particularly fine String Quintet in C Major (with two cellos), Opus 163. Outstanding works with piano are the Trio in B Flat, Opus 99 and a Quintet for Piano, Violin, Viola, Cello and Double Bass, Opus 114. This work, like the D Minor String Quartet, also contains a set of variations on a melody from one of the composer's songs, in this case *Die Forelle* (*The Trout*) and hence is always known as the *Forellen* Quintet.

One of Schubert's finest songs, *Der Wanderer* (*The Wanderer*), furnished the theme for a long and impressive piano piece the *Wanderer Fantasy* (1822). The title, *Fantasy,* indicates the formal freedoms exhibited by the work, a composition in four sections whose structure anticipates the later symphonic poem.[1]   Franz Liszt, the father of the symphonic poem, was sufficiently intrigued by Schubert's work to make an arrangement of it for piano and orchestra (1851).

But it is as a composer of songs (German: *Lieder*) that Schubert is preëminent.   As is usually the case, he had been preceded by many lesser composers in this form, notably the composers of *Singspiele*— plays of a popular nature in which dialogue was interspersed with songs and duets.   Nor should the contributions to the song literature of Mozart and Beethoven be forgotten.   But it remained for Schubert to bring this particular type of fusion of poetry and music to the fore.

The Art-Song

The *art-song,* to use a term that distinguishes the form now being discussed from the anonymous *folk song,* is a trained composer's setting of a poem for voice and accompanying instrument.   Some modern composers have used prose texts.   The accompanying instrument is almost invariably the piano, sometimes aided by another instrument such as the viola or the clarinet.   Songs are occasionally written for voice and orchestra or they may, in rare instances, be entirely unaccompanied.

Inasmuch as a song is a musician's interpretation of a poem, the form is a combination of the work of two creative artists, the poet and the composer.   It is a fusion of two media of communication, rhythmic speech and music, two auditory phenomena that readily combine to form a vivid and effective means of expression.   So strong is this power of combination that some inspired musical settings associate themselves indissolubly with their poems and become part of their very being.   For example, a knowledge of Schubert's setting of *Der Erlkönig* of Goethe alters one's reading of the poem for all time.

As with all vocal forms, the listener's enjoyment of the song in its totality depends in large measure on his knowledge of its text.   Many of the world's great songs have been written by German composers, who have employed poems either written in or translated into their own tongue.   The translation of these poems into English verse, while feasible, is almost invariably difficult to bring about without changes

[1] See page 287.

in word order and distortion of the subtler shades of meaning. Destruction of the unity of text and music is often the result. *Traduttori—traditori* (Translators are traitors). A study of the German language holds no greater reward than the pleasure to be derived from a knowledge of its extensive wealth of lyric poetry as so happily interpreted by such great German masters of song as Schubert, Schumann, Brahms, Wolf and Richard Strauss.

Considered structurally, songs are usually divided into three types. The first, the *strophic* type, is a song in which each of the various stanzas of the poem has received an identical setting. Schubert's famous setting of Goethe's *Heidenröslein* (*Little Heather Rose*) is a representative sample. A *modified strophic* song is one in which most of the stanzas have identical settings, while one or two, because of the demands of their text, have received a different treatment. *Die Forelle* (*The Trout*) is typical.

The third type is always described by the untranslatable German adjective *durchkomponiert* (approximate translation: "composed throughout"). The *durchkomponiert* song follows no rigid formal pattern; its design and plan are dictated entirely by the poem. In its comparative freedom from formal considerations the *durchkomponiert* type offers excellent possibilities for expressive combination of poetry and music, and many of the world's great songs fall into this category.

Schubert's Songs

Schubert was primarily a creator of melodies, tunes capable of expressing all shades of emotion and yet retaining a simplicity and a directness of utterance that frequently recall the naturalness of folk song. The most distinctive feature of Schubert's vocal writing is the manner in which he has reconciled the purely musical demands of his melodies with the rhetorical implications of his poems. There are hundreds of beautiful melodies in the songs of Schubert; but despite their perfection of outline, there are practically no errors in accentuation. With this lyrical gift there was coupled a wide knowledge of the expressive possibilities of the human voice. All of Schubert's songs are eminently singable.

But Schubert does not always utilize pure melody as a means of setting poetry. Declamation is frequently employed, and in a manner which is thoroughly realistic. Magnificent examples of the dramatic effectiveness with which Schubert utilizes declamation are to be found in such songs as *Der Wanderer* (*The Wanderer*), and *Der Doppelgänger* (*The Phantom Double*).

The piano accompaniment of a Schubert song may either provide a simple rhythmic and harmonic support, create a mood, or describe or portray persons, things, or situations mentioned in the poem. Or, by the use of harmonic coloring, it may throw words or phrases into high relief. It was Schubert who raised the piano accompaniment to a position of importance; and it was he who first endowed it with a measure of self-sufficiency, occasionally laying greater emphasis on it than on the voice. In the creation of delineative piano figures Schubert's genius seems inexhaustible, and the range of subjects for which he found musical representation is enormous. The following examples chosen from among the better-known songs will serve to demonstrate this phase of Schubert's art.

The mood of *Heidenröslein* (*Little Heather Rose*) is created by this innocent little figure which makes its appearance between the verses:

Ex. 2

The accompaniment of the celebrated *Ständchen* (*Serenade*) is merely the reproduction of the sounds of a guitar:

Ex. 3

Die Forelle (*The Trout*) has a piano accompaniment that apparently describes the trout's darting to and fro in the brook:

Ex. 4

Die Post (*The Post*), from a cycle of twenty-four songs entitled *Die Winterreise* (*The Winter Journey*), possesses an introduction that portrays the galloping of the horses drawing the post-coach and reproduces the notes of the postillion's horn:

Ex. 5

The opening measures of *Der Leiermann* (*The Hurdy-Gurdy Man*), the concluding song of the *Winterreise* cycle, not only duplicate the sounds of the hand-organ, but also suggest the bleakness of winter:

Ex. 6

Beethoven had shown the expressive possibilities of modulation [2] in his instrumental works. Schubert, who was well-acquainted with Beethoven's compositions, makes persistent use of modulation as a means of differentiating the various sections of the poem, or of emphasizing emotional crises. In this respect his style is an anticipation of that of Richard Wagner. Vivid contrasts of major and minor are also fre-

[2] See page 39.

quent. That many of Schubert's songs have been called "miniature dramas" is due in large measure to his ability to create continued dramatic interest through utilizing the attention-sustaining potentialities of skilful modulation.

Of the many great Schubert songs, two have been selected for closer examination here as typical illustrations of his art: *Gretchen am Spinnrade* and *Der Erlkönig*. Both are fine examples of *durchkomponiert* songs.

"GRETCHEN AM SPINNRADE"

The text of *Gretchen am Spinnrade* (*Gretchen at the Spinning-Wheel*) is an excerpt from Part I of Goethe's *Faust*. The rejuvenated Faust has fallen deeply in love with Gretchen, a simple village maiden. Her bewilderment at being the object of the affections of a man of his apparent station in life is expressed as she sits alone in her room and spins. Her anxiety finds utterance in the first two lines: *"Meine Ruh' ist hin, Mein Herz ist schwer"* ("My peace is gone, My heart is heavy"). The Schubert setting of these lines accentuates the four important words, *Ruh', hin, Herz, schwer,* by making them much longer than the others and placing them on the strong beat of the measure; and the word *Herz* is made doubly prominent by elevation in pitch:

Ex. 7

The piano accompaniment, which, with the exception of one momentary halt, continues throughout the song, is based on an undulating figure which portrays the spinning-wheel, and which, by means of tension-creating harmonic alterations typical of Schubert's style, reflects the mental state of Gretchen:

Ex. 8

Gretchen commences to describe her beloved: *"Sein hoher Gang, Sein' edle Gestalt"* ("His high bearing, His noble appearance"). Her recital of his attributes becomes increasingly ecstatic and culminates in *"Und ach, sein Kuss!"* ("And ah, his kiss!"). The setting of these four words is an example *par excellence* of Schubert's art: the voice part suddenly breaks into free declamation; *Sein Kuss* is thrown into high relief by a preceding pause, by elevating it in pitch, by suddenly terminating the restless figures of the piano accompaniment, and by prolonging the word *Kuss* and underscoring it with a strikingly dissonant chord:

Ex. 9

From this point on there is a gradual decrease in the intensity of Gretchen's utterance. Schubert has taken the liberty of repeating the first two lines at the conclusion of his setting, with excellent dramatic effect. The facts concerning the composition of the song are almost incredible: Schubert wrote it in October, 1814, in one afternoon; he was then a youth of only seventeen. It was the first of his sixty-eight settings of texts by Goethe.

"DER ERLKÖNIG"

Der Erlkönig (The Erl King), composed in 1815, is Schubert's most famous song. Its text is also a poem of Goethe, the title of which is the result of an incorrect translation from the Danish. The correct German word should have been *Elfenkönig* (Elf King). The poem tells of a father who rides through the night clutching his sick son to his bosom. The wild gallop is vividly represented by a rain of repeated notes that constitute an accompaniment so energetic and so taxing that few pianists are capable of playing it adequately:

Ex. 10

With the exception of the first and last verses, which are in the third person, the poem consists of a series of utterances by three characters —father, son, and Erl king. A faithful setting of the poem demands, therefore, that these individuals be clearly differentiated despite the fact that only one voice is employed. Schubert has solved the difficulty in masterly fashion by continual change of key, by change in the tempo of delivery, and by change in the style of vocal writing. When, for example, the Erl king enticingly invites the child to his realm, the key changes to the bright B-flat major, and the Erl king sings this melodic passage:

Ex. 11

The anguished cries of the terror-stricken child are written in a declamatory manner, and are intensified in the piano by chords which produce piercing dissonances, as, for example, when the E-flat of *Vater* impinges against the C and D of the accompaniment:

Ex. 12

Der Erlkönig is a striking instance of the manner in which Schubert employs modulation as an intensifying medium. After each successive alluring promise of the Erl king, the child cries to its father. Each of these cries is made more intense than the preceding one through being pitched in a higher key. Schubert writes the gripping last lines—*"In seinen Armen das Kind war tot"* ("In his arms the child was dead")—in pure declamation, with a dramatic pause before the last two words.

Suggested Readings

The most useful and one of the most reliable treatises on Schubert is *The Music of Schubert,* edited by Gerald Abraham (New York, 1947). An excellent Schubert bibliography will be found in the work. Otto Erich Deutsch, *Schubert, A Documentary Biography* (London, 1946), contains a wealth of pertinent material and is one of the most dependable sources of factual information on the composer. Schubert's life and times are attractively described in Karl Kobald, *Franz Schubert and His Times* (New York, 1928), and Newman Flower, *Franz Schubert: the Man and his Circle* (London, 1928), (new and revised edition, London, 1949). Sir George Grove, the first editor of the famous *Dictionary of Music and Musicians* which now bears his name wrote for it a compendious treatise on Schubert, a contribution which has the dimensions of a book. The *Musical Quarterly* for October 1928 is a Schubert number with many valuable articles.

Detailed studies of individual works are to be found in *The Music of Schubert* mentioned above; Richard Capell, *Schubert's Songs* (London, 1928); Donald Francis Tovey, *Essays in Musical Analysis* (London, 1935); and Willi Kahl, "Schubert" in Cobbett's *Cyclopedic Survey of Chamber Music* (London, 1929).

Chapter XVII

CARL MARIA VON WEBER

CARL Maria von Weber has often been called the father of German opera. Like other musical paternities, the extent of this fatherhood is somewhat exaggerated, for the German people already possessed two great operas in their own tongue—Mozart's *Die Zauberflöte* and Beethoven's *Fidelio*. But while the language of these works was German, their libretti and the many older conventions to be found in them prevented their having popular appeal. The roots of von Weber's art are to be found more in the German *Singspiel* [1] with its emphasis on national legends and fairy tales. In raising this form to a position of dignity, von Weber displaced the stylized Italian opera and brought a truly indigenous German opera into being. Rooted in the people, in their folklore and their folk music, the "romantic opera" quickly established itself as a significant art form. In its later perfection at the hands of von Weber's most ardent disciple, Richard Wagner, it became one of the most important manifestations in the history of music.

Born November 18, 1786, at Eutin, near Lübeck, von Weber spent the first years of his life in the atmosphere of the theater. His father, a former soldier, court official, and musician, now turned actor, had organized the several members of his family into a theatrical troupe which wandered through Germany performing in the principal towns. Von Weber received his first musical instruction from his father and an older stepbrother; but as had been the case with both Haydn and Schubert, possession of a fine voice earned him a place in an institution, in this instance, the choirboys' school at Salzburg. Here he received training at the hands of Michael Haydn, a younger brother of

[1] See page 218.

the more famous Joseph. In 1803 he journeyed to Vienna and placed himself under the tutelage of the then celebrated Abbé Vogler.[2] Vogler was an ardent student of folk music and directed von Weber's interest to it, an interest that was to have magnificent results.

Von Weber's active musical career commenced when he was nineteen years old; on Vogler's recommendation, he was given the post of opera conductor in the theater at Breslau. Operatic conducting was von Weber's principal activity throughout his lifetime, with the exception of an interval of six and a half years. Part of this time was spent as private secretary in the service of Duke Ludwig of Württemberg at his dissolute court at Stuttgart, and the rest in travel and concert appearances as a piano virtuoso. From 1813 to 1816 he directed operas in Prague, and from 1817 till his untimely death in 1826 he was Kapellmeister in charge of German opera at Dresden. As an operatic conductor, von Weber aroused antagonism in his colleagues because of his exacting methods of rehearsal and the painstaking care that he bestowed upon every aspect of an operatic presentation, including acting, costuming, and stage-setting as well as music. He was one of the first orchestral conductors to use a baton.

All of von Weber's great zeal as an operatic conductor was dedicated to one cause—the furtherance of German opera. Most of the important opera houses of the period were parts of the musical establishments of various royal houses, and the predominating taste of the sovereigns who dictated the destinies of these opera houses was Italian. Italian musicians were engaged to direct them and Italian operas were given preference. The two great German operas already in existence, *Die Zauberflöte* and *Fidelio,* were performed infrequently if at all. The German language was considered vulgar, and regular performances in the native tongue were usually given only in the smaller public theaters. The situation that existed at the Saxon capital, Dresden, during von Weber's nine years of service there was thoroughly typical of the times. The King of Saxony had two Kapellmeisters in his employ, the Italian Morlacchi and the German von Weber. All the honors and royal approbation were bestowed upon the now-forgotten Italian. Despite the fact that von Weber organized and conducted a splendid German opera company, his efforts were not appreciated,

2 The Abt Vogler of Browning's poem.

CARL MARIA VON WEBER

and he and the art for which he stood were almost completely ignored by the Royal House. The situation at Berlin, where the Italian Spontini held sway, paralleled that at Dresden, and in all of his relations with the Prussian king, von Weber, as the representative of German opera, met with a condescension and an apathy that bordered on insult.

Von Weber was catapulted into fame when his opera *Der Freischütz* was given in Berlin on June 18, 1821. The applause at the first performance, which was unattended by the Prussian Court, was tumultuous; so great was the enthusiasm of the audience that the overture and one of the choruses had to be repeated. No other opera in the history of the German theater had ever met with such ready acceptance and with such popular demonstrations of approval. Within eighteen months there were fifty performances of the work in Berlin alone. The fame of the work spread quickly, and it was not long before it was heard not only on all the German stages, but in foreign capitals as well. A performance in English took place in New York as early as 1825. *Der Freischütz* was followed by *Euryanthe,* given in Vienna in 1823, and *Oberon,* produced in London in 1826; but neither of these works, despite many features of merit, achieved the artistic level of their forerunner.

The fame of von Weber rests almost entirely on his one masterpiece; of the two later operas only the brilliant overtures are regularly performed today. And great though the fame of *Der Freischütz* may be, it has never become a repertory piece in America. (Only seventeen performances of it have been given by the Metropolitan Opera.) An earlier work for piano, *Invitation to the Dance* (1819), was salvaged from the fragments of an uncompleted opera and dedicated by von Weber to his wife. An orchestration of the work, frequently heard today, was made by Hector Berlioz in 1841 to be inserted as ballet music in the performances of *Der Freischütz* in Paris. Wholesale mangling of operas was not infrequent at that time, and garbled versions of works often appeared. At earlier Paris performances of *Der Freischütz* various liberties had been taken with the text, and the title of the work had been changed to *Robin des Bois.*

Like Mozart's and Schubert's, von Weber's life was tragically brief. While *Der Freischütz* won him tremendous popular acclaim, the failure of *Euryanthe* to achieve a comparable success all but broke von Weber's heart. Continued exasperation slowly wore him down; and in a desire to provide for his wife and children he accepted an offer to compose *Oberon* for England, and to make the long and arduous journey to London to conduct the première of the work. The financial results of this London venture were disappointing, however, and von Weber's bitter sense of failure served further to undermine his already fragile constitution. He died of tuberculosis in London on June 5, 1826, and was buried there. Eighteen years later his body was brought back to Germany, largely as a result of the efforts of the devoted Richard Wagner.

The Romantic Opera

Typical texts of romantic operas are based on medieval epics, on folklore, especially on legends dealing with supernatural manifestations, or on exotic subjects distantly removed in time or place. But no matter how fantastic the plot or how extreme the various elements of the supernatural or marvelous, the entire action is treated seriously. Hand in hand with this imaginative aspect there goes an effort to achieve realism, particularly in the handling of scenes dealing with folk life. Local incidents and customs receive detailed and sympathetic treatment from which, however, sentimentality is seldom absent. In its representation of native folk life and customs the romantic opera serves to awaken nationalistic feelings, and it is interesting to note that the two greatest composers of romantic operas, von Weber and Wagner, were both ardent nationalists.

The musical elements of romantic opera present an interesting study in contrasts. For the evocation of distinctive atmosphere, the delineation of supernatural occurrences, and the intensification of feeling and emotion, the orchestra plays an important role. Its idiom becomes more and more complex and its colorings increasingly subtle; its harmonic language is significantly enriched through the increased use of dissonant chords and striking modulations. Equally complex are some of the vocal ensembles on the stage and the great arias of the more important characters. But on the other hand a conscious attempt to achieve simplicity and realism can be seen in the folk-like choruses that impart local color to romantic opera.

Almost all of the salient features of romantic opera appear in the culmination of the style in Wagner's *Lohengrin* (1848). Its text has for its source the legend of the Swan Knight. The supernatural aspects of the drama are rendered credible by the orchestra, as, for example, in the description of the Holy Grail by violins playing in their higher registers. Elsa tells of her dream of the coming of her rescuer, Lohengrin, and Lohengrin describes his lineage and mission in long, involved arias. Large ensembles appear on the stage and are entrusted with involved choral music. But equally typical of romantic opera is the tender and simple "Bridal Chorus."

Der Freischütz: the Text

As an example of the text of a romantic opera, the libretto of *Der Freischütz,* with its emphasis on folk customs and its depiction of supernatural phenomena, may be briefly summarized here. It was written by Friedrich Kind and is based on a tale appearing in Apel and Laun's *Gespensterbuch* (*Ghost Book*). The title, *Der Freischütz,* means "the free-shooter," one who shoots with magic bullets.

The action takes place in Bohemia shortly after the end of the Thirty Years' War (ca. 1648).

Act I. A clearing in the forest.

The peasants have assembled for a shooting contest. Max, a young huntsman, is unsuccessful in his display of marksmanship. He aspires to the hand of Agathe, daughter of the chief forester; but in order to become the chief forester's son-in-law, he must demonstrate publicly his skill with a rifle. In desperation, Max falls easy prey to the designing Caspar, a grisly huntsman in league with the Evil One, Samiel. Max agrees to meet Caspar at midnight in the haunted Wolf's Glen to assist in the casting of magic bullets which, thanks to the power of Samiel, never fail to hit their mark.

Act II, Scene 1. A room in the Chief Forester's house.

Agathe, distressed by various unlucky omens, awaits Max. She prays to Heaven to protect him. Max arrives and is joyfully greeted by Agathe. She tells him of the ominous portents. He refuses to heed her warning and rushes off to the Wolf's Glen.

Scene 2. The Wolf's Glen.

Caspar converses with the invisible Samiel to whom he has forfeited his life in exchange for magic bullets. He proposes to Samiel that Max be accepted as a substitute. Max arrives on the scene and the two huntsmen proceed to cast the magic bullets. Samiel has allowed them seven. Six will strike their mark; the seventh will go as Samiel directs. During the casting of the bullets all kinds of supernatural manifestations occur in the haunted glen. Wild boars and wheels of fire rush across the stage, a terrible storm arises, dogs howl, a ghostly hunting party is heard, owls hoot, trees fall down, and so forth.

Act III, Scene 1. The forest.

Max has already fired three of the four magic bullets which Caspar gave him. He begs Caspar for another. Caspar refuses. Max now has only one bullet left for the crucial contest.

Scene 2. The Chief Forester's house.

Clad in her bridal dress, Agathe kneels before a small altar and utters a fervent prayer. The maidens of the village, following local custom, bring Agathe her bridal wreath; but when it is unwrapped it turns out to be a funeral wreath. Greatly perturbed by this additional omen of misfortune, Agathe and the maidens depart for the shooting contest.

Scene 3. A clearing in the forest.

The populace has assembled for the shooting contest that is to take place in the presence of their Prince. The huntsmen sing lustily of the joys of forest life. Max takes aim at a pigeon flying overhead and fires. Agathe with a shriek sinks unconscious to the ground, and Caspar, who has been perched in a tree, falls dead. The bullet which Max had fired was the seventh, Samiel's. Samiel had intended it for Agathe; but she was beyond his power, and so he had claimed Caspar as forfeit. General consternation ensues. Agathe is revived. Max confesses that he has used magic bullets. The Prince orders him to be banished; but a kindly and wise old hermit appears and intercedes for him. Max is pardoned and told that after a trial year of service as a forester, he may marry Agathe. There is general rejoicing and thanks to God for the defeat of the forces of evil.

Der Freischütz: the Music

The music that von Weber created for this highly imaginative libretto cloaks it with vividness and credibility. The vocal writing, particularly in the choruses, is distinctly folk-like in character, so that the listener readily imagines that he is hearing villagers singing actual folk songs. With one exception, a peasant's march in Act I, the melodies of *Der Freischütz* are original; it was von Weber's study of folk music that enabled him successfully to simulate its style. There is no better proof of the inherently folk-like nature of several of the choruses of this opera than the fact that they immediately became very popular and were even sung on the streets by students. So well known are they in Germany today that they may be said actually to have become folk music; and some have found their way, with new texts, into English and American hymnals.

The most striking feature of *Der Freischütz* is the manner in which the orchestra is employed. Von Weber was one of the first operatic composers to utilize fully the dramatic potentialities of many of the orchestral timbres. He himself stated in a letter to a young musician that "the composer must bring out the essential character of his work by means of tone-colors." [3] Colorful use is made of the horns in the numerous scenes dealing with life in the forest. The low tones of the clarinet, coupled with tremolando and pizzicato effects in the lower strings, are used to represent Samiel and the forces of evil. The most original use of the orchestra is to be found in the Wolf's Glen scene. The astonishingly realistic orchestral effects introduced by von Weber in this gruesome episode have become well known through widespread imitation, but for their time they were quite revolutionary. It must be borne in mind that *Der Freischütz* was completed in 1820, and that it antedated Beethoven's Ninth Symphony by three years. In no previous opera had the orchestra played so important a part in the action of the play, and von Weber's vivid demonstration of its dramatic potentialities was an important influence in the development of the orchestral technique of composers such as Hector Berlioz and Richard Wagner.

OVERTURE TO "DER FREISCHÜTZ"

The well-known overture to *Der Freischütz,* a musical synthesis of the drama, is based almost entirely on thematic material heard in it. Using the sonata form, von Weber portrays in the overture the scene of the action and the conflict of the opposing forces of good and evil. The influence of the dramatic plan of the Beethoven overtures is obvious. In his capacity as opera conductor, von Weber had broken many lances for Beethoven's *Fidelio.*

After a portentous introduction, the use of horns indicates that the action takes place in the forest:

[3] Julius Kapp, *Carl Maria von Weber* (Berlin, 1922), page 226.

Ex. 1

Tremolos in the strings, the ominous low notes of the clarinet, and the dull thuds of the kettledrums and double basses, pizzicato, are associated in the opera with the Evil One, Samiel. The episode is an outstanding example of von Weber's coloristic use of the orchestra:

Ex. 2

The tempo now becomes fast, and the clarinets, over an agitated accompaniment in the strings, give out another theme associated with the forces of evil that are enveloping Max:

Ex. 3

A tempestuous outburst of the orchestra is drawn from the music accompanying the violent storm that terminates the scene in the Wolf's Glen (Act II):

Ex. 4

The transition to the second group is accompanied by a moving clarinet solo, an instrumental version of Max's cry of despair:

Ex. 5

The second group begins with the celebrated melody that is identified with Max's redeemer, Agathe:

Ex. 6

The development, a dramatic working out of Examples 3 and 4, is brought to a hushed end by Example 6. Von Weber, always willing to forsake convention for dramatic expediency, does not repeat the exposition literally. The first group, representing the forces of evil, is heard again, but instead of repeating the second group, von Weber first interposes a violent climax in which the Samiel thuds (Example 2) reappear. Three tense pauses are then followed by the repetition of Example 6 in the bright key of C major. The forces of good have been victorious. The close of the overture is drawn from the jubilant finale of the opera.

Suggested Readings

Adequate treatments of von Weber in English are limited to Philipp Spitta's article in Grove's *Dictionary of Music and Musicians* (New York, 1927), and Lucy and Richard Stebbins, *Enchanted Wanderer, the Life of Carl Maria von Weber* (New York, 1940). The latter work contains a splendid bibliography. For more extensive information, the life of von Weber by his son Max Maria, *Carl Maria von Weber, Ein Lebensbild* (Leipzig, 1866), should be consulted. A detailed study of *Der Freischütz* appears in Ernest Newman's *Stories of the Great Operas,* Vol. II (Garden City, New York, n. d.). Informative essays on the three frequently played overtures are included in *Philip Hale's Boston Symphony Programme Notes,* edited by John N. Burk (Garden City, New York, 1935). The literary aspects of von Weber's activity may be found in the *Sämtliche Schriften von Carl Maria v. Weber* (Leipzig, 1908).

Chapter XVIII

FELIX MENDELSSOHN

THE REPUTATION that Felix Mendelssohn enjoys today rests on a few works, imperishable masterpieces that could not have been written by any other composer. The nature of Mendelssohn's compositions, combined with his own personal charm and refinement, caused him to be one of the most popular musicians of his day, and made him the object of almost universal praise and adulation. That this uncritical excess of enthusiasm should be followed by a wave of depreciation was to be expected. Today, however, the status of Mendelssohn has attained a fair degree of equilibrium, and the unique, even if circumscribed, nature of his talents is generally conceded.

Felix Mendelssohn, born in Hamburg on February 3, 1809, was the son of a wealthy banker and the grandson of a celebrated philosopher. The family moved to Berlin when he was three years old, and he grew up there in an atmosphere of culture and refinement. His education, in which music was not given undue emphasis, was entrusted to numerous private tutors. He appeared as pianist in his tenth year, and two years later he commenced active composition under the tutelage of Carl Zelter. All his youthful works were performed before the gatherings of distinguished men and women who frequented the Mendelssohn household. One of his most celebrated compositions, the overture to Shakespeare's *A Midsummer Night's Dream,* was written in 1826, when he was only seventeen years old. In 1829 Mendelssohn played a large part in awakening interest in the music of Bach by reviving and directing his *St. Matthew Passion,* in all probability the first performance of the work since the death of its composer in 1750. He visited England in the same year, and at his appearances as a pianist, as organist, and as conductor of his own works he laid the foundation for his great popularity in that country. A visit to Scotland led him to compose the *Scotch* Symphony and the overture *Fingal's Cave.* The trip to England was followed by extensive travel on the Continent.

His first important post was that of music director of the Rhine town of Düsseldorf; but after two years he resigned to become conductor of the famous Gewandhaus Orchestra at Leipzig. In 1843 he added to his duties the post of director of the newly established Leipzig Conservatory. Despite all his official obligations, the round of receptions, and his prolific activity in composition, he managed to find time to participate in the affairs of the school. In 1846 he completed his great oratorio *Elijah,* which had its first performance in Birmingham, England, in the same year. Mendelssohn himself conducted, and so great was his popularity there that four choruses and four arias were encored. But the strain of countless public appearances and his many official obligations had undermined his health. The sudden death of his beloved sister Fanny in 1847 was the final blow, and he himself passed away in November of the same year at the age of thirty-eight.

During his short but active career Mendelssohn had enriched the musical life of Europe in many ways other than through his own compositions. His revival of the *St. Matthew Passion* of Bach was not his only act in that then neglected composer's behalf: as an organist he played Bach's music frequently; as a conductor he presented many of the cantatas. Handel oratorios often appeared on his programs. Mendelssohn was also responsible for many performances of the formidable Ninth Symphony of Beethoven. Beethoven's Fourth and Fifth Piano Concertos, as well as Mozart's Concerto in D Minor, were often played by him when he appeared as piano soloist with orchestra. It was Mendelssohn who conducted the first performance of the Schubert Symphony in C Major after Schumann had discovered the music in Vienna; and the first two of Schumann's four symphonies had their premières under his direction.

The atmosphere in which Mendelssohn had been brought up, the contacts which the wealth and social positon of his family permitted him to make, and his wide travels all helped to make him a cultured, polished gentleman capable of moving in the highest levels of society with ease. He was, for example, a favorite of Queen Victoria and

Prince Albert. He possessed more than the usual number of accomplishments, for, in addition to his musical talents, he was a fluent writer of letters, a gifted painter of water colors, and an energetic sportsman. A brilliant conversationalist, he was endowed with much personal charm and was always the center of any gathering.

Mendelssohn's Style

While these personal traits may have made Mendelssohn a thoroughly desirable participant in a soirée, they also left an indelible stamp on his music, which is equally polished, equally refined, and correct almost to a fault. The music of Mendelssohn, like the voice of its creator in the drawing room, is always suave, gracious, and well-mannered. It never becomes intense or boisterous, and anything that might offend the more fastidious is absent from it.

Mendelssohn was the most conservative of the romantic composers. He adhered to classical forms, and all of his works exhibit a perfection of formal outline that puts them almost in a class with those of Mozart. But the listener often feels that this formal perfection has been achieved a bit too self-consciously. Mendelssohn's melodies, which he created with facility, seldom strike a note of intensity or pathos. Many are somewhat saccharine, and possess an almost cloying sentimentality. Rhythmic and harmonic monotony is often found in his works, particularly in the highly characteristic shorter piano pieces, the *Songs Without Words;* yet their charm cannot be denied.

Only a small fraction of Mendelssohn's prodigiously long list of compositions retains any permanence in the modern repertory. Pianists have always enjoyed playing the lyrical short pieces, the *Songs Without Words,* though they may have been deluded by the spurious titles that have become attached to them. While lacking the popularity of the more frequently performed *Rondo Capriccioso,* Opus 14, the seventeen *Variations sérieuses,* Opus 54, are probably Mendelssohn's finest work for the piano.

The larger works for orchestra include two colorful symphonies, the Third in A Minor (*Scotch*) and the Fourth in A Major (*Italian*). Both of these works are classical in form though romantic in color and spirit. Neither has any program other than the adjectival title. In addition to the music for Shakespeare's play, *A Midsummer Night's*

FELIX MENDELSSOHN

Dream, there is an overture, *Fingal's Cave.* The Concerto for Violin in E Minor, one of the great staples in the form, has two interesting deviations from the classical tradition of the concerto: the initial exposition for orchestra alone is eliminated; and the work begins almost immediately with the violin solo. And the single cadenza, in the first movement, is not left to the performer to improvise but is written out for him by the composer.

Public appreciation of the fine oratorio *Elijah* has been slowly waning and complete performances of this dramatic work are no longer common. Several excerpts from it, however, are given frequently in churches, despite the fact that it was originally designed for presentation in the concert hall.

The most praiseworthy features of Mendelssohn's art are the skilfulness of his orchestration and delicacy of his scherzos. Mendelssohn handled the orchestra in a thoroughly original manner and drew from it tonal effects that were truly romantic. In his symphonic works he aimed more for clarity and contrast than sonority or brilliance. The fairy-like quality of a work such as the overture to *A Midsummer Night's Dream* remains unrivaled; the colorful scoring of the *Fingal's Cave* overture even elicited praise from Wagner.

The Mendelssohn scherzos are wholly unlike those of any other composer. They are light-footed, elfin, playfully humorous pieces. Whether written for piano, string quartet, or orchestra, they possess a transparency of texture and a lucidity of statement in which Mendelssohn has never been surpassed.

The Concert Overture

The overtures *A Midsummer Night's Dream* and *Fingal's Cave* are not overtures in the true sense at all, for neither was conceived as a preliminary to a drama. The former work was designed for the concert hall and was not linked to Shakespeare's play until seventeen years later. In his use of the term overture Mendelssohn is responsible for a new designation—*concert overture.* Additional confusion has been created by the practice of calling fantasias on popular melodies overtures—for example, Brahms' overture, *The Academic Festival,* Tchaikovsky's overture, *1812,* Rimsky-Korsakoff's overture, *The Russian Easter.*

MUSIC FOR SHAKESPEARE'S "A MIDSUMMER NIGHT'S DREAM"

As has been previously stated, the overture to Shakespeare's *A Mid-summer Night's Dream* was composed in 1826. In 1843 King Frederick William of Prussia commissioned Mendelssohn to write incidental music for the play. Of the twelve numbers which were composed for this purpose, two are played on concert programs in conjunction with the overture—the *Nocturne* and the *Scherzo*.

Of the content of the overture, Mendelssohn himself has written:[1] "It follows the play closely, however, so that it may perhaps be very proper to indicate the outstanding situations of the drama in order that the audience may have Shakespeare in mind or form an idea of the piece. I think it should be enough to point out that the fairy rulers, Oberon and Titania, appear throughout the play with all their people, now here, now there; and thereafterwards come in, first a Duke Theseus of Athens, who goes hunting in the forest with his bride; then two pairs of lovers, who lose and find one another again; then a troop of rude clumsy journeymen, playing their boorish jokes; and at last the elves again, making fun of everyone—these are the elements from which the play is put together. At the end, after everything has been satisfactorily settled and the principal players have joyfully left the stage, the elves follow them, bless the house and disappear with the dawn. So the play ends and my overture too."

The overture, which is in sonata form, begins with four delicate wood-wind chords of magical effectiveness:

Ex. 1

These are followed by a nimble pianissimo passage for violins divided into three, later four, parts. The mischievous nature of this episode identifies it with the elves:

[1] *The Musical Quarterly,* April, 1933, page 184, quoted by Georg Kinsky from V. Hase, *Breitkopf und Härtel: Gedenkschrift und Arbeitsbericht II* (Leipzig, 1919).

Ex. 2

It is rudely interrupted by the fortissimo entrance of the full orchestra with this vigorous tune:

Ex. 3

In the course of a forte statement of Example 2, the bray of the "translated" Bottom is portrayed by the tuba, which takes the place of the now obsolete ophicleide for which Mendelssohn scored:

Ex. 4

The second group commences with a theme associated with the young lovers, Lysander and Hermia, and given out by the clarinet:

Ex. 5

This is immediately followed by another theme of the same type, which, according to Adolph Marx, a friend of the composer, depicts the wanderings of the lovers:

Ex. 6

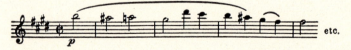

A jovial episode that follows is later employed for the "bergomask" dance, which is performed after the presentation of the interlude by "the hard-handed men, that work in Athens here" (Act V):

Ex. 7

The call of hunting horns brings the exposition to a close.

The development, based almost entirely on Example 2, is a master-piece of orchestral coloring. As the strings continually toy with the theme, all manner of delicate figures are tossed off by the wood winds. A series of loud blares from the horns reminds us that the lovers are lost in the forest. The transition to the recapitulation is effected by the chords which were heard at the outset (Example 1). The coda commences with Example 2, but after a few wood-wind chords gives way to this beautiful transformation of Example 3, gently played at a slower tempo by the violins over sustained wood-wind chords:

Ex. 8

The melody of Example 8 appears at the very end of the incidental music for the drama, where it is played by the orchestra as Oberon says:

> With this field-dew consecrate,
> Every fairy take his gate;
> And each several chamber bless,
> Through this palace, with sweet peace:
> Ever shall in safety rest,
> And the owner of it blest.

The work closes with an even more delicate version of the wood-wind chords with which it opened. Mendelssohn's overture ranks as one of the finest musical interpretations of Shakespeare among the large num-ber of works inspired by that master's plays.

The celebrated *Scherzo*, entr'acte between Acts I and II, is an *Allegro vivace* in sonata form. Wood winds give out the weightless first theme in the elfin staccato so characteristic of Mendelssohn:

Ex. 9

The second group begins with a playful subject assigned to all the strings except the double basses, and accompanied by crisp chords in the wood winds:

Ex. 10

The development devotes itself to delicate manipulation of Example 9. The coda contains a celebrated solo for the flute. The entire movement is a striking example of the delicacy with which Mendelssohn could write for orchestra. Music from the *Scherzo* appears in the course of the famous dialogue between Puck and the fairy with which Act II begins.

The *Nocturne* serves as an entr'acte between Acts III and IV. The forest and the two pairs of lovers who lie asleep in it are portrayed by a beautiful horn solo, whose warm lyricism recalls the style of many of the *Songs Without Words:*

Ex. 11

The festive *Wedding March,* played after Act IV, is one of the least typical and at the same time, needless to say, the most frequently performed of all of Mendelssohn's compositions.

Suggested Readings

Sir George Grove's lengthy article in his *Dictionary of Music and Musicians* (New York, 1927) remains the most complete treatise on Mendelssohn in English. Excellent critical studies are included in Daniel Gregory Mason, *The Romantic Composers* (New York, 1906), and *The Heritage of Music,* H. P. Foss, editor (London, 1934). *Mendelssohn's Letters,* edited by G. Selden-Goth (New York, 1945), is a fine selection the value of which is enhanced by reproductions of many of the composer's drawings. Commentaries on the orchestral works appear in Donald Francis Tovey, *Essays in Musical Analysis* (London, 1935), and *Philip Hale's Boston Symphony Programme Notes,* edited by John N. Burk (Garden City, N. Y., 1935).

Chapter XIX

ROBERT SCHUMANN

ROBERT Schumann, one of the great leaders of the Romantic Movement, was born on June 8, 1810, in Zwickau, a town in Saxony about forty miles from Leipzig. His father was a bookseller and publisher, and the boy grew up in a cultured atmosphere. As a youth Schumann not only played the piano and composed but also showed decided literary propensities. An important influence on him at this time was the extravagantly romantic German writer, Jean Paul Richter. Schumann read his works with avidity and in his enthusiasm compared Richter to Bach. In 1828 Schumann commenced the study of law at Leipzig, continuing later at Heidelberg; but his interest in music outweighed all other considerations, and he finally abandoned law to make himself a piano virtuoso. Returning to Leipzig in 1830, he commenced active study under the pedagogue Friedrich Wieck.[1] Typical romantic impatience caused him to experiment with an apparatus designed to develop strength in the fingers, and thus to accelerate technical mastery. Unfortunately the device was too efficient and permanently lamed one of the fingers of his right hand.

The career of a virtuoso being closed to him, Schumann turned to composition, and for a time was the pupil of a local Kapellmeister, Heinrich Dorn. His literary tendencies remained strong, however, and in 1834, when still a young man of twenty-four, he associated himself with a group of Leipzig musicians and writers in the publication of a critical journal, the *Neue Zeitschrift für Musik*. Shortly after the magazine was founded, Schumann became its editor and contributed

[1] Wieck ran a small circulating library in Leipzig. In 1828 a boy of fifteen, whose enthusiasm for music had been awakened by hearing a Beethoven symphony, decided to become a musician himself and borrowed a manual of harmony from Wieck's library. His name was Richard Wagner.

many excellent and discerning articles to it. In his characteristically whimsical manner Schumann made the magazine an organ of expression for an imaginary league, the *Davidsbund* (the League of David, that is, the opponents of Philistinism). He also signed many of his articles with the pseudonyms *Florestan, Eusebius,* or *Raro,* each name typifying a different aspect of his own personality. *Florestan* represented to Schumann the fiery and impetuous part of his nature; *Eusebius,* the gentle and meditative; while the more logical *Raro* strove to reconcile these contrary viewpoints. These pseudonyms were used for musical as well as literary works.

For four years Schumann conducted an ardent courtship of Wieck's daughter and pupil, Clara. Wieck objected to the match because he saw in it the end of the virtuoso career that he had planned for Clara. Schumann finally took the matter before a court of law; Wieck was forced to consent, and the marriage took place in 1840. In his newly found happiness Schumann devoted himself assiduously to composition, and the first year of his marriage was characterized by the writing of a large number of songs. The Schumanns, in their mutual devotion, were an artistic couple comparable to the Brownings. In addition to Clara, an important influence on Schumann during this period at Leipzig was Felix Mendelssohn, who took a lively and sympathetic interest in Schumann's compositions.

For a short time Schumann was on the faculty of the Leipzig Conservatory; but the peculiar nature of his personality prevented his having any success as a teacher. After some years of residence in Dresden (1844-1850) he accepted an invitation to become music director of the Rhine town of Düsseldorf. Temperamentally unfitted for conducting, however, and suffering from mental disturbances, Schumann failed to meet the expectations that his fame as a composer had engendered, and after much unpleasantness, he withdrew in 1853. Shortly before leaving Düsseldorf he was visited by the twenty-year-old and as yet unknown Johannes Brahms. In his enthusiasm for Brahms' compositions, Schumann wrote a prophetic essay entitled *"Neue Bahnen"* (New Paths) for the *Neue Zeitschrift für Musik.* This article, Schumann's last, created much interest. The manner in which his prophecy was fulfilled testifies to Schumann's acumen as a critic.

Schumann's mental aberrations now became more frequent, and in

ROBERT SCHUMANN

1854 he attempted suicide by throwing himself into the Rhine. It was necessary to confine him in an asylum until his death in 1856. His wife, who survived him by forty years, returned to the concert stage. Despite the responsibilities of caring for a large family, she won for herself a reputation as a great artist and interpreter, particularly of her husband's works. Schumann's widow continued her husband's friendship with Brahms and his interest in Brahms' compositions.

Unlike so many of his contemporaries, Schumann was a shy, retiring individual who had great difficulty in expressing himself by means of the spoken word. He was phlegmatic only superficially, however. His literary works are animated and penetrating, and are often enlivened by apt wit. Most of the composers of his generation were critically appraised by Schumann in the *Neue Zeitschrift* and many of his evaluations of their music have stood the test of time.

Characteristics of Schumann's Music

Any evaluation of Schumann's music must be made with the awareness that his training was pianistic and that his genius found its greatest freedom of expression when writing for that instrument All of his compositions up to his Opus 23 are for the piano. And it should also be borne in mind that Schumann's faculties as a creative artist declined as he grew older. With few exceptions most of his finest and most representative compositions were the products of his earlier years. One of his greatest compositions for piano solo, for example, the *Fantasie,* Opus 17, was written in 1836, when Schumann was 26 years old.

Schumann's unique gifts are observed at their best in his shorter works; the larger compositions often exhibit formal deficiencies that may be attributed in the main to Schumann's zest and exuberance in the handling of his material. But, as many critics have pointed out, a mastery of the larger musical designs comparable to that of Beethoven was not achieved by most of the romantic composers.

Rhythmic novelty, particularly syncopation and cross-accents, lends an element of freshness to Schumann's music. Melodic lines are for the most part lyrical, be the medium instrumental or vocal, and invariably deeply felt. The texture of his works is full and rich, occasionally to the point of heaviness. The best characterization of Schumann's music was given by the composer himself when he labeled his Piano Sonata in F Sharp Minor, Opus 11, "by *Florestan* and *Eusebius*," for these two fictitious characters with whom Schumann identified himself so strongly embody his two most typical stylistic traits—impetuosity and animation on the one hand and warm lyricism and fanciful reverie on the other.

Schumann created no intrinsically new forms. Nor can it be said that his works had a strong influence on any composer other than Brahms. Many of his works bear titles; but the implications of these indications are more fanciful than specific and in most instances they are, to quote Schumann:[2] "nothing more than delicate directions for performance and understanding" added to the music after it had been created and designed to indicate to both player and listener the composer's poetic intent.

Schumann's activity as a composer may be divided into several phases. His first important composition, a work for piano, was written in 1830, and until 1840, the year of his marriage, he confined himself entirely to this instrument. The year 1840 has been called the "song year," the period having been devoted to the creation of songs. In similar fashion, the year 1841 was devoted to the composition of orchestral works, and the following year to chamber music. Later works of importance were the Second, Third, and Fourth Symphonies, the last a reinstrumentation of a product of the "symphony year," the concerto for piano and the concerto for violoncello. Schumann also made settings of several scenes from Goethe's *Faust,* and of Byron's poem *Manfred.* The overture to the latter ranks as one of his best orchestral works. An opera, *Genoveva,* proved unsuccessful.

Piano Music

Schumann's piano music forms an important part of the repertory of the modern recitalist. In addition to three sonatas and a splendid set of variations entitled *Symphonic Études,* there are numerous sets of characteristically romantic shorter pieces appearing under group superscriptions such as *Papillons (Butterflies), Novelletten (Romantic Tales), Phantasiestücke (Phantasy Pieces), Nachtstücke (Nocturnes), Kinderscenen (Scenes from Childhood), Album für die Jugend (Album for the Young),* and the ever-popular *Carnaval.* The last-men-

[2] *Robert Schumanns' Briefe,* edited by F. G. Jansen (Leipzig, 1886), page 147.

tioned work, one of the most frequently played of Schumann's piano compositions, may be analyzed in some detail.

"CARNAVAL"

Schumann entitles this work, his Opus 9, composed in 1834-1835, *Carnaval. Scènes mignonnes composées pour le pianoforte sur quatre notes* (Little scenes composed for the piano, based on four notes). As he explained in a letter, the four notes represent the name of the town Asch from which an earlier love, Ernestine von Fricken, had come. The four letters also happen to be the only musical letters in Schumann's name. In the German language they represent four tones: *H* in German corresponds to our B-natural, *As* to our A-flat, while the pronunciation of the letter *S* is the same as *Es* denoting our E-flat. Of the various combinations that are possible, Schumann employs:

AS C H—A-flat, C, B

and

A S C H—A, E-flat, C, B

Schumann was fond of using devices of this sort as a basis for musical works. His first important composition is a series of variations on a family name ABEGG, while *The Album for the Young* contains a *Greeting to GADE,* a prominent contemporary.[3]

The *Carnaval* describes a masked ball in a kaleidoscopic series of twenty pieces, most of which are based on a combination of notes derived from ASCH. The pieces bear descriptive titles that, although superimposed after the work was completed, serve as excellent clues to their subject matter. The first number of the set, *Préambule,* is longer than most of the others and functions as an overture. It contains no reference to the musical letters. Number 2, *Pierrot,* and Number 3, *Arlequin,* describe individuals in costumes associated with the stereotyped figures of the Italian *Commedia dell' Arte.* Number

[3] For a detailed account of music based on letters of the alphabet see Hans David, "Themes From Words and Names" in *A Birthday Offering to Carl Engel,* edited by Gustave Reese (New York, 1943).

4, *Valse noble,* is one of Schumann's rare pieces in dance style. Number 5, *Eusebius,* and Number 6, *Florestan,* constitute a revealing pair of self-portraits. Number 7, *Coquette,* and Number 8, *Réplique* (Reply), are another musical pair. At this point in the work there appear some short cryptic figures in the bass register, the three *Sphinxes.* These brief quotations of the generating musical letters are usually omitted in performance. Number 9, *Papillons* (Butterflies), employs the same title that Schumann had used for an earlier set of pieces, the twelve *Papillons,* Opus 2; but it has no other connection with them. Number 10, *Lettres dansantes* (Dancing Letters), is a fast and delicate waltz based on ASCH and SCHA. The *Chiarina* of Number 11 is none other than the Clara Wieck whom Schumann later married. (*Chiarina* is the Italian equivalent of the German *Clärchen.*) Number 12, *Chopin,* describes the Polish composer, whom Schumann so admired, by reproducing the style of one of his nocturnes. The young lady of the town of Asch, the Ernestine von Fricken of whom Schumann had once been enamored, is the subject of Number 13 under the name *Estrella.* Schumann himself describes Number 14, *Reconnaissance,* as a "recognition scene." Number 15, *Pantalon et Colombine,* describes more clowns of the variety already encountered in Numbers 2 and 3. Number 16, *Valse allemande* (German Waltz), is interrupted by a brilliant *Intermezzo* bearing the name of the violinist Paganini, the demoniacal performer who had created such a sensation in Europe and whose playing had influenced many composers. Number 17, *Aveu* (Confession), Schumann describes as "an avowal of love," and Number 18, *Promenade,* as "a stroll such as one takes with one's lady at a German ball." The brief *Pause,* Number 19, quotes from the opening *Préambule* and leads directly into the final *Marche des Davidsbündler contre les Philistins* (March of the Members of the League of David against the Philistines), an animated account of the triumph of the romantic spirit over its reactionary enemies. The *Davidsbund* is, of course, the fanciful league that Schumann created to combat Philistinism in art. To ridicule the anti-progressive Philistines, Schumann introduces an old and well-known German tune *Der Grossvater Tanz* (The Grandfather Dance), a melody which he had used before in his *Papillons.* The march, in addition to manipulating the musical letters, contains many allusions to the *Préambule* with which the work opened.

The colorful series of pieces which comprise the *Carnaval* afford an excellent demonstration of romantic writing for the piano. The work is in essence a set of variations on a whimsically derived theme treated with singular imaginativeness in a way that is often more apparent to the eye than to the ear. A few examples will show how the musical letters give rise to distinctive melodic patterns:

Ex. 1: No. 3—*Arlequin* (A-S-C-H)

Ex. 2: No. 11—*Chiarina* (AS-C-H)

Ex. 3: No. 13—*Estrella* (AS-C-H)

Ex. 4: No. 20—*Marche des Davidsbündler contre les Philistins* (AS-C-H)

But despite the attempt to construct the work on the musical implications of a few letters of the alphabet, the entire composition remains a loose series of mood delineations. Schumann recognized the weakness and the virtue of the *Carnaval* when in writing to his friend and fellow composer Moscheles he said of it: "As a whole it is entirely lacking in artistic value; the manifold and diverse states of the soul are all that interest me." [4] The first public performance of *Carnaval*

[4] *Robert Schumanns' Briefe*, edited by F. G. Jansen (Leipzig, 1886), page 87.

was given by Franz Liszt, who played ten numbers from the work at his concert in Leipzig on March 30, 1840.

Songs

As a writer of songs Schumann is the direct successor to his greatly admired Schubert. Like Schubert, Schumann composed his songs with amazing spontaneity; about 150 songs were written in 1840, "the song year." Many of these songs were inspired by Clara. Schumann's literary sensitivity is shown by his choice of poems, notably those by Eichendorff and Heine. The character of the songs ranges from the simple, warm lyricism of *Der Nussbaum* (*The Walnut Tree*) to the animated *Die Beiden Grenadiere* (*The Two Grenadiers*) with its typically romantic introduction of the *Marseillaise*. Many of the songs possess significant instrumental postludes.

PIANO CONCERTO IN A MINOR

Schumann's Piano Concerto in A Minor, Opus 54, completed in 1845, is the direct successor to the piano concertos of Beethoven. The solo part is not written in a virtuoso style and lacks the brilliancy demanded of concertos by the prevailing taste of the time. The work, for example, possesses only one cadenza, written by Schumann himself. This cadenza does not afford the customary opportunity for the display of technical facility, but is rather a poetic interlude for the solo instrument. Schumann abandoned the double exposition formerly employed for the concerto, and, as in the Mendelssohn Violin Concerto, the soloist shares with the orchestra the exposition of the thematic material. The contrast of impetuous and lyrical moods in this work again shows the hands of its joint authors, *Florestan* and *Eusebius*

The first movement of the concerto, an *Allegro affettuoso* (lively, with feeling), although in sonata form, is improvisational in style. In its original version it had been a *Phantasie* for piano and orchestra which Schumann composed in 1841. Two movements were added to it four years later and the whole entitled *Concerto*. It begins with a brief prefatory gesture on the part of the piano, after which the woodwind instruments give out the beautiful first theme:

Ex. 5

The second group commences not with a new theme, but with a subject that is essentially another version of Example 5:

Ex. 6

The long development begins with an idyllic *Andante espressivo* in which the piano presents this version of the principal theme:

Ex. 7

Further elaboration leads to the recapitulation, which is largely a repetition of the exposition and ends with the cadenza. In the lively coda the principal theme appears in a march-like form:

Ex. 8

The second movement, which Schumann calls an *Intermezzo,* is written in the style of a *romanza* [5] and is in three-part form. The

[5] See p. 170.

manner in which Schumann unites piano and orchestra as strands in a common texture is seen to best advantage in this movement. The opening, for example, consists of a dialogue between the piano and the strings:

Ex. 9

The middle section is based on an expansive song-like theme played by the cellos:

Ex. 10

The Intermezzo proceeds without pause into the last movement, but not before the first movement has been furtively recalled by the wood winds:

Ex. 11

The last movement, an *Allegro vivace* in sonata form, is an excellent example of the rhythmic originality found so often in Schumann's music. The buoyant first theme is given out by the piano:

Ex. 12

The rhythmic complexity of the theme which appears at the beginning of the second group renders it especially attractive:

Ex. 13

The energetic development is followed by a somewhat curtailed recapitulation. The coda, which is quite long and discursive, contains some beautiful passage-work for the piano.

Orchestral Music

Schumann composed four symphonies, which, although rich in content, suffer from the composer's inability to handle the larger forms with ease. The best movements of these works are the shorter ones in slow tempi, in which Schumann's essentially lyrical style appears at its best. Schumann was one of the few great composers who did not have an adequate grasp of the art of orchestration. The scoring of his symphonies tends to be thick and monotonous, more pianistic than orchestral. The wealth of beautiful music in these works, however, atones for their mechanical defects.

Chamber Music

Schumann's "chamber music year" was 1842, during which he wrote his most important compositons in this category: the three string quartets, Opus 41, and the celebrated Quintet in E-flat Major for piano and strings, Opus 44. The latter work was the first combination of these ostensibly incompatible instrumental groups. It has justifiably won a place for itself as one of the world's most popular chamber-music compositions.

Suggested Readings

The standard biography is Frederick Niecks, *Robert Schumann* (New York, 1925). The article on Schumann in Grove's *Dictionary of Music and Musicians* (New York, 1928) was written by Philipp Spitta. Although given to overpraise of Schumann's music, it contains much accurate information about the composer's life. A good selection from Schumann's writings appears in *On Music and Musicians,* translated by Paul Rosenfeld (New York, 1946). His piano music is treated in detail in Ernest Hutcheson, *The Literature of the Piano* (New York, 1948), the chamber music in *Cobbett's Cyclopedic Survey of Chamber Music* (London, 1929), and the orchestral works in *Philip Hale's Boston Symphony Programme Notes,* edited by John N. Burk (Garden City, New York, 1935).

Chapter XX

FRÉDÉRIC CHOPIN

FRÉDÉRIC Chopin belongs with the small number of composers who have confined themselves exclusively to one medium of musical expression. With the exception of a few undistinguished pieces, all of Chopin's music was written for the piano. The mechanical improvement that the piano had undergone in the early part of the nineteenth century had greatly increased its potentialities, and these were effectively revealed in Chopin's compositions.

Chopin was a Pole. He was born not far from Warsaw on February 22, 1810, and was brought up in that city, receiving a somewhat limited general education. His musical talents manifested themselves when he was quite young, and when he was eight years old he appeared publicly as a pianist. His piano instructor was a local teacher, Adalbert Zwyny, who, when the boy had reached his twelfth birthday, declared he had nothing more to teach him. Studies in composition were undertaken under the guidance of the capable Joseph Elsner. Chopin's Opus 1 was published when he was fifteen years old. It is important to note that Chopin as a boy came in close contact with the folk music of his native country. In 1830 he left Warsaw on a concert tour, in the course of which he appeared in the principal German cities. His destination was Paris, and it was here that he made his home for the rest of his short life.

His reception in Paris was an enthusiastic one, and he quickly became an idol of the salons as well as a teacher whose services were much in demand. He was on friendly terms with many of his fellow-artists in Paris, notably Franz Liszt, with whom he appeared at a concert given for the benefit of Hector Berlioz' fiancée, Henrietta Smithson. The number of his public appearances was, however, quite small. As opposed to the prevailingly exhibitionistic tendencies of the day, his pianistic style was of an intimate nature, successful only in a small hall. From 1837 to 1847 he was intimate with the eccentric French writer of romantic novels, George Sand (Mme. Amandine Dudevant). His tragic life came to a premature end when he finally succumbed to the ravages of tuberculosis in 1849.

Chopin and the Piano

Chopin made many important innovations in the art of writing for the piano. Many of these had their origin in the attempt to overcome the fundamental limitation of the instrument—its inability to produce sustained tones. The usual solution of this problem consists of some repetitive figure in which the tones of a chord are sounded in quick succession and thus give rise to a unified harmonic impression, much as the quickly repeated images of the motion picture merge into a unified optical sensation. In the discussion of the F minor Sonata of Beethoven (page 185) the accompanying figures of Examples 3 and 4 demonstrate the manner in which chords may be sustained by repetition of their elements. Chopin's method, however, was to attenuate these chords over a much wider span, producing a figure of greater clarity and also of greater rhythmic interest. The following illustration, from the Ballade in F minor, Opus 52, is typical of Chopin's chord spacing:

Ex. 1

None of the chords written in this fashion would possess any effectiveness whatsoever if the piano did not have a "damper" pedal, the one at the extreme right. When this pedal is depressed, all the dampers are lifted from the strings. Those strings that have been struck will continue to sound while many others are free to vibrate in sympathy

FRÉDÉRIC CHOPIN
(*Painting by Eugène Delacroix*)

with them. The result is that instead of a single tone, many tones are produced, the fusion of all resulting in a rich, full sonority. Intelligent use of this pedal is an indispensable factor in the artistic performance of Chopin's works.

Chopin's Style

Although Chopin's compositions bear only generic titles, they represent some of the most typical products of the romantic school. His style is essentially lyrical, based on an intimate and poetic type of melody of highly original stamp. Some of these melodies may seem somewhat sentimental and effeminate; but many others are just as vigorous and dramatic. His harmonic language is often bold and original in its treatment of dissonance, and many of the chordal progressions to be found in his works anticipate the methods of other composers, notably Wagner.[1]

Examination of the list of Chopin's works shows that he wrote almost exclusively in the shorter forms. His two sonatas (Opus 35 in B-flat minor, and Opus 58 in B minor) exhibit formal deficiencies. Each is more a series of four independent pieces than a unified work. The two concertos for piano possess the same formal defects in addition to rather inept orchestration. The consistently beautiful shorter pieces, however, are among the most highly treasured compositions in the literature of the piano.

Before passing to a detailed discussion of these forms, a few of their general characteristics may be pointed out. Two of the more outstanding of these are elegance and refinement. Chopin's sensitive nature shrank from excesses of any kind, yet his music does not lapse into the conventionalities of the equally fastidious Mendelssohn. A third feature of Chopin's art is its variety, even within the limitations of the shorter forms. Of the fifty-one mazurkas, for example, no two are alike. A fourth feature is the manner in which Chopin embellishes his melodies by embroidering them with brilliant festoons of notes containing many delicately implied dissonances. The following excerpt from the Ballade in G minor, Opus 23, is a beautiful example of these tonal sprays:

[1] See Example 3, page 264.

Ex. 2

The nineteen *Nocturnes* are Chopin's most popular pieces, since many of them are easier to play than most of his other compositions. Chopin found the designation *Nocturne* in the works of a contemporary Irish composer, John Field. The nocturne is a short piece in three-part form, pensively lyrical in style, and often tinged with a quiet melancholy. The title indicates a characteristically romantic interpretation of moods of the night.

The twenty-four *Préludes, Opus 28,* comprise a collection of short poetic pieces in a wide variety of moods and, like the similarly named pieces of each book of Bach's *Well-Tempered Clavier,* utilize each of the major and minor keys. The term prélude takes on new meaning here, for in the hands of Chopin the form loses its earlier improvisational character and becomes a brief and highly concentrated treatment of a single musical idea, the result of which is a typically romantic "mood piece." Some of Chopin's most inspired creations can be found among these terse miniatures.

The twenty-four *Études,* Opus 10 and Opus 25, are works designed ostensibly for the development of instrumental technique (*Étude*— French for "study"). But like the *Inventions* of Bach, they are more than mere mechanical exercises, and the artistic inspiration that pervades them overshadows the mechanical problems of piano playing with which they profess concern. Chopin said of them, "In writing my études I tried to put not only science but also art into them." [2] Almost all of the *Études* are three-part forms and each is constructed on only one motive, the proper execution of which constitutes the pianistic problem. Many of them are technically very difficult, and several are brilliant and showy enough to make them effective exhibition pieces for virtuoso

[2] C. Wierzynski, *The Life and Death of Chopin* (New York, 1949), page 177.

pianists.   The fire and the energy that are communicated in a fine performance of many of the *Études* are just as typical of Chopin as the
languid melancholy of the more popular *Nocturnes*.   The various
names, for example, *Black-Key, Revolutionary,* and *Butterfly,* given to
some of them, as is usually the case with epithets of this type, did not
originate with their composer.

The four *Scherzos* have nothing in common with the scherzos of
Beethoven other than triple rhythm and rapid tempo.   Nor are they
humorous pieces.   They are vigorous and forceful works, rich in emotional content.   With the exception of the first, which is in three-part
form, their formal construction follows no conventional pattern.

In using the term *Ballade* as a title for four extensive pieces, Chopin
seems to have implied that they are narratives in music.   They are
said to have been inspired by poems of the great Polish poet, Adam
Mickiewicz.   The four Ballades are extensive pieces worked out on a
large scale.   In their grandeur of conception and range of expression
they serve as an effective refutation of the common classification of
Chopin as a composer of pleasing music for the delectation of the
Parisian salons.

The influence that the music of his native country had upon Chopin
is shown most clearly by his dance music.   The *Waltzes* are idealized
versions of a German dance form; but the *Mazurkas* and the *Polonaises*
are genuinely Polish.   They typify another aspect of the romantic interest in folk life.   While still a boy, Chopin had manifested a keen
interest in the dances of the Polish peasants.

The *Mazurka* is a lively peasant dance, whose name is derived from
the Polish region in which it originated, Mazovia.   It is lively in
tempo and is in triple rhythm, usually with a strong accent on the
third beat.   In his fifty-one mazurkas Chopin has effectively caught
the mood of this dance.   While preserving its fundamental rhythmic
scheme and occasionally employing modal melodies of a folk-like nature, he has raised it to a high artistic level through originality of
melodic elaboration and by advanced harmonic treatment.   A frequently cited example of the modernity of Chopin's harmony is this
progression from the Mazurka in C-sharp minor, Opus 30, No. 4, a
far cry indeed from the simple harmonies of a peasant dance:

Ex. 3

The other Polish dance which Chopin has immortalized is the *Polonaise*. This is not a peasant dance like the mazurka, but a majestic processional dance of courtly origin. It is in well-accented triple rhythm and stately tempo. It owes its French name to the fact that a French prince, Henry, Duke of Anjou, reigned as King of Poland for thirteen months. At a great reception, which he held in Cracow in 1574, the assembled Polish nobles passed in ceremonial procession. Through Henry and his followers the stately music that accompanied this procession was brought to Paris; and, as was the case with many other dances, it eventually acquired both the French name and the French characteristics that we have already observed in the suites of Bach. Chopin in his twelve polonaises has restored the original courtly grandeur and pomp of the form. In no other works is he so intensely Polish, so ardently nationalistic.

POLONAISE IN A-FLAT MAJOR, OPUS 53

Chopin's most characteristic Polonaise is the brilliant one in A-flat Major, Opus 53, one of his most eloquent compositions. It is in three-part form. The sixteen opening measures serve as a tension-creating preliminary to the triumphant first theme:

Ex. 4

The middle section begins with a trumpet-like melody accompanied by a celebrated series of repeated bass figures, an unrelenting *ostinato* that has made this Polonaise a favorite recital piece:

Ex. 5

The return to the main section is preceded by a wistful interlude from which march rhythms are absent:

Ex. 6

The main section is repeated in an abbreviated version. After a brief coda, in which the opening theme (Ex. 4) and the ostinato of the middle section (Ex. 5) appear in close juxtaposition, the Polonaise concludes with a series of forceful chords.

Suggested Readings

The centennial in 1949 of Chopin's death resulted in the appearance of several studies on the Polish master. Among the more valuable are Casimir Wierzynski, *The Life and Death of Chopin* (New York, 1949), probably the best biography, Herbert Weinstock, *Chopin, The Man and His Music* (New York, 1949), and Arthur Hedley, *Chopin* (New York, 1949). Readers with a knowledge of harmony will find much illuminating comment in Gerald Abraham, *Chopin's Musical Style* (London, 1939). Among the older works on Chopin the following still have value: James G. Huneker, *Chopin: The Man and His Music* (New York, 1913) and William Murdoch, *Chopin, His Life* (London, 1934). Pianists of modest attainments anxious to expand their knowledge of Chopin will profit from consultation of Ernest Hutcheson, *The Literature of the Piano* (New York, 1948).

Chapter XXI

HECTOR BERLIOZ

THE LIFE and the music of the French composer Hector Berlioz represent one of the most typical manifestations of the romantic spirit. An impetuous and intense individual, Berlioz possessed a rich imagination that, coupled with an apparently inexhaustible store of energy and enthusiasm, drove him to compose a series of grandiose works, imposing in their dimensions and novel in their content. But like his German predecessor, von Weber, he composed one work that in its artistically revolutionary implications has won for him an undeniable position of importance in the development of the expressive powers of music. This work, the name of which might well be the title of a novel based on the composer's own life, is the *Symphonie fantastique (Fantastic Symphony)*. Estimates of Berlioz' stature as a composer have always ranged from enthusiastic praise to vehement condemnation. Wagner spoke of the Berlioz orchestra as a "miraculous mechanism" whose heights and depths had been explored with "a truly amazing perceptivity." [1] Debussy, on the other hand, said of him: "He is not a musician at all. He creates the illusion of music by means borrowed from literature and painting." [2] The only feature of Berlioz' work on which all of his critics seem to be in agreement is his great skill in orchestration.

Hector Berlioz, the son of a country doctor, was born in the small town of La Côte Saint-André, near Grenoble, on December 11, 1803. As a boy he showed keen interest in music; but his early musical training was confined to a few flute and guitar lessons, plus an almost negligible amount of theoretical instruction. An amateur's proficiency

[1] C. F. Glasenapp, *Wagner-Encyklopädie* (Leipzig, 1891), Vol. I, page 119.
[2] Léon Vallas, *The Theories of Claude Debussy* (London, 1929), page 38.

in the playing of the two above-mentioned instruments constituted the sum total of Berlioz' ability as an instrumental performer during his entire lifetime. When Berlioz was eighteen his father sent him off to Paris to study medicine; but the opera house proved more attractive than the dissecting room, and medical studies were eventually abandoned in favor of music. The ambitious youth set to work composing with great zeal despite his lack of technical training, and when he was twenty-one years old he ventured to present a Mass of his own composition with an orchestra of 150 players. Eventually he was enrolled as a pupil in the Paris Conservatoire, but he found formal instruction irksome. He learned instrumentation by following operatic performances from score, and so well did he come to know the repertory of the opera house that mistakes in playing or "improvements" in the score would cause this tall, red-headed individual to rise from his seat in the midst of a performance and in a loud voice question the rectitude of the proceedings.

In 1827 he fell madly in love with Henrietta Smithson, an Irish actress whose performances in the plays of Shakespeare had made her the idol of Paris. The tortures of this "interminable and inexhaustible passion" drove Berlioz to complete his masterwork, the *Fantastic Symphony,* which was first performed on December 5, 1830. In 1833 he finally married Henrietta, whose fame as an actress had, in the interim, dwindled to the vanishing point. Their marriage turned out unhappily, and after ten stormy years they separated.

Berlioz presented many concerts of his own works in Paris. But to his chagrin, no lasting public acclaim ensued, and his compositions, almost invariably calling for musical forces of gigantic dimensions, were regarded more as ephemeral novelties than as significant art works. He also held the positon of critic on the important *Journal des débats,* and the writing of *feuilletons* occupied much of his time.

But if Paris denied Berlioz the recognition for which he longed, other European cities, particularly those of Germany and Russia, gave him a full measure of acclaim. He was particularly triumphant in the concerts he directed at St. Petersburg and Moscow, and notable performances of his works were given at Weimar by Liszt. Despite all the reports sent back to Paris, however, the Parisian public failed to become enthusisatic about either Berlioz or his music. The continued

HECTOR BERLIOZ

postponement and eventual failure of his opera *Les Troyens* (*The Trojans*) was the final rebuff to his unsuccessful efforts to win recognition in his own land.   He died in 1869, a bitter and disappointed man.

No brief summary of the life of Berlioz does full justice to the hectic career of this extraordinary individual.   His unbounded imagination permeated his life as well as his compositions, and his *Mémoires* are a revealing account of the outstanding incidents of his career.   In characteristic fashion, Berlioz omitted no detail from them, and even considered it necessary to include a lurid account of the exhumation of Henrietta's corpse.   In fact, although the Parisian public did not appreciate Berlioz as a composer, it did hold a good opinion of his literary abilities.   His *feuilletons* appeared in collected form, and one series, *Les Soirées de l'orchestre* (*Evenings in the Orchestra*), ran through two editions within his lifetime.

The principal works of Berlioz are the *Fantastic Symphony;* the "dramatic" symphony *Romeo and Juliet;* the symphony *Harold in Italy;* the "dramatic legend" *The Damnation of Faust;* the two unsuccessful operas *Benvenuto Cellini* and *The Trojans;* and two gigantic choral works, a *Requiem* and a *Te Deum.*   Of these only the following may be heard today with some degree of regularity: the *Fantastic Symphony,* the *Queen Mab* scherzo from the *Romeo and Juliet* symphony, three orchestral excerpts from *The Damnation of Faust;* the overture to the opera *Benvenuto Cellini,* and the concert overture *The Roman Carnival,* originally the introduction to the opera's second act.

The importance of Berlioz is in no manner commensurate with the amount of his music heard today.   With rare exceptions, almost every contemporary composer and not a few successors were indebted to him.   His ideas and methods, even if somewhat unsuccessful in their realization at his own hands, were such as to command attention.   It was necessary, however, for composers of greater talent, such as Liszt, Wagner, and Strauss, to bring them to fruition.

Berlioz and Program Music

The avowed aim of Berlioz was to write descriptive music, that is, program music.   Inspired by the symphonies of Beethoven, he attempted to portray in his compositions not only such easily recognizable aural images as the sounds of nature but also the flow of moods and feelings. As he writes in his memoirs, "The prevailing characteristics of my music are passionate expression, intense ardor, rhythmical animation, and unexpected effects. When I say passionate expression I mean an expression intent on enforcing the inner meaning of its subject even when the feeling to be expressed is gentle and tender or even profoundly calm." But in his desire to achieve realism in the portrayal of emotional states Berlioz sacrificed formal considerations. His larger works, therefore, despite their obvious sincerity of purpose, tend to become vague and diffuse, and while moments of great beauty and effectiveness are frequent, lack of organization militates against the success of the whole. The melodic inventiveness of Berlioz was also of an inferior order unconcealable by the rhythmic novelty and striking timbres of his works. Furthermore, some of his choices of subjects for musical portrayal were questionable. One of the movements of the *Fantastic Symphony,* for instance, describes decapitation by the guillotine, and the finale of *Harold in Italy* depicts a drunken orgy of murderous brigands. But his procedures were entirely original at the time, and they served as a strong impetus for the widespread development of program music which took place during the nineteenth century.

Orchestration

Parallel with Berlioz' furtherance of the programmatic concept went an intense study of the delineative possibilities of the orchestra. His famous manual of instrumentation, originally a series of *feuilletons,* is an imaginatively written compendium in which every orchestral instrument is painstakingly discussed and its timbre and expressive potentialities clearly set forth. It was revised by Richard Strauss in 1905, and is still a basic work. Berlioz' mastery of instrumentation was universally conceded during his lifetime, and it is in this sphere that his influence has been greatest. All of his scores abound in passages in which the orchestral instruments, both as entities and as groups, are handled with the greatest originality and effectiveness. The same fertility of orchestral imagination that created the heaven-storming sonorities of the *Rakoczy March* from the *Damnation of Faust* also brought forth the delicate *Dance of the Sylphs* from the same work, as well as a masterpiece of orchestral gossamer, the *Queen Mab* Scherzo from the *Romeo and Juliet* Symphony. This scherzo may well be regarded as Berlioz' greatest triumph in instrumentation.

Musical Symbolism

The dramatic plan of the *Fantastic Symphony* and of *Harold in Italy* led Berlioz to employ musical phrases specifically associated with elements of their programs. The "beloved one" of the *Fantastic Symphony* is described throughout the work by a recurrent theme that the composer calls an *"idée fixe"* (fixed idea). The wandering pilgrim Harold is portrayed not only in terms of a distinctive melody but also by a striking tone color, that of a solo viola intended, says Berlioz, "to figure as a more or less active personage of constantly preserved individuality." Although the quasi-symbolic use of characteristic phrases with specific associations had been of frequent occurrence in opera (e.g., *Der Freischütz*), Berlioz' employment of it in symphonic music was novel. Its influence may be seen in works like the *Faust Symphony* of Liszt (1857) and in Richard Strauss' *Don Quixote* (1897), with the personification of its hero by a solo cello.

THE FANTASTIC SYMPHONY

The *Fantastic Symphony* is the composite result of Berlioz' desire to chronicle musically the experiences of an ardently romantic man of twenty-six; the strong influence upon him of Beethoven's symphonies, notably the *Pastoral;* his reaction to Goethe's *Faust* with its macabre gathering of witches on the Brocken; his reading of such contemporary works as De Quincey's *Confessions of an English Opium Eater,* in a French translation by Alfred de Musset (1828); and his feverishly intense and for a long time unreciprocated love for the actress Henrietta Smithson. Although the composer refers to her in his *Mémoirs* as "the heroine of this strange and painful drama," the common belief that the symphony was inspired by Berlioz' unrequited love for the portrayer of Shakespeare's Juliet and Ophelia cannot be conclusively substantiated. The *idée fixe* of the symphony, specifically indicated by the composer as a description of "the beloved one," was not inspired by Henrietta at all: it had been first composed by Berlioz for an unsuccessful choral work. And the opening melody of the symphony's introductory section had been part of a song written fourteen years previously when Berlioz was only twelve years old.

The program of the symphony was published in a Parisian newspaper several months before the work was performed, and a copy was given to every member of the audience at the première. Evidently Berlioz was aware that the novel content of his work was in need of some literary clarification. The first of the five versions of the program contains this statement: "Each part of this instrumental drama being merely the musical development of given situations, the author deems it indispensable to set forth the subject matter in advance. The following program should therefore be considered as the spoken text of an opera serving to introduce the musical numbers, of which it decides the character and determines the expression."[3] But when the score of the work was published sixteen years later the composer cast doubts on both the closeness of the program's connection with the music and the listener's obligation to have prior knowledge of it. Although the program still stands at the head of the printed score, it is prefaced by this admonition: "It is not absolutely necessary that the program be distributed, and only the titles of the five movements need be retained; for the symphony can itself afford (so the composer hopes) a musical interest independent of all dramatic intention."

The version of the program that appears in the score reads as follows:

Program of the Symphony

A young musician, of a sickly sensitivity and an ardent imagination, poisons himself with opium in a fit of lovesick despondency. The dose of narcotic, too weak to kill, plunges him into a heavy sleep accompanied by strange visions, in the course of which his emotions, his feelings, his memories, translate themselves in his sick brain into musical thoughts and images. The beloved one herself has become for him a melody, like a fixed idea which he finds and hears everywhere.

Part I

Reveries, Passions.

He first recalls the discomfort of the soul, the emptiness of passions, the fits of melancholy, the causeless joys which he experienced before having seen the one whom he loves; then the volcanic love which she suddenly inspired in him, his delirious anguish, his jealous rage, his returns to tenderness, his religious consolation.

[3] Julian Tiersot, "The Berlioz of the Fantastic Symphony," *The Musical Quarterly* (July 1933), page 310.

Part II

A Ball.

He finds his beloved again at a ball in the midst of the excitement of a brilliant fête.

Part III

Scene in the Fields.

One summer evening in the country, he hears two shepherds piping away in turn at their herdsman's tune. This pastoral duet, the setting of the scene, the light murmur of the trees gently stirred by the wind, some grounds for hope which he had recently imagined, all conspire to bring back to his heart an unaccustomed calm; but she appears again, he suffers anguish of heart, agitated by sorrowful presentiments: were she to deceive him... One of the shepherds takes up the simple melody, the other does not reply. The sun goes down.... Distant rumbling of thunder... Solitude... Silence...

Part IV

March to the Scaffold.

He dreams that he has killed the one he loves, that he is condemned to death, and led to the scaffold. The procession moves ahead to the tones of a march now somber and wild, now brilliant and solemn, in which the dull thud of heavy steps follows without transition upon a most clamorous uproar. In the end, the fixed idea reappears for an instant like the last thought of love interrupted by the fatal stroke.

Part V

Dream of a Witches' Sabbath.

He sees himself at a witches' sabbath in the midst of a troop of terrible shadows, of sorcerers, of monsters of all kinds reunited for his funeral. Strange noises, groans, bursts of laughter, distant cries to which other cries seem to answer. The beloved melody again reappears; but it has lost its noble and modest character; it is no more than a dance tune, ignoble, trivial and grotesque; it is she who comes to the witches' sabbath... roars of joy at her arrival.... She participates in the diabolical orgy.... Funereal tolling, burlesque parody of the *Dies irae.* Witches' dance. The witches' dance and the *Dies irae* together.

H. Berlioz

Despite the implications of the program, only the last of the five movements involves any radical departures from conventional symphonic form. The first movement *Reveries and Passions* presents no striking deviation from the formal plan of a corresponding movement in a Beethoven symphony. The *Ball* is a symphonic waltz; the *Scene in the Fields,* a pastoral with an obvious indebtedness to

Beethoven. The fourth movement, the *March to the Scaffold,* while novel in concept, is a symphonic processional piece analogous to the Funeral March of Beethoven's *Eroica* Symphony and to certain sections of his Ninth Symphony. The *Dream of a Witches' Sabbath,* a demonic dance, is, from the formal standpoint, the only truly novel movement of the five. Thus it is the subject-matter of the symphony, the passionate communication of the composer's own emotions through unrestrained and completely original exploitation of orchestral sonorities, that won for it such acclaim in its day and still maintains it as a monument of romantic art, the first great symphony to break with the classical tradition.

Only a few of the many striking orchestral effects can be enumerated here: the brilliant arpeggios and scales for two harps at the opening of the *Ball;* the dialogue between oboe and English horn and the passage for four kettledrums in the *Scene in the Fields;* the rattles and groans produced by cellos, double basses, horns and kettledrums in the *March to the Scaffold* and the startling use of percussion instruments later in the movement. The *Witches' Sabbath,* an immense catalogue of diabolic sonorities, contains what are probably the first instances of solo passages for the small E-flat clarinet, and for two tubas. At the height of the orgy, violinists and violists are directed to play their instruments percussively by rapping the strings with the backs of the bows, an orchestral effect known as *col legno*—with the wood.

The musical phrase which is associated with "the beloved one" reappears throughout the symphony; hence its designation by Berlioz as an *idée fixe.* It is important, however, to notice that the *idée fixe* undergoes transformation from movement to movement and does not appear merely as an arbitrary and invariable symbol.

In the first movement, *Reveries, Passions,* the *idée fixe* appears as:

Ex. 1

In the second movement the orchestra plays an animated waltz whose strains are interrupted by this version of the *idée fixe:*

Ex. 2

In the third movement, *Scene in the Fields,* the reappearance of "the beloved one" in the thoughts of the artist is again portrayed by the *idée fixe:*

Ex. 3

A short fragment of the *idée fixe* is heard in the fourth movement, the *March to the Scaffold,* just before the loud chord describing the fall of the knife. It is not until the last movement, the *Dream of a Witches' Sabbath,* that the *idée fixe* is radically transformed. Berlioz changes the melody to "a dance tune, ignoble, trivial and grotesque" and makes it doubly vulgar by assigning it to the E-flat clarinet, a high-pitched instrument that imparts a shrewish quality to the music:

Ex. 4

The last movement also contains one of Berlioz' most imaginative strokes, the introduction by two tubas of a melody based on the medieval chant for the dead, the *Dies irae (Day of Wrath)*, a traditional part of the Requiem Mass of the Catholic Church. In its original form the chant is:

Ex. 5

Di - es i - rae, di - es il - la,   Sol-vet   sae - clum in fa-vil - la,

Berlioz not only introduces the *Dies irae,* but later proceeds to parody it by altering its rhythm and having it played as a lively dance tune by pizzicato strings:

Ex. 6

Berlioz' use of this liturgical chant was followed by Franz Liszt in his *Totentanz (Dance of the Dead)* for piano and orchestra (1859), Camille Saint-Saëns in the symphonic poem, *Danse macabre* (1874), and by Sergei Rachmaninoff in the *Isle of the Dead* (1907) and his *Rhapsody on a Theme of Paganini,* for piano and orchestra (1934).

Suggested Readings

The long needed definitive biography and critical reappraisal of Berlioz in English appeared in 1950 (Boston). Entitled *Berlioz and the Romantic Century,* it is the richly-documented work of the cultural historian, Jacques Barzun, an astute critic of Berlioz. The exhaustive but frequently unreliable French biography, the three volume work of Adolphe Boschot, appeared with these titles: *La jeunesse d'un romantique, Hector Berlioz 1803-31* (Paris, 1906); *Un Romantique sous Louis Philippe, Hector Berlioz 1831-42* (Paris, 1908); *Le Crépuscule d'un romantique; Hector Berlioz, 1842-69* (Paris, 1913). An abridged version of this work was published as *Une Vie romantique, Hector Berlioz* (Paris, 1919), revised edition, 1939. The valuable *Memoirs of Hector Berlioz* are available in an edition enriched by the commentary of Ernest Newman (New York, 1932). A defense of Berlioz against his numerous critics and a scholarly refutation of the many misconceptions that have grown up around his art are to be found in the *Berlioz* of Tom S. Wotton (London, 1935). Details of Berlioz' contribution to orchestral technique can be read in Adam Carse, *The History of Orchestration* (London, 1925) and the same author's *The Orchestra from Beethoven to Berlioz* (Cambridge, England, 1948).

Chapter XXII

FRANZ LISZT

THE LONG and brilliant career of Franz Liszt spans one of the most glamorous periods in the history of music. He was born on October 22, 1811, at a time when Beethoven was occupied with the composition of his Seventh Symphony. The whole romantic movement unfolded itself during his lifetime, and he not only lived to see the triumph of Wagner, but survived him by three years. His playing as a boy was heard by Beethoven, and as an old man by individuals who lived well into the present century.

Liszt's birthplace was the town of Raiding, then in Hungary. His father, an employee of the same Esterhazy family that had engaged Haydn, was an amateur cellist and had often played in the Eisenstadt orchestra under Haydn's direction. When Liszt was only ten years old he was taken to Vienna by his father and placed under the tutelage of Carl Czerny, the friend and pupil of Beethoven and the composer of the dull but efficient piano studies known to every pupil today. Not long afterwards he appeared before the Viennese public as a pianist and aroused great enthusiasm. Beethoven was present at a concert given by Liszt on April 13, 1823, and is said to have rushed forward at the end of the performance and kissed the phenomenal child on the forehead. The great composer was stone-deaf at the time and must have appreciated the visual rather than the aural aspects of Liszt's playing.

Father and son now removed to Paris, where efforts to gain admittance to the Conservatoire were unsuccessful because the boy was not of French birth. With the exception of occasional concert tours, Liszt spent the next eleven years of his life in the French capital and grew up under French influences. The total amount of musical instruc-

FRANZ LISZT

tion, instrumental as well as theoretical, that he received during his entire lifetime consisted merely of his year of piano study under Czerny and some exercises in composition in Vienna and Paris. His Parisian appearances soon brought him much fame, and he became a familiar figure in the salons of the city. Here he came in contact with other artists of strongly romantic tendencies.—Hugo, de Musset, Balzac, Dumas, Heine, and Delacroix. He was also on terms of close artistic friendship with Chopin, and with Berlioz, whose ideas awakened a particularly sympathetic response. The playing of the virtuoso violinist Paganini inspired him to perfect a comparable pianistic facility. Liszt also met and fell in love with the Countess d'Agoult, a brilliant figure of the Parisian salons, who wrote extensively under the pen name Daniel Stern. In 1835 the pair removed to Switzerland, and during the five years in which they lived together, three children were born to them. The second child, Cosima, eventually became the wife of Richard Wagner.

After his separation from the Countess, Liszt commenced a series of concert tours. During the years 1840-1847 he appeared in every city of importance in Europe. Every concert was a triumphal event. So great was Liszt's fame that the passport which he carried bore the following as a description of him—"Celebritate sua sat notus" [1] ("Sufficiently known through his fame"). During his travels in Russia, he became friendly with the Princess Carolyne Sayne-Wittgenstein, a wealthy and cultured noblewoman. She fled from Russia in 1848, met Liszt in Austria, and went with him to Weimar, where Liszt, having given up his concert tours, had become music director at the court of the Grand Duke. The Princess, who was exceedingly devout, possessed a strong personality which greatly influenced Liszt's development as a composer. Intricacies of ecclesiastical law prevented their marriage.

During his thirteen years at Weimar (1848-1861) Liszt, despite poor facilities and official indifference, devoted himself wholeheartedly to the performance of contemporary operatic and symphonic music. Such were his efforts that Weimar became a Mecca for composers, and had the ruling house seen fit to support his assiduity with commensurate financial backing, the glories of the days of Goethe and Schiller would assuredly have been revived. Despite the obstacles put

[1] Peter Raabe, *Liszts Leben* (Stuttgart and Berlin, 1931), page 55.

in his path, Liszt performed valiant deeds for his fellow musicians.
Of the forty-three operas that he presented at Weimar, no less than
twenty-four were by contemporary composers, notably Berlioz and
Wagner. Of these operas the most important was Wagner's *Lohengrin,* which had its première in 1850. Many of Liszt's own orchestral
works were also given their first performances here, but he did not
lavish as much attention upon them as he did on the works of other
composers. Amidst all these labors he still found time for teaching and
for participation in the varied social activities of the court and of his
own home, the *Altenburg,* over which the Princess presided.

Of all the composers that Liszt befriended during his lifetime,
Richard Wagner stands out as the one who received the most understanding and encouragement. Liszt, who was an ardent admirer of
the latter's operas, conducted three of them at Weimar, presented
extracts from them at symphonic concerts, and transcribed excerpts
from them for piano solo. A firm believer in Wagner's genius and
its ultimate destiny, Liszt encouraged all of his efforts and even gave
him financial assistance. But as was true of so many of Liszt's bene-
factions, the relationship was rather one-sided. Although Liszt had
been of incalculable assistance to him, Wagner never conducted a single
one of Liszt's numerous orchestral works.

Discontentment with the reception of his efforts at Weimar finally
caused Liszt to resign his post in 1861. He went to Rome, where he
studied theology, and in 1865 was admitted to a monastic order. Although he took clerical garb largely to gratify the Princess, Liszt had
possessed strong religious feelings from early manhood. During his
stay in Rome he frequently played before the Pope, Pius IX. But
his clerical obligations did not exclude secular activity, and he appeared
in various European capitals as conductor of his own works and occasionally as soloist. Most of his compositions of this period were
sacred choral works. During the summers Liszt, who despite his age
possessed unusual vitality, returned to Weimar to devote himself to
the pupils who came from all over the world to receive instruction from
him. His interest in Wagner continued, and he was an honored guest
at the opening of the theater at Bayreuth in 1876. Liszt died at Bayreuth on July 31, 1886. Although he was seventy-five years old, he had
appeared publicly as a pianist only twelve days before his death.

The personality of Franz Liszt is not easy to describe. By means of selected evidence it can be proven that he was essentially a poseur possessed of a wonderful mechanical dexterity, or, with equal facility, that he was one of the world's most sincere artists. He himself seems to have been conscious of this dual personality. It is for some of his proclivities as an instrumental virtuoso that one can find the most fault with Liszt. During his concert tours he pandered to public taste in a way that seems quite objectionable today: a note of sensationalism was seldom absent from either his concert manner or the programs he presented.

But while Liszt was a master showman, he was not motivated merely by a desire for pecuniary gain. Huge as the receipts from his concerts were, he gave the greater part of them to local charities. Other worthy causes also received his help. He was a prime mover in the formation of societies for the publication of the music of Bach, Handel, and Mozart, and he gave a substantial sum of money for the erection of a Beethoven monument at Bonn. In all his relationships with other musicians he was kind and sympathetic. Busy as his life was, he found time for extensive teaching. Only talented pupils were accepted by him, and they received their instruction absolutely free. Liszt lacked many of the weaknesses usually associated with virtuosi. Fêted everywhere, received by almost every crowned head in Europe, the recipient of many honors, medals, and decorations, the most celebrated performer of his time, he was essentially a modest individual, particularly with regard to his own works, and his mode of life was unusually simple and unpretentious.

Although Liszt received little formal schooling, he was a man of wide culture whose personality was just as dominating in the salon as it was in the concert hall. He read avidly, and in addition came in contact with the best minds of his day. His wide travels also left a strong impress upon him. He never mastered the Hungarian tongue, although he took an active interest in Hungary and its music. All of his numerous prose works were written in French, and in many respects the art of Liszt stands closer to French culture than to German or Hungarian.

In discussing the musical importance of Liszt, one again finds a diversity as confusing as it is impressive. He was not only a pianist but also a writer of eight volumes of prose[2] and a large number of letters, a teacher, a conductor, and a composer of some seven hundred works.

Piano Music

Franz Liszt was the greatest pianist the world has ever known. Under his hands the sonorities and the variety of timbres to be obtained from the piano were so augmented that an entire evening's performance on the instrument could be given in a large hall. He did away with the custom of performing publicly only with orchestra, and he may thus be credited with being the originator of the piano recital. It is interesting to note that when Liszt commenced to appear as a solo performer his seeming audacity met with considerable censure, particularly from those musicians who envied his ability to fill a hall completely while saving the usual expenses for orchestra. Unfortunately, all of Liszt's accomplishments as a pianist are buried with him. The phonograph was invented only nine years before his death, and no attempt was made to record his playing on what was then but a primitive instrument. Contemporary opinions were unanimous in stating that Liszt made the piano sound like an entire orchestra.

It is nevertheless possible to obtain a fairly close approximation of Liszt's technical procedures by examining the music which he wrote for his recitals. His works abound with rapid passages in tenths as well as octaves, simultaneous use of several registers of the piano calling for great surety in leaping, adroit crossing of the hands, trills, tremolos, elaborate arpeggios, repeated notes, and brilliant ornamental cadenzas utilizing the higher octaves of the piano. Every finger of both hands is kept continually occupied. The two staves usually employed for piano writing often proved insufficient, causing Liszt to introduce a third. His playing was based largely on free play of the arms, and by introducing a higher chair than had been customary, he found it possible to apply their full weight. The achievement of mere volume, however, was not Liszt's sole aim. There are many passages in his piano works that for delicacy and sheer beauty of tone-color have never been excelled.

[2] It has been conclusively shown that many of the articles bearing Liszt's name are in reality the works of either the Countess d'Agoult or the Princess Carolyne Sayne-Wittgenstein. See Emile Haraszti, "Franz Liszt—Author Despite Himself," *The Musical Quarterly* (Oct. 1947).

Over two hundred diverse works of various composers were arranged by Liszt for piano solo. These arrangements, in which much freedom of treatment is to be found, he called *transcriptions,* a term which he was the first to employ. Many of the transcriptions were written merely to serve as vehicles for the display of Liszt's technique; they are still used by many modern virtuosi for the same purpose. An examination of the list of compositions transcribed by Liszt for piano, all of which he performed, will illustrate not only his talents as a pianist, but also his ability to obtain orchestral sonorities from the instrument. Among the works so treated are the nine symphonies of Beethoven, the *Symphonie fantastique* of Berlioz, and even so intrinsically orchestral a composition as the overture to Wagner's *Tannhäuser.* The more artistic transcriptions are those of the organ fugues of Bach and the songs of Schubert. Liszt's performances of his pianistic versions of the works of these two composers played an important part in making them known to the public.

The nature of Liszt's original compositions is such as to make generalization difficult. It is invariably necessary to bear in mind his one great weakness—deference to public taste; he was often called a "slave of the public." Some of his works are somewhat banal, while others lack the essential note of sincerity. On the other hand, not a few of his efforts are the result of a genuine artistic impulse. Although Liszt was well acquainted with the compositions of the great masters, his own works were apparently uninfluenced by them and seldom employed conventional forms. The majority are programmatic in character. The programmatic indications, however, are generally of a poetic nature, and Liszt makes no attempt at detailed treatment. The following titles used for piano works are typical: *Waldesrauschen (Forest Murmurs), Au bord d'une source (At the Spring), Après une lecture de Dante (After Reading Dante), Consolations.* The harmonic procedures of Liszt, characterized by their novel and extensive use of chromaticism, constitute one of his most original contributions to the language of music.

In the original compositions for piano one finds again a curious mixture of shallow sentimentality, empty pretense, and indulgence in virtuoso display, combined with true poetic feeling and an excellent facility in using the instrument as a means of delineating moods and situations. Many of the shorter pieces possess definite charm. The nineteen Hungarian Rhapsodies, based on Hungarian melodies, bespeak Liszt's later interest in the music of his native land.

PIANO SONATA IN B MINOR

The monumental Sonata in B minor, written in 1852-1853 and dedicated to Schumann, is Liszt's greatest original composition for the piano. It is not a sonata in the customary sense, for none of its three movements is cast in the conventional sonata form. These three movements, prefaced by a brief introduction, are welded to one another in a manner that makes the sonata one large musical unit. Liszt has labeled them *Allegro energico, Andante sostenuto, Allegro energico.* Unlike almost all of Liszt's compositions, the work has no program. Its formal construction is based on a method of thematic development which Liszt himself called "transformation of themes," that is, the use of one or more themes as the basis for an entire composition, no matter how many movements it may possess. In these movements the themes appear in a variety of transformations. The technical procedure, therefore, is rooted in the older variation form, now utilized in a more poetic, if less organized, manner. While Liszt's use of this formal device had been anticipated by Berlioz in the *idée fixe* of his *Symphonie fantastique,* he employed it so frequently and so imaginatively in all his larger works that it has been extensively adopted in some form or other by many later composers.

The sonata, whose uninterrupted playing time is approximately thirty-three minutes, is based on four themes. The first theme, a descending scale figure, appears in the slow introduction:

Ex. 1

The first movement proper commences with the second theme, a forceful leaping figure given out in octaves:

Ex. 2

This is followed at once by the third theme, an emphatic repeated-note motive:

Ex. 3

After a long development of these three motives, the fourth theme, a somewhat pompous *Grandioso,* makes its appearance:

Ex. 4

Of the numerous transformations that all of these four themes undergo in the course of the three movements, the most important is the following variant of Example 3, transformed into a treble melody and augmented:

Ex. 5

Works for Piano and Orchestra

Of the nine works for piano and orchestra, the Concerto No. 1, in E-flat Major, is the most important. Its first performance at a Court concert in Weimar (February, 1855) must have been a thrilling occasion, for the composer himself was the soloist, and Berlioz was the conductor. Although the piano part is written in Liszt's best virtuoso style, the orchestra is not used merely as a background but is assigned a role equal in importance to that of the solo instrument. The form of this work, which differs materially from the conventional design of the concerto, is analogous to that of the B minor Sonata. The concerto is a long single movement, divisible, however, into four sections in contrasted tempi. Of the many transformations to which the four themes of the work are subjected, one of the most striking is the change made in a theme which appears at the opening of the slow second section as:

Ex. 6

At the beginning of the last section, an *Allegro marziale,* this becomes a vigorous march:

Ex. 7

The scherzo-like third section contains the deservedly famous piquant solo for the triangle:

The *Totentanz* (*Dance of the Dead*) for piano and orchestra, one of Liszt's finest creations, seldom attains the recognition of public performance because of the great virtuosity demanded of the soloist. Inspired by a celebrated fourteenth-century fresco, *The Triumph of Death,* on one of the walls of the Campo Santo in Pisa, Italy, it consists of a powerful series of variations on the *Dies irae,* the chant for the dead.[3] With its combination of the macabre and the churchly, it is one of the best examples of the emphasis on both the diabolic and the religious which characterizes several of Liszt's larger works. Other instances are the B minor Piano Sonata and the *Faust* Symphony.

The Symphonic Poems

With the abandonment of his virtuoso career and the commencement of his activity at Weimar, Liszt directed his energies to composition in the larger forms, particularly for orchestra. The principal fruit of this activity was a series of twelve symphonic poems, the term *symphonic poem* being Liszt's own creation. Although the symphonic poem cannot be said to have a specific form, certain attributes are almost invariable. The principal characteristic of the symphonic poem is its attempt at orchestral representation of some poetic concept in a work which, no matter what its length or number of changes of tempo may be, is performed as a single movement. The form that this movement may take is based on the same principle of thematic transformation employed in Liszt's Sonata in B minor and his Piano Concerto in E-flat major; but the nature of these transformations is determined by the poetic concept that the work seeks to communicate. The symphonic poem is, therefore, a species of program music, the program of which may consist either of a poem affixed to the score or merely of a suggestive title. Each and every symphonic poem, while abjuring any rigid form, possesses its own definite musical logic, which for many listeners is sufficient in itself. But while the symphonic poem exhibits the same

---

[3] See page 275.

principles of balance and thematic development that have been observed in its predecessor, the classical symphony, its formal plan is dictated by the poetic idea. The development of the symphonic poem is one of the most important phenomena of the romantic movement.

"LES PRÉLUDES"

Of the twelve symphonic poems of Liszt, only one, *Les Préludes,* has remained in the symphonic repertory. The work takes its title from one of the *Méditations poétiques* of the French poet and statesman, Alphonse de Lamartine (1790-1869), paraphrased by Liszt and printed as a preface to the score.[4] Lamartine's poem, which portrays man's life as but a series of preludes to the final song of death, contrasts the ephemeral joys of pastoral existence with the dangers of war. The orchestral composition which Liszt entitled *Les Préludes* was originally, however, the overture to an uncompleted work for male chorus, *Les quatre éléments* (*The Four Elements*). This overture was revised and enlarged at a later date, supplied with the extract from Lamartine, and eventually published as a symphonic poem in 1856. Inasmuch as the music preceded the poem, the listener is under no compulsion to approve of the fitness of Liszt's choice of poetic preface. Examination will show that *Les Préludes* is a well-constructed work that in its musical self-sufficiency stands in no need of explanation in terms of the now faded sentiments of Lamartine.

Les Préludes consists of four well-contrasted sections prefaced by a short introduction and merged into a single movement. The entire work is based on two themes, which are subjected to numerous transformations—melodic, harmonic, and rhythmic. The first theme, a short motive of three notes, makes its appearance in the introduction as part of a broad passage for strings:

Ex. 8

In the *Andante maestoso,* which follows, this theme appears in these variants:

---

[4] It is the fifteenth *Méditation* of the second series (1822).

Ex. 9
(a)

and

(b)

The second theme is a suave cantabile melody assigned on its first appearance to the violas and horns:

Ex. 10

This first section, in its presentation of these two themes contrasted in mood and tonality, functions as an exposition, the content of which is developed in the three succeeding sections.

The stormy section which follows begins with another variant of the first theme, which, after a somewhat prosaic and unconvincing chromatic succession, assumes this form:

Ex. 11

This portion of the work is rather bombastic and illustrates in its theatricality that aspect of Liszt's art with which critics have found the most fault.

The third section, the finest of the entire composition, is a beautiful *Allegretto pastorale* whose mood is established by a series of colorful passages in the wind instruments, beginning with this horn call:

Ex. 12

The cantabile second theme (Example 10) reappears in the pastoral section in combination with a motive derived from the horn call:

Ex. 13

The last section, an *Allegro marziale animato,* is based on a series of variants of the two basic themes, both of which have now taken on a martial character.   Two typical transformations are:

Ex. 14
(a)

and

(b)

The work is brought to an impressive if somewhat noisy close with a repetition of the variant of the first theme quoted in Example 9(a).

Two fine orchestral works of Liszt are based on the character Faust. The first, entitled *Mephisto Waltz* (*The Dance in the Village Tavern*), is based on an episode in the *Faust* of the Hungarian poet Lenau. The impressive *Faust* Symphony, based on Goethe's play, is considered by many to be Liszt's finest orchestral composition.   Liszt's interest in Goethe's work had been awakened by the settings of portions of it by Berlioz, to whom the symphony was later dedicated.

The Influence of Liszt

No discussion of Liszt is complete without mention of his personal relationships with contemporary composers. All of Liszt's manifold and energy-consuming activities did not prevent him from finding time to receive other composers, play over and discuss their compositions with them and give them sympathetic advice and encouragement. The long list of individuals so befriended is, of course, headed by the name of Richard Wagner, and includes Brahms, Saint-Saëns, and Franck. Many of these composers were young men who were attempting to create national musical literatures in their own lands, and they found in Liszt, who had pointed the way with his Hungarian Rhapsodies, an inspiring counselor. Among the nationalistically minded composers so influenced were the Russians, Balàkireff, Borodin, and Rimsky-Korsakoff; the Bohemian, Smetana; the Norwegian, Grieg; and the Spaniard, Albéniz.

There is no more convincing proof of the importance of Liszt in the history of music than the firm manner in which his various innovations have taken root. His contributions to piano writing have been freely utilized by many later composers. The piano pieces of Maurice Ravel, for example, afford evidence of this. The symphonic poem, in particular, has found universal acceptance as an art form. Such works as the great series of symphonic poems by Richard Strauss, *The Sorcerer's Apprentice* of Dukas, and *The Afternoon of a Faun* of Debussy, as well as many of the instrumental works of César Franck, trace their ancestry back to the symphonic poems of Liszt.

Suggested Readings

An adequately detailed and up-to-date biography of Liszt in the English language is lamentably lacking. The lengthy "authorized" biography, Lina Ramann, *Franz Liszt als Künstler und Mensch* (Leipzig, 1880-94), is, despite its wealth of detail, neither impartial nor reliable. Only the first of its three volumes has been translated into English (London, 1882). The most dependable work is Peter Raabe, *Liszt: Leben und Schaffen* (Stuttgart and Berlin, 1931). It contains a useful catalogue of Liszt's compositions. Chapter V of Ernest Hutcheson, *The Literature of the Piano* (New York, 1948) is a lively and well-considered discussion of Liszt's works for piano. An interesting collection of impressions of Liszt by his contemporaries appears in James Gibbons Huneker, *Franz Liszt* (New York, 1927). The *Musical Quarterly* for July, 1936, is a Liszt issue containing many important articles.

Chapter XXIII

ITALIAN OPERA OF THE
EARLY NINETEENTH CENTURY

E VER since the opening of the first opera house in Italy in 1637, operatic performances have played an important part in Italian life. Creative musical activity in Italy during the latter half of the eighteenth century and the entire nineteenth century was confined almost exclusively to the writing of operatic music. Well-patronized theaters existed in most of the larger cities and towns, and a vast quantity of music was written for performance on their stages. The predilection that the Italian people have shown for the opera in preference to any other type of music has existed to this day.

Italian opera, with but few exceptions, has always placed its emphasis more on fine vocalism and ingratiating melody than on dramatic propriety. It has not been so much a play enhanced by music as a form of musical entertainment, in which accomplished singers have delighted their audiences with beautiful melodies expertly delivered in a language rich in mellifluous vowels, and consequently well adapted to song and to vocal display. For this reason Italian opera has always enjoyed great popularity everywhere. This popularity has at times been excessive and has occasionally served to impede public recognition of other types of operatic compositions of a less colorful nature. The harsh manner in which German composers such as von Weber spoke of the Italian opera was more of a reaction to what they considered an unjust discrimination than a true aesthetic judgment. The comment that Beethoven made about one of the most famous Italians explains why German composers found the competition difficult: "Rossini is a talented and melodious composer; his music suits the frivolous and sensuous spirit of the times; and his productivity is so great that he needs only as many weeks as the Germans need years to write an opera." [1]

Rossini

Of the many composers who were busily fulfilling the requirements of the Italian opera theaters during the early part of the nineteenth century, one met the popular demand for effective vocal writing and tuneful melody with such perfection that his fame spread far beyond the borders of his native land. His name was Gioacchino Rossini, and he was born in February 1792, in the small Adriatic seaport of Pisaro. He wrote his first opera when he was eighteen years old, and before his twenty-second birthday had several successes to his credit. His greatest opera, *Il Barbiere di Siviglia* (*The Barber of Seville*), was composed in 1816 within the space of two weeks.

Rossini's fame grew with each new opera. In 1822 he journeyed to Vienna, where every performance of his works was a great personal triumph. While in Vienna he called on Beethoven, who spoke of *The Barber of Seville* with the highest praise. In the following year he went to London and was again the object of much adulation. So great was his importance in the operatic world that the French government appointed him to a high-salaried post. His activity in Paris culminated with the presentation of *William Tell* in 1829, after which Rossini, although only thirty-seven years old, abandoned operatic composition entirely, an act of renunciation that has never been completely explained. From 1829 until his death in 1868 he lived in retirement, first in Italy and for the last thirteen years of his life in Paris, where his residence was the center of many brilliant musical gatherings. The only significant composition to be written during these thirty-nine years of retirement was a choral work, the *Stabat Mater*. Of the thirty-eight operas which Rossini composed, only one, *The Barber of Seville,* remains a staple of the operatic repertory.

Rossini was regarded, during his lifetime, as a daring innovator; but to show the origin of this reputation would necessitate an extended examination of the Italian operas written before his day. It is important to note, however, that *The Barber of Seville* is the oldest Italian opera to hold a firm place in the repertory. Rossini eliminated

[1] Thayer-Krehbiel, *The Life of Ludwig van Beethoven* (New York, 1921), Vol. III, page 77.

GIOACCHINO ROSSINI

the time-honored prerogative of the virtuoso singer to elaborate at will upon the music that the composer had written. He brought about this change not by dispensing with showy passages entirely, but by writing them out in a specific manner and demanding that the singers adhere to them literally.[2] His skill in writing for the voice is evident everywhere in his works. He was one of the first composers to give a bass voice a prominent role in a serious opera. Rossini abbreviated the long and tedious recitatives that had encumbered the older Italian opera, and made them more interesting musically by having their accompaniments played by the orchestra. In the realm of orchestration he far excelled any of his contemporary Italian composers. He possessed a decided gift for orchestral color, excellent examples of which are to be found in his many fine overtures, notably that to *William Tell,* with the highly original section for five solo cellos in its opening *Andante.*

Rossini was, above all, a facile melodist. His melodies, though rarely as expressive as those of Mozart or Schubert, are bright and spirited, and possess a crispness and a spontaneity that are unique. They are almost always set forth in a purely homophonic style. To Rossini's discredit may be mentioned his frequent lapses of taste, particularly the incessant use of clichés such as the celebrated Rossini *crescendo.* This device, one of the composer's most persistent mannerisms, consisted of the repetition of a short phrase over an obvious accompaniment, commencing *pianissimo* and working up to a *fortissimo* in a somewhat mechanical manner. It earned for him the opprobious nickname, "Signor Crescendo."

Opera Buffa

Rossini's masterpiece, *The Barber of Seville,* is a perfect example of *opera buffa* (comic opera), a type of opera in which Rossini's talents showed themselves at their best. The opera buffa had developed from the comic interludes that had appeared in the previous century between the acts of an *opera seria* (serious opera). In many respects the opera buffa was unrestricted by the conventions which hindered

---

[2] This has not prevented singers from taking all manner of liberties with Rossini's music. Contemporary performances of the aria "Una voce poco fa" (originally for mezzo-soprano) from *The Barber of Seville* might well be compared with the printed version of the music.

the development of opera seria. The number of characters was not rigidly fixed; low male voices might be utilized; the libretto did not have to be historical or legendary, but might deal with events in the lives of the common people; emphasis was placed on effective characterization, tuneful arias, and vivacious ensembles; the action moved speedily. In short, the opera buffa was not only excellent music, it was also excellent theater. The first successful opera buffa was *La serva padrona* (The Maid as Mistress) composed by Giovanni Pergolesi (1710-36) in 1733. This charming little work has had many performances in America.

The text of *The Barber of Seville* was adapted from the celebrated comedy of the same name by the French dramatist Beaumarchais, whose *Marriage of Figaro* had been set by Mozart. The action, dealing with the contest between the young Count Almaviva and the dour Dr. Bartolo for the hand of the latter's ward, Rosina, is replete with intrigue, skilfully manipulated by the town factotum, the barber Figaro. Rossini's sparkling music, ever elegant and patrician, characterizes the various parties to the intrigue and at the same time provides all of the singers with excellent opportunity to display their vocal technique. Rossini himself was quite a wit, and the many farcical situations afforded by the plot elicited a fitting musical response from him.

The famous overture to *The Barber of Seville* had done service for two other operas before Rossini decided to attach it to the work with which it is now associated. It first saw the light of day as the introduction to an opera, *Aureliano in Palmyra,* which dealt with an adventure of the Roman Emperor, Aurelian, in the Syrian desert. This work was unsuccessful, but its overture was salvaged and attached to *Elisabetta,* an opera based on an episode in the life of Queen Elizabeth of England. Rossini actually wrote an overture employing Spanish themes for *The Barber of Seville,* but this was lost, and since he was either too occupied or too indifferent to write another overture, he borrowed the one from *Elisabetta.* This incident not only is typical of the manner in which Rossini continually re-used material from his older works, but it also indicates what dramatic significance Italian composers of this era attached to the overture. Inconstant as its dramatic affiliations may have been, however, the overture to *The Barber of Seville* is thoroughly representative of Rossini's art.

Grand opéra

William Tell stands apart from Rossini's other operas. It was written to a French text and in the tradition of the French opera, and it laid the foundation for the French *grand opéra* of the nineteenth century. The *grand opéra* was based on an historical text, made effective use of large crowd scenes, and emphasized extravagantly staged spectacles, the delineation of local color, and the intense portrayal of emotions. It differed from the German romantic opera largely in the character of its subjects, which were factual rather than fictitious. The greatest exponent of *grand opéra* was the German composer Jakob Meyerbeer (1791-1864), a foreigner who, like Rossini and Gluck before him, dominated operatic activity in Paris over a long period.[3] None of his once famous operas, *Les Huguenots* (1836), *Le Prophète* (1849), and *L'Africaine* (1864) are given today, although they remained repertory works until well into the twentieth century.

Before taking leave of Rossini it should be emphasized that his artistic activity came to an end in 1829, and that he should be grouped chronologically as a contemporary of von Weber and Schubert.

Bellini and Donizetti

The successors of Rossini in the sphere of Italian opera were Vincenzo Bellini (1801-1835) and Gaetano Donizetti (1797-1848). Of Bellini's ten operas, the sole contribution to the modern repertory is *Norma* (1831). His style, in contradistinction to that displayed by Rossini, was thoroughly lyrical. Bellini's melodies possess an elegant and poetic character and a certain elegiac quality that awakened a particularly strong response in Chopin, in many of whose works there are persistent echoes of his music.

Donizetti, like Rossini, composed operas with incredible speed; within sixteen years he wrote no less than sixty-six dramatic works. Of this impressively long list only one opera has survived—*Lucia di Lammermoor,* written in 1835. The celebrated "Mad Scene" in the third act of this opera is a great *tour de force* for coloratura soprano. Donizetti, like Bellini, was primarily a creator of beautiful if slightly

---

[3] Jean Baptiste Lully (1639-1687), director of *Les Petits-Violons* of Louis XIV and the first great writer of French opera, was an Italian.

trite melodies. Both composers lacked Rossini's command of the orchestra, and the orchestral writing in their works ranges from a thin guitar-like accompaniment to noisy, blatant use of the brass instruments; but of true orchestral coloring there are only slight traces.

It has often been customary to compare the works of the Italian operatic composers with those of Richard Wagner. Wagner's adherents, in their zeal for his works, adopted a belittling attitude toward Italian opera. Wagner himself, however, spoke of both Rossini and Bellini in terms of high praise and had the greatest respect for their works, many of which he conducted. He also wrote a long article on Rossini in which he spoke of him as "the first truly great and reverable man I had as yet encountered in the art world." [4]

SUGGESTED READINGS

Francis Toye, *Rossini: A Study in Tragi-Comedy* (New York, 1934), is a lively study of the composer and his age. No adequate treatises on Bellini and Donizetti exist in English. Discussions of *The Barber of Seville* and *William Tell* are included in Ernest Newman, *Stories of the Great Operas* (Garden City, New York, Reprint 1948). Detailed treatments of the operatic types discussed in this chapter and of their principal exponents will be found in Donald J. Grout, *A Short History of Opera* (New York, 1947).

[4] *Richard Wagner's Prose Works,* translated by Wm. Ashton Ellis, Vol. IV, page 271.

Chapter XXIV

RICHARD WAGNER

THE ARTISTIC life of Richard Wagner was a continuous and undaunted struggle for the attainment of one objective: a fusion of dramatic poetry and music into an artistic whole—the music drama. Wagner's convictions on the application of music to the drama amounted almost to an obsession. This monomania drove him relentlessly forward to the composition of gigantic operatic works that, judged by the standards of the period, possessed no possibilities whatever of being performed. Wagner's works, literary as well as musical, stirred up a hornet's nest of discussion and engendered violent displays of partisanship. No other composer was so enthusiastically praised or so bitterly reviled during his lifetime. In the face of all this, Wagner not only completed a great series of music dramas, but also built a theater to be devoted exclusively to their production. Grandiose as Wagner's conceptions were, all were successfully realized on the operatic stages of Europe during his lifetime. The music dramas are now the very foundation of the operatic repertory, and excerpts from them are among the works frequently performed at orchestral concerts.

Wilhelm Richard Wagner, born at Leipzig on May 22, 1813, was the ninth child of Friedrich Wagner, a clerk in the local police court. Wagner's father had shown some dramatic inclinations, and a brother and two sisters were actively engaged on the stage during his youth. The father died not long after Wagner's birth, and in the same year the widow married Ludwig Geyer, an artistically-minded individual, gifted not only as an actor but also as a painter and a dramatist. Wagner's youth was spent in Dresden, where he conceived an intense admiration for the local Kapellmeister, Carl Maria von Weber, and his works. He had as yet not demonstrated any strong musical bent;

RICHARD WAGNER

as a student his interests were predominantly literary, and before his fifteenth birthday he had made some translations from Homer and had written a tragedy, modeled largely after Shakespeare. Violin studies were undertaken with much indifference. Wagner, like Berlioz, was not an instrumental virtuoso; nevertheless, he possessed in later years a pianistic ability adequate for the performance of extracts from his own works in the privacy of his home.

In 1827 the family, which had again been left fatherless, returned to Leipzig. Wagner's conversion to music dates from the following year, when he heard a Beethoven symphony, the Seventh, for the first time. He at once borrowed a textbook of harmony from a local lending library,[1] neglected school, and devoted himself avidly to rather amateurish efforts at composition. An eccentric *Concert-Overture,* played in 1830 at a concert given in the Leipzig Theater, was his first composition to be given a public performance. In 1831 he enrolled as a *studiosus musicae* at the University of Leipzig and for some time gave himself over to the excesses in which students of the time were prone to indulge. But his stay at the university was soon terminated in favor of his all-absorbing interest in music.

Wagner now placed himself under the tutelage of an able theorist, Christian Theodor Weinlig, who as Cantor of St. Thomas' Church occupied the position that had been held by Johann Sebastian Bach in the previous century. Wagner was subjected to a severe contrapuntal discipline by Weinlig, who at the end of six months dismissed him with the remark that he had nothing more to impart to him. The compositions of this period of Wagner's life were almost entirely instrumental works of a not particularly promising nature.

Wagner's active musical career commenced in 1833 when he became chorus master at the opera theater at Würzburg. Subsequently he directed operatic performances at Magdeburg and at Königsberg, where in 1836 he married an actress, Minna Planer. In the following year Wagner and his wife journeyed to the distant Baltic seaport of Riga where he became Kapellmeister at the German Theater. Here he composed the first two acts of his first important opera, *Rienzi,* whose libretto he had adapted from the novel of the English writer, Bulwer-Lytton. But Wagner was forced to flee from Riga because of

[1] See page 246, footnote.

the huge burden of debt that his extravagances had incurred. This unfortunate habit of continually accumulating debts that he could not possibly repay persisted throughout his lifetime.

The harassed Kapellmeister and his wife took passage on a small sailing vessel bound for London; but the boat was blown far off its course by storms, and the voyage that normally consumed eight days lasted for three and one half weeks. Events on this journey later found their way into *Der fliegende Holländer* (*The Flying Dutchman*). The pair stayed in London for only a brief period and then headed directly for Paris, where Wagner hoped to make a name for himself in what was then the center of the operatic world. He was unsuccessful in his plans, however, and for two and one half years he earned a miserable living by journalistic hack writing and such lowly musical tasks as arranging operatic tunes for cornet and piano. While in Paris he completed *Rienzi* and *Der fliegende Holländer*. *Rienzi* was accepted for performance by the Dresden opera in 1841, and the composer returned to Germany to supervise its production (October 20, 1842). The work was a great success, and in the following year Wagner was appointed to the comparatively well-paid post of Kapellmeister at Dresden. Here he gave fine performances of the operas of Mozart and Gluck. In 1846 he conducted what was to all intents and purposes a "revival" of the Ninth Symphony of Beethoven, the result of which was to restore to an important place in the repertory what had been a neglected and undervalued work. The operas *Tannhäuser* and *Lohengrin* were composed at Dresden, the former being performed in 1845. Wagner, despite the fact that he was a Royal Kapellmeister, had taken an important part in the political agitation then current in Dresden; and when the popular unrest broke out in 1849 in a soon suppressed insurrection, he was an active participant. Wanted by the authorities, he took refuge for a few days with Liszt at Weimar and eventually made his way over the border into Switzerland.

For the next eleven years Wagner was an exile from his native land. He settled in Zurich where his principal activity for the first few years was the writing of his great theoretical treatise *Oper und Drama* (*Opera and Drama*), completed in 1851, and the composition of the dramatic poem *Der Ring des Nibelungen* (*The Ring of the*

Nibelungen), which was to be the libretto for the cycle of four operas of the same name. The poem was finished and privately printed in 1852. The musical setting of it was begun in 1853, after a period of six years in which Wagner had written only a very small amount of music, and during which his style had undergone a complete metamorphosis. *Das Rheingold,* the first opera of the *Ring* cycle, was finished in 1854 and *Die Walküre,* the second, in 1856.

About this time Wagner became intimate with Mathilde Wesendonk, the wife of a wealthy Swiss merchant. In 1857 he was forced to cease work on *Siegfried* because of straitened finances. He now turned to the composition of what he naïvely described to Franz Liszt as a "simple" opera, easy to perform and consequently financially remunerative. The "simple" opera turned out to be one of his most difficult works—*Tristan und Isolde,* finished in 1859 and not performed until 1865. *Tristan und Isolde* was in some respects the direct result of his hopeless love for Mathilde Wesendonk. His relationship with Frau Wesendonk served to accelerate what had been going on for years—his drifting away from his wife Minna. They separated in 1861 after twenty-five years of a union in which neither had found happiness. *Tristan und Isolde* was followed by the great comic opera, *Die Meistersinger von Nürnberg* (*The Mastersingers of Nuremberg*), which was commenced in 1861 but was not completed until 1867. In the interim he had, in 1861, revised and expanded the first scene of *Tannhäuser* for a performance of the work in Paris. After six months of heartbreaking rehearsals, the revised opera was finally given three presentations at which the members of the fashionable Jockey Club, incensed because Wagner had not written the traditional second-act ballet of French opera, created so much disturbance that the work was withdrawn. His enforced exile from Germany was terminated in 1860 when he received a partial amnesty which excluded him from Saxony only. This restriction was removed two years later.

The long series of disappointments which had been Wagner's fate since his flight from Dresden came to an end when Ludwig II, the young King of Bavaria, became interested in him after hearing a performance of *Lohengrin.* In 1864 he dispatched a messenger to find Wagner and bring him to Munich. Ludwig now took him under his protection and for a long time supplied him with funds. Cabals were formed against Wagner in Munich, and as the result of much criticism of the king's partiality to him, he withdrew to Switzerland. But the king's interest, both financial and artistic, continued to sustain him for many years.

From the year 1864 dates also the beginning of Wagner's relationship with the daughter of Franz Liszt, Cosima Liszt von Bülow, then the wife of the celebrated pianist-conductor Hans von Bülow. In 1866 Cosima left von Bülow to live with Wagner at Triebschen on Lake Lucerne. They were married in July, 1870. Three children had already been born to them, the youngest a son, Siegfried. Wagner's conduct with Cosima for a long time estranged him from his father-in-law and best friend, Liszt, and also caused an abatement of the king's interest in him. In his new-found happiness Wagner completed *Die Meistersinger von Nürnberg* and turned again to the long-neglected *Siegfried*. It was not until 1874, twenty-six years after its inception, that the composition of *Der Ring des Nibelungen* was brought to an end with the completion of *Götterdämmerung* (*The Twilight of the Gods*).

From the commencement of his labors on *Der Ring des Nibelungen* Wagner had been convinced that it could not be mounted in any of the theaters of Europe. At first he planned to erect a theater for the performance of the Ring operas in Zurich; at another time he mentioned locating it on the banks of the Rhine. The friendship with King Ludwig resulted in the drawing up of plans for a festival theater to be erected in Munich, but these were abandoned when the popular opposition to Wagner's presence at the Bavarian Court caused his withdrawal to Switzerland. In 1871 Wagner decided to build his own theater at Bayreuth, a small Bavarian town centrally located in Germany, yet far enough away from a city and in the heart of a beautiful countryside. To raise the necessary funds, Wagner Societies were established in the principal cities of Germany and even in London and New York. The cornerstone of the *Festspielhaus* was laid in 1872 on Wagner's fifty-ninth birthday, and the event was celebrated by a magnificent performance of Beethoven's Ninth Symphony with Wagner conducting. After herculean labors on the part of all concerned, the theater was opened to the public on August 13, 1876, and *Der Ring des Nibelungen* was performed on four nights (August 13,

14, 16, 17) before a distinguished audience. While the first festival
was an unqualified artistic success, the financial results were disappointing, and the season ended with a large deficit.

A desire to wipe out this deficit was responsible for Wagner's journey
to London in the following year. Here he directed eight concerts
comprising extracts from his operas. His works met with an enthusiastic response, but the expenses were large and the profits small.
Shortly after his return to the Continent Wagner finished the poem
of his last opera *Parsifal*. This work was completed in January, 1882,
and Bayreuth reopened its doors for the première in July of the same
year. At the same time an excellent traveling company under the
impresario Angelo Neumann was busy performing *Der Ring des
Nibelungen* in the principal German cities. Audiences flocked to the
presentations, and Wagner's name was on every tongue. The composer's success was now complete, but the exertions attendant upon
the mounting of *Parsifal* at Bayreuth had seriously undermined his
health. He died in Venice in February, 1883, and was buried in the
garden of his villa *Wahnfried* in Bayreuth.

It is doubtful that the personality of any other artist rivaled in complexity that of Richard Wagner; yet probably no other artist has so
completely revealed himself. Wagner left no stone unturned in the
expression of his ideas. Not only did he write the text and the
music for thirteen operas, but he also penned ten volumes of prose,
including wordy essays on many non-musical topics, and approximately
six thousand letters. At social gatherings it was always Wagner who
monopolized the conversation. Unlike Liszt, he was not particularly
interested in the music of contemporary composers. He continually
imposed upon such of his friends as were willing to put up with
his demands. In short, he rode roughshod over everyone without feeling any qualms of conscience. But this cannot be attributed wholly
to vanity or conceit. It was, rather, the result of a limitless faith in
himself and in his ideas, which would brook no opposition. This
faith, which did not disdain to sacrifice the careers of others for the
attainment of its own selfish purposes, also enabled Wagner to create
gigantic masterworks at a time when his cause seemed almost hopeless. Even when he was a young man he was convinced that he
would become a person of importance. In 1835, when he was only

twenty-two years old and still a fledgling operatic conductor, he began to keep careful notes for his autobiography.

The Fates were kind to Wagner and granted him a long life; he died a few months before his seventieth birthday. Yet he was never in perfect health, and suffered from various stomach disorders and painful skin maladies. The life and the works of Wagner constitute a phenomenon so unusual and so provocative that more books have been written about him than about almost any other creative artist. He was, beyond doubt, one of the most important characters of the nineteenth century and one whose influence made itself felt in many non-musical fields.

The Earlier Operas

The operas of Wagner that are regularly performed today may be divided into two groups: (1) the earlier works—*Der fliegende Hollän-der, Tannhäuser,* and *Lohengrin,* and (2) the works of his maturity— the four *Ring* operas: *Das Rheingold, Die Walküre, Siegfried,* and *Götterdämmerung; Tristan und Isolde, Die Meistersinger von Nürn-berg,* and *Parsifal.* The three earlier operas are, when compared to the works of contemporary composers, masterpieces whose chief fault is that they are overshadowed by Wagner's later creations. In *Tann-häuser* and *Lohengrin* Wagner broke with the convention of dividing an opera into a series of "numbers"—set pieces such as arias and duets —and the unfolding of the drama is therefore continuous. The vocal writing of these earlier operas is essentially lyrical, and the orchestra occasionally plays a subordinate role. Pageantry and procession are still employed in a manner that contributes little to the drama, but nevertheless justifies the interpolation of effective music; for example, the entrance of the guests in the second act of *Tannhäuser.* These earlier works are, as the composer himself called them, "romantic operas" in the accepted sense of the word; but, as regards the nature of the text, effectiveness of characterization, and treatment of the or-chestra, they are worthy forerunners of the music dramas.

THE MUSIC DRAMAS

Our analysis of the works of Wagner will be restricted to the second group, the music dramas. In the sense that Wagner's methods struck a decisive blow at the abuses that prevailed in the opera house at the time, he may be called a reformer. But on closer observation it becomes apparent that whatever Wagner's contributions may have been, they were merely incidental to the reassertion of that concept of the application of music to the drama that had guided the Florentine progenitors of the opera. It will be recalled that the earliest opera writers wrote works in which music was utilized only as a means for heightening the effectiveness of dramatic poetry. The situation that prevailed during the first half of the nineteenth century, despite the reforms of Gluck and the innovations of von Weber, is beautifully summed up by Wagner in his treatise *Opera and Drama*. He writes that the error in the art-genre of opera had been "that a means of expression (music) has been made the end, and the end of expression (the drama) has been made a means." [2] The music-dramas of Wagner restored music to its initial role as an aid in the accomplishment of a dramatic purpose.

The Texts

Wagner's first departure from accepted convention was his choice of text. With the exception of *Die Meistersinger von Nürnberg,* the subjects of both the romantic operas and the music-dramas are derived from mythology or folk legend. The reason why Wagner went to mythology for his texts is stated by him in *Opera and Drama:* "The incomparable thing about the mythos is that it is true for all time, and its content, how close soever its compression, is inexhaustible throughout the ages. The only task of the poet was to expound it." [3] Wagner has in every instance treated his materials with the greatest freedom, and some of his libretti, especially *Der Ring des Nibelungen* and *Tristan und Isolde,* occupy an important place in the long list of literary works inspired by folk legend or medieval epic. *Der Ring des Nibelungen* is one of the most significant of the ten or more Nibelungen plays turned out by German dramatists during the nineteenth century. Of these, three antedate Wagner's setting. The myths were recast by Wagner into dramas whose plots are somewhat confused, and sometimes, as in *Der Ring des Nibelungen,* contradictory. Wagner's claim

---

[2] *Richard Wagner's Prose Works*, translated by W. A. Ellis (London, 1893), Vol. II, page 17.
[3] *Ibid.*, page 193.

to distinction as a dramatist rests largely upon his ability to create characters and portray emotions; his attempts at allegorical philosophizing are generally held to be long-winded and unconvincing. But he has created such strongly defined characters as *Brünnhilde, Isolde, Wotan, Tristan,* and *Hans Sachs,* whose names are common coin; and his *Tristan und Isolde* has even been given as a play, without the music. Furthermore, these texts and these alone brought forth the music.

With the exception of the early *A Faust Overture* and the *Siegfried Idyll,* the latter written for Cosima's birthday, all of Wagner's purely instrumental works are of an inferior order. Of the three marches that he composed, the *Huldigungsmarsch* (*March of Homage*) written to honor King Ludwig, the *Kaisermarsch* celebrating the German victory at the close of the Franco-Prussian war, and the *Centennial March* written by commission for the Philadelphia Exposition in 1876, not one can be compared with the march from the second act of *Tannhäuser.*

The Wagner operas are frequently deficient in stage action; in several scenes of a work like *Tristan und Isolde* action is almost entirely lacking. The listener may, therefore, find it difficult to grasp all the implications of an opera unless he has familiarized himself with its text in advance. This prior study should never be undertaken with the aid of any versified translation. The poetry of Wagner is complex even in the language in which it was written. Recourse is had to alliterative verse in *Der Ring des Nibelungen* and parts of *Tristan und Isolde.* Most versified translations make the text even more confused and serve to cast Wagner and opera in general into disrepute. Good prose translations are available and should be freely used—before the performance. An intimate knowledge of the text is the *sine qua non* for the enjoyment of a Wagner opera.

The manner in which Wagner combined his dramatic poetry with music to produce the music drama had been anticipated by Bach in his cantatas and by Schubert in his songs, for example. The problem, simply stated, was to associate music with speech in two ways—first by cloaking the speech with music, second by writing instrumental music to be performed simultaneously with the vocal music, the two in combination producing an artistic result that is incomparably greater than the sum of its parts. We shall now proceed to examine the constituent parts of the music drama, but in so doing it must not be forgotten that they are always coexistent and have only limited meaning apart from one another.

The Voice

For Wagner, the singer was simply a vocalist to whom was entrusted the task of delivering words in a style that may be described as melodious declamation, a fusion of speech and song. The manner in which the poetry is set has as its aim the augmentation of the accents and cadences of speech and is indifferent to the metrical scheme of the poetry itself. Music becomes, therefore, a medium for illumination of the text by means of which words, or important parts of words, can be brought out in high relief. The vocal writing is not melodious in the usual sense, for it does not consist of a series of clear-cut, easily recognizable tunes capable of ready extraction, but is a part of what Wagner called "endless melody." This melody is not broken up into arias or choruses, but flows along in uninterrupted association with the poetry, the illumination of which is its sole aim. At certain emotional climaxes, such as "Wotan's Farewell" (*Die Walküre*), the voice part may become pure song. But it is seldom that any of the music entrusted to the singer can be regarded as having any existence apart from the text that it cloaks.

The Orchestra.

Associated with the voice in the creation of the "endless melody" is a large orchestra, which, according to Wagner's demands, must not be visible to the audience. The orchestra of the music-dramas differs from all previous operatic orchestras in that its role is not subordinate to that of the stage action, but parallels it throughout. The orchestra is not merely accompanist or commentator, but rather a dramatic protagonist that expresses itself concurrently with another medium of communication—the spoken word raised to the level of musical speech. It is on the complete fusion in the mind of the listener of three simultaneously operating factors—action, the spoken word, and music —that the Wagnerian music drama depends for the attainment of its objective. In his *Opera and Drama* Wagner has enumerated some of the potentialities of the orchestra.[4] He points out that the orches-

[4] *Ibid.*, page 316.

tra has a faculty of speech that is unique in its ability to utter the
unspeakable; that is, the orchestra can express those ideas or emotions
for whose communication the spoken word is inadequate.   The orchestra can, furthermore, ally itself with gesture; it can recall past situations and past emotions; it can express foreboding or, on occasion,
predict what is to come.   The orchestra is in reality an organ of expression of vast potentialities. Wagner has employed it to impart
verisimilitude to the stage action; to give a distinctive color to each
scene; to vivify the words as given out by the singer; to recall past
events; to prophesy future events; to tell the audience what characters
on the stage themselves do not know; to establish the mood of either
an entire opera or an opening scene by means of an instrumental prelude; to deliver a moving commentary.   All these functions are performed by means of a continuous flow of music that is coexistent
with the stage action.   As commentator, interpreter, and prophet, the
orchestra may be compared with the chorus of the Greek drama.

Wagner's concept of the role of the orchestra demanded that that
body of instruments be enlarged.   The greatest augmentation of the
orchestral forces was called for in the *Ring* operas. Here Wagner
demanded four instruments each of the flute, the oboe, and the clarinet
groups; that is, three flutes and a piccolo, three oboes and an English
horn, three clarinets and a bass clarinet.   The horn quartet was doubled,
a bass trumpet was added to the trumpet group, and a contrabass
trombone to the trombones; Wagner also specified that new instruments, now called "Wagner tubas" (though in reality modified horns),
be played in occasion by the second horn quartet.   He carefully specified the required number of string instruments, though in this respect
he had been anticipated by Berlioz in the *Symphonie fantastique*.
Wagner turned the genius of each and every orchestral instrument to
his own dramatic purpose, and for each he opened up new avenues
of expression and revealed hitherto hidden possibilities of execution.
Many devices that were at first deemed impracticable have now become the common property of all orchestral composers.   But Wagner's
art of orchestration did not emphasize single instruments so much as
instruments in combination.   The richness and fullness of any Wagner
chord, no matter how softly it may be played, can be attributed to
his ability to create subtle mixtures of tone colors in which no par-

ticular timbre predominates and a perfect balance is achieved. There is no better demonstration of Wagner's contribution to the vocabulary of orchestral language than a comparison of the sonority of one of his orchestral chords with one from a symphony of Haydn, Mozart, or Beethoven.

The Wagner orchestra pours forth what appears to be "endless melody." Closer examination will show, however, that this endless melody is comprised of very short phrases deftly interwoven in a tapestry-like manner that entirely obliterates the junction points. The apparent jointlessness of a Wagner score is due to the composer's mastery of modulation and his ability to fuse successive orchestral colors. He himself wrote in a letter to Mathilde Wesendonk:[5] "It now seems to me that the finest and most profound feature of my art is the art of transition, for its entire texture consists of such transitions."

The Leading Motive (Leitmotiv)

The orchestral language is made more specific through repetition of certain phrases that have identified themselves with some aspect of the drama as enacted on the stage, a person, a thing, a phenomenon of nature, or some abstract concept. These phrases have been called leading motives, and are short, striking, easily recognizable themes. They make their appearance in the orchestra at some salient moment, or on some occasions appear as vehicles for the text. In any case their associations are vivid. It is of the utmost importance to realize that the leading motives are not labels which bob up mechanically whenever the persons, things, or ideas associated with them appear or are mentioned. The motives are subjected to an intensive system of variation that casts a strong and revealing light on the transformations that their associated persons, things, or ideas have undergone. The variations may be of all conceivable types—melodic, harmonic, rhythmic, or instrumental.

A few examples will illustrate the dramatic potency of this variation technique. The following theme appears for the first time in Das Rheingold as the light of dawning day illumines the abode of the gods, Walhall (Valhalla):

[5] Richard Wagner an Mathilde Wesendonk, Tagebuchblätter und Briefe (Berlin, 1904), page 189.

Ex. 1

Ruhiges Zeitmass

It thus definitely associates itself with *Walhall* and, by transference, with Wotan, its lord. In the succeeding opera, *Die Walküre,* Wotan foresees the tragic end of the gods, and this is expressed by the orchestra in an intense variant of Example 1:

Ex. 2

The following buoyant horn call is associated with the young Siegfried, the child of the forest:

Ex. 3

In *Götterdämmerung* Siegfried has reached man's estate and has become the husband of the Valkyrie maiden, Brünnhilde. Before he appears on the stage, this transformation of the motive associated with him indicates how he himself has been transformed:

Ex. 4

And after Siegfried is slain, the long orchestral interlude[6] that serves as his eulogy concludes with:

Ex. 5

Wagner was not the first operatic composer to make use of recurring phrases as unifying dramatic elements. The procedure may be observed as far back as the works of Monteverdi; and it had also been anticipated in instrumental music in such works as the *Symphonie fantastique* with its *idée fixe* and in the symphonic poems of Liszt. No other composer, however, has approached Wagner in his ability to use the leading motive as a plastic factor in the development of a drama.

For purposes of identification the leading motives were supplied with names, not by Wagner, but by writers of didactic commentaries on the music dramas. It must be borne in mind, however, that many of the leading motives are associated with dramatic situations of a complex emotional hue, and that as a result the names assigned to them are merely suggestive. The use of these names is not objectionable provided the listener realizes that they are only arbitrary labels representing a third person's summaries in prose of the dramatic functions of the motives. To "translate" the sounds of these motives as they are given out by the orchestra is tantamount to defeating Wagner's purpose in employing them.

Chromaticism, the use of semitonal progressions within the framework of the diatonic scale, was carried to new extremes by Wagner, particularly in *Tristan und Isolde* and *Parsifal*. The following excerpt from the Prelude to Act III of the former work typifies the chromatic idiom, both harmonic and melodic, that pervades these operas. The melody includes every note of the chromatic scale from C to C with the exception of B-natural, and the bass descends in half steps:

---

[6] This interlude is played in the concert-hall under the designation *Siegfried's Funeral March* (or *Funeral Music*).

Ex. 6

This procedure serves in large measure to obliterate our awareness of definite tonality. In many respects Wagner's chromatic idiom, with its breaking down of older concepts of the function of the scale and the chord, is prophetic of twentieth-century procedures.[7] It is only fair, however, to point out that the works of Liszt were important influences on Wagner's harmonic vocabulary, as Wagner himself acknowledged.

The Preludes

Wagner seems never to have made up his mind about the function of the overture, despite the preachments to be found in an essay on the overture, which he wrote in 1841.[8] No less than three different types of preliminary pieces are to be found in his works. Up to and including *Tannhäuser* they bear the designation *Overture,* afterwards they are called *Vorspiel* (Prelude). In none of these introductions does Wagner adhere to the sonata form, which had been employed by his great predecessors Beethoven and von Weber. The first type of prelude is found in the four *Ring* operas wherein the orchestral preliminary is simply an introduction to the first scene. Examples of the second type are the preludes to *Lohengrin, Tristan und Isolde,* and *Parsifal.* In these Wagner has confined himself to symbolizing in music the basic concept of the entire opera. The third type shows a close affiliation with the dramatic overture of Wagner's predecessors in that it is a condensation of the entire opera. In this category are the overtures to *Der fliegende Holländer,* and *Tannhäuser,* and the prelude to *Die Meistersinger von Nürnberg.* A notable feature of almost all the operas is the presence in each of a beautiful and sig-

[7] See page 424.
[8] *Richard Wagner's Prose Works,* translated by W. A. Ellis (London, 1898), Vol. VII, page 151.

nificant third-act prelude, not at all like the old *entr'acte* music, but rather an important instrumental introduction, an overture to the act.

Because of their vividness of portrayal, their richness of orchestration, and their wealth of beautiful melody, the Wagner overtures and preludes have acquired an existence apart from the operas that they were intended to preface and are now included among the most frequently performed orchestral works. While they are dominated throughout by a dramatic purpose, their formal structure, although following no conventional pattern, is such as to make them intelligible concert pieces.

Like that of Bach and Beethoven, the art of Wagner does not permit satisfactory illustration by means of selected examples. Each of his works has a markedly individual character, and it would be difficult to state which opera is the most typical. One of the music dramas, however, *Die Meistersinger von Nürnberg,* is beautifully condensed in its prelude, one of Wagner's finest. A study of this composition will therefore serve as an excellent introduction to Wagner's art.

PRELUDE TO "DIE MEISTERSINGER VON NÜRNBERG"

The action of *Die Meistersinger* takes place in the Bavarian city of Nuremberg during the sixteenth century. The *Meistersinger* were tradesmen and artisans banded together in a powerful guild whose aim was to foster the creation of songs. The high artistic purpose of the *Meistersinger* was thwarted by their belief that works of art could be created according to an elaborate set of rules, mastery of which was a prerequisite to membership in their order. The leader of the guild was the liberal-minded cobbler-poet, Hans Sachs. The essential conflict of the opera is the struggle between the conservative spirit in art, as typified by the *Meistersinger* and carried to an extreme by the ridiculous town clerk Sixtus Beckmesser, and the progressive youthful spirit that is impatient with the outworn canons of the past, and desires to create art according to its own lights. The symbol of this viewpoint is a young knight, Walther von Stolzing, who comes into conflict with the pedantic regulations of the *Meistersinger* when he aspires to win the hand of Eva Pogner, daughter of a goldsmith who is a member of the guild. At a contest of song held on the meadow outside of Nuremberg, Walther triumphs over Beckmesser, his opponent in love as well as in art. The opera closes with a magnificent address by Hans Sachs, in which he reconciles the seemingly contradictory viewpoints and points out the debt of the new to the old.

The prelude to the opera may be divided into three sections, the third of which refers back to the first in a manner that, although quite free, creates the impression of a three-part form. The work commences with the resplendent theme of the *Meistersinger,* the earnest, dignified custodians of art:

Ex. 7

This is considerably extended by the full orchestra, and finally gives way to a rapturous wood wind melody identified with young Walther's love for Eva:

Ex. 8

A brilliant scale passage in the violins then serves to introduce another theme of the *Meistersinger,* a march-like fanfare adapted by Wagner from an actual *Meistersinger* melody encountered by him in an old tome which treated of their customs:

Ex. 9

This leads to one of Wagner's richest passages of orchestral polyphony, based on a theme that reappears at the close of the opera as Hans Sachs delivers his praise of German art:

Ex. 10

An agitated interlude, describing young Walther's perturbations of heart, is followed by the middle section. This commences with a theme that is associated with Walther and also becomes part of the Prize Song heard in Act III:

Ex. 11

The course of this beautiful melody is interrupted by an impetuous phrase derived from a song sung by Walther in Act I, and symbolic of his impatience:

Ex. 12

After a sudden change of instrumentation Wagner depicts the playful apprentices. The music is a light, gamboling version of the *Meistersinger* motive quoted in Example 7 and is given out with irreverent incisiveness by the wood winds:

Ex. 13

The conclusion of the prelude is practically identical with the close of the opera, in which Hans Sachs reconciles the old and the new.

Wagner effects a reconciliation of these opposing viewpoints by contrapuntal combination of their musical symbols:

Ex. 14

The prelude concludes with a triumphant pronouncement of the *Meistersinger* motive (Example 7) followed by jubilant fanfares by the trumpets. The concert version of the prelude brings it to a full close; in the opera itself there are no terminating chords and the music leads directly into the first scene.

SUGGESTED READINGS

Ernest Newman, *The Life of Wagner* (New York, 1933-1946), a monumental work in four volumes, is the most authoritative treatment in any language of this difficult subject. No study of Wagner should be undertaken without prior consultation of this richly documented narrative of Wagner's turbulent career. G. A. Hight, *Richard Wagner: A Critical Biography* (London, 1925), is an accurate treatise that also contains synopses and critical discussions of the operas. The Wagner autobiography, *My Life* (New York, 1911), is a valuable work which must be read with discretion. It extends only to the year 1864.

Of the countless critical writings on Wagner the following are particularly noteworthy: George Bernard Shaw, *The Perfect Wagnerite* (New York, 1909); Ernest Newman, *Wagner as Man and Artist* (New York, 1924); and the same author's *Fact and Fiction about Wagner* (New York, 1931); Lawrence Gilman,

Wagner's Operas (New York, 1937); Jacques Barzun, *Darwin, Marx, Wagner: Critique of a Heritage* (Boston, 1946).

There are many collections of Wagner letters available in English. The best selection is that of Wilhelm Altmann, *Letters of Richard Wagner* (New York, 1927). *Richard Wagner's Prose Works* (London, 1893-1899) is an eight volume series of translations by W. A. Ellis of all the important essays.

The best introduction to the texts and music of the operas may be obtained from Ernest Newman, *Stories of the Great Operas* (Garden City, New York, Reprint, 1948). Newman's later work, *The Wagner Operas* (New York, 1949), is a much more detailed treatment and a worthy companion to his great biography of Wagner. Gertrude Hall has made excellent translations of the texts of the operas into English prose in the *The Wagnerian Romances* (New York, 1925).

Chapter XXV

ITALIAN OPERA OF THE
LATE NINETEENTH CENTURY

AT THE same time that Wagner was formulating new operatic standards with his music dramas, an Italian contemporary, Giuseppe Verdi, was content to follow in the footsteps of Rossini, Bellini, and Donizetti. But while adhering in the main to the basic traditions of Italian opera, Verdi won for himself a position as Wagner's most formidable rival in the realm of dramatic music.

Giuseppe Verdi

Giuseppe Verdi was born in the Parmesan hamlet of Le Roncole on October 10, 1813, the son of a poor innkeeper. He was thus only a few months younger than Wagner. He received his first instruction in music from a local organist and displayed so much talent that when he was eighteen years old fellow townsmen provided him with funds for study in Milan. The conservatory in that city refused to admit him, however, and he therefore became the pupil in composition and orchestration of an excellent teacher, Vincenzo Lavigna, a member of the orchestra of Milan's famous opera house, *La Scala*. Verdi's earliest opera, which showed strong influences of Bellini, was performed in 1839, but his first great success was scored with *Nabucco,* which had its première in 1842. This was also the year in which the opera *Rienzi* brought Wagner his first taste of fame. The chronicle of Verdi's life after the triumph of *Nabucco* is largely a record of his operas.

The successive stages of Verdi's evolution as a creative artist may be divided into three periods. All the operas of the first period (1839-1850) have now disappeared from the repertory. The second period

(1851-1867) includes some of Verdi's most popular works—*Rigoletto* (1851), *Il Trovatore* (1853), and *La Traviata* (1853). In the last period (1871-1892) are found his three great masterpieces—*Aïda* (1871), *Otello* (1887), and *Falstaff* (1892). Verdi wrote twenty-six operas in all, about twice as many as Wagner. The success that most of his works achieved brought him a considerable income; but despite the wealth that he accumulated, he always remained a simple peasant at heart. He died in 1901.

Verdi and Nationalism

It was not until 1871 that the various Italian states were unified to form what is now the sovereign state of Italy; during the period in which most of the operas of Verdi were written, political disturbances aiming at the overthrow of the Austrian domination were rife throughout the peninsula. The libretti of some of Verdi's operas contained scenes which could be interpreted in terms of revolutionary sentiments, and operatic audiences of the day were prone to see in them representations of their own national aspirations. As a consequence, patriotic demonstrations in the theater were frequent occurrences. In addition, the letters of Verdi's name were the same as the initial letters of the Sardinian king, whom the Italian nationalists wished to see King of Italy. Audiences could therefore defy the Austrian authorities by shouting *"Viva Verdi"* at the end of a performance, as a disguise for *Vittorio Emanuele, Rè d'Italia.* Verdi himself was an ardent patriot; but his nationalistic tendencies, as far as his music was concerned, consisted of a devotion to an Italian style of operatic composition with the rigid exclusion of German influences. His brand of nationalism was, like Wagner's, more intuitive than purposeful.

Libretti

Many of the libretti of Verdi's earlier operas employ lurid, violent plots from which sanguinary elements are seldom absent. *Rigoletto,* a tense drama whose principal character is a hunchbacked jester who unwittingly becomes a party to the murder of his beloved daughter, is a representative example. *La Traviata,* on the other hand, based on a play of the younger Dumas, is a refined work in which much of the action takes place in the drawing rooms of the Paris of the 1840's.

GIUSEPPE VERDI

Aïda, the scene of which is laid in ancient Egypt, has one of the most uncomplicated of all operatic texts and at the same time is replete with colorfully exotic pageantry and spectacle. The libretti for *Otello* and *Falstaff* were fashioned from Shakespeare by a fellow-composer, Arrigo Boïto (1842-1918), the creator of a celebrated Faust opera, *Mefistofele* (1868).

Style

The most striking feature of Verdi's operatic style is his power of portraying a dramatic situation in eloquent vocal melody. The popularity of Verdi is attributable to the vigorous, forceful nature of the broad tunes that abound in his operas—virile melodies that, despite their occasional adaptability to the hand organ, possess a highly dramatic flavor. Verdi's sole aim was truthfulness of dramatic presentation; none of his operas was written to serve as a medium for the display of vocal pyrotechnics. Like most Italian opera composers, he had a consummate knowledge of the expressive powers of the human voice; and it is from the dramatic potency of straightforward melody rendered by an accomplished vocalist that the effectiveness of his operas derives.

The melodic simplicity with which Verdi could express intense emotion is well exemplified in the conclusion of the aria in the second act of *La Traviata,* when Violetta implores her beloved Alfredo to remain steadfast in his love for her:

Ex. 1

Prose translation: Love me, Alfredo, as I love you, Farewell!

A touchingly beautiful instrumental version of this melody appears in the Prelude to Act I of the opera.

In Verdi's last three operas, *Aïda, Otello,* and *Falstaff,* the orchestra assumed a much more significant role, and, in the last two, the traditional division into set pieces was abandoned in favor of a continuous flow of music. But the human voice still remained the dominant musical factor. The analogy between these later developments in Verdi's style and some of the innovations of Wagner at once brought forth the comment that Verdi had fallen under Wagnerian influences— an accusation that he bitterly resented. The idiom of the last operas, while in a limited sense analogous to that of Wagner, was the result not of any external influence, but rather of Verdi's natural evolution as a composer.

Otello and *Falstaff,* remarkable products of Verdi's old age (the latter was written when he was eighty years old), rank with the world's greatest musical dramas. Masterly characterizations are achieved through expressive declamation, noble melodic lines and subtle orchestral participation in the intensification of emotion. The composer of the melodramatic *Rigoletto* and *Trovatore,* with their direct homophonic idioms, brought his long career in the theater to a close with the witty *buffo* comedy *Falstaff* whose concluding scene is one of the liveliest and most effective fugues ever written, a humor-saturated setting of *"Tutto nel mondo è burlá. L'uom è nato burlone."* ("All the world is a jest. Man is born a fool.")

Like the works of Rossini, many of Verdi's operas are distorted and mangled today by the vanity of performers. A distinguished English composer-critic of Italian origin, Ferruccio Bonavia, writes with justifiable indignation: "To assign to him his place among famous men is difficult while his works are still performed by those who have not the necessary technique or intelligence, who never hesitate to deal arbitrarily with his directions, by singers who turn every high note into an occasion to display their endurance. But most of those who have taken the trouble to clear away from his music the incrustations accumulated during years of license, and have discovered how many moments there are even in the earlier operas in which everything earthly has been fused away and only the fire of passion remains, will not hesitate to place him among the great epic poets of music." [1]

The Manzoni Requiem

The death in 1873 of the Italian poet and patriot, Alessandro Manzoni, affected Verdi so deeply that he composed a Requiem Mass in

[1] *The Heritage of Music,* Edited by H. J. Foss (London, 1934), Vol. II, pages 222-3.

his memory. The text of the Requiem Mass is rich in dramatic suggestion, and Verdi responded to it with the same instinct for dramatic representation that characterized his operas. The charge has been made that the idiom of the Requiem is too theatrical. There are, to be sure, episodes in the Requiem that recall the style of Verdi's operatic music, but the sincerity and depth of conviction that pervade the work as a whole cannot be questioned.

Verismo

Two operas that appeared in Italy at the close of the nineteenth century are now the Siamese twins of the operatic repertory—Mascagni's *Cavalleria rusticana* (*Rustic Chivalry*), first performed in 1890, and Leoncavallo's *I Pagliacci* (*The Clowns*), which appeared two years later. These operas set the fashion for *verismo,* a type of operatic realism. The texts of these works, based on events in the lives of common people, are compact and terse and are presented in one tightly drawn act; emotional climaxes are frequent, and the bloody denouements are swift.

From the musical standpoint the most important feature of these operas is the close association of text and music. The orchestra plays a comparatively important role, and the manner of writing for it suggests the influence of at least the harmonic language of Wagner; but as is customary in Italian opera, the voice remains supreme. The music of these works is, however, not of a consistently high order, and the effectiveness of many of the melodic ideas is negated by overinflation. It must be conceded, however, that an opera like *I Pagliacci* is a remarkably effective integration of drama and music. Neither Mascagni nor Leoncavallo ever succeeded in fulfilling the promise of these two operas, and the numerous dramatic works that followed them have failed to win a firm place in the operatic repertory.

Puccini

The successor to Verdi was Giacomo Puccini (1858-1924), a composer of exceptional attainments. Puccini's style, although far from eclectic, was a fusion of three important features of nineteenth-century opera: the expressive melody of Verdi, the dramatic potency of *verismo,* and the illuminative commentary of the Wagner orchestra. Puccini's masterworks are *La Bohème* (1896), *Tosca* (1900), and *Madama But-terfly* (1904); he also wrote a first-rate one-act comic opera *Gianni Schicchi* (1918). A colorful and masterfully set opera on a Chinese fairy tale, *Turandot,* remained unfinished when Puccini died in 1924. The closing scene was written from the composer's sketches by Franco Alfano. Given its première in 1926, *Turandot* is the youngest of the "standard" operas.

In addition to his lyric gifts, his exceptional command of harmonic resources, and his fine sense of the theater, Puccini possessed an excellent grasp of orchestral values. His orchestration is colorful, if none too original, and the many picturesque scenes that occur in his operas owe their effectiveness as much to the orchestra as to the scene painter. Puccini also made use of the leading motive, although in a somewhat limited fashion.

SUGGESTED READINGS

The best works on Verdi are Ferrucio Bonavia, *Verdi* (London, 1930), Francis Toye, *Giuseppe Verdi, His Life and Works* (New York, 1931), and Dynaley Hussey, *Verdi* (New York, 1940). The eminent novelist, Franz Werfel, com-piled a selection of Verdi's letters, *Verdi: the Man in His Letters* (New York, 1942). Richard Specht, *Puccini, The Man, His Life, His Work* (New York, 1933), is a translation from the German. The principal operas of Verdi and Puccini are described in detail in Ernest Newman, *Stories of the Great Operas* (Garden City, New York, Reprint, 1948). The sources of the oriental melodies used by Puccini in *Madame Butterfly* and *Turandot* are given in Mosco Carner's illuminating article, "The Exotic Element in Puccini," *The Musical Quarterly* January, 1936. Donald J. Grout, *A Short History of the Opera* (New York, 1947), contains many well-considered criticisms of late Italian opera and much valuable information.

Chapter XXVI

JOHANNES BRAHMS

THE OPENING of the festival theater at Bayreuth in 1876 was a great triumph for Wagner, the creator of music-dramas. But Wagner, the writer on music, went down to defeat when the First Symphony of Johannes Brahms was performed at Karlsruhe less than three months after Bayreuth had opened its doors. Strange as his words may sound today, Wagner had confidently declared that the expressive possibilities of absolute music had been exhausted in the symphonies of Beethoven; he maintained that Beethoven himself had shown in his Ninth Symphony that instrumental music would have to find its salvation in an alliance with poetry. The compositions of Brahms are outstanding in the list of works that might be cited in refutation of Wagner's dictum.

Johannes Brahms, born in Hamburg on May 7, 1833, was the son of a musician who played the double bass in the orchestra of the town theater. The father taught his son to play the violin, the cello, and the horn. And as a child, Brahms helped augment the family income by playing at dances. When he was seven years old he commenced the study of the piano under a local teacher, Otto Cossel, and made such rapid progress that by the time he was ten Cossel prevailed upon the learned theorist and then well-known composer Eduard Marxsen to accept the boy as his pupil. Marxsen's teaching was an important influence on the development of Brahms. A well-schooled musician, he focused the attention of his pupil on the works of Bach and Beethoven. It is interesting to note that at Brahms' first appearance as a recitalist (September, 1848) he performed a fugue of Bach. Up to his twentieth year he led a somewhat desultory life in Hamburg. Although it was necessary for him to give lessons, play at dances,

327

make arrangements, and do other musical hack work, he found time not only for serious study of the technical aspects of composition, but also for the writing of some piano pieces.

The arrival in Hamburg of a Hungarian violinist, Eduard Reményi, was an important factor in Brahms' career. Reményi, who was impressed by Brahms' ability as an accompanist, suggested that they embark on a concert tour together. The pair left Hamburg in April, 1853, and in the course of their travels played at Hanover, where Reményi's compatriot and former fellow-student, the violinist Joseph Joachim, was concertmaster of the Royal Orchestra. Joachim quickly perceived the unusual nature of Brahms' talents and directed him to what was then the Mecca for all young musicians—the *Altenburg,* Liszt's residence at Weimar. Brahms stayed in Weimar for six weeks. Liszt was enthusiastic over his compositions and looked on him as a new adherent of his group. Brahms, however, found himself repelled by all that Weimar represented.

Another artistic contact for which Joachim was also directly responsible proved more fruitful. On September 30, 1853, Brahms called on Schumann, who was then music director at the Rhine town of Düsseldorf. Schumann was so impressed with Brahms and with his compositions that he wrote the celebrated article *Neue Bahnen* (New Paths) for the *Neue Zeitschrift für Musik,* the important musical magazine whose editor he had once been. The essay, which hailed the twenty-year-old Brahms as a composer from whom the world might some day expect great choral and orchestral works, had two important results—it served to make Brahms' name known in all the musical circles of Europe, and it placed on his shoulders the responsibility for fulfilling Schumann's prophecy. The enthusiastic Schumann also wrote to the well-known music publishers, Breitkopf and Härtel, and persuaded them to undertake the publication of Brahms' compositions. From that time until Schumann's death three years later, Brahms was in intimate contact with him.

Through the intercession of two pupils of Clara Schumann, Brahms was given a post at the small court of Lippe-Detmold in 1857. His duties were light, and he had ample time for composition and for frequent trips to Hamburg, where he conducted a small chorus of women's voices. In 1859 he appeared as soloist at Leipzig in his monu-

JOHANNES BRAHMS

mental Piano Concerto in D minor, his first composition of symphonic dimensions. This somewhat austere work was roundly condemned by all except, paradoxically enough, the adherents of Liszt.

Brahms resigned his post at Lippe-Detmold in 1860 and spent two years in Hamburg, where he hoped to receive the position of director of the Philharmonic Society. His name again figured in the public press when he, Joachim, and two other musicians drew up an indiscreet declaration in which they deplored and condemned the artistic tenets of Liszt and his disciples. From that time on Brahms was *persona non grata* with the Weimar group.

Inasmuch as Hamburg did not see fit to honor its native son with a post, Brahms, like his predecessor Beethoven, turned toward Vienna. He appeared in the musical capital as pianist and composer in November, 1862, and established enough of a reputation to warrant his being made conductor of a choral organization, the *Singakademie;* but he resigned his post after presenting four programs on which the works of older masters, particularly Bach, held an important place. Vienna remained Brahms' residence, but after resigning the conductorship of the *Singakademie* he travelled extensively.

In 1868 his great choral work, *Ein Deutsches Requiem* (*A German Requiem*) was sung in Bremen. The performance was an unqualified success, and the numerous repetitions in all the larger German towns served to bring the composer's name to the attention of the world at large. The Requiem was followed by other important choral works, *Rinaldo,* the *Liebeslieder* (*Love Songs*), the *Alto Rhapsody,* the *Schicksalslied* (*Song of Destiny*), and the *Triumphlied* (*Song of Triumph*). The last named, composed in commemoration of the German victory in the Franco-Prussian War, was received with excesses of enthusiasm wherever it was performed. In 1872 Brahms was reinstalled as a choral director at Vienna. For three years he was director of the *Singverein,* the chorus of the *Gesellschaft der Musikfreunde* (Society of the Friends of Music). This was the last of the three small posts which Brahms held during his lifetime. None can be said to have been very important, nor did they contribute much to what was outwardly a fairly uneventful life.

The last two decades of Brahms' life were free from any official en-

tanglements, but his work was frequently interrupted by arduous concert tours on which he appeared as performer and conductor. As yet
he was known as a composer only of piano, chamber, and choral
music. Brahms, with characteristic reserve, had withheld his First
Symphony until 1876, at which time he was already forty-three years
old. The Second Symphony followed in the next year. Within the
next ten years he had added to the list of his symphonic works two
more symphonies, a violin concerto, a second piano concerto (in B-flat
major), and a double concerto for violin and violoncello. In 1879 the
University of Breslau conferred upon him a doctor's degree, *honoris
causa,* in acknowledgment of his being, as the diploma said "the foremost living German master of the art of strict composition." As a
gesture of appreciation Brahms composed the *Academic Festival* Overture, based on German student songs and conducted it in the Great
Hall of the university. The University of Cambridge had given him
an honorary Doctor of Music degree in 1877. Brahms died at the
height of his fame on April 3, 1897, and was buried close to Beethoven
and Schubert. The prophecy that Schumann had made forty-four
years before had been fulfilled.

The long list of distinguished men and women who enjoyed the
friendship of Brahms is headed by Clara Schumann, the widow of
his great benefactor. Brahms was extremely devoted to her and sent
many of his compositions to her for criticism before publishing them.

The personality of Brahms resembled that of Beethoven in that it
was concealed from the world by a rough exterior. To strangers he
seemed crude and almost ill-mannered. Among friends he was thoroughly charming, genial, and witty, usually quite exuberant, and fond
of jokes. He never married and had the typical old bachelor's fondness for children. They, in turn, were attracted to the stubby little
man with the beard, who almost invariably had some candy in his
pocket for them. Brahms was essentially modest; he hated publicity
and any sort of public function. He was particularly reserved about
his own works, and his estimate of himself as a composer extended
almost to self-depreciation. Although he was widely read and as his
letters attest, possessed no slight literary facility, Brahms' only literary
effort was the unfortunate manifesto signed in 1860.

Brahms and Wagner.

Richard Wagner, his theories, and his music-dramas had been revolutionary enough to engender much opposition on the part of those individuals who chose to remain faithful to the older music. Unfortunately for Brahms, the anti-Wagnerites selected him as their symbol of musical rectitude. The Wagner faction retaliated with much venom, and Wagner himself was not above writing slanderous statements about his younger contemporary. While Brahms may have had his private opinions, he never indulged in any public defamation of Wagner. It may be remarked, parenthetically, that he had an excellent knowledge of the music dramas and admired much in them. But he could not evince any enthusiasm for them as entities.

Few traces of the celebrated squabble remain today. With the passing of time it has become clear that Wagner and Brahms operated in spheres that were remote from each other and wholly unantagonistic. The controversy between them was really a battle between the heirs of Beethoven, each with definite ideas as to how the magnificent heritage should be utilized. Wagner elected to put the orchestral language of Beethoven to use in the service of the drama; Brahms, on the other hand, was content to follow unquestioningly in Beethoven's footsteps and confine himself to the forms which he had employed.

Brahms' Position in the History of Music

The position of Brahms in the history of music is in some ways unique, for according to the style of his works his rightful place is directly after Beethoven and Schumann. It would be no exaggeration to say that he wrote as if von Weber, Berlioz, Liszt, and Wagner had never existed. The implications of this statement are clear when one recalls that Brahms was no less than twenty years younger than Wagner. One looks in vain in the list of his works for piano pieces with fanciful titles, for program symphonies, or for symphonic poems. In the sphere of instrumental music he restricted himself to the forms of Bach and Beethoven—the variation, the sonata and its allied forms, such as the symphony, the string quartet, the concerto; and his concept of these forms, as opposed to those of such of his contemporaries as employed them, remained truly classical and wholly unaffected by the formal innovations of Liszt. It is therefore with a considerable degree of accuracy that Brahms is often called a neo-classicist.

Brahms also shows his kinship with Bach and Beethoven in his predilection for, and mastery of, the variation form. There are two splendid sets of variations for the piano that are frequently performed: the *Variations and Fugue on a Theme of Handel* (Opus 24), and the twenty-eight *Variations on a Theme of Paganini* (Opus 35).

The latter work uses a theme found in the twenty-fourth of the great Italian virtuoso's *Caprices* for violin solo, where it also serves for a set of variations. Brahms was inspired to write his own set after hearing his friend Joachim play Paganini's work. In Brahms' version the theme, a short binary melody, appears as follows (right hand only):

Ex. 1

The wholly uncharacteristic pianistic exhibitionism of these variations is explained by the peculiar circumstances of their origin: they were designed as virtuoso études and initially published as *Studies for the Pianoforte*. The enormous difficulties involved in performing them led so devout an admirer of Brahms as Clara Schumann to dub the work *"Hexenvariationen"*[1] ("Witches Variations"). A more recent treatment of this blithe little tune is the *Rhapsody on a Theme of Paganini* (1934), a colorful and deservedly popular composition for piano and orchestra by the Russian, Sergei Rachmaninoff.

The orchestral *Variations on a Theme of Haydn* (Opus 56a) were composed in 1873, and thus precede the First Symphony by three years. The theme, called by Haydn "Chorale of St. Anthony," is a movement of a work composed for the military band of Prince Esterhazy.[2]

[1] *Letters of Clara Schumann and Johannes Brahms,* Edited by B. Litzmann (New York, 1927), Vol. I, page 159.

[2] See page 137.

Brahms retains the initial wind instrument color of Haydn's melody
by assigning the theme to oboes and bassoons:

Ex. 2

The set of eight variations, a series of pieces in diverse styles based on
some element of the theme and sharing its form, is followed by a
monumental *Finale,* itself a set of variations in that it is a passacaglia [3]
on a basso ostinato derived from the theme.

Brahms returned to his beloved variation form for his last symphonic essay, the final movement of his Fourth Symphony. Here again
he utilizes the passacaglia form so closely identified with Bach. On
a simple scale-wise melody of eight measures—

Ex. 3

Brahms writes a magnificently designed series of thirty variations
each of the same length as the theme, and then closes the movement
with a forceful coda in which the theme is treated with greater freedom.

But the neo-classicism of Brahms was not the equivalent of a sterile
eclecticism based on close study of classical models. Although he used
the forms of earlier masters, one of whom had preceded him by one
and one half centuries, he treated them in a highly individual manner,
and the characteristics of his musical style are well marked.

[3] See page 95.

Characteristics of Brahms' Music

The instrumental music of Brahms reveals a degree of concentration comparable to that already encountered in the works of Beethoven. In the sphere of absolute music Brahms must be acknowledged one of the greatest masters of the art of development. This mastery was the joint product of a fertile imagination and a rich technical equipment. The writing of a new work was for Brahms, as for Beethoven, a prolonged act of labor. He, too, subjected his works to severe self-criticism. It is said that he composed and destroyed over twenty string quartets before publishing one work in this difficult form. As a consequence of this attitude, the formal design of his works exhibits a perfection that is not to be found in the works of his more impetuous, though not one whit more romantic, predecessors. Brahms' attitude toward composition is perhaps best summed up in a statement made to a friend, George Henschel, who later became the first conductor of the Boston Symphony Orchestra: "One ought never to forget that by actually perfecting *one* piece one gains and learns more than by commencing or half-finishing a dozen. Let it rest, let it rest, and keep going back to it and working at it over and over again, until it is completed as a finished work of art, until there is not a note too much or too little, not a bar you could improve upon. Whether it is *beautiful* also, is an entirely different matter, but perfect it *must* be." [4]

Most of Brahms' finest themes are lyrical in character, and although entirely original, often bear a strong resemblance to folk song. It is often his custom to commence a first movement with a song-like theme rather than with an incisive dramatic one. These cantabile subjects are usually of considerable breadth. During the course of an extended movement they are frequently subjected to elaborate polyphonic treatment. As a harmonist Brahms again reverted to the idiom of his forebears and abjured the sensuous chromaticism and frequent modulation of the Liszt-Wagner school. One of the most attractive features of his style is his rhythmic originality. In this respect he was far in advance of Wagner. Syncopations, cross-accents, combinations of rhythms, and irregular groupings of phrases abound in his music.

Beauty of thematic material, conciseness of development, and per-

[4] George Henschel, *Personal Recollections of Johannes Brahms* (Boston, 1907), page 39

fection of form were much more weighty considerations with Brahms than questions of tone color. His classical spirit is again shown in his comparative indifference to the new coloristic potentialities of both the piano and the orchestra, which had been demonstrated by Chopin and Liszt on the one hand, and by Berlioz and Wagner on the other. Brahms' writing for both piano and orchestra is often thick and muddy. In his writing for the former he shuns virtuosity for its own sake, and such difficulties as arise are only incidental to the music itself. His orchestration is lusterless and sonorous, lacking contrast and brilliance. In characteristic fashion Brahms made no use either of the newer instruments that had recently found a place in the orchestra or of the mechanical improvements that had given older instruments like the brasses greater melodic freedom.

Piano Music

Brahms' compositions for the piano occupy an important place in the repertory of contemporary recitalists. That the public was late in granting them the recognition that is their due can be attributed largely to the fact that none of the piano pieces is "brilliant" in the usual sense. As has been pointed out previously Brahms ignored contemporary trends, and all his works, with the exception of the previously discussed *Variations on a Theme of Paganini,* are totally lacking in technical bravura. Brahms apparently aimed at fullness rather than brilliancy in his piano writing, but the frequent doublings and progressions in thirds and sixths, particularly in the lower register of the instrument, often make for thickness and muddiness. Almost all of the piano works exhibit the rich polyphonic texture and the rhythmic complexity so characteristic of his style.

Of the three piano sonatas, all earlier works, the Third, in F minor (Opus 5), is considered the finest. The numerous shorter pieces bear titles such as *Capriccio, Intermezzo, Rhapsody, Ballade.* These indications cannot be construed literally; nor does Brahms' use of them approximate that of other composers. They are subjective character pieces filled with a romantic fantasy that expresses itself without the aid of any external program. The great works in variation form have already been mentioned.

Like many great composers, Brahms had his lighter moments. His predilection for Bach and Beethoven did not prevent his possessing an unbounded enthusiasm for the works of his good friend, the Viennese "Waltz King," Johann Strauss, composer of the celebrated *Beautiful Blue Danube*. Brahms' own essays in the dance form so closely identified with the city of his adoption have also become very popular. They comprise the sixteen Waltzes for Piano, four hands (Opus 39); and the *Liebeslieder* (*Love Songs*), for Piano, four hands, and Vocal Quartet, (Opus 52, Opus 65). The four sets of Hungarian Dances, also for piano duet, include some of Brahms' most popular compositions. Brahms' interest in the folk music of Hungary had probably been aroused by his contact with Reményi. The Hungarian Dances are artistic arrangements of traditional gypsy tunes whose original spirit has been effectively reproduced.

Songs

As a song writer Brahms also held aloof from contemporary practices of combining poetry and music; in his choice of poems and in his setting of them he was predominantly lyrical rather than dramatic. His vocal writing does not aim to bring out the details of the poem by subtleties of declamation, but endeavors instead to portray its underlying mood by cloaking it with beautiful melody. Many of these melodies possess a simplicity which recalls folk song. Of the approximately two hundred Brahms songs the greater part is in strophic form. The piano accompaniments are full and rich but again do not aim to subject the poem to detailed treatment. The majority of the songs are love songs, a type thoroughly congenial to Brahms' essentially lyrical temperament. The *Vier ernste Gesänge* (Four Serious Songs), Opus 121, occupy a special place in the list of Brahms' compositions. Written in the last year of his life, and utilizing Biblical texts treating of death, they constitute an intimate personal document revealing his attitude toward the end that he knew was not far away.

Chamber Music

Of all the romantic composers only Schubert, Mendelssohn, and Schumann had ventured to devote themselves extensively to chamber music. The more ardent spirits of the movement were too concerned with the piano, the orchestra, and the theater. The nature of chamber music is such as to require mastery of form and power of sustained development. Fanciful programs are seldom used; nor can coloristic facility be used as a cloak for paucity of invention. Of all the successors of Beethoven, Brahms was the only one who possessed the inspiration and the craftsmanship to write chamber music works worthy of a place beside those of his great forerunner. Brahms' output in the field of chamber music comprises twenty-four works, including three fine string quartets (Opus 51, No. 1, in C minor, Opus 51, No. 2, in A minor, and Opus 67, in B-flat major); a great piano quintet (Opus 34, in F minor); three celebrated sonatas for violin and piano (Opus 78, in G major, Opus 100, in A major, and Opus 108, in D minor); and a splendid Quintet for Clarinet and String Quartet (Opus 115, in B minor).

PIANO QUINTET IN F MINOR, OPUS 34

The Piano Quintet in F Minor, Opus 34, Brahms' only composition for this particular combination of instruments, is one of his most famous chamber music works. Its present form is the result of two recastings; Brahms originally conceived the work as a string quintet with two cellos, and later arranged it as a sonata for two pianos before giving it its final instrumentation in 1864.

The first movement, in sonata form, commences with a powerful subject of typical breadth:

Ex. 4

The genial *Andante, un poco Adagio,* in A-flat major, is a simple lyrical movement in three-part form. The first theme with its characteristically Brahmsian thirds and sixths is given out by the piano:

Ex. 5

The second violin and viola give out the expansive melody of the middle section:

Ex. 6

Although the third movement, in C minor, is labeled *Scherzo,* the prevalence of duple rhythms throughout creates the effect of a march. Characteristic syncopations and a brief fugato may be observed in the main section, the crowning glory of which is this bold tune in C major:

Ex. 7

A quiet *Trio,* in C major, offers a brief moment of relaxation in this otherwise energy-crammed movement.

The last movement, which reverts to the original F minor, is opened by a calm introduction in a slow tempo, after which the movement proper, in sonata form, begins with an engaging melody given out by the cello.

Ex. 8

The second group opens with a more sustained theme of characteristic rhythmic interest:

Ex. 9

The development, which concerns itself with the initial motive of Example 8, is quite brief and hence the recapitulation undergoes considerable amplification. The long and typically vigorous coda employs a rhythmic modification of the first theme.

Orchestral Music

As has been stated previously, the first of the four Brahms symphonies did not appear until 1876. Widespread popular acceptance of these works was delayed because of the partisan struggle then prevailing. Brahms' own adherents caused the pro-Wagner faction further irritation by calling the First Symphony the "Tenth." Hans von Bülow found himself moved to excesses of enthusiasm and called public attention to the fact that the names of the three great German composers began with B by coining the slogan, "Bach, Beethoven, Brahms."

The four symphonies are in many respects the culmination of Brahms' career as a composer of instrumental music. Each is a masterpiece, each is typical Brahms throughout, yet each has its own decided individuality and presents its own special problems. The Third, in F major, completed in 1883, is probably the easiest to grasp since it is the shortest, the most colorful, and the most cheerful of the four.

SYMPHONY NO. 3, IN F MAJOR

The first movement, an *Allegro con brio,* opens vigorously with a three-note scheme, *a,* that pervades the entire movement and recurs, furthermore, in the last. As this theme terminates, another vigorous theme, *b,* is announced by the violins over *a* as a bass:

Ex. 10

The second group is in the key of A major and employs a new rhythm, $\frac{9}{4}$. The clarinet gives out this song-like theme in which a small group of notes is continually altered:

Ex. 11

The $\frac{6}{4}$ rhythm in which the movement began is restored as the oboe recalls theme *a* of Example 10; and after a few measures of pleasant dialogue in the wood winds in which theme *a* is again heard, the exposition concludes with a series of syncopated chords. In the development, which is somewhat short, Example 11 is changed into a forceful $\frac{6}{4}$ rhythm and assigned to the violas, cellos, and bassoons. Theme *a* again appears, first as a beautiful horn solo:

Ex. 12

It then proceeds to work its way upward from the bass and after considerable dramatic suspense finally serves to usher in the recapitulation. The coda subjects theme *b* to extensive development of a forceful character. The movement closes with peaceful reminiscences of themes *a* and *b*, quotations of the former in the wood winds being followed by the descent of the latter in the violins.

The second movement, an *Andante,* begins with a simple folk-like subject announced by clarinets and bassoons. Cadences that give the effect of echoes are sounded between the phrases by the lower strings:

Ex. 13

This melody is repeated with figuration, and after a subdued transitional passage is followed by another folk-like subject entrusted to the clarinet and the bassoon:

Ex. 14

The distinctive feature of this theme is the two repeated notes with which it begins. Brahms makes much of this two-note motive during the course of this movement, and it reappears in the fourth movement. The exposition of the thematic material of the movement concludes with a series of announcements of this motive in various registers of the orchestra.

A short development, in which the first theme is subjected to ornamental variation and is presented in various keys, is followed by an abbreviated recapitulation. A beautiful feature of the movement is the broad, expansive coda. This begins with a new subject whose origin can be traced back to the first theme (Example 13):

Ex. 15

Solemn chords in which the trombones play an important part bring the movement to a quiet end.

None of the third movements of the Brahms symphonies is a scherzo. With the exception of the Fourth Symphony, they are of a graceful, lyrical character, short and unpretentious. The third movement of the Third Symphony is a simple three-part form. The theme of the first section, of typical length and rhythmic interest, is sung by the cellos and begins as follows:

Ex. 16

Repetitions of this are heard in the violins and later in the wood winds. The middle section, in A-flat major, begins with a lilting phrase in the wood winds:

Ex. 17

The repetition of the first section, while containing the same thematic material, is scored in an entirely different fashion. The opening cello passage, for example, is now entrusted to a solo horn.

The last movement, an *Allegro,* is fiery and impetuous and abounds in vivid contrasts. It begins in subdued fashion and in a minor key with:

Ex. 18

The course of this subject is interrupted by a chorale-like passage that recalls the second theme of the second movement (Example 14):

A vigorous *tutti* leads to the second group which begins with a boisterous theme played by the cellos and the first horn:

Ex. 19

Several other themes appear in the exposition. The protracted development is based on Example 18 and is subtly joined to the recapitulation. The coda begins with a wistful statement of Example 18 played by muted violas:

Ex. 20

The solemn tones of Example 14 are now chanted by the wood winds, and the entire symphony is brought to a romantic close with a quotation of the opening theme of the first movement, *b* of Example 10.

Other important orchestral works of Brahms are the *Variations on a Theme of Haydn,* the *Tragic* Overture, and the *Academic Festival* Overture.

The Concertos

The neo-classic outlook of Brahms is again shown by his four concertos, two for piano (D minor and B-flat major), one for violin, and a double concerto for violin and violoncello. In all these works Brahms has restored the double exposition that Mendelssohn and Schumann had discarded; and in the violin concerto he permits the soloist to interpolate his own cadenzas. The B-flat major piano concerto occupies an unusual place in the literature inasmuch as it has four movements and no cadenzas whatsoever. The concertos, like those of Beethoven, are not vehicles for virtuoso display. All are works of great dignity whose thematic content and masterly development place them on an equal footing with the four symphonies.

VIOLIN CONCERTO IN D MAJOR, OPUS 77

The Violin Concerto in D major, Opus 77, was dedicated to and first performed by the composer's friend, Joseph Joachim.[5] Joachim served in an advisory capacity during the composition of the work and assisted in various technical details.

The first movement commences with a *cantabile* theme sung by bassoons, horns, and lower strings:

Ex. 21

The second group includes a lyrical subject of much charm:

Ex. 22

The second movement is based on a simple folk-like theme given out by the oboe:

[5] See page 197.

Ex. 23

The last movement is an animated *Allegro giocoso,* whose first theme, announced by the soloist, reflects Brahms' interest in Hungarian music:

Ex. 24

Choral Music

Of Brahms' numerous compositions for chorus and orchestra the most important is the *Deutsches Requiem (German Requiem)*. The Requiem is not music for the ritual of any church. Its text, in the German language, is composed of seven Biblical excerpts selected by Brahms himself. The initial idea for a work of this type was Schumann's. Brahms, as Schumann's disciple, apparently honored his memory by bringing the plan to fruition. Brahms' mother died in 1865, and what is now the fifth movement was added in her memory to the already completed work.

Suggested Readings

The best single volume on Brahms' life and music is *Brahms, His Life and Work* by Karl Geiringer, second edition revised and enlarged (New York, 1947). Another valuable treatise is Walter Niemann, *Brahms* (New York, 1929). The monumental eight-volume biography in German, Max Kalbeck, *Johannes Brahms* (Berlin, 1904-14), while containing much significant data, is none too reliable. It includes some entirely unsubstantiated descriptions of the sources of inspiration or the content of some of the major works. Interesting biographical data with questionable psychiatric interpretations appear in Robert Haven Schauffler, *The Unknown Brahms* (New York, 1933).

Analyses of the compositions appear in Edwin Reeves, *Historical, Descriptive and Analytical Account of the Entire Works of Johannes Brahms* (London, 1912-36); Max Friedlaender, *Brahms' Lieder* (London, 1928); and Daniel Gregory Mason, *The Chamber Music of Brahms* (New York, 1933). Numerous penetrating discussions of major works by Donald Francis Tovey, a devoted admirer of Brahms, appear throughout his collection of *Essays in Musical Analysis* (London, 1935-39).

Chapter XXVII

NATIONALISM IN MUSIC

ALTHOUGH strongly nationalistic tendencies developed among many nineteenth century composers, musical nationalism was not in itself an entirely novel manifestation. Like all other human beings, composers have at all times been influenced by their immediate cultural heritage and by the traditions, customs, and characteristic idioms of expression of the ethnic groups into which they were born. But their musical modes of expression seldom are unmixed; the works of Bach, for example, show his familiarity with characteristic features of both French and Italian styles. Analogous influences can be encountered in the works of other composers.

Despite borrowings from other cultures most composers have succeeded in imprinting an undeniably national stamp on their works. Mozart's *Le Nozze de Figaro,* for example, with its Italian libretto and adherence to the then prevalent Italian operatic tradition, remains a truly Austrian work. And there are many listeners who can detect regional characteristics within the confines of one national group. Brahms' North German background is held to make itself felt in his work; Schubert's music is everywhere conceded to be typically Viennese; and Bavarian tendencies are claimed for some features of the music of Richard Strauss.

Nineteenth century composers were not the first to make use of folk song and folk dances in art music. The extensive use of the fifteenth century folk song, *L'homme Armé* by Renaissance composers has already been mentioned.[1] There are instances of borrowing from peasant tunes and dances, for example, in some of the symphonies and

---

[1] See page 58.

string quartets of Haydn, himself the creator of a great patriotic song, *Gott erhalte Franz den Kaiser.*[2]

The nationalism of the nineteenth century differs from these earlier efforts, however, in its fervent self-awareness and the complete cognizance of its aims. Its first great exponent was Carl Maria von Weber, the self-consciousness of whose work was a natural reaction to the predominance of Italian opera in the German theaters. Similarly, the rise of nationalism in the non-German countries was either a protest against domination by German composers, a reaction to the political oppression of minorities, or the result of military defeat. These protests took the form of a self-imposed resistance to an art that was not indigenous to the soil on which it was conceived. This act of abnegation was the result not of a stiff-necked pride, but rather of a conviction that blind imitation leads only to sterility and that great art must find its roots in it own soil. Whether a composer uses themes actually taken from native music or not is unimportant. The music of most great composers, however, is written in their national musical language, the idioms of which have found simplest expression in their country's folk songs and dances. These features become most apparent when they have their origin in countries whose modes of expression are most removed from our own. Thus the works of Slavonic composers, Russian or Bohemian, sound more nationalistic to our ears than do the symphonies of Brahms, which are, in a sense, equally nationalistic.

Works, operatic or symphonic, based on national history or landscape and employing national musical idioms have often aroused patriotic emotions in native listeners. Hence performances of Sibelius' *Finlandia* were forbidden by the Czarist regime when Finland was a part of the Russian Empire prior to the First World War. Similarly, performances of the operas and symphonic poems of Smetana were prohibited in Czechoslovakia when it was under the domination of Hitler.

Precisely as many romantic works have now become classics, many compositions conceived in an ardently nationalistic spirit have carried their message far beyond their local borders. A typical example is Richard Wagner's *Die Meistersinger von Nürnberg.*

[2] See page 151.

Nationalism, because of its exclusiveness, contains the ferment of its own decay. The nineteenth-century movements as movements of discovery or of liberation from foreign domination were essentially progressive, inasmuch as they brought to light a great store of hitherto hidden or neglected folk music and served to establish national musical literatures. But the great danger of nationalism is that it may become chauvinistic or lend itself to extra-artistic purposes.

Czech Nationalism

Before the First World War, Bohemia, part of what is now Czechoslovakia, was included in the Austro-Hungarian Empire. The Bohemians were subjected to much oppression at the hands of their Austrian masters, and like most oppressed minorities they jealously guarded their own customs and language and exhibited a strong self-awareness as an ethnic group. The interest in Czech music *per se* followed closely on the revival of the Bohemian language and was contemporaneous with the development of a Bohemian literature, all in the face of Austrian decrees establishing German as the sole official language. The two outstanding Czech composers, Smetana and Dvořák, were both zealous patriots, the former's nationalistic activities even making it seem advisable for him to leave Bohemia for a period of years.

Bedřich Smetana

The individual who first brought to light the artistic potentialities of the great store of Czech music was Bedřich Smetana (1824-1884). As a young man he came under the influence of Franz Liszt, and some of his first works were symphonic poems. Smetana's great masterpiece is the opera *The Bartered Bride,* produced in Prague in 1866. It is the great folk opera of Czechoslovakia and has been performed in the National Theater at Prague more than one thousand five hundred times. In its nationalistic implications, its wealth of folk melody, and its emphasis on Czech peasant life, *The Bartered Bride* is comparable to von Weber's *Der Freischütz.* One of the most distinctive features of the score is the series of intriguing dances, which in their catchy melodies and intricate rhythms stem directly from Czech peasant dances, notably the *polka.* The brilliant overture is based on the finale of the second act, the scene in which the bride is ostensibly sold.

Smetana's love for his homeland was also expressed in a cycle of six symphonic poems entitled *My Country*. Of these the second, *The Moldau* (Vltava), the name of the river that flows past Prague, is frequently performed. Smetana's symphonic poem describes its rise from two springs, as well as various occurrences on its banks, including a peasants' wedding for the description of which the composer introduces a typical Bohemian polka:

Ex. 1

Antonin Dvořák

Antonin Dvořák (1841-1904) is best known to American audiences by the Symphony in E minor, *From the New World,* an orchestral work which is thoroughly Bohemian in idiom despite the fact that it was written while the composer was resident in America. Dvořák, like his compatriot Smetana, was an ardent nationalist, and during the four years he spent in this country as director of the now defunct National Conservatory of Music in New York he endeavored to instill a nationalistic outlook in his American pupils.

The New World Symphony had its first performance at a Carnegie Hall concert of the New York Philharmonic Orchestra on December 15, 1893. While some of the themes of the work bear resemblances to American tunes, the composer categorically denied making use of any native American music. The celebrated English horn solo of the *Largo* of the symphony:

Ex. 2

is heard now in a variety of questionable versions, vocal as well as instrumental. The beautiful movement of which it forms a part was inspired, according to a statement made by the composer to the eminent

ANTONIN DVOŘÁK

American critic, Henry E. Krehbiel, by the reading of the account of Hiawatha's wooing that appears in Longfellow's famous poem. Dvořák admired *Hiawatha* and once contemplated writing an opera based on it.

Dvořák may be likened to Schubert, for he too had a seemingly inexhaustible store of melody that he expressed with great spontaneity. Of his long list of compositions, only a few are heard in America today. In addition to the New World Symphony, there are a spirited overture, *Carnaval,* a fine cello concerto, the String Quartet in F major, Opus 96, written in this country and often called The American Quartet; and the characteristically nationalistic *Slavonic Dances,* originally written for piano duet and later orchestrated by the composer.

NORWEGIAN NATIONALISM

Edvard Grieg

The fate that has overtaken most of the creations of the Norwegian composer Edvard Grieg (1843-1907) shows that nationalistic feeling alone is not sufficient for the creation of lasting art works. The distinctive charm of Norwegian folk music was first brought to the attention of the world through Grieg's numerous piano pieces, songs, incidental music for Ibsen's *Peer Gynt,* works for string orchestra, sonatas for violin and piano, and above all the well-known concerto for piano. Grieg appears at his best only in the shorter forms. He was incapable of any sustained thematic development, and the initial attractiveness of many of his melodies palls through mechanical repetition, the obviousness of which is not concealed by a sentimentalized chromatic harmonization. Mannered as many of Grieg's works are, they contain much beautiful music, even if not of the most exalted type.

SUGGESTED READINGS

Rosa Newmarch's authentic *The Music of Czechoslovakia* (London, 1942) discusses Smetana, Dvořák and their works in considerable detail. While there is as yet no adequate English biography of Smetana, several books on Dvořák are available. Among the best are Paul Stefan, *Antonin Dvořák* (New York, 1941); and Alec Robertson, *Dvořák* (London, 1945). David Monrad-Johansen, *Edvard Grieg* (Princeton, 1938), is the authoritative life of the Norwegian minor master. *Grieg,* a symposium edited by Gerald Abraham (London, 1948), consists of a comprehensive series of critical essays.

Chapter XXVIII

RUSSIAN NATIONALISM

NATIONALISM as an artistic creed brought forth its finest products in Russia, thanks to the existence of two rich sources from which it was able to draw its materials—the great wealth of Russian folk song and the music of the old Russian Church.

The extent of the Russian state and the number of diverse ethnic groups included within its borders, plus the traditional musicality of these groups, are responsible for the fact that the country is so rich in folk music. This music has always been assiduously cultivated by the common people. It has also been the object of careful study on the part of professional musicians, and there is hardly a Russian composer whose style has not been influenced by it, consciously or unconsciously.

To Western ears the most striking characteristic of Russian folk music is its use of modal scales,[1] the preservation of which can be attributed to the centuries of isolation from Western influences. Scales like our conventional major and minor are also used, but with a curious fluctuation between them, producing a somewhat uncertain tonality. A definite Oriental influence may be observed in the florid passages executed upon one syllable. Rhythmic irregularity is another pronounced characteristic. The emotional extremes to which the national temperament is prone are also continually reflected in its folk music, with a resultant expressiveness that has earned for it a widespread appreciation outside of its native land.

The Russian Church, one of the branches of the Orthodox Eastern Church (the Greek Catholic Church), unlike the Roman Catholic Church, kept its liturgical music free from secular influences for several centuries. The modal characteristics of this music, traceable to

[1] See page 36.

its Byzantine origin, therefore remained pure and undefiled and, because of the role of the church in the life of the people, exercised considerable influence on their folk music.

During the reign of Catherine the Great (1762-1796) an earnest attempt was made to plant the art and culture of Western Europe on Russian soil. Music was not neglected, but the emphasis fell principally on Italian opera, many composers of which were brought to St. Petersburg. The string quartets of Haydn and Mozart were frequently played by the private ensembles of the nobility. It will be recalled that Beethoven had dedicated his Opus 59 quartets to the Russian ambassador to Vienna, Count Rasoumovsky. Another Russian nobleman, Prince Galitzin, commissioned three of Beethoven's last quartets.

Glinka and Dargomijsky

The composer who overthrew the Western European domination of Russian music and established a truly national school was Michael Glinka (1803-1857). Although his operas *A Life for the Czar* (1836) and *Russlan and Ludmilla* (1842) had not been the first dramatic works to use Russian folk melodies, they were the first to breathe a truly Russian spirit. *A Life for the Czar,* like *Der Freischütz,* laid the foundation for a distinctly national school of opera. Glinka's successor was Alexander Dargomijsky (1813-1869), the composer of the opera *The Stone Guest.* The libretto of this work was a poem by Pushkin based on the Don Juan story utilized by Mozart in his *Don Giovanni.*

"THE FIVE"

During the 1860's a group of five young men living in St. Petersburg took upon themselves the task of building a national school of composition on the foundations laid by Glinka. This coterie, known as "The Five," consisted of Mily Balakireff (1837-1910), César Cui (1835-1918), Nicholas Rimsky-Korsakoff (1844-1908), Alexander Borodin (1833-1887), and Modeste Mussorgsky (1839-1881). With the exception of Balakireff, all were initially amateurs. Although bent upon creating truly Russian compositions, they did not escape the influence of the new forces then making themselves felt in Western music—

the works of Berlioz and Liszt; most of Wagner's, however, they bitterly condemned. The group, as an entity, broke up about 1875.

Balakireff

Balakireff was the rather tyrannical leader of the group. He had come by his role of mentor in a natural fashion, for he was the only member of the band who at the time of its inception possessed a reasonable amount of technical proficiency. The other members of the group subjected themselves to his guidance, and, even though his methods were not of the best, he served as an unfailing source of inspiration to his disciples. His work in stimulating the artistic growth of his fellow-composers is his chief claim to fame, for the number of his compositions is small and performance of them infrequent. The best known is *Islamey,* a virtuoso piano piece reflecting the Orientalism of the times.

Cui

Cui was an officer of artillery, who in addition to being a composer was also a regular contributor of articles on music to the leading journals of Russia and France. Of his numerous compositions, including several operas, the only one likely to be heard today is a little piece called *Orientale.* His importance in the development of a Russian national school rests entirely on his work in popularizing its objectives through his journalistic activities.

Rimsky-Korsakoff

Rimsky-Korsakoff had been trained for the career of officer in the Imperial Russian Navy. As a midshipman on a Russian clipper he visited the United States in 1863-1864. While still in the navy he composed a symphony, a symphonic poem, and an opera. In 1873 he was made inspector of naval bands, a civilian post. The demands of this position laid the foundation for his intimate knowledge of wind instruments. Through long years of self-imposed discipline he finally mastered all of the technical elements that enter into the art of composition. Thus he eventually became the best equipped of all the members of "The Five" and supplanted Balakireff as its mentor. His kind and sympathetic nature made him an excellent teacher, and

NICHOLAS RIMSKY-KORSAKOFF

the list of musicians who received instruction from him during his long professorship at the St. Petersburg Conservatory includes such famous composers as Liadoff, Glazunoff, Stravinsky, Prokofieff, and Respighi.

The music of Rimsky-Korsakoff is one of the finest examples of the fusion of a wide knowledge of national music and a thorough command of the technique of composition. He was primarily a composer of operas, of which all except one are based on either national history or national legend. But the works by which he is best known in America are three purely orchestral compositions composed within a short time of one another. These are the *Capriccio Espagnol* (*Spanish Caprice*) (1887), the symphonic suite *Scheherazade* (1888), and the overture *The Russian Easter* (1888). His finest music, however, is found in the satirical opera *Le Coq d'or* (*The Golden Cockerel*). Completed in 1907, the political innuendoes of the libretto made the opera fall under the censor's ban. It was not performed until 1909, a year after the composer's death.

Most Russian composers have shown a singular skill in handling the orchestra; but of them all Rimsky-Korsakoff is the most outstanding in this regard. His scores abound in original and effective orchestral passages vividly colored and sharply contrasted. As opposed to the German composers, Rimsky-Korsakoff strove to achieve brilliancy rather than sonority. As an innovator in the art of orchestration he ranks with his French forebear Berlioz and, like him, also wrote a valuable textbook on the subject. His melodies are gracefully conceived and always possess a certain charm, but they are more pleasing than moving. All are pervaded by either Russian or Oriental elements.

OVERTURE, "THE RUSSIAN EASTER"

The Russian Easter overture is not only an example of Rimsky-Korsakoff's skill as an orchestrator, but is also an instance of direct usage of national music—in this case that of the Russian Church, on several of whose canticles, as the composer relates in his autobiography, the work is based. He writes: "This legendary and heathen side of the holiday, this transition from the gloomy and mysterious evening of Passion Saturday to the unbridled pagan-religious merry-making on the morn of Easter Sunday, is what I was eager to reproduce in my Overture." [2] The work is dedicated "to the memory of Mussorgsky and Borodin." The opening *Lento mistico* presents in dark colors a theme derived from the hymn *Let God Arise:*

Ex. 1

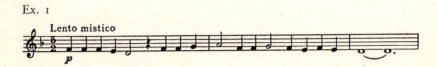

After a short cadenza for the violin, a solo cello, delicately accompanied by flutes and harp, intones the hymn *An Angel Wailed:*

Ex. 2

The two hymns are heard alternately, and there are beautiful solo passages for flute, violin, cello, and clarinet. The tempo now changes to an *Allegro* and the hymn *Let Them Also that Hate Him Flee before Him* is heard in the violins:

Ex. 3

This is followed by a joyous dance-like motive that appears frequently throughout the overture:

Ex. 4

The excitement subsides and a beautifully scored theme derived from the hymn *Christ is Risen* is introduced.

[2] Rimsky-Korsakoff, *My Musical Life* (New York, 1923), page 249.

Ex. 5

After development of Examples 4 and 5, a pontifical recitative for trombone is introduced, apparently in imitation of the chant of a priest. The rest of the overture consists of a series of brilliant episodes based on the themes already quoted; but there is more of vivid change of orchestral timbres than of thematic development. The work comes to a close with a grandiose pronouncement of *Christ is Risen* (Example 5), solemnly intoned by the bass instruments amidst fanfares of trumpets and the peal of bells, the sound of which, according to the composer, is an "invariable feature of ancient Russian life." [3]

Some of Rimsky-Korsakoff's colleagues either possessed a knowledge of the orchestra inadequate for the scoring of their works or else died before completing them. Rimsky-Korsakoff, feeling deeply his obligation to his friends and to the music of his native land, devoted much time to revising or completing their works. Among these acts of kindness may be mentioned the completion and revision of Dargomijsky's *The Stone Guest,* the revision of Borodin's Symphony in B minor as well as the completion and orchestration of parts of his opera *Prince Igor* (with the assistance of his pupil Glazunoff); and notably the revision of almost all of Mussorgsky's works, including his masterpiece, the opera *Boris Godunoff.* Despite his kindliness Rimsky-Korsakoff was somewhat pedantic in his reshaping of Mussorgsky's great opera, and his "corrections" of what he deemed to be Mussorgsky's "harmonic incoherence" [4] now appear as a presumptuous obliteration of pioneering inspiration. But, as Carl Van Vechten has pointed out in his introduction to Rimsky-Korsakoff's autobiography, "it must be remembered that Rimsky-Korsakoff meant it all for the best, that he did no more for his dead friend than he was constantly doing for himself, and that he made it possible for Mussorgsky's music-drama to be performed not only in Russia but also out of it."

[3] Op. cit., page 281.
[4] Op. cit., page 280.

Borodin

Borodin crowded a tremendous amount of activity into his lifetime. He was a physician, professor of organic chemistry at the St. Petersburg Academy of Military Medicine, a prime mover in the formation of a medical college for women and subsequently a member of its staff, a writer of several learned treatises on chemical subjects, as well as a musical dilettante who played the piano and cello fairly well and composed the opera *Prince Igor,* two symphonies, two string quartets, a few short pieces, and some songs.

With the exception of the descriptive orchestral piece, *On the Steppes of Central Asia,* all of Borodin's instrumental music is written in the traditional Western European form—the sonata. In this respect he differs from his colleagues, most of whose instrumental music shows the influence of Berlioz and Liszt. Keenly nationalistic, he possessed a facile melodic gift enabling him to create many beautiful melodies that, while thoroughly original, are imbued with the spirit of folk music. His works possess buoyancy and freshness; their form is at all times devoid of complications, and their orchestration is colorful without being sensational.

SYMPHONY NO. 2, IN B MINOR

Borodin's Second Symphony, in B minor, is probably the finest piece of absolute music produced by any member of "The Five." Completed in 1876, the symphony was composed while Borodin was also working on his historical opera *Prince Igor* as well as on a ballet whose scenes were laid in pre-Christian Russia. This preoccupation with the history of early Russia had its influence on the symphony; for, as Rimsky-Korsakoff narrates in his autobiography, the writer, Vladimir Stassov, librettist of *Prince Igor,* called the work the *"Paladin* Symphony" (Paladin: a peer or a knight). Stassov, who became the literary champion of "The Five," also wrote of the symphony: "The old Russian form predominates. I may add that Borodin himself has often told me that in the adagio [the third movement] he intended to recall the songs of the old Slavonic *bayans* [traveling minstrels]; in the first movement, the assembling of the old Russian princes, and in the finale, the banquets of the heroes to the tones of the *guzla* [a harp-like plucked string instru-

ALEXANDER BORODIN

ment] and bamboo flute, amid the enthusiasm of the people." [5]
Stassov gives no clue to the descriptive purpose of the second movement.

The first movement, in sonata form, opens with a vigorous presentation of its principal theme, a striking subject that remains unharmonized until its seventh measure:

Ex. 6

The second group, in the related key of D major, begins with a lyrical cello melody whose rhythmic attractiveness is characteristic of much of Borodin's music:

Ex. 7

The development places special emphasis on Example 6, which now appears in new rhythmic patterns and in contrasting registers of the orchestra. The recapitulation, which in true Beethoven manner serves as the climax of the development, begins with Example 6, amplified in orchestral sonority by the addition of instruments and elongated by doubling the time values of its notes (augmentation [6]). The coda, in which brilliant wood wind colors figure prominently, leads up to the final statement of Example 6, even more powerful in its instrumentation and now augmented to four times its original length.

The second movement, a *Scherzo* in conventional three-part form to which a coda is affixed, begins with a dissonant chord designed to effect a modulation from the B minor tonality of the first movement. It was suggested to Borodin by Balakireff, who considered the original start in F major to be too abrupt a change. The *Scherzo,* a *Prestissimo* in the uncommon rhythm of $\frac{1}{1}$, contains a striking repeated-note *ostinato* figure appearing initially in the horns and later transferred

[5] Alfred Habets, *Borodin and Liszt* (London, 1895), page 56.
[6] See page 89.

to the trumpets and then to the wood winds. The *Trio,* much more relaxed in mood, is an *Allegretto* in $\frac{6}{4}$. To the accompaniment of wood winds, harp and triangle, the oboe sings a melody strongly reminiscent of the *Prince Igor* whose creation paralleled that of the symphony:

Ex. 8

The *Scherzo* is repeated and is followed by a terse coda that ends in a soft chord for clarinets and horns.

The third movement, free in form and bardic in style, suggests Slavonic minstrelsy in its song-like themes played by solo wind instruments to the accompaniment of the harp. To the sound of harp chords a brief introductory passage for clarinet is followed by a long melody sung by a solo horn:

Ex. 9

The horn melody, although alternating with other themes, has the most important role in the movement. After some manipulation of motives drawn from it, it appears in a richly scored orchestral tutti. The short clarinet figure of the opening reappears and, as the horn intones the initial motive of its theme in augmentation, the movement comes to a tender close. This, however, is not designed to have any element of finality, for the composer directs an immediate transition to the last movement.

The fourth movement, in the bright key of B major, is in sonata form. A tense introduction is given over to allowing the principal theme of the first group to take its final shape as an impulsive dance tune given out by full orchestra in typically Russian rhythmic irregularity:

Ex. 10

The second group begins quietly with another dance theme given to the clarinet:

Ex. 11

The development consists largely of dramatic rhythmic modifications of the two themes quoted above. The recapitulation contains some wholly new and strikingly beautiful changes in orchestral texture, the true author of which may well be Rimsky-Korsakoff. (He assisted Borodin in revising the orchestration of the symphony, the original score of which had been marred by excessive use of the brass.)

Borodin told his friends that some of the folk songs and dances he had collected for use in his *Prince Igor* and had not used in that opera had gone into the Second Symphony. Listeners familiar with the well-known orchestral arrangement of the *Polovtsian Dances* from the opera will easily perceive the strong kinship that exists between the stage work and its symphonic relative.

Mussorgsky

When Mussorgsky first joined Balakireff's group he was an ensign of the guards in the Russian army. The son of prosperous parents, he had been brought up on the land and had early in life acquired an interest in the life of the Russian peasants. As a student at the Military Academy he received some desultory piano instruction, and through the friendly interest of a priest, Father Krupsky, became acquainted with the music of the Church. This was the sum total of his musical equipment when he met Balakireff at the home of Dargomijsky and was inducted into his circle. For a short time he was Balakireff's pupil; but Balakireff lacked the ability to impart knowledge systematically, and Mussorgsky learned practically nothing from him. This lack of formal instruction accounts for both the

MODESTE MUSSORGSKY

strength and the weakness of Mussorgsky's style. He resigned from the army in 1859; but with the liberation of the serfs in 1861 his income dwindled, and by 1863 he found it necessary to accept a clerkship in the Russian civil service. The last eighteen years of his life were thus spent at routine tasks. But despite the stultifying nature of his governmental post, he managed to find time for composition. His premature end, which was hastened by debasing poverty, vile surroundings and acute alcoholism, was brought on largely by the failure of his contemporaries to recognize his unique genius. His works were quickly forgotten after his death. Mussorgsky's biographer, von Riesemann, has pointed out that the revival of interest in his music was the result largely of the untiring activity, during the early part of the twentieth century, of a French singer, Madame Olenine d'Alheim.[7] The list of his works that are performed today includes two operas, *Boris Godunoff* and *Khovanchina,* an orchestral work, *A Night on Bald Mountain,* a series of piano pieces, *Pictures at an Exhibition,* and many particularly fine songs.

Mussorgsky's sole aim in his masterpiece, the "musical folk-drama" *Boris Godunoff,* was accuracy of delineation, and every other consideration was sacrificed to the attainment of this one end. In an uncompleted autobiographical sketch prepared for a German musical dictionary, he states his *credo* quite bluntly: "Art is a means of communicating with people, not an aim in itself. This guiding principle has defined the whole of his creative activity . . . he considers the task of musical art to be the reproduction in musical sounds not merely of the mood of the feeling, but chiefly of the mood of human speech." [8] Mussorgky's letters contain many expressions of his interest in the lives of the common people and his firm belief that the composer should find his inspiration in their speech and other distinctive characteristics. In his desire, therefore, to depict accents of speech and subtleties of character, Mussorgsky developed a musical idiom born of a distrust of conventional methods, simple and direct in its utterance, and of immediate and telling effectiveness. It is this facility in rapid vivid expression that has earned for Mussorgsky the title "realist." No better

[7] Oskar von Riesemann, *Moussorgsky* (New York, 1929), page 386.

[8] *The Musorgsky Reader,* translated and edited by Jay Leyda and Sergei Bertensson (New York, 1947), page 420.

example of Mussorgsky's skill in instantaneous delineation of character and movement can be cited than the sixth of his set of piano pieces, *Pictures at an Exhibition,* a double portrait entitled "Two Polish Jews, rich and poor."

To Western ears the most obvious feature of Mussorgsky's music is its strongly modal character. Inasmuch as he had received practically no formal training, he evolved a harmonic language which, in its freedom from the restraint of established convention, was thoroughly original and in many respects prophetic. The use of a modal idiom in itself produced new chordal sequences; but in addition Mussorgsky did not hesitate to write any chordal progression as long as it served his dramatic purpose. The entire instrumental prelude to the Coronation Scene in *Boris Godunoff,* for example, is constructed on only two chords, effectively juxtaposed:

Ex. 12

His modulations are usually abrupt but never capricious. At no time did Mussorgsky strive for novelty or consciously aim to be different. The weak feature of his works is their orchestration, and it is in the improvement of the instrumentation, more than in any other respect, that the Rimsky-Korsakoff revisions have proved valuable.

Boris Godunoff was presented for the first time in 1874. It was well received by the public, but the professional critics condemned the work rather harshly for its "amateurishness." It was not until early in the twentieth century that its true artistic significance was realized. The work is now the great Russian national opera, the Russian analogue of the German *Der Freischütz* and the Czech *The Bartered Bride*.

Mussorgsky adapted his libretto from the Russian poet Pushkin's historical drama of the same name. It is a somewhat loosely constructed series of scenes based on the usurpation of the Russian throne by Boris Godunoff in 1598. The principal dramatic protagonist, however, is the Russian people, effectively represented in several animated choral episodes.

The voice parts of *Boris* are written in a melodious recitative that is not interrupted to allow interpolations of arias or ensembles except where dramatically justified. Mussorgsky has made use of a few themes derived from folk songs. One of the best known of these, employed as a hymn of praise during the Coronation Scene, had been utilized by Beethoven in the third movement of his second Rasoumovsky quartet (Opus 59, No. 2). Mussorgsky's version is:

Ex. 13

Rimsky-Korsakoff also introduced it into his opera, *The Czar's Bride*.

One of Mussorgsky's friends was the architect Victor Hartmann. Hartmann died prematurely, and a showing of his watercolors and drawings was later held to honor his memory. Mussorgsky has left a record of his visit to this exhibition in a series of ten piano pieces entitled *Pictures at an Exhibition*. An interesting feature of the pieces is the appearance of four short interludes entitled *Promenades,* a series of whimsical self-portraits of the composer as he wanders from picture to picture. The *Promenades* are based on a theme of characteristic rhythmic interest:

Ex. 14

A brilliant and yet understanding orchestration of these colorful pieces, made in 1923 by the French composer Maurice Ravel, appears frequently on symphonic programs and has done much to popularize Mussorgsky's art.

Tchaikovsky

Peter Ilitch Tchaikovsky (1840-1893) was among the first Russian composers to win widespread recognition. He conducted his works in the major cities of Europe, was given an honorary doctor's degree by the University of Cambridge, and was invited to America to conduct his compositions at the opening of Carnegie Hall in 1891. His long popularity in America dates back to 1875, when his Piano Concerto in B-flat minor was given its world première by Hans von Bülow in Boston. The reason for this ready acceptance of Tchaikovsky's works is that they were conceived along the lines of Western European music and yet possessed certain sensational elements attributable to the composer's native temperament. Tchaikovsky was not an ardent musical patriot, nor did he have a very high regard for "The Five" and their theories. Yet like all artists his language was that of his native land, and despite obvious Western influences his music, even if not the product of a self-conscious nationalism, is as typically Russian as that of his zealous contemporaries. The differences between his works and those of "The Five" are to be explained in terms of personality and technical facility rather than in degrees of nationalistic sentiment. It should not be overlooked that Borodin, whose works won the wholehearted approval of his colleagues, was as much influenced by Western European music as was Tchaikovsky.

Like his fellow Russian composers, Tchaikovsky did not initially plan a professional musical career for himself. It was not until his twenty-first year that he began any serious study; and it was not until his twenty-third year that he gave up a clerkship in the Ministry of Justice to devote himself entirely to music. He was freed from financial care by the interest that a wealthy widow, Nadejda von Meck, took in him. For thirteen years she gave him an annual allowance, but stipulated that they were never to meet; and accordingly their sole contact was through correspondence. Tchaikovsky was thus enabled to devote himself to composition unhindered, and the list of his works is a long one. Among the more frequently performed compositions are the Fourth, Fifth, and Sixth Symphonies, the last of which is entitled *Pathétique* by the composer, the overture-fantasia *Romeo and Juliet,* the Piano Concerto No. 1, in B-flat minor, the Violin Concerto, the suite from the ballet *The Nutcracker,* and a few chamber music works. Two noisy orchestral pieces, the *Marche Slav* and the overture *1812* were written to order for patriotic celebrations. Two of his eight operas, *Eugen Onégin* and *Pique Dame,* have been performed at the

PETER ILITCH TCHAIKOVSKY

Metropolitan Opera House, but although still given in European theaters they have gone into eclipse in this country.

The instrumental works of Tchaikovsky are unrestrained expressions of his own emotions. But these are emotions of a peculiar kind; for Tchaikovsky, despite his successes as a composer, was a morbidly sensitive individual, subject to recurrent periods of depression. This despondency was freely expressed in his music, sometimes intruding into his gayest movements. The degree to which Tchaikovsky revealed his woes amounts in some cases to a form of self-pity. This morbidity reaches its high point in his last work, the *Pathétique* Symphony, the concluding movement of which is an *Adagio lamentoso*. But to stress the melancholy of Tchaikovsky is to place a false emphasis on one aspect of his art. Of all the Russian composers he stands out as the foremost master of symphonic form. Each of his last three symphonies is constructed with great skill and with considerable mastery of the intricacies of the larger forms. A distinctive feature of the Fourth and Fifth Symphonies is the use of a recurring "motto theme." But Tchaikovsky does not follow conventional models slavishly; the greater part of the first movement of the Fourth Symphony, for example, is a passionate waltz, and the third movement of the Sixth Symphony is a brilliant and exciting march. Tchaikovsky's melodies are usually of a broad, sweeping character. They are rarely modal and usually lack the folk-like qualities of those of "The Five"; but actual folk tunes are occasionally utilized, as in the last movement of the Fourth Symphony. His orchestration is particularly colorful and owes its effectiveness to the habitual employment of the orchestral instruments in sharply contrasted independent groups. Each melodic line therefore stands out with the greatest clarity. A characteristic of Tchaikovsky's style, which has caused occasional adverse criticism, is his predilection for sensational climaxes, usually reached via an ascending series of short sequential passages stretched out over a long pedal.[9]

SYMPHONY NO. 4, IN F MINOR

As a typical example of Tchaikovsky's music, his Symphony No. 4, in F minor, Opus 36, has been chosen for examination here. It was completed in 1878 and dedicated "To My Best Friend" (Mme. von

[9] See page 50.

Meck). In a long letter to Mme. von Meck, the composer has given his own interpretation of the meaning of the work.[10]

The first movement begins with an incisive repeated-note motive for horns and bassoons:

Ex. 15

In his explanatory program Tchaikovsky has called this motive "the kernel of the entire symphony. This is Fate, that inevitable force which checks our aspirations toward happiness ere they reach their goal." The connection between this opening and that of the Fifth Symphony of Beethoven is obvious and is admitted by Tchaikovsky himself. In a letter to a fellow musician he writes that his work is "in reality, a reflection of Beethoven's Fifth Symphony; I have not copied its musical contents, only borrowed the central idea." [11] The main section of the movement, a *Moderato con anima* in the style of a waltz, is in the conventional sonata form. The melancholy principal subject is given out by the violins and the cellos, playing in octaves:

Ex. 16

Repetitions of this theme are followed by a characteristic ascent to a climax. The second group begins with a whimsical clarinet solo in A-flat minor:

Ex. 17

[10] Modeste Tchaikovsky, *The Life and Letters of Peter Ilitch Tchaikovsky*, abridged English version by Rosa Newmarch (London, 1906), page 275.
[11] *Op. cit.*, page 294.

Upon repetition of this theme in B major by the flute and oboe, an undulating *cantabile* melody in the cellos is combined with it:

Ex. 18

The exposition is brought to a thrilling conclusion as all the strings except the double basses play this broad theme, also in B major:

Ex. 19

The beginning of the development is heralded by the return of the motto theme (Example 15) in the trumpets. There is an intense working out of Example 16 interrupted three times by vigorous pronouncements of the motto theme by the trumpets. The recapitulation is considerably abridged. The coda introduces two transformations of a motive found in the third measure of Example 15. The first of these is a quiet wood wind melody:

Ex. 20

and the second a lively string figure:

Ex. 21

The second movement is a simple three-part form, the first theme of which is sung by a solo oboe:

Ex. 22

The middle section is based on a march-like theme, stiffly announced by clarinets and bassoons:

Ex. 23

The return of the first section is a fine instance of one of Tchaikovsky's favorite orchestral idioms: the theme is played by the first violins while various wood wind instruments alternate at embroidering it with piquant arabesques based on scale patterns. Graceful episodes of this kind can be used as evidence to support the occasional allegation that Tchaikovsky is more a composer of ballet music than a symphonist.

The third movement, marked *Scherzo,* is in the usual three-part form. It is the finest example of the manner in which Tchaikovsky continually divides his orchestra into contrasting groups—in this instance strings, pizzicato throughout the movement, wood winds, and brass. At no time do these groups lose their independence. The *Scherzo* itself is given to the strings alone, the *Trio* to the wood winds and the brasses. All these groups indulge in sharp retorts in the coda.

The last movement, according to the composer, depicts a popular festival and is an expression of "simple, vigorous, primitive joy." It is a wild, orgiastic movement with many climaxes ably punctuated by the cymbals. A Russian folk song, *In the field there stood a birch tree,* serves as its principal thematic element and appears in several variations:

Ex. 24

A second theme, march-like in character and noisily orchestrated, appears before and during the variations on the folk song:

Ex. 25

The motto theme makes a dramatically unexpected appearance in the midst of the tumult, after which a long and boisterous coda exploits some of the possibilities of Example 25.

SUGGESTED READINGS

The best general books on Russian music are by the authoritative English writer Gerald Abraham. These are *Studies in Russian Music* (New York, 1936) and *On Russian Music* (New York, 1939). With M. D. Calvocoressi, Abraham has written *Masters of Russian Music* (New York, 1936).

Reliable and informative works on individual composers and their music are:

Victor I. Seroff, *The Mighty Five, The Cradle of Russian National Music* (New York, 1948).

Gerald Abraham, *Borodin, The Composer and His Music* (London, 1927).

Oskar von Riesemann, *Moussorgsky* (New York, 1929).

M. D. Calvocoressi, *Mussorgsky* (New York, 1946).

Jay Leyda and Sergei Bertensson, Translators and Editors, *The Musorgsky Reader* (New York, 1947).

N. A. Rimsky-Korsakoff, *My Musical Life* (New York, 1928).

Herbert Weinstock, *Tchaikovsky* (New York, 1943).

Wladimir Lakond, Translator and Editor, *The Diaries of Tchaikovsky* (New York, 1945).

Gerald Abraham, Editor, *The Music of Tchaikovsky* (New York, 1946).

No detailed biographies of Balakireff or Cui are available in English. A resumé of *Boris Godunoff* appears in Ernest Newman, *More Stories of Famous Operas* (Philadelphia, 1946).

Chapter XXIX

FRENCH NATIONALISM

B EFORE the Franco-Prussian War (1870-1871), French composers
  could win appreciation in their homeland only if they confined
themselves to the production of operas; and these operas had to follow a tradition that had been established by foreign composers. Since
1831 the favorite operatic composer at Paris had been a German, Jakob
Meyerbeer.[1] Instrumental music was neglected. It will be recalled
that works of Berlioz had been treated with indifference by his fellow-
countrymen during his lifetime.

The disastrous results of the Franco-Prussian War served to rally
French composers to their own artistic defense. Capitalizing on patriotic sentiment, they formed an organization, the *Société Nationale de
Musique* (National Music Society), whose professed aim was "to aid
the production and the popularization of all serious musical works,
whether published or unpublished, of French composers."[2] The Society was responsible for the growth of a French school of great
importance, a school which definitely marked the end of German
hegemony in the sphere of music. Through the existence of this organization worth-while works of native composers were assured a hearing. The long list of important French compositions, including many
now universally known, that had their first performance at the Society's
concerts indicates the significant role that the organization played.
The necessarily limited scope of the activities of the Society was also
responsible for the diversion of emphasis from operatic to instrumental
music and, consequently, for the creation of a national literature of
chamber and symphonic music. Of the many composers who were

---

[1] See page 297.
[2] Romain Rolland, *Musicians of Today* (London, 1928), page 268.

active in the affairs of the Society during its early years, the names of several remain well known today: Camille Saint-Saëns, César Franck, Edouard Lalo, Jules Massenet, Emmanuel Chabrier and Vincent d'Indy. Saint-Saëns resigned in 1886. Franck was the president until his death in 1890, although he had refused the title.

The French nationalistic movement differed from those taking place around it in that it was not at all preoccupied with folk music. Nor was its purpose a purely chauvinistic one having as its goal the exclusion of German music from French concert halls. Its aim was purely the establishment of a French school of instrumental composition as proof that German composers held no monopoly in this sphere. But like their fellow nationalists in other lands, these French composers could not entirely escape the influence of either the innovations in form made by Liszt or the new harmonic language and orchestral texture of Wagner. These influences were so strong and the adoption of them so fruitful that these French composers may be considered among the outstanding successors of Liszt and Wagner; for the majority of German composers who attempted to follow in Wagner's footsteps were uninspired imitators. Curiously enough the influence of Berlioz was negligible, although the Franco-Prussian War helped bring about the final awakening of popular interest in his music as well. Most of the French composers of the last quarter of the nineteenth century were of essentially classical temperament, and the romantic endeavors of their predecessor failed to arouse any desire for emulation on their part.

Saint-Saëns

Camille Saint-Saëns (1835-1921) was an enormously gifted composer whose works impress more with the precision of their musical logic than with the significance of their content. A virtuoso pianist and organist, Saint-Saëns wrote poetry and plays, dabbled in astronomy and mathematics, and composed in all types and forms. His works are characterized by the presence of suave well-turned melodies, fluently expressed orchestration, and flawless structure, all combining to create the impression of intellectual elegance with a strong classical bent. Of Saint-Saëns' symphonic poems, all conceived under the influence of Liszt, only the *Danse macabre* with its waltz transformation of the *Dies irae* remains in the repertory. The Biblical opera *Samson et Dalila*

was produced in 1877 in Weimar, thanks to Liszt's efforts in the composer's behalf.   Virtuoso instrumentalists often perform his Violin Concerto No. 3, in B minor, and two of his five piano concertos, the Second,
in G minor, and the Fourth, in C minor.   But it is usually held that
Saint-Saëns' masterpiece is his Symphony No. 3, in C minor, a splen-
didly integrated piece of musical craftsmanship in which organ and
piano (played by two pianists) are added to the orchestra.   The four
movements of the symphony share one theme, thus displaying the
cyclical form so common in French music of the time and discussed
on page 379.

Franck

César Franck (1822-1890), the father of the French school, was a
Belgian by birth; but he spent the greater part of his life in Paris and
was to all intents and purposes a Frenchman.   The life of Franck may
be likened to that of Bach, for he also was an obscure church organist
who received little recognition during his lifetime.   If it had not been
for the Société Nationale, it is doubtful if much of his music would
ever have been performed at all.   Such works as were given a public
hearing were indifferently received, and it was not until the last year
of his life that he was accorded any expression of public approval.
From 1860 until his death Franck was the organist of the church of
Ste.-Clotilde in Paris.   He was not only a great virtuoso, but also a
master of improvisation.   Liszt heard him improvise at Ste.-Clotilde in
1866 and in his enthusiasm compared Franck to Bach.   In addition to
his church post Franck later held the position of professor of organ
at the Paris *Conservatoire.*

Despite his duties at Ste.-Clotilde and the *Conservatoire,* the drudgery
of private instrumental instruction, and his ceaseless creative labors, he
found time to be an inspiring teacher of composition.   With the exception of Liszt, no other great composer has possessed the humanity
and the disinterestedness of Franck towards his pupils, and it is therefore not to be wondered at that they worshiped him as "le père Franck."
It was through these pupils as well as by his own compositions that
Franck laid the foundation for the French school.   Among the better
known of this band of disciples were Henri Duparc, composer of some
fine songs; Vincent d'Indy, composer of the symphonic variations *Istar,*

CÉSAR FRANCK

who later became his master's biographer and artistic successor; the gifted but short-lived Ernest Chausson, composer of the well-known *Poème* for violin and orchestra, and a splendid symphony. The following were not pupils of Franck but came within the orbit of his artistic influence: Gabriel Pierné, Emmanuel Chabrier of *España* fame, and Paul Dukas, composer of the orchestral scherzo, *L'Apprenti sorcier* (*The Sorcerer's Apprentice*), another of the many works inspired by Goethe.

Franck's tolerance apparently extended to his criticism of his own works, for of the great quantity of music that he turned out with such methodical earnestness, only a comparatively small amount merits performance today. His fame as a creative artist rests on the following compositions, all late works: the Prelude, Chorale and Fugue, and the Prelude, Aria and Finale for piano solo; the Symphonic Variations for piano and orchestra; the Sonata for Violin and Piano in A major; the String Quartet in D major; the Piano Quintet in F minor; the Symphony in D minor (Franck composed only one work in each of these categories); several pieces for organ of which the *Pièce héroïque* is the best known; and an oratorio, *Les Béatitudes*.

Franck's Style

Franck as a composer invites comparison with Brahms, for his outlook was thoroughly classical, and, as examination of the list of his great works shows, he was a master of the larger forms. But here the analogy ends. Brahms was indifferent to most of what was going on around him. Franck, while still employing the classical forms, introduced into them many of those additions to the vocabulary of music for which Liszt and Wagner were largely responsible.

The first of these features is the principle of thematic transformation employed by Liszt in his symphonic poems. Franck applies this to large-scale absolute music by recurrently introducing one theme, suitably modified, in each of the several movements comprising a work, thereby creating a community of interest in the movements that serves to integrate them into a unified whole. The procedure had, of course, been anticipated by Berlioz with the *idée fixe* of the *Symphonie fantastique,* and it had already been utilized in the works of Liszt and Tchaikovsky. An instrumental work so constructed is called a *cyclical*

form.   An excellent example is Franck's Piano Quintet in F minor.
Here the theme that pervades the three movements of the work makes
its appearance in the first movement in this form:

Ex. 1

In the course of the slow middle movement it recurs as:

Ex. 2

Its final appearance is as a *pianissimo* reminiscence in the middle of
the coda of the last movement:

Ex. 3

Franck's harmonic language stems directly from the chromaticism
of Liszt and Wagner and carries it on to new levels.   His harmonic
idiom is characterized by continual modulation, often so excessive as
to obscure tonality, by elusive cadences, and by a great frequency of
semitonal progressions.   The Franck melodies, unlike those of his
German contemporary Brahms, are uniformly short-breathed and have
a curious tendency to cluster about a focal note.   The theme from the
Piano Quintet quoted above is typical.

But the music of Franck, like that of all the great masters, eludes
characterization in terms of a particular brand of musical syntax.   The
underlying spirit of his works is one of deep sincerity and earnestness
that while reserved in its utterance is of a highly personal nature.

PRELUDE, CHORALE AND FUGUE

The noble Prelude, Chorale and Fugue for piano, first performed at
a concert of the Société Nationale in 1885, is one of the results of
Franck's close contact with the music of Bach.   But in typical fashion

he has utilized the old forms in the spirit of the late nineteenth century. Between the units of the customary prelude and fugue combination he has inserted a movement that, although written for an instrument, is appropriately entitled "Chorale." The three movements, which are joined one to the other, comprise a cyclical form whose motto theme may be represented as:

Ex. 4

The Prelude, in the improvisational style associated with the form, commences with a series of toccata-like *arpeggio* figures out of which the motto theme emerges as:

Ex. 5

The Chorale is based on two themes, the first of which is a transformation of the motto theme:

Ex. 6

The second theme is a meditative air of touching simplicity:

Ex. 7

The subject of the four-voiced Fugue is another transformation of the motto theme:

Ex. 8

The development contains a fine example of inversion,[3] the fugue subject appearing as:

Ex. 9

The development reaches a climax and is followed by a section that Franck entitles *come una cadenza* (like a cadenza).   This commences with reminiscences of the opening arpeggios of the Prelude into which the melody of Example 7 is eventually introduced with great delicacy. A long crescendo finally culminates in a dramatic contrapuntal combination of the chorale melody and the fugue subject.   The entire work is brought to a close with a rather banal series of fanfares derived from Example 7.

SYMPHONY IN D MINOR

The celebrated Symphony in D minor, completed in 1888, is Franck's best-known composition and occupies an important place in the symphonic repertory as a universally accepted classic.   The work is ostensibly in only three movements but, as will be shown later, the second movement combines the functions of a slow movement and a scherzo.

The first movement is in sonata form, but the slow introduction and the entire first group are repeated literally in a different key.   The introduction opens with a solemn questioning motive that had already found employment in Beethoven's String Quartet in F major (Opus 135), in Liszt's *Les Préludes,* and in Wagner's *Die Walküre:*

Ex. 10

The introduction also contains a tranquil melody harmonized in Franck's characteristically chromatic manner:

[3] See page 89.

Ex. 11

The introduction is now followed by the conventional *Allegro* commencing with an energetic diminution of Example 10:

Ex. 12

The introductory and allegro sections are now repeated in F minor. After a brief transition the key shifts to F major, the key of the second group. Two important themes are heard in the new tonality. Both exhibit Franck's predilection for melodies that pivot on one note, in this instance:

The first, a quiet limpid theme, is given out by the strings with effective imitation in the outer parts:

Ex. 13

After some characteristically elusive modulations the music attains the level of a *fortissimo* and the second theme of this group appears in jubilant syncopation:

Ex. 14

Franck takes leave of this motive rather reluctantly, and it is only after much pensive manipulation of it that the development finally gets under way. This section, although of considerable length, is filled with dramatic interest through ingenious treatment of the subject matter. It culminates in a grandiose canonic statement of Example 10 in a slow tempo and in its original key of D minor. After some remote modulations the recapitulation settles down into the conventional restatement of the exposition. The coda consists of an extended crescendo over a modulating ground bass derived from Example 14:

Ex. 15

The movement is brought to a triumphant conclusion with another canonic statement of Example 10.

As has already been mentioned, the second movement is in reality two movements telescoped into one. Its first section corresponds to the usual slow movement. The introduction, for strings pizzicato and harp, also serves as accompaniment for the principal theme, a plaintive melody in B-flat minor sung by the English horn:

Ex. 16

A wholly unexpected modulation turns the course of this theme into B-flat major, in which key another melody appears as a contrasting middle section:

Ex. 17

Example 16 now returns for what is ostensibly a *Da capo*. But the procedure is abandoned, and after a few tentative starts the muted strings commence a delicate passage in the mood of a Mendelssohn scherzo:

Ex. 18

The scherzo part of the movement also has its contrasting middle section, a graceful tune given out by the clarinet:

Ex. 19

The Scherzo returns, and after two preliminary trials in different keys appears in combination with Example 16 in the tonic key of B-flat minor:

Ex. 20

The beautiful coda is based on variants of Examples 17 and 19 and concludes with a *pianissimo* chord of B-flat major adorned by a quiet harp arpeggio.

The last movement starts out as though it planned to follow the normal sonata form pattern. The suave first subject is given out by the bassoons and cellos:

Ex. 21

The second group in B major introduces a solemn theme scored for brass alone—an excellent example of the influence of Wagner:

Ex. 22

Instead of proceeding to develop these themes Franck returns to the material of the second movement, and the English-horn melody (Example 16) is heard again. After this interruption the development of Examples 21 and 22 commences and reaches a climax in the presentation by the full orchestra of Example 16. This is followed by the introduction of two themes from the first movement, Example 10 and Example 14. The coda, like the corresponding section in the first movement, is worked out over a modulating ground bass; and the movement terminates with a canonic treatment of its first theme, Example 21.

Suggested Readings

The formation of the Société Nationale is described by Romain Rolland in the chapter "The Awakening" included in his *Musicians of Today* (London, 1928). The work of Franck and his pupils receives copious treatment in Edward Burlingame Hill, *Modern French Music* (Boston, 1924). Vincent d'Indy's *César Franck* (London, 1910), is the work of a pupil and disciple, and tends, therefore, to be generous in its praises. Norman Demuth, *César Franck* (New York, 1949), is an uneven work that, despite some occasional factual errors, has much to recommend it. No full-scale life of Saint-Saëns is as yet available.

Chapter XXX

POST-WAGNERIAN MUSIC
IN GERMANY AND AUSTRIA

OF THE numerous German and Austrian composers who ventured to follow in the footsteps of Wagner, only a handful escaped being mere imitators. The composers achieving the greatest success were those who effected a transference of the Wagnerian technique to non-operatic spheres by utilizing the Wagner orchestra and Wagner's methods of thematic development for symphonic music, and his manner of associating the spoken word with instrumental music for the art song. The only significant German dramatic work of the immediate post-Wagnerian era which adhered faithfully to Wagnerian precepts and yet showed an individual style was the fairy opera *Hänsel und Gretel* of Engelbert Humperdinck (1854-1921), produced at Weimar in 1893.

Richard Strauss

The most outstanding German composer since Wagner was Richard Strauss, born in Munich June 11, 1864 and dying on Sept. 8, 1949 at the age of eighty-five. His career was long and brilliant and despite initially adverse criticisms, a large number of his works became repertory pieces during his lifetime. Strauss' father was a famous horn player of ultraconservative temperament, who saw to it that his precocious son received a thorough musical training at the hands of various Munich pedagogues. Most of Strauss' earlier works were written in a conventional idiom, and for a time his musical development seemed to be progressing in the direction of Brahms. An early symphony of Strauss written in the best classical tradition was given its première under Theodore Thomas in New York in 1884. Strauss' conversion

RICHARD STRAUSS

to the aesthetic principles embodied in the works of Liszt and Wagner is attributed by the composer himself to his contacts with a contemporary musician, Alexander Ritter, who was not only close to the Weimar circle but also had married a niece of Wagner. Strauss described Ritter's influence upon him as follows: "He urged me on to develop the expressive, the poetic in music after the example set by Berlioz, Liszt and Wagner." [1]

Strauss' Tone-Poems

The result of Ritter's exhortations was to divert Strauss' creative gifts into the channels of program music. During the interval 1887-1898 a notable series of symphonic poems, or as the composer called them, "tone poems" (*Tondichtungen*), came from his facile pen. Of these the following have become firmly established in the modern orchestral repertory: *Don Juan* (1888), *Tod und Verklärung* (*Death and Transfiguration*) (1889), *Till Eulenspiegels lustige Streiche* (*Till Eulenspiegel's Merry Pranks*) (1895), *Also sprach Zarathustra* (*Thus Spake Zarathustra*) (1896), *Don Quixote* (1897), *Ein Heldenleben* (*A Hero's Life*) (1898). The high artistic level of the tone poems has not been attained by Strauss in his later program symphonies, the *Symphonia domestica* (1903) and the *Alpensymphonie* (*Alpine Symphony*) (1915). Although the tone poems are directly descended from the symphonic poems of Liszt, Strauss, thanks to the wide scope of his imagination and to his complete mastery of all of the many factors that enter into the art of orchestral composition, invested the symphonic poem with an entirely new musical significance. This technical mastery is particularly evident in his sense of form, in his polyphonic skill, and in his orchestration.

Don Juan is the only work of Strauss that is closely modeled after a poem, in this instance the *Don Juan* of the Hungarian poet Nicolaus Lenau. Although a poem by the composer's friend Alexander Ritter prefaces the score of *Tod und Verklärung,* the verses were written after the work was completed and hence may be regarded as an *ex post facto* literary interpretation bearing the composer's approval. None of the other tone poems possesses a detailed literary program. *Till Eulenspiegel, Don Quixote,* and *Also sprach Zarathustra* are rather

[1] Max Steinitzer, *Richard Strauss* (Stuttgart, 1927), page 56.

freely conceived musical elaborations of the basic ideas involved in three works of literature. *Ein Heldenleben* is frankly autobiographical.

Although all the Strauss tone poems are pure program music, their formal aspects are completely satisfying, and the music remains comprehensible without any reference to the program. Strauss has maintained that he recognizes no difference between absolute music and descriptive music, and that a program is merely an incentive to the creation of a new musical form. The formal plan of each of the tone poems represents a notable advance over Liszt's system of "transformation of themes," although that device has been freely employed, and *Don Juan* and *Tod und Verklärung* show the strong influence of Strauss' great predecessor. In *Till Eulenspiegel* Strauss reverts to the classical rondo. In *Don Quixote* the adventures of the knight are described in a series of variations. *Ein Heldenleben* is a huge orchestral movement whose formal outlines bear a very close resemblance to those of the classical sonata form.

The texture of the tone poems is extraordinarily rich and full, due to Strauss' superlative command of orchestration and to his natural inclination toward a polyphonic manner of expression. Some of the finest examples of Strauss' contrapuntal facility are to be found in *Ein Heldenleben*. But this fluency also leads Strauss to present his listener's ears with polyphonic complexities which in their wealth of melodic freight occasionally defeat their own purpose.

Strauss possessed unusual melodic gifts. His melodies, most of which are conceived along large lines, display impetuosity and vigor, and a characteristic boldness. The opening theme of *Ein Heldenleben* (quoted on page 33) and the horn theme of *Till Eulenspiegel* (quoted on page 393) are typical examples of the great pitch range of many of Strauss' melodies. A curious feature of his melodic idiom, however, is the frequency with which it lapses into a straightforward diatonic tunefulness which, while far from commonplace, is somewhat difficult to reconcile with the more complex melodic formations abounding in his works. Although almost every composition of Strauss exhibits this quality of *Gemütlichkeit* (geniality), it may best be observed in his opera *Der Rosenkavalier* (*The Rose Cavalier*).

Strauss' Orchestration

The works of Strauss have established new standards of orchestration as well as of orchestral performance. The composer took Wagner's orchestra, but discovered new usages for its constituent instruments and added to their number. Strauss wrote almost habitually for large orchestras. A performance of *Ein Heldenleben,* for example, requires an orchestra of one hundred and five players. This insistence on large orchestras originated in Strauss' apparent need for great volume of tone, a need which is met not only by using a large number of instruments, but also by making frequent use of their intense upper registers; he occasionally went so far as to write passages beyond the normal ranges of the orchestral instruments. As a result of Strauss' originality in this sphere his works have played an important part in the development of the art of orchestration. But it should be noted that all the many devices for which he is responsible were the outcome of a need for a more accurate means of musical communication, and not mere attempts at musical eccentricity. The demands which Strauss made on the orchestral instruments, by breaking down traditional concepts regarding their range and their capabilities, have done much to raise standards of orchestral proficiency. This has been particularly apparent in the case of the brass instruments, from the players of which great virtuosity is demanded. The Strauss tone poems, despite their age, remain among the more difficult of orchestral works.

Strauss' uncanny skill at using the orchestra as a delineative agency has won for him the appellation of "realist." In *Don Quixote,* for example, he has produced an amazingly effective imitation of the bleating of a herd of sheep by having muted brass instruments play querulous dissonances in a rapidly tongued tremolo called "flutter-tonguing." The same work also calls for a wind machine. In *Ein Heldenleben* Strauss revenged himself on those critics who had belittled his works by depicting them in a series of haggling, carping passages given out by wood-wind instruments. To overemphasize the realistic aspects of Strauss' orchestral wizardry, however, is to do him an injustice. Few composers have achieved the rich glow which emanates from certain contemplative sections of *Don Juan, Don Quixote, Ein Heldenleben,* and the *Symphonia domestica.*

"TILL EULENSPIEGELS LUSTIGE STREICHE"

To *Till Eulenspiegel* has been accorded the place of honor among Strauss' tone poems. Of all his works it is the most concise in form, the most human in its sympathies, the most universal in its outlook. Above all it bears the stamp of sincerity, a quality that, unfortunately, is not to be found in all of Strauss' music. The full title of the work is *Till Eulenspiegels lustige Streiche, nach alter Schelmenweise—in Rondeauform,* the translation of which is: *Till Eulenspiegel's Merry Pranks, after the old roguish manner—in rondo form.*

Till Eulenspiegel is said to have lived in the fourteenth century. He was a clever knave who used his wits to perpetuate all manner of tricks on pompous, dull-witted members of the bourgeoisie. According to the medieval *Volksbuch* of a Dr. Thomas Murner, in which Till's life and exploits have been chronicled, he even succeeded in evading a sentence of death that had been passed upon him, and his end was a peaceful one. In Strauss' musical account of Till Eulenspiegel's career, however, the rogue's life terminates on the gallows.

When Strauss composed *Till Eulenspiegel* he merely gave the above title, hoping that "after the old roguish manner" would indicate the mischievous nature of his piece. The accounts of Till's exploits were household tales in Germany, and Strauss naturally assumed that his musical narrative would need no further elucidation. In reply to a request for an explanatory program to accompany the première of the piece, Strauss declared that it was impossible to give a detailed description of its contents. But his refusal included the following provocative statement: "Let us therefore leave it to the hearers themselves to crack the nuts the rogue hands to them. By way of helping them to a better understanding, it seems sufficient to point out the two Eulenspiegel motives, which, in the most manifold disguises, moods, and situations pervade the whole up to the catastrophe, when, after he has been condemned to death, Till is strung up to the gibbet. For the rest, let them guess at the musical jokes which a rogue has offered them." [2]

Strauss has stated that his work is in rondo form, but his conception of the rondo form is a late nineteenth-century one. The rondo element

[2] Henry T. Finck, *Richard Strauss, The Man and His Works* (Boston, 1917), page 174.

in Till consists of the frequent reappearance of the two motives associated with the hero; but as opposed to classical practice, these motives
undergo many transformations. The recurring feature of the work
is, therefore, the personality of the knave as seen in his various exploits.

The first of the two motives upon which the composition is based
is given out in genial fashion by the violins in a short prologue:

Ex. 1

The second basic motive, of characteristic breadth and of much rhythmic originality, is entrusted to a solo horn:

Ex. 2

Of these two motives, the first is subjected to the greater number of
transformations. One of the most typical variants is a saucy figure,
given out on its first appearance by the E-flat clarinet,[3] the small clarinet
which Berlioz had used so spectacularly in the *Symphonie fantastique:*[4]

Ex. 3

In a subsequent episode the same theme is broken up into fragments:

Ex. 4

The following transformation of the second theme evidently depicts
one of Till's wooings. The composer has marked it *liebeglühend*

---

[3] Although Strauss' score calls for the slightly larger D-clarinet, the E-flat instrument is
habitually used.

[4] See page 275.

(ardently loving) and has directed that the violins add a humorous touch by playing a *glissando* at the end of the phrase:

Ex. 5

Strauss, in characteristic fashion, cannot resist the temptation to effect a combination of motives derived from the two basic themes:

Ex. 6

Till is finally apprehended and after a short trial, whose atmosphere is created by low-pitched repeated chords and snare-drum rolls, is condemned to death. The composer himself has stated that the following stentorian figure given out by bassoons, horns, trombones, and tuba represents the pronouncement of the death sentence:

Ex. 7

The penetrating shriek of the E-flat clarinet, later joined by the oboes and English horn, describes Till's end on the scaffold. A flutter in a flute adds the typically Straussian touch of realism:

Ex. 8

The work ends with a whimsical epilogue which seems to indicate that Till's demise is not to be taken too seriously.

Till Eulenspiegel is a fine example of humor in music, though, to be sure, a different type of humor from that of Beethoven. Touches of the humor and geniality which characterize so much of *Till Eulenspiegel* also manifest themselves in Strauss' other works.

Strauss' Songs

Although Strauss' primary importance is in other types of composition, he has made a few significant contributions to the repertory of song. His song production taken as a whole, however, has been uneven, and in many instances surprisingly unoriginal. The only successful works in this genre are the predominantly lyrical songs, many of which have won wide popularity and well deserve to be classed with the great German *Lieder*. Of them, *Traum durch die Dämmerung* (*Dream at Twilight*) seems to have been Strauss' particular favorite. A fragment of it appears among quotations from the tone poems in "The Hero's Works of Peace" section of his *Ein Heldenleben*.

Strauss' Operas

Strauss had written operas as early as 1892, but his great triumphs in operatic composition did not occur until after the advent of the twentieth century. Of Strauss' fifteen operas, four are conceded to be great masterworks and are seemingly destined for a long life on the world's operatic stages. These are *Salomé* (1905), *Elektra* (1909), *Der Rosenkavalier* (1911), and *Ariadne auf Naxos* (1912). *Salomé* utilizes a German translation of the famous one-act play of Oscar Wilde. For *Elektra, Der Rosenkavalier,* and *Ariadne,* as well as three other operas, Strauss had as his librettist a distinguished man of letters, the Austrian poet and dramatist, Hugo von Hofmannsthal (1874-1929). The vocal writing, particularly in *Salomé* and *Elektra,* is often cruel and inhuman, although there are occasional moments in which the voices are allowed to shake off the tremendous orchestral weight mercilessly loaded upon them. The operas are further testimonials of Strauss' ability to manipulate a huge orchestra with telling effectiveness. Wagnerian influences are evident in the use of leading motives, but Strauss' motives often lack distinction, a defect that their elaborate orchestral development cannot conceal. The emphasis that Strauss places upon the orchestra often relegates the voice to a secondary position, with consequent impairment of the intelligibility of the words.

Der Rosenkavalier, one of the world's great comic operas, contains some notable departures from Strauss' normal operatic methods. The work includes vocal ensembles of ravishing beauty and numerous Viennese waltzes, the charm of which more than atones for the historical error which Strauss perpetrated in introducing them into an opera whose action takes place about the middle of the eighteenth century, many years before the waltz had achieved popularity in Vienna.

Strauss lived to see many of his compositions, which once created such a stir, become widely-accepted classics. But while his craftsmanship increased with the years, his inventive power and his faculty for self-criticism waned considerably. No truly great work came from his pen after *Ariadne,* and the last thirty-eight years of his life appear as the anti-climax of a long and significant career.

Anton Bruckner

Among Wagner's most reverent disciples was the intensely religious Austrian composer Anton Bruckner (1824-1896). Bruckner, initially a country schoolmaster, was for some time organist at the cathedral at Linz and later held the position of professor of theory and organ at the Vienna Conservatory. His works include eight symphonies and three movements of an uncompleted ninth, in addition to a considerable amount of sacred choral music. All of Bruckner's symphonies are large-scale compositions in which the influence of Wagner's harmonic procedures and methods of orchestration is particularly evident. Bruckner was an intensely earnest soul for whom composition was an act of devotion. His symphonies, however, are prolix and diffuse— fervent passages of great inspiration alternating with sections that are merely pious attenuations of commonplace materials. The works of Bruckner have achieved great popularity in Germany and Austria. American audiences, however, have on the whole failed to be impressed by them.

Gustav Mahler

Gustav Mahler (1860-1911) is usually grouped with Bruckner, for he is also a composer of colossal symphonies, nine in number, in addition to an impressive orchestral song cycle in six movements, *Das Lied von der Erde* (*The Song of the Earth*). Mahler had spent many years at the conductor's desk and had thus acquired an intimate knowledge of the inner workings of the orchestra. Hence the orchestration of his works, planned with great attention to detail, is rich and colorful. Four of his symphonies contain important vocal parts. The loftiness of Mahler's conceptions and the overwhelming intensity that characterized his life as well as his music may fail to make themselves apparent to most listeners because of the composer's tendency to indulge in overstatement and overelaboration. The Second Symphony, in C minor (1894), for greatly augmented orchestra, soprano, alto, and chorus, with its stirring finale, an exalted setting of Klopstock's *Resurrection* Ode, may be regarded as typical of Mahler's style.

The inordinate length of many of Mahler's works has been another hindrance to their ready acceptance in America, but no orchestral conductor who has had unswerving faith in Mahler and his music (Bruno Walter, for example) has ever failed to stir an audience with a rendition of one of his symphonies. The position of Mahler in musical art is still a disputed one; but performances and recordings of his works are continually increasing in number.

Hugo Wolf

Wagner's methods of combining poetry and music were transferred to the song by the Austrian composer, Hugo Wolf (1860-1903). Wolf, however, was no mere imitator of Wagner. Proceeding from Wagner's assumption that the purpose of a musical setting was to heighten the effectiveness of poetry, Wolf developed new standards of declamation, new harmonic methods, and new ways of employing the piano in association with the voice.

Wolf's period of productivity, extending from 1888 to 1897, was amazingly brief; the majority of his songs were written before 1891. It was Wolf's custom to make a thorough study of one particular poet and, after having thoroughly absorbed his literary style, to commence setting his poems to music. Once composition was begun, Wolf turned out one master song after another at a furious rate. His fifty-one settings of Goethe's poems, for example, were written within the space of three months. The greater part of Wolf's creativeness is included in the following six groups of songs: fifty-three Mörike songs, twenty

Eichendorff songs, fifty-one Goethe songs, forty-four songs from the *Spanisches Liederbuch* (*Spanish Song Book*) of Heyse and Geibel, forty-six songs from the *Italienisches Liederbuch* (*Italian Song Book*) of Heyse, and three sonnets by Michelangelo.

Wolf's vocal writing is predominantly declamatory. His declamation, however, is not to be confused with that of Wagner. Wagner's methods were designed to meet the needs of the operatic stage and involved settings of dramatic poetry of heroic proportions. Wolf, on the other hand, dealt largely with short lyrical poems, every nuance of which stands revealed through the subtleties of his declamation. Wolf's emphasis on a declamatory style, while resulting in a certain melodic impoverishment of the vocal part, adds immeasurably to the significance of the poem. It also demands that the listener have some knowledge of the poem prior to hearing it sung. It is worthy of note that whenever Wolf performed his songs before his friends it was always his custom to preface his renditions by careful and expressive readings of the texts he had set.

An important feature of Wolf's style is the utter objectivity of his approach to poetry. In a letter to Engelbert Humperdinck, the composer of *Hänsel und Gretel,* he spoke of himself somewhat humorously as "an objective lyricist who can pipe in all keys." [5] This objectivity, combined with an acute literary sensitivity, was responsible for the success with which Wolf met the diverse needs of his poems. Wolf's attitude toward his poets is shown by the titles he gave his collections, for example, *Gedichte von Goethe für eine Singstimme und Klavier von Hugo Wolf* (*Poems by Goethe set for voice and piano by Hugo Wolf*).

The above title also indicates Wolf's concept of the function of the piano in his songs. He lists it as an associate of the voice; the word "accompaniment" is significantly absent. Wolf assigns to the piano a role that in its relation to the poem is somewhat analogous to that of the Wagnerian orchestra. Like Wagner's orchestra, the piano in Wolf's hands is an instrument capable of expressing subtle shades of emotion, of accurately delineating character, and of creating atmosphere. Unlike Wagner, however, Wolf is capable of expressing a great deal in an amazingly short space. Many of his songs are master-

[5] Ernst Decsey, *Hugo Wolf* (Leipzig and Berlin, 1903-06), Vol. II, page 77.

pieces of condensation; Wolf may well be called one of the greatest of musical miniaturists. Like Schubert, Wolf realized the dramatic possibilities of carefully planned modulation. He had, in addition, thoroughly digested Wagner's harmonic methods, notably his chromaticism. Wolf's songs abound in harmonic procedures of great originality and telling psychological effectiveness.

SUGGESTED READINGS

Almost all the extensive treatises on Richard Strauss are sadly out of date. The reader who is restricted to English will have to content himself with Henry T. Finck's opinionated work, *Richard Strauss; The Man and His Works* (Boston, 1917). The principal German works, all of which are quite detailed, are Max Steinitzer, *Richard Strauss* (Stuttgart, 1927); Richard Specht, *Richard Strauss und sein Werk* (Leipzig, 1921); and Roland Tenschert, *Richard Strauss* (Vienna, 1944). A provocative article on Strauss appears in Cecil Gray, *A Survey of Contemporary Music* (London, 1927).

Discussions of Strauss' principal orchestral works appear in *Philip Hale's Boston Symphony Programme Notes,* Edited by John N. Burk (Garden City, New York, 1935). *Elektra* and *Der Rosenkavalier* are described at length in Ernest Newman, *More Stories of Famous Operas* (Philadelphia, 1946).

The best source of information on Bruckner and Mahler is Dika Newlin, *Bruckner, Mahler, Schoenberg* (New York, 1947). A stimulating appreciation by a devoted disciple, Bruno Walter, *Gustav Mahler,* appeared in English translation in 1941 (New York).

The amount of material on Wolf in the English language is wholly out of proportion to his importance as a composer. Only one full length treatment is available: Ernest Newman, *Hugo Wolf* (London, 1907). The second volume of *The Heritage of Music,* H. J. Foss, Editor (London, 1934), contains a good article on Wolf by Walter Ford. The standard biography is the four-volume work of Ernst Decsey, *Hugo Wolf* (Leipzig and Berlin, 1903-6).

Chapter XXXI

JEAN SIBELIUS

IT IS difficult to assign a position in the development of music to the great Finnish symphonist Jean Sibelius. He may conceivably be grouped, on a geographical basis, with such nationalistic composers as Grieg or Borodin, but he is of far greater artistic stature than any of the nineteenth-century nationalists. While most of his great works have been composed during the twentieth century, Sibelius is no modernist in the conventional sense of the term. The style of his writing, the forms that he has chosen, and his indifference to contemporary trends recall the situation of Brahms in the previous century. His larger works, like those of Brahms, were slow in winning public recognition; but today his preëminence as the foremost contemporary master of the symphony is unquestioned.

Sibelius was born on December 8, 1865, at Tavastehus, Finland. His family were cultured members of the middle class. As a boy he played the violin and made some amateurish attempts at composition; but, like Wagner, he showed no signs of any unusual musical aptitude during his youth. Like Schumann and Tchaikovsky, Sibelius was for a short time a student of law before he decided to devote himself exclusively to music. After a period of study in Helsinki he left Finland in 1889 for further instruction in Berlin and Vienna. He returned to his native land in 1892. A few years later the Finnish government conferred an annual allowance upon him, with the highly beneficial result that he has been freed from all financial care, and has been able to devote himself to composition without interruption. With the exception of occasional appearances as conductor of his own works, his life has been uneventful. Sibelius came to America in 1914 to conduct his compositions at a festival held at Norfolk, Connecticut.

Yale University conferred the degree of Doctor of Music upon him at this time, and three of his compositions were played at the commencement ceremonies.   He is today Finland's foremost citizen.

Of the many works of Sibelius, the following may have won a firm place on American programs: two symphonic poems, *En Saga* and *Finlandia;* a "Legend" for orchestra, *The Swan of Tuonela;* and five of his seven symphonies, Nos. 1, 2, 4, 5, 7, the last of which dates from 1924; and a fine violin concerto, among the few great compositions in this category.   An eighth symphony, on which Sibelius has apparently been working for many years, has not yet been released.

Sibelius was the first composer of his nationality to win international recognition.   Inasmuch as his music had a peculiar flavor, it was but logical that its divergences from prevailing idioms should be attributed to the influence of Finnish folk music.   Sibelius, however, is no self-conscious nationalist.   At no time has he employed actual Finnish folk tunes in his music.   Attempts have also been made to explain Sibelius in terms of the peculiar topography and climate of Finland; but the roots of Sibelius' style probably rest on much less tangible concepts, such as his own personality, as well as on the racial characteristics of the Finnish people.   One of Sibelius' strongest traits of character is his love of nature.   He has expressed himself in this regard as follows: "It pleases me greatly to be called an artist of nature, for nature has been truly the book of books for me.   The voices of nature are the voices of God, and if an artist can give mere echo of them in his works, he is fully rewarded for all his efforts." [1]   It is in this sense that Sibelius' style may be viewed as the outcome of the unique character of the Finnish scene.

Sibelius' specifically national works are the numerous programmatic pieces on subjects from Finnish folklore, including the works inspired by the great Finnish epic *Kalevala,* of which *The Swan of Tuonela* is the best known.   The popular and hackneyed *Finlandia* was written to serve as incidental music for a series of historical tableaux produced in Helsinki in 1899.   It is regrettable that this bombastic work and the trite *Valse triste* are Sibelius' most frequently heard composi-

---

[1] Quoted by Philip Hale in a Boston Symphony Orchestra program book, from an article in *Musical America* for January 14, 1934.

JEAN SIBELIUS

tions, for neither is typical, and the emphasis placed upon them has served to delay recognition of his more substantial creations.

Sibelius' best works are his seven symphonies, none of which bears a descriptive title or a program. These symphonies, like those of Beethoven and Brahms, are highly individual in character, and generalizations concerning them are both difficult and hazardous. With the exception of the Seventh Symphony, which is in one movement initially designated as a *fantasia sinfonica,* the formal outlines of the symphonies do not represent radical departures from conventional procedures. The various movements retain a degree of independence unusual for an age in which the constructional principles fostered by Liszt had become standard usage in symphonic composition.

The feature of Sibelius' style that makes him a worthy associate of the world's greatest symphonists is the degree of concentration to be found in his works. His thematic material is brief and concise, its development a natural process of organic evolution that remains under firm control and is not the product of either caprice and fancy on the one hand, or pedantry and mere craftsmanship on the other. The rhythmic, melodic, and harmonic aspects of his writing, like those of Brahms, are thoroughly original without constituting a radical departure from accepted methods. Sibelius is responsible for no new theories, no innovations.

In an era in which orchestral color as an end in itself seems to have become an indispensable factor in orchestral composition, Sibelius, in a manner which again recalls Brahms, has resisted the temptation to exploit the coloristic potentialities of the modern symphony orchestra. His orchestration, while lacking in sensuous appeal, is at all times thoroughly colorful, but the color of any given passage in his works is an integral part of the music itself and not an added condiment. Sibelius has also found an orchestra of more modest size to be adequate for his purposes. The instrumentation that he specifies for his Third, Fourth, and Seventh Symphonies, for example, is practically identical with that of the Fifth Symphony of Beethoven.

The English writer Gerald Abraham has aptly said of Sibelius: "By general consent he is a symphonist first and foremost; whatever he may have done in other fields, his reputation rests at present on his symphonies and will stand or fall with them in the future. If we wish to understand Sibelius, we must begin by studying his symphonies."[2]

SYMPHONY NO. 2, IN D MAJOR

At the risk of placing misleading emphasis upon a single composition, Sibelius' Symphony No. 2, Opus 43, composed in 1901-1902 has been chosen for examination here. The history of this now well-known and greatly admired symphony in America exemplifies the slow rate of acceptance of many of Sibelius' works: The New York Philharmonic Orchestra did not play the symphony until 1916. Between 1925 and 1932 it was entirely absent from all New York orchestral programs.[3]

The first movement of the Second Symphony may be divided into three sections that are somewhat analogous to the various parts of a movement in sonata form. The first section, an exposition, is given over entirely to the presentation of several terse and well-contrasted melodic fragments. The first of these is a rising figure in the strings:

Ex. 1

This is followed by a blithe tune for the oboes and clarinets, the conclusion of which is echoed in a slower tempo by the horns:

Ex. 2

An episode in the bassoons leads to this melody played by unaccompanied violins:

---

[2] Gerald Abraham, ed., *The Music of Sibelius* (New York, 1947), page 14.

[3] From a review of a performance of the symphony by Francis D. Perkins, *The New York Herald-Tribune*, May 3, 1940.

Ex. 3

A series of sequences for the strings, pizzicato, leads up to this vehement subject given out by the wood winds over a string figure based on Example 1:

Ex. 4

The second section of this movement is akin to the familiar symphonic development, but instead of breaking individual themes up into smaller units, Sibelius joins them into larger wholes. The third section might be described as a greatly abridged recapitulation.

The second movement begins with a kettledrum roll. This is followed by a long pizzicato passage in the lower strings over which the bassoons eventually enter with this forlorn tune:

Ex. 5

With the entrance of the violins the pace of the movement is accelerated, giving rise to a dramatic episode that culminates in an intense phrase:

Ex. 6

After a particularly forceful presentation of this theme in the full brass, two lyrical themes of singular expressiveness are heard. The first appears in a richly scored passage for divided strings, later joined by wood winds:

Ex. 7

The second of these themes is sung by the oboes and clarinets:

Ex. 8

The greater part of the movement is now repeated, with dramatic intensification of the orchestration and changes in key. Trills in the wood winds, a vigorous scale passage for the strings, and fragments of previously heard melodies bring the movement to a somber close.

Although specific indications are lacking, the two contrasting sections of the third movement may be regarded as the familiar combination of Scherzo and Trio. The predominant note of the Scherzo is established by an epigrammatic motive:

Ex. 9

While the strings maintain the rapid pace of Example 9, flutes and bassoons intone:

Ex. 10

The brief Trio contains an oboe tune that is as beautiful as it is simple:

Ex. 11

Both Scherzo and Trio are repeated, but with change of orchestration, after which a tense bridge passage effects a dramatic transition to the concluding movement.

The last movement lacks the complexity of its predecessors; it is in the conventional sonata form and is based on two well-contrasted subjects. The first of these, an impressive martial theme, is given out by the upper strings over a stubborn accompaniment in the trombones, timpani, and double basses:

Ex. 12

The second group begins with a folk-like tune for the wood winds accompanied by an *ostinato* figure in the strings:

Ex. 13

The exposition ends with this stentorian figure in the trumpets and trombones:

Ex. 14

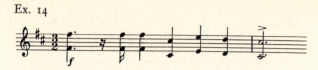

The brief development is based largely on Examples 12 and 14. In the recapitulation, the second group is materially lengthened and its underlying *ostinato* is intensified by a dramatic accumulation of instrumental weight. The coda consists of a triumphant presentation of Example 12 by the full orchestra, with trumpets and trombones blaring forth this version of it over a thunderous kettledrum pedal:

Ex. 15

SUGGESTED READINGS

The most useful work on Sibelius is the collection of essays edited by Gerald Abraham and entitled *The Music of Sibelius* (New York, 1947). The brief but informative work by Cecil Gray, *Sibelius* (London, 1931), has points of merit. There are two works of a biographical nature: Karl Ekman, *Jean Sibelius* (New York, 1938), and Bengt de Törne, *Sibelius: A Close-up* (London, 1937). Alfred H. Meyer's article, "Sibelius: Symphonist," in *The Musical Quarterly,* January, 1936, catalogues the elements of the composer's style. Discussions of the more frequently performed works appear in *Philip Hale's Boston Symphony Programme Notes,* edited by John N. Burk (Garden City, New York, 1935), and in Volumes II, III and VI of Donald Francis Tovey, *Essays in Musical Analysis* (London, 1935-39).

Chapter XXXII

CLAUDE DEBUSSY

THE EFFORTS of the Société Nationale in behalf of French music had, to be sure, created a French musical literature worthy of a place beside the great masterpieces of Germany; but hard as Franck and his contemporaries may have striven, they did not free themselves entirely from the German yoke. The final break was not made until the very end of the nineteenth century, and it was brought about by the advent of a new musical style in the works of one composer, Claude Debussy. The new style is known today as Impressionism. Unlike Romanticism or Nationalism, Impressionism, insofar as music was concerned, was not a movement in which many artists participated. It was the highly personal idiom of one man, which, like other individual styles, has attracted imitators, few of whom, however, have been able to transcend its limitations.

Claude Debussy was born on August 22, 1862, at St. Germain-en-Laye, a small town about thirteen miles from Paris. His parents, humble shopkeepers, moved to Paris shortly after his birth, and almost all of Debussy's life was spent in that city. He studied the piano for a time under a pupil of Chopin, and when he was eleven years old entered the Paris *Conservatoire*. In 1879 he was engaged as household pianist by the selfsame Madame von Meck who had assisted Tchaikovsky.[1] Debussy went with Madame von Meck to Switzerland and Italy and finally to Moscow, where he became acquainted with a few of the compositions of Rimsky-Korsakoff and Borodin, those of the latter exercising a considerable influence upon him. The works of Mussorgsky were little known at the time, and Debussy's wide knowledge of them dates from a later period in his life. Debussy spent

[1] See page 368.

CLAUDE DEBUSSY

eleven years in all at the Paris Conservatory, not without creating a reputation for himself as a wilful breaker of academic rules of harmony. In 1884 he won the coveted *Prix de Rome* which entitled him to three years at the Villa Medici; but he did not stay in Rome the required length of time, and 1887 found him back in Paris. No compositions of merit resulted from this Roman sojourn.

Upon Debussy's return several forces helped to mold his artistic outlook and musical style. The first of these was his keen interest in Wagner; Debussy visited Bayreuth in 1888 and 1889. Not a few aspects of Debussy's harmonic style are traceable to Wagner's methods, particularly as displayed in *Tristan und Isolde*. Another molding force was his presence at two concerts of Russian music that Rimsky-Korsakoff conducted at the great International Exposition held in Paris in 1889. At these concerts Debussy had his first real contact with Russian symphonic music. A much more important part of the exposition so far as Debussy was concerned, however, was the performance of native musicians from Java and French Indo-China. The highly exotic flavor and particularly the unique scales of this Oriental music stirred his imagination.

The fourth and apparently the strongest formative influence at this time was his association with a group of artists and writers who were the prime movers in the symbolist and impressionist movements, notably Stéphane Mallarmé and Paul Verlaine. Debussy met many kindred spirits among the artists who frequented Mallarmé's salon and found himself in sympathy with their attempts to suggest fleeting moods or emotions in a manner that placed special emphasis on fidelity of representation of sensory impression to the obscuration of detail. Mallarmé himself described their aim as: "To evoke in a deliberate shadow the unmentioned object by allusive words." [2]

A fifth influence was his discovery of the music of Mussorgsky. The directness of Mussorgsky's style, unhampered as it was by academic considerations, met with Debussy's enthusiastic approval. It seemed to him to be the ideal escape from the tyranny of conventional standards as well as from the complexities of Wagner. Mussorgsky's influence on Debussy was, however, purely catalytic; Debussy regarded him as a precedent, but not as a model. It is important to notice that,

[2] Edward Lockspeiser, *Debussy* (London and New York, 1936), page 38.

with the exception of the music of Wagner, all these influences were such as to confirm Debussy's deep-seated iconoclasm.

Debussy's life in Paris was rather uneventful. His public appearances were comparatively rare. Although a fine pianist, he seldom played in public; he lacked ability as a conductor, and he appeared in some of the larger European capitals as director of his own works largely because of financial exigencies. His compositions, particularly the opera *Pelléas et Mélisande,* aroused much controversy so that Debussy, even if not universally appreciated, was at least well known. Debussy, like Schumann before him, was an astute critic and contributed numerous articles to Parisian periodicals. Despite their ironic tone and the caustic manner in which Debussy aired his anti-Wagnerian prejudices in them, these articles contain much sound criticism of the music, the musicians, and the musical instruction of his day. During his last years Debussy's productivity as a composer fell off considerably, due in large measure to a wasting sickness. He died on March 25, 1918.

Included among Debussy's more important works are many beautiful songs, notably those with poems by Baudelaire, Verlaine, and Mallarmé; many fine piano pieces; a string quartet (1893); *L'Après-midi d'un faune (The Afternoon of a Faun)* (1894); *Nocturnes* (1899); *La Mer (The Sea)* (1905); *Iberia* (1908) for orchestra; and the opera *Pelléas et Mélisande* (1902).

Impressionism

Debussy's music, like that of his romantic predecessors, was only one manifestation of a well-defined movement in the arts. This movement reached its zenith during the latter part of the nineteenth century in the compositions of Debussy, in the poetry of Mallarmé and Verlaine, and in the paintings of Manet, Monet, Pissaro, Sisley, and Renoir; the designation *Impressionism* given to it is said to have had its origin in a painting of a sunrise at sea which Monet entitled *Impression: soleil levant* (1874). The symbolist poets stressed imagery and mood in writing; their aim was to capture the feeling of a fleeting impression rather than factually to describe sensory impressions. The result of this restriction to indirect suggestion was a certain vagueness. It is important to observe, however, that the symbolists let no accepted convention retard what they considered to be their presentation of artistic truth. Mallarmé, for example, invented a new punctuation and a new grammatical construction for his verse. The impressionistic style in painting, again in opposition to traditional procedures, excluded detail and precision, and concentrated on the reproduction of an object exactly as the artist saw it. The impressionist painters thus strove for a higher degree of realism than that permitted by adherence to orthodox standards.

The music of Debussy echoes the work of these poets and painters in its departure from conventional standards of melodic construction, its total avoidance, with the exception of the string quartet, of orthodox formulas, its suppression of detail, its emphasis on atmosphere, and, above all, its peculiar subtlety. Debussy has described his music as follows: "I desired for music that freedom of which it is capable perhaps to a greater degree than any other art, as it is not confined to an exact reproduction of nature, but only to the mysterious affinity between Nature and the Imagination." [3]

The impressionism of Debussy also constituted a revolt against orthodox standards, in this case standards of harmonic procedure, of dissonance, and of the function and progression of chords. The first of the Debussy innovations involved a new concept of dissonance: dissonance was now regarded as an end in itself and not an episode on the route to an eventual consonance. Each of the chords in this excerpt from a piano piece, *La Cathédrale engloutie* (*The Engulfed Cathedral*), for example, is dissonant; none is resolved according to older canons of harmonic propriety:

Ex. 1

Debussy was especially fond of concatenations of dissonant chords of the type shown by this excerpt from *Pelléas et Mélisande,* Act I, Scene 3:

---

[3] Leon Vallas, *Claude Debussy: His Life and Works* (London, 1933), page 85.

Ex. 2

It will be observed that both examples contain successions of parallel fifths, a procedure which recalls the *organum* [4] of a thousand years previous.

The second important feature of the impressionistic idiom is the frequent use of modal scales.[5] An example of Debussy's use of one of the modes has been cited on page 37. Debussy also used the pentatonic or five-tone scale, one of whose forms can be created by striking only the black keys of the piano. The pentatonic scale, while extensively used for much Western folk music, has certain Oriental connotations and consequently is aptly introduced in Debussy's piano piece *Pagodes*. A less restricted use of this scale is found in his *Nuages* (*Clouds*) in a beautiful episode for flute and harp:

Ex. 3

The most unusual scale employed by Debussy is the whole-tone scale.[6] Although the absence of half steps limits the melodic potentialities of this particular scale pattern, its harmonic implications are both numerous and valuable and have been a fructifying influence in the development of modern harmony. Debussy's use of this scale is best exemplified by a piano piece *Voiles* (*Sails*), from which this typical whole-tone passage is quoted:

[4] See page 44.
[5] See page 36.
[6] See page 38.

Ex. 4

The various innovations of Debussy listed above were important factors in the development of modern music. Debussy treated chords as units that could be arranged in successions apparently at variance with conventional standards and yet of undeniable beauty. But with this new usage of chords, their older tonality-fixing function was either weakened or wholly obliterated. In addition, many of the scales employed by Debussy, particularly the whole-tone scale, lack the pronounced tonal centers of the conventional major and minor scales. But Debussy's artistic use of them has resulted in the creation of entirely new concepts of melodic and harmonic values.

Debussy's break with tradition, despite its radical nature, was motivated purely by a desire to achieve new beauties and to create an idiom more sensitively attuned to what he wished to communicate. (It is interesting to note that Debussy harbored a deep admiration for another colorist, Carl Maria von Weber.) It is difficult to divorce Debussy's style from the literary or pictorial subjects that he delineated in his works, almost all of which bear descriptive titles. Typical designations, which might have served with equal facility for impressionistic paintings, are *Jardins sous la pluie* (*Gardens in the Rain*), *L'Isle joyeuse* (*The Isle of Joy*), *Reflets dans l'eau* (*Reflections on the Water*), *Poissons d'or* (*Goldfish*), *Des Pas sur la neige* (*Footprints in the Snow*), *Feuilles mortes* (*Dead Leaves*). Like the Impressionists in other arts, Debussy suggests rather than actually portrays. His music has an elusiveness, a reticence, a delicacy of touch, that, while giving his works a definitely personal cast, have at the same time often robbed them of emotional depth, persuasiveness, and vitality. The scope of his art is narrow, but within its limits Debussy has created works of consummate beauty.

Piano Works

The literature of piano music has been considerably enriched by Debussy, and his many short descriptive pieces for the instrument have become standard recital fare. Debussy ranks with Liszt and Chopin as a significant contributor to the development of pianism. His compositions abound in colorful passages based on new concepts of sonority involving subtle adjustment of dynamic values, skilful use of the pedals, and imaginative employment of the lower register with its wealth of faint yet effectively dissonant overtones.

Pelléas et Mélisande

Pelléas et Mélisande, Debussy's only opera, is a setting of the play by the Belgian symbolist Maurice Maeterlinck. The work was of almost revolutionary significance, for it represented the first really new contribution to the technique of dramatic composition since the music drama of Wagner. The most important feature of the opera is the manner in which the orchestra has been employed. The orchestral music of *Pelléas et Mélisande* is not a vigorous torrent that is vitally bound up with the stage action, but a sensitively conceived commentary that, despite its poignancy and profundity, remains comparatively restrained. The vocal parts are written in a chant-like recitative from which tuneful elements are almost entirely absent. Despite all Debussy's vindictiveness toward Wagner, he has utilized the Wagnerian leading motive, although in a much less complex fashion. Throughout the work Debussy has achieved a remarkably successful fusion of spoken word, music, and stage action. But the highly rarefied atmosphere of the opera has prevented it from achieving any great measure of popularity.

Orchestral Music

Debussy's orchestral works, of which the more important have been mentioned, exhibit a style of orchestral writing that was at marked variance with the accepted standards of his time, particularly those whose origins were traceable to Wagner's influence. Debussy placed his emphasis not on volume or brilliancy of tone, but rather on delicacy and subtle contrast. Here again his contribution has been an important one. The exquisite refinement of his writing and the delicacy of texture of his works, all brought about with the greatest economy of means, were based on technical devices that have now become a definite part of the vocabulary of modern orchestration. It is in his masterful use of orchestral color as an expressive medium that Debussy shows his closest affinity with the painters of the impressionist school.

PRÉLUDE À L'APRÈS-MIDI D'UN FAUNE

The *Prélude à l'après-midi d'un faune* is Debussy's most celebrated orchestral work. This composition, which had its première in 1894 at a concert of the Société Nationale, is based on a pastoral poem by Mallarmé. The poem, called by the English critic Edmund Gosse "a famous miracle of unintelligibility," describes the musings of a faun, a Roman god of the woods and fields, of human shape but with a tail, short horns, and goat's feet. The faun, drowsy and surfeited with wine, attempts to recall his pursuits of nymphs and naiads. But the effort is too much for him, and he falls asleep in the warm rays of the sun.[7] Debussy's title *Prélude* is difficult to interpret, but it seems to suggest that the music was conceived as a sort of introduction to Mallarmé's poem. According to the composer the music evokes "the successive scenes of the faun's desires and dreams on that hot afternoon."[8] Mallarmé, who was quite pleased with Debussy's interpretation of his poem, said that the music had conveyed its "nostalgia and light with subtlety, malaise and richness."[9] The work is scored for a small orchestra that includes two harps, and from which trumpets, trombones, tuba, and kettledrums are absent.

The mood of the poem is quickly established in the opening measures with the languorous presentation of the principal theme by a solo flute:

Ex. 5

---

[7] A sensitive rendering into English of Mallarmé's famous eclogue made by Aldous Huxley appears in Mark van Doren (Editor), *An Anthology of World Poetry* (New York, 1928), page 77.

[8] Leon Vallas, *Claude Debussy: His Life and Works*, page 102.

[9] E. Lockspeiser, *op. cit.*, page 168.

Beautifully scored repetitions, in which the flutes play an important role, are followed by the introduction of a more animated theme by the oboe:

Ex. 6

doux et expressif

Motives derived from this theme are developed, and after a brief forte episode another melody is announced in the wood winds:

Ex. 7

This is also brought to a climax, after which Example 5 returns in an augmented form, played first by the flute and then by the oboe, interrupted, however, by fleeting episodes in which harp *glissandi* and querulous wood wind passages play an important role. At the conclusion of the work Debussy makes colorful use of the antique cymbals, tiny plates which give out a bell-like tone of definite pitch when struck together. Just before the final chords muted horns and violins give out an exquisitely harmonized and characteristically impressionistic version of the principal theme in a hushed and far-distant *pianissimo*:

Ex. 8

Suggested Readings

The most authentic life of Debussy is Leon Vallas, *Claude Debussy: His Life and Times* (London, 1933). Oscar Thompson, *Debussy, Man and Artist* (New York, 1937), contains much significant anecdotal material not included in Vallas' work. Edward Lockspeiser, *Debussy* (London and New York, 1936), is also valuable. The section captioned "The Reaction Against Romanticism: Impressionism" in Gerald Abraham, *A Hundred Years of Music,* Second Edition (London, 1949), is an able and penetrating discussion of the impressionist movement and its principal composers.

Debussy's provocative writings have been assembled and classified in Leon Vallas, *The Theories of Claude Debussy* (London, 1929). Debussy's own collection of his criticisms have appeared under the title *Monsieur Croche, The Dilettante Hater* (New York, 1928).

Discussions of the better-known orchestral pieces appear in *Philip Hale's Boston Symphony Programme Notes,* Edited by John N. Burk (Garden City, New York, 1935). Ernest Hutcheson writes engagingly of the piano pieces in his *The Literature of the Piano* (New York, 1948). *Pelléas et Mélisande* and its unique position in the history of opera are informatively discussed in Vol. II of Donald J. Grout, *A Short-History of Opera* (New York, 1947). The plot of the opera is given in considerable detail in Ernest Newman, *More Stories of Famous Operas* (Philadelphia, 1946).

Chapter XXXIII

CONTEMPORARY TRENDS

THE FIRST half of the twentieth century has witnessed the appearance of several seemingly new musical idioms and styles, which, despite their apparent novelty, are the results of the centuries-long evolution of musical materials and their manipulation. Whether or not some of these new methods will achieve permanency remains to be seen. The value of several, however, has been well demonstrated by many outstanding composers, not through theoretical treatises but through persistent use of these idioms in works that are now widely accepted. The catalogue of music of the twentieth century already includes a number of "classics."

New Rhythmic Concepts

Almost all the newer rhythmic devices employed by contemporary composers find their origin in a desire to achieve freedom from the monotony of a rhythmic system based on pulse groups of uniform character, usually the recurring patterns of two or three pulses or some multiple thereof that characterize most of the music of their predecessors from about 1600 to 1900. Earlier composers had achieved contrast in their rhythmic patterns by the use of syncopation, by cross rhythms, or by a sudden change in pulse grouping, as, for example, in the Scherzo of the Third Symphony of Beethoven:

Ex. 1

Contemporary composers, however, produce rhythmic patterns of great dynamic impact through frequent and irregular change of accent patterns with resulting asymmetric rhythms.

The most convincing examples of the effectiveness of asymmetric rhythms occur in *Le Sacre du printemps* (*The Rite of Spring*), music for a ballet of the same name by Igor Stravinsky, born in Russia in 1882 and since 1939 resident in America. A pupil of Rimsky-Korsakoff, Stravinsky was brought to the attention of the world by the impresario Serge Diaghileff, who invited him to compose music for his *Ballet Russe,* then performing in Paris. For Diaghileff's company Stravinsky wrote *L'Oiseau de feu* (*The Firebird*) in 1910, *Petrouchka* in 1913, and *Le Sacre* in 1914. *Le Sacre,* a barbaric spectacle portraying fertility rites in prehistoric Russia, concludes with a frenzied *Danse sacrale,* a solo dance in which a chosen virgin dances herself to death. For so violent a choreographic representation Stravinsky writes music characterized by continued change of rhythm, reinforced by acute dissonance and brusque orchestration. Here is a typical sequence of the tortured sound patterns of the *Danse sacrale:*

Ex. 2

The first performance of *Le Sacre* in Paris was accompanied by rude behavior on the part of a hostile audience. But by 1941 the idiom of Stravinsky's music had become conventional enough for Walt Disney to employ a portion of *Le Sacre* for one of the sections of his color cartoon film *Fantasia.* The extent of Stravinsky's enrichment of our musical resources is indicated by the many testimonials from fellow composers. Virgil Thomson, for example, describes *Le Sacre* as "probably the most influential work of music composed in our century and the most impressive in performance." [1] Other contributions of Stravinsky will be discussed later in this chapter.

[1] Virgil Thomson, *The Art of Judging Music* (New York, 1948), page 23.

IGOR STRAVINSKY

(*Sketch by Picasso*)

The jaunty vigor of the rhythms of American jazz has also found its way into the music of the concert hall. On February 22, 1924, Paul Whiteman (1891-   ) and his band presented in Aeolian Hall, New York, a program entitled "An Experiment in Modern Music" at which the history-making *Rhapsody in Blue* of the song writer George Gershwin (1898-1937) had its première. A year later Gershwin played the solo piano part at the first performance of his Concerto in F, one of the most successful of the many applications of jazz techniques to traditional forms. Although the rhythmic subtleties of the displaced accent encountered in American "popular" music had been used and exploited by serious composers before Gershwin (Debussy's "The Golliwog's Cake-Walk" from his piano suite, *Children's Corner* (1908), and Stravinsky's *L'Histoire du Soldat* (1918)), most of the conspicuous usages are of later date than the *Rhapsody in Blue*. Particularly worthy of citation for the skillful employment of the resources of jazz are the *The Rio Grande* (1929) for chorus, solo piano and orchestra by the English composer Constant Lambert (1905-   ), and the last movement of Maurice Ravel's (1875-1937) Piano Concerto in G major (1931). The novel and colorful harmonic resources and the highly enterprising devices of instrumentation associated with jazz have also been utilized; but its distinctive methods of performance with their emphasis on improvisation and freedom of intonation defy reproduction by musicians trained in other types of performance.

Polytonality

Polytonality is produced by the simultaneous employment of several tonalities within a musical texture. Usually only two tonalities are utilized. The simultaneous use of two keys guarantees independence to the constituent parts of the music through blocking any possibility of their fusing into conventional chords. The aim of the composer of polytonal music, then, is an old one: independence of part writing. But now it is attained by denying to the parts that which was long held to be their inalienable right: a common tonality. The dissonances produced by polytonality are, of course, unresolved.

The best known of the many contemporary uses of polytonality appears in Stravinsky's already mentioned ballet *Petrouchka,* in which the despair of the frustrated marionette is described by the juxtaposition of two mutually remote chords, C major (exclusively on the white keys of the piano) and F♯ major (exclusively on the black):

Ex. 3

Today polytonality is a common idiom and numerous examples of its application might be cited. The ease with which listeners of all degrees of musical experience may assimilate it is convincingly shown in the central role it plays in the type of American popular music known as "bebop."

Atonality

In one of the early chapters of this book melody was defined as "a meaningful succession of simple tones." Obviously the crucial term in this definition is the word "meaningful." Modern composers have done nothing to warrant a change in the definition. But they have created successions of tones whose relationship to each other may not be as clear to the listener as those of their predecessors.

It will be recalled that the melodies written by earlier composers could be described in terms of the various scales on which they were based and the definite feeling for tonality that they produced. This feeling for tonality remained intact during the nineteenth century despite the extensive use of chromaticism with its emphasis on semitonal progressions, melodic and harmonic, and its frequency and diversity of change of tonalities (Liszt, Wagner, Strauss). The logical extension of the chromaticism of the nineteenth century is a system that denies the twelve tones of the chromatic scale the relationships imparted to them by conventional major and minor scales and permits the composer to use these now autonomous tones at will. With the composer free to utilize the twelve tones of the chromatic scale according to relationships determined solely by himself and not by prior concepts of tonal patterns, a music is produced completely lacking in conventional tonality. The result is called *atonality*. The individual whose name is most closely associated with its promulgation and establishment as a musical idiom is the Austrian composer Arnold Schoenberg, who was born in Vienna in 1874, and who, in 1933, after a long and successful career as composer and teacher in Europe, migrated to America. Schoenberg himself disapproves of the negative implications of the term atonality and insists that his music is the result of "composing with twelve tones which are related only with one another." [1]

The organizing device of the twelve-tone technique of atonal music is an arbitrary series of the tones of the chromatic scale, arranged beforehand for any given work. This basic series is usually called either *tone-row, row,* or *set.* Here, for example, is the pattern of twelve tones from which Schoenberg creates his Variations for Orchestra, Opus 31 (1918).

Ex. 4

Three other versions of the row of a twelve-tone work are obtained by using devices which had been employed hundreds of years before by composers of polyphonic music. These additional forms are: (a) inversion of the row, produced by changing the direction of each interval, ascending intervals becoming descending, and vice versa; (b) retrograde (crab motion) version, produced by reversing the row and working backward from the last to the first tone; and (c) retrograde inversion, produced as in (a) by changing the direction of the intervals of the retrograde sequence. Each of the four patterns of the row, furthermore, can be started on any of the twelve tones of the chromatic scale. Hence forty-eight different versions of it are available to the composer.

The operation of the twelve-tone system can be effectively shown by Ernst Křenek's *Twelve Short Piano Pieces Written in the Twelve-Tone Technique,* Op. 83. Křenek, who was born in Vienna in 1900 and has lived in America since 1938, achieved world-wide fame as the composer of a jazz opera *Jonny spielt auf* (1926). He adopted the atonal idiom about 1931 and has since composed extensively in it be-

[1] Arnold Schoenberg, *Style and Idea* (New York, 1950), page 107.

sides writing a spirited defense of the system in his book *Music, Here and Now* (New York, 1939).

Křenek's piano pieces are designed "to correspond with the capacity and the interest of normally advanced students and amateurs" and hence may be classified as *Gebrauchsmusik,* (see the discussion later in this chapter). The descriptive titles were given to them after they were completed. As brief pieces with a minimum of demand on the player's mechanical resources, they constitute an excellent introduction to the twelve-tone technique.

In the preface to the pieces the composer gives the four forms of their generating row:

Ex. 5

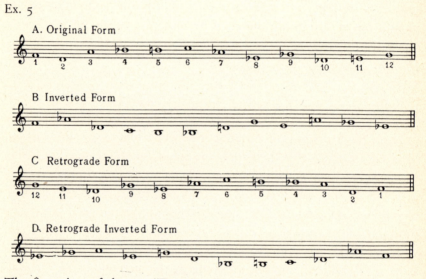

The first piece of the set, "Dancing Toys," utilizes the original form of the row in the following manner:

Ex. 6

(Numbers inserted beside the notes correspond to tones of the row.)

Copyright, 1939, by G. Schirmer, Inc.

Some of the most successful applications of the twelve-tone system appear not in the works of Schoenberg but in the compositions of his devoted disciple, the Austrian Alban Berg (1885-1935). Berg's opera, *Wozzeck,* written in the atonal idiom and completed in 1921, was produced in Berlin in 1925. The intensity of the emotional response that Berg's music, despite the strangeness of its idiom, engendered in those who heard it accounts for the frequency of performance of this opera: up to the end of 1936 it had been given 166 times in 19 cities.[2] Excerpts from the opera appear occasionally on orchestral programs. An unusually sensitive and appealing Violin Concerto (1935), dedicated "to the memory of an angel," has as its concluding movement an *Adagio* in which Berg incorporates into his atonal texture the solemn diatonic melody of a Lutheran chorale as found in Bach's church cantata No. 60, *O Ewigkeit, du Donnerwort.* The concerto has been performed extensively in this country.

Despite the number of successful compositions in the atonal style, the idiom remains strange and forbidding to most listeners. Some critics hold it to be a hyper-intellectual cerebral effort. Others will readily admit its powers of communication for sensitive listeners capable of intense concentration. Its partisans emphasize its "logic"; its detractors claim that it is music whose patterns appeal more to the eye than to the ear.

Unintelligible though this music may be to many listeners, it should be borne in mind that its distinguished creators, like their forebears, have resorted to new styles because of what seemed to them the exhaustion of older idioms. Schoenberg's complete mastery of the tonal language of Wagner and Strauss, for example, is shown by his earlier works, the String Sextet, Opus 4, *Verklärte Nacht* (1899), popular in the composer's adaptation for string orchestra, and the *Gurrelieder* (1901), both melodious, richly scored compositions. For a concert given in Vienna in 1909 that included some pieces in the then new twelve-tone technique, Schoenberg felt called upon to state the reasons for his change of style. Recalling his older *Gurrelieder,* Schoenberg said of his newer works: "...it seems opportune to show...that it is not lack of invention or of technical skill, nor of the knowledge of the other demands of contemporary aesthetics, that has urged me in

2 René Leibowitz, *Schoenberg and His School* (New York, 1949), page 155.

this direction, but that I am following an inner compulsion that is stronger than education, and am obeying a law that is natural to me, and therefore stronger than my artistic training."[3] The question of whether the older styles are exhausted or not and whether tonality must give way to atonality will be answered not by theoreticians and writers on music but by the creative musicians of our times and the audiences to whom their communicative efforts are addressed.

Neoclassicism

Several modern composers have attempted to recreate the styles of the seventeenth century, mostly through forms associated with the name of Bach. The concerto grosso, the fugue, and the toccata, with their restraining emphasis on clarity of form and their demand for vital music undiluted by personal or literary associations, have appealed to composers anxious to free themselves from the emotional demands of late romantic music. To this attempt to revive the spirit of classicism the term *neoclassicism* has been given.

The prime mover in the neoclassical movement was Igor Stravinsky, who, after his initial successes with folkloristic ballet, produced in 1923 an octet for wind instruments, polyphonic in texture, classical in its proportions and devoid of extramusical connotation. The composer said of the work, "This sort of music has no other aim than to be sufficient in itself."[4] Later works of neoclassical character by this versatile creative artist are a Concerto for Piano and Orchestra (1924), a Sonata for Piano (1924), an opera-oratorio *Oedipus Rex* (1927), a *Symphony of Psalms* for Chorus and Orchestra (1930), a Symphony in C (1940), a Symphony in Three Movements (1945), a Concerto for String Orchestra (1946), and a Mass in C (1948).

The neoclassical idiom leans strongly to contrapuntal textures whose constituent strands are made to impress themselves on the listener's ear more in their horizontal aspects as melodic lines than in their harmonic relationship as chords. That is, the melodic independence of the parts is secured through the use of dissonance and sharply contrasted orchestral timbres. From this practice are derived the terms "dissonant counterpoint" or "linear counterpoint" in use today.

[3] Egon Wellesz, *Arnold Schoenberg* (London, 1924), page 27.
[4] Program Book of the International Composers' Guild (New York, April 17, 1927).

The contrapuntal virtuosity possessed by many contemporary writers of music is convincingly demonstrated in the tour-de-force executed by the many-sided French composer, Darius Milhaud (1892-   ) with his two string quartets Nos. 14 and 15 (1948). Either quartet may be played alone; or both quartets may be played simultaneously to produce a third work, an octet.

The vitality with which the neoclassical idiom can be employed appears at its best in the works of another European composer who has taken up residence in America, Paul Hindemith (1895-   ), an eminently practical instrumentalist, composer, writer and teacher, thoroughly objective in his outlook. The catalogue of his compositions embraces a large number of sonatas for various instruments, ensemble music, symphonies, concertos, choral works and operas. From the most recent of his operas, *Mathis der Maler* (*Matthias The Painter*), composed in 1934, Hindemith has extracted three instrumental movements and ordered them as a symphony. The titles of the movements, "Angelic Concert," "Entombment," and "The Temptation of St. Anthony" refer to panels of a famous sixteenth century altarpiece painted by Matthias Grünewald, originally in the town of Isenheim in Germany and now in the museum at Colmar. Hindemith's opera, based on historical events, has been performed several times in Europe but is still awaiting presentation in America. It deals with a peasants' revolt in which Grünewald plays a prominent part. (Recent scholarship has established Grünewald's correct name to be Mathis Gothart Nithart.) The "Angelic Concert" introduces a thirteenth century German Crusader's hymn, *Es sungen drei Engel* (*Three Angels Sang*), as a solemn chant in the trombones. Near the end of the last movement two Catholic chants *Lauda Sion Salvatorem* (*Praise Thy Saviour, Zion*) and an *Alleluia* appear. The close association of the music with a work of pictorial art does not detract from its neoclassical quality, all the result of a sound polyphonic texture, a logical development of thematic elements, and a finely proportioned form.

A marked predilection for neoclassical idioms characterizes the compositions of the American composers Roy Harris (1898-   ) and Walter Piston (1894-   ), both writers of large scale symphonic works that often employ such classical forms as the passacaglia and the fugue.

Gebrauchsmusik

Gebrauchsmusik is the German word for "useful music," a type of functional music that was assiduously cultivated in Germany after World War I. The aim of composers of *Gebrauchsmusik* is a laudable one: to supply amateurs with worthwhile music in the modern idiom but with a minimum of technical difficulties. Despite the appearance of a new name to describe it, *Gebrauchsmusik* represents an attempt to recreate an important feature of some of the music which flourished before the nineteenth century with its development of virtuoso ap-plauding audiences: music to be played and not to be heard, the sort of music that, for example, Bach wrote in his partitas for harpsichord, described by him as "for the delectation of amateurs." [5]

One of the first exponents of *Gebrauchsmusik* was Paul Hindemith, whose *Sing-und Spielmusiken für Liebhaber und Musikfreunde, Opus 45 (Music for Singing and Playing by Amateurs and Friends of Music)*, written in 1928, has this introduction: "This music is written neither for the concert hall nor for artists. It aims to afford interesting and modern musical practice for individuals who want to sing or play either for their own pleasure or before a small group of kindred spirits. To achieve this end, no great technical demands are made on the per-formers." [6] One of the best examples of Hindemith's many pieces of *Gebrauchsmusik* is his opera written for performance by children, *Wir Bauen eine Stadt (We Build a City)* (1930).

In writing *Gebrauchsmusik* contemporary composers have returned to the eighteenth century concept of the composer as a craftsman fash-ioning an artistic product for specific consumers. This limitation has been no more confining than the analogous restrictions which held sway in the days of Bach, Handel, Haydn and Mozart. The musical needs as well as the technical limitations of the American amateur have been happily met, for example, by Aaron Copland (1900-   ), one of America's greatest composers, with his *The Second Hurricane* (1937), "a play-opera for High School performance." Kurt Weill (1900-1950), a German composer who came to America in 1935 and

---

[5] See page 79.

[6] Translated from the facsimile of the original in Heinrich Strobel, *Paul Hindemith* (Mainz, 1928).

achieved great success as a writer of music for many outstanding Broadway productions, utilized an American folk tune, *Down in the Valley,* for his folk opera of the same name (1948). This attractive work was specifically written for performance by college students. And the English musician, Benjamin Britten (1913-), composer of one of the most successful operas of recent times, *Peter Grimes* (1945), has written a clever little work, *Let's Make An Opera,* subtitled "Entertainment for Young People" (1949). This is a musical stage work with an adult cast and is designed for an audience of children who themselves are required to participate in the action by acting as a chorus. Their part consists of four songs, original compositions by Britten, learned by them in a rehearsal held before the performance of the opera and effectively worked into its presentation.

Composer and Listener

Gebrauchsmusik represents one way of bridging the gulf between the composer and his hearers that the increasing complexity of musical speech has brought into being. But there are other solutions to the problem. Some composers, for example, have attempted to bring their art closer to the everyday experiences of average listeners by depicting characteristic aspects of twentieth century civilization in programmatic pieces. Here the validity of the musical means can at least be gauged by the listener's own background. Typical of this sort of composition are: the celebrated description of a steam locomotive, *Pacific 231* (1923), by the Swiss composer Arthur Honegger (1892-); Philip James' (1890-) prize-winning commentary on the activity of a radio station *Station WGZBX* (1931); Randall Thompson's (1899-) satirical settings of H. L. Mencken's gleanings from the American press, *Americana* (1932), for mixed chorus and piano; and Ernst Křenek's musical version of a list of names of railroad stations, *The Santa Fe Timetable* (1947), for mixed chorus *a cappella*.

Other musicians, with the distinguished Aaron Copland in the lead, have tried different methods of bringing the composer closer to his listeners. Copland, many of whose earlier works had been in an idiom which may have been forbidding to average audiences, began to cultivate a deliberately simple style in 1934. In his clear-thinking book,

Our New Music (New York, 1941, page 229), he wrote as follows of his audiences: "It made no sense to ignore them and continue writing as if they did not exist. I felt that it was worth the effort to see if I couldn't say what I had to say in the simplest terms." The results of this gesture have been many tuneful works in a modern idiom, attractively scored, straightforward without being banal, and thoroughly American in spirit. Among them may be mentioned the music for the motion picture *Our Town* (1940), and the music for the ballets *Billy the Kid* (1938), *Rodeo* (1942), and *Appalachian Spring* (1944). The last named includes a fine set of variations on an American folk song, a hymn of the Shaker sect, " 'Tis the Gift to be Simple."

For some composers the cultivation of a simple style has not resulted from a personal choice but has been imposed from above by the totalitarian state. In February 1948 the composers of Russia, for example, including such internationally recognized musicians as Sergei Proko-fieff (1891-   ), Aram Khatchaturian (1903-   ), and Dmitri Shos-takovitch (1906-   ), found all their works officially condemned and themselves accused of having "lowered the high public role of music and narrowed its significance, limiting it by the satisfaction of distorted tastes of esthetic individualists." Prokofieff, one of the foremost living composers, and his comrades now saw their symphonies and operas characterized as exhibiting "a passion for muddled neuropathic combinations which transform music into a cacophonic and chaotic heaping of sounds." The critical manifesto of the Central Committee of the Communist Party went on to demand of Russian composers "recognition of the truthfulness and reality of music, of its deep organic connection with the people and their music and songs," and to require from them "high professional art with simultaneous simplicity and accessibility of musical works." [7] The gulf between composer and listener was now to be eliminated by ukase and the artistic merits of a composition determined by the vagaries of a "party line" aesthetic. What the result will be for the creative artists now deprived of the freedom of utterance that Beethoven was so instrumental in winning for them remains to be seen. [8]

---

[7] From a Moscow dispatch in *The New York Times*, February 12, 1948.

[8] For a complete documentation of this formidable attempt to set up ideological standards for music see Nicolas Slonimsky, *Music Since 1900*, Third Edition (New York), pages 684-709.

A Classification of Contemporary Composers

Aaron Copland, is, as has been noted above, much concerned with the average listener and his grasp of the music of his times. In an article "A Modernist Defends Modern Music" written for *The New York Times* of December 25, 1949, Copland emphasizes the variety of musical styles to be encountered today and proceeds to guide the listener by listing the principal composers in terms of the accessibility of their idioms. As a critical estimate by a man who is himself a highly esteemed composer, Copland's classification deserves literal quotation here:

Very easy: Shostakovitch and Khatchaturian, Francis Poulenc, Erik Satie, early Schoenberg and Stravinsky, Vaughan Williams, Virgil Thomson.
Quite approachable: Prokofieff, Roy Harris, Villa-Lobos, Ernest Bloch, William Walton.
Fairly difficult: late Stravinsky, Béla Bartók, Chavez, Milhaud, William Schuman, Honegger, Britten, Hindemith, Walter Piston.
Very tough: middle and late Schoenberg, Alban Berg, Anton Webern, Varese, Křenek, Charles Ives, Roger Sessions.

As the famous aphorism of the French naturalist Georges Buffon (1707-1788) tells us, "The style is the man himself."

SUGGESTED READINGS

Among the many available books on contemporary music the following may be listed as being particularly useful: Gerald Abraham, *This Modern Stuff,* Second Edition (London, 1939); Ernst Křenek, *Music Here and Now* (New York, 1939); Aaron Copland, *Our New Music* (New York, 1941); John Tasker Howard, *This Modern Music* (New York, 1942); Adolfo Salazar, *Music in Our Time* (New York, 1946); Marion Bauer, *Twentieth Century Music,* Revised Edition (New York, 1947); Nicolas Slonimsky, *Music Since 1900, Third Edition* (New York, 1949); and David Ewen (Editor), *The Book of Modern Composers,* Second Edition (New York, 1950).

The impact of Stravinsky on modern music is attested by the extent of the literature dealing with him and his works. From this large catalogue these may be selected: Eric White, *Stravinsky, His Life and Work* (New York, 1948); Minna Ledermann (Editor), *Stravinsky in the Theater* (New York, 1949); Merle Armitage (Editor), *Igor Stravinsky* (New York, 1949). A book by a friend who is also an accomplished composer, Alexander Tansman, *Stravinsky* (New York, 1949), is particularly competent in its treatment of its subject. Stravinsky's own views on music may be read in his *An Autobiography* (New York, 1936) and his *Poetics of Music* (Cambridge, Mass., 1947), the latter from the six lectures that Stravinsky delivered at Harvard University.

1835-1921

Additional information about Schoenberg may be found in Egon Wellesz, *Arnold Schoenberg* (London, 1924); Merle Armitage (Editor), *Schoenberg* (New York, 1939), and in the partisan works of Dika Newlin, *Bruckner—Mahler—Schoenberg* (New York, 1497), and René Leibowitz, *Schoenberg and His School* (New York, 1949). Schoenberg has stated some of his own ideas on the twelve-tone system in his *Style and Idea* (New York, 1950). No full length discussions of Berg or Hindemith are as yet available in English.

American composers of today are authoritatively discussed by John Tasker Howard in his *Our Contemporary Composers—American Music in the Twentieth Century, Third Edition* (New York, 1946). Claire Reis, *Composers in America,* Revised and Enlarged Edition (New York, 1947), contains a brief biographical sketch of almost every American composing serious music today and a complete catalogue of his works.

INDEX OF MUSICAL EXAMPLES

GENERAL INDEX